Shojo Beat

ANONYMOUS NOISE

Ryoko Fukuyama

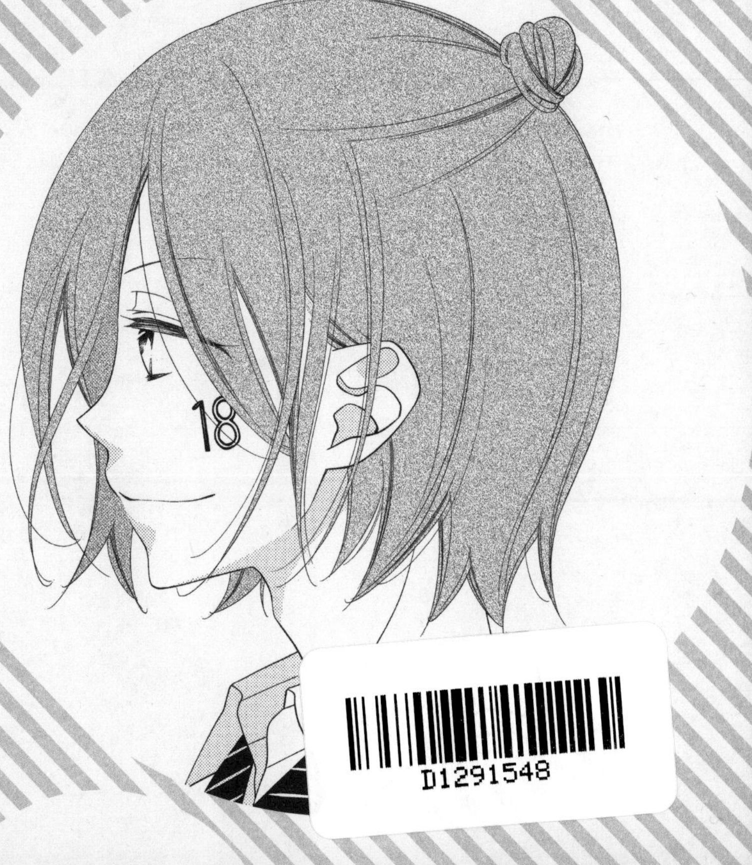

Anonymous Noise
Volume 18

CONTENTS

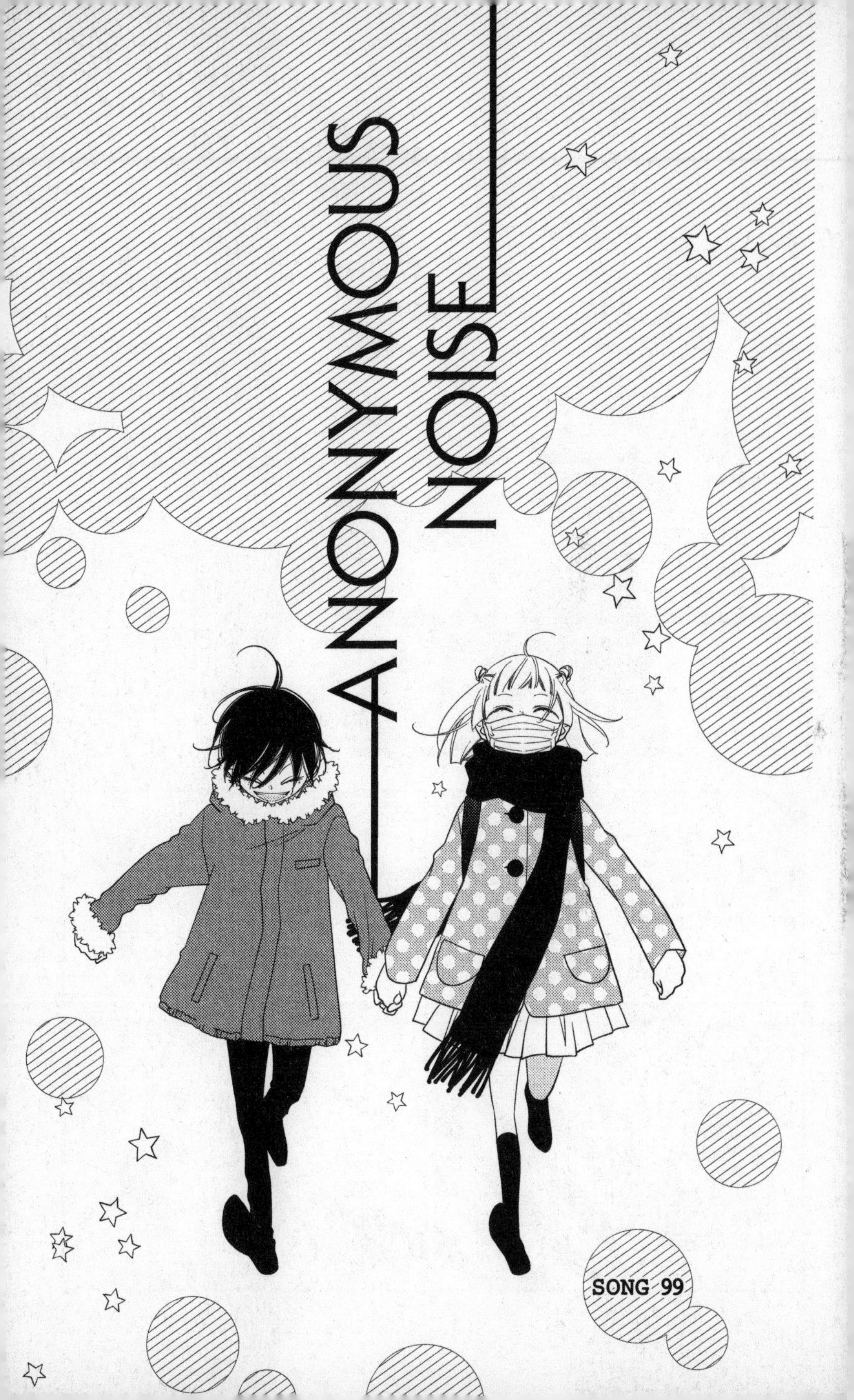
ANONYMOUS NOISE
SONG 99

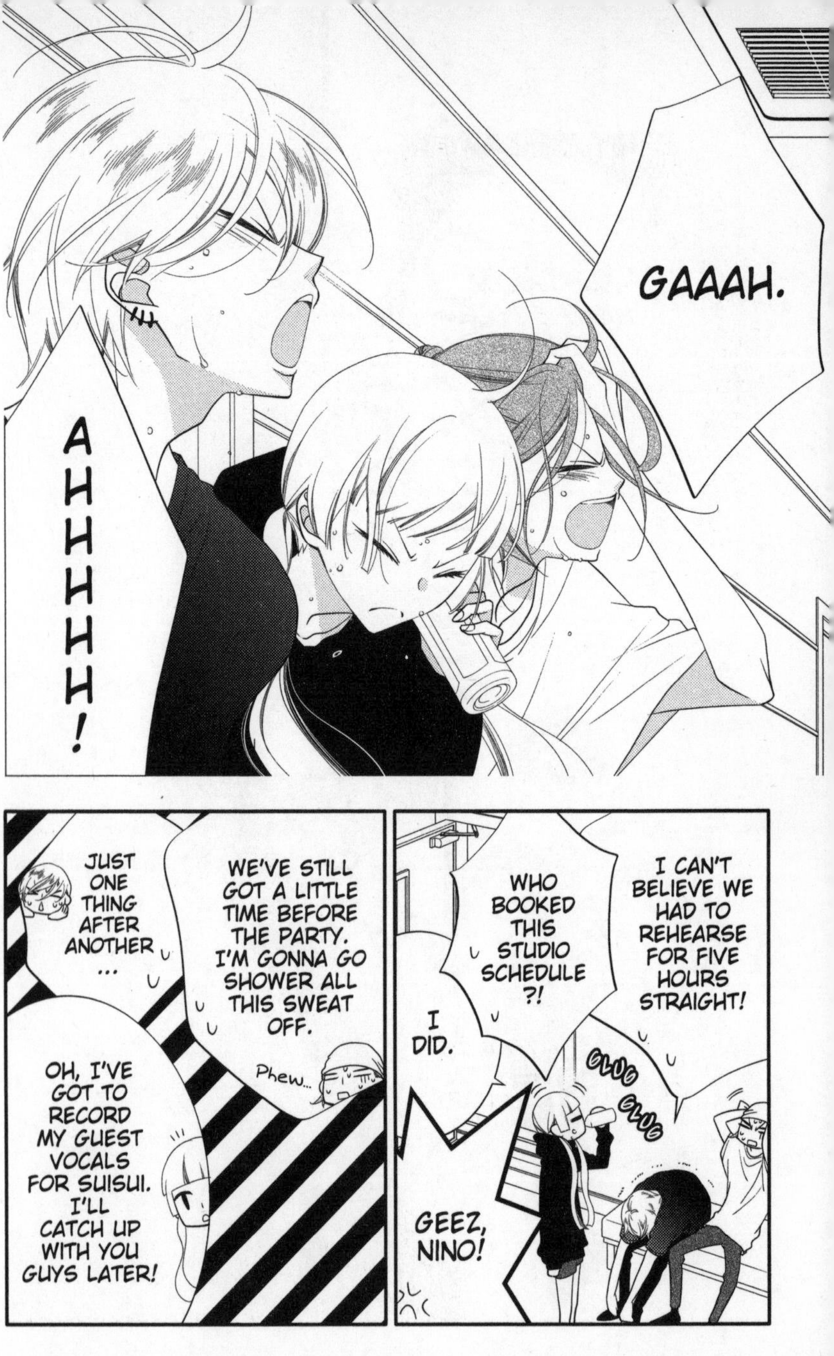
GAAAH.
AHHHHH!
I CAN'T BELIEVE WE HAD TO REHEARSE FOR FIVE HOURS STRAIGHT!
WHO BOOKED THIS STUDIO SCHEDULE?!
I DID.
GLUG GLUG
GEEZ, NINO!
WE'VE STILL GOT A LITTLE TIME BEFORE THE PARTY. I'M GONNA GO SHOWER ALL THIS SWEAT OFF.
JUST ONE THING AFTER ANOTHER...
Phew...
OH, I'VE GOT TO RECORD MY GUEST VOCALS FOR SUISUI. I'LL CATCH UP WITH YOU GUYS LATER!

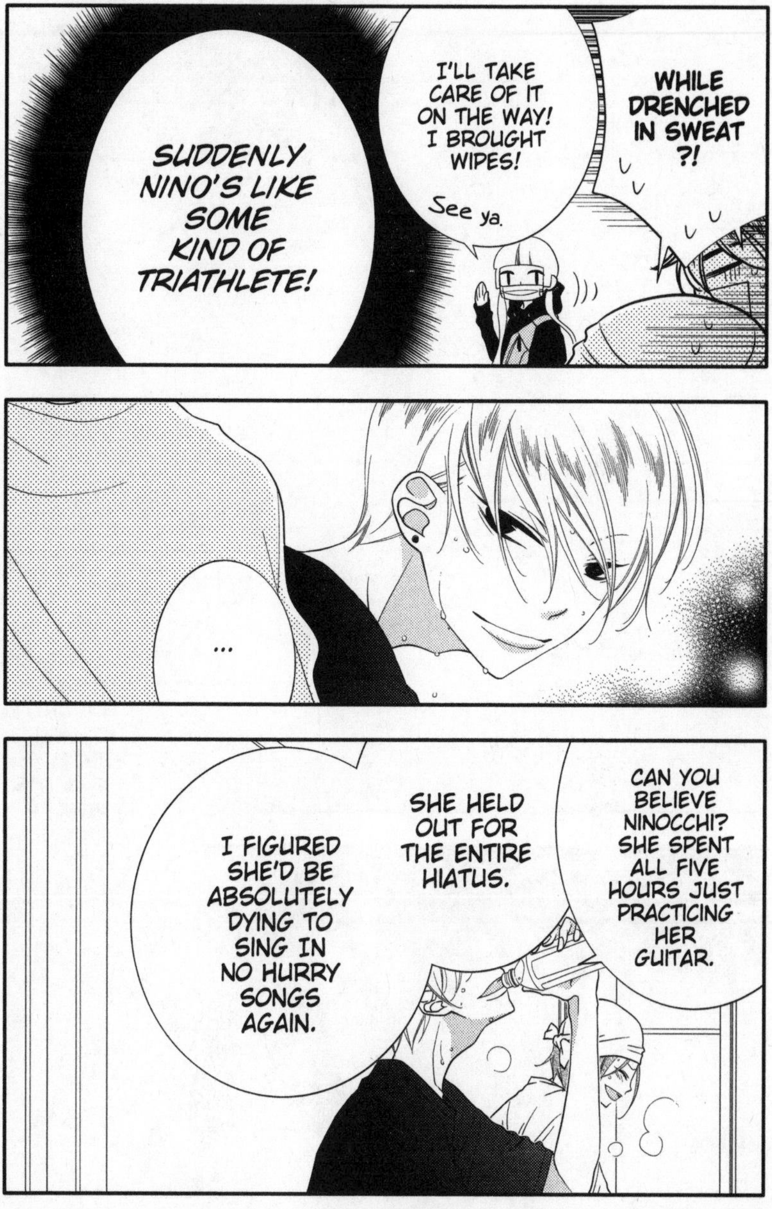
WHILE DRENCHED IN SWEAT?!
I'LL TAKE CARE OF IT ON THE WAY! I BROUGHT WIPES!
See ya.
SUDDENLY NINO'S LIKE SOME KIND OF TRIATHLETE!
...
CAN YOU BELIEVE NINOCCHI? SHE SPENT ALL FIVE HOURS JUST PRACTICING HER GUITAR.
SHE HELD OUT FOR THE ENTIRE HIATUS.
I FIGURED SHE'D BE ABSOLUTELY DYING TO SING IN NO HURRY SONGS AGAIN.

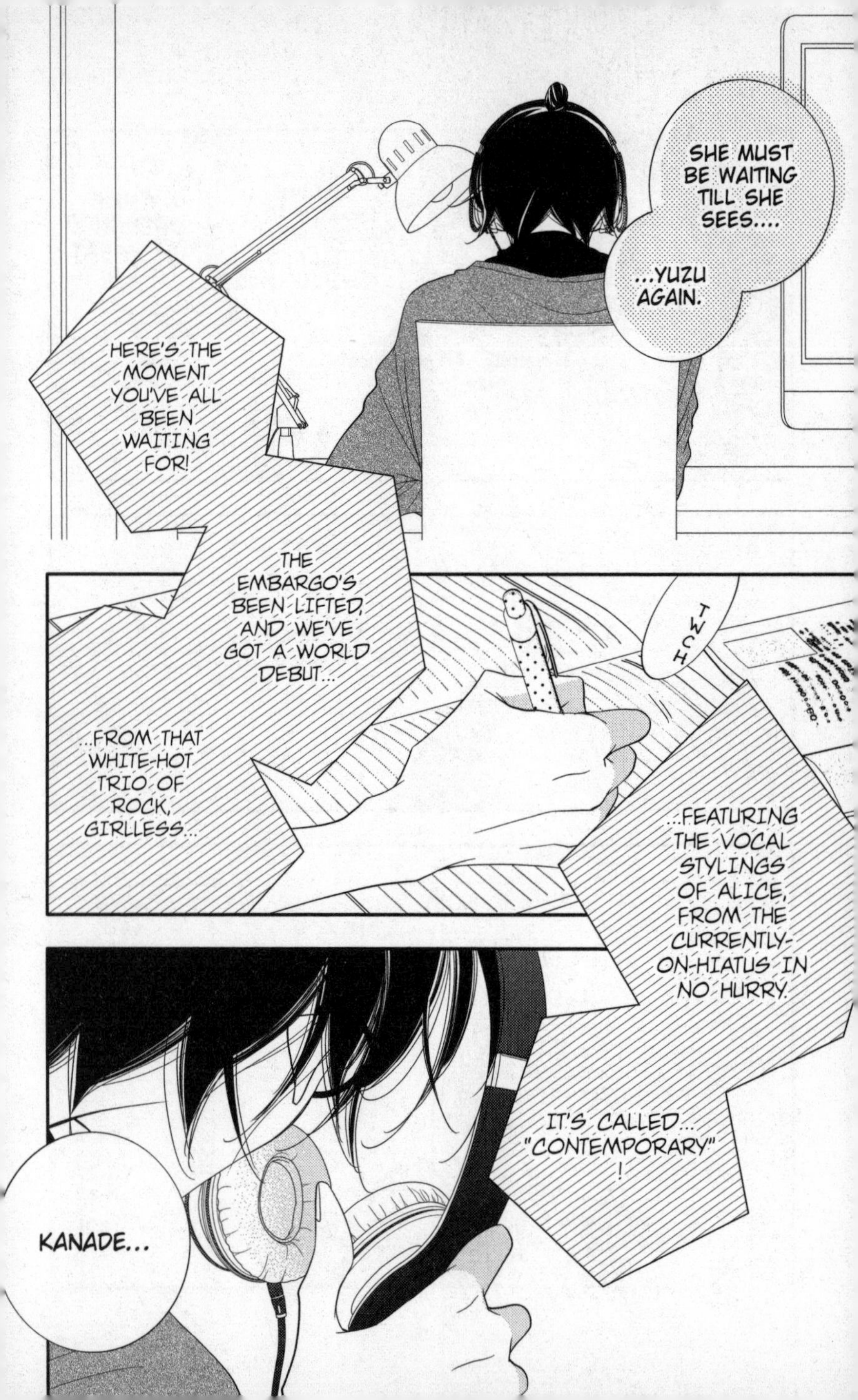
SHE MUST BE WAITING TILL SHE SEES....
...YUZU AGAIN.
HERE'S THE MOMENT YOU'VE ALL BEEN WAITING FOR!
THE EMBARGO'S BEEN LIFTED, AND WE'VE GOT A WORLD DEBUT...
TWCH
...FROM THAT WHITE-HOT TRIO OF ROCK, GIRLLESS...
...FEATURING THE VOCAL STYLINGS OF ALICE, FROM THE CURRENTLY-ON-HIATUS IN NO HURRY.
IT'S CALLED... "CONTEMPORARY"!
KANADE...

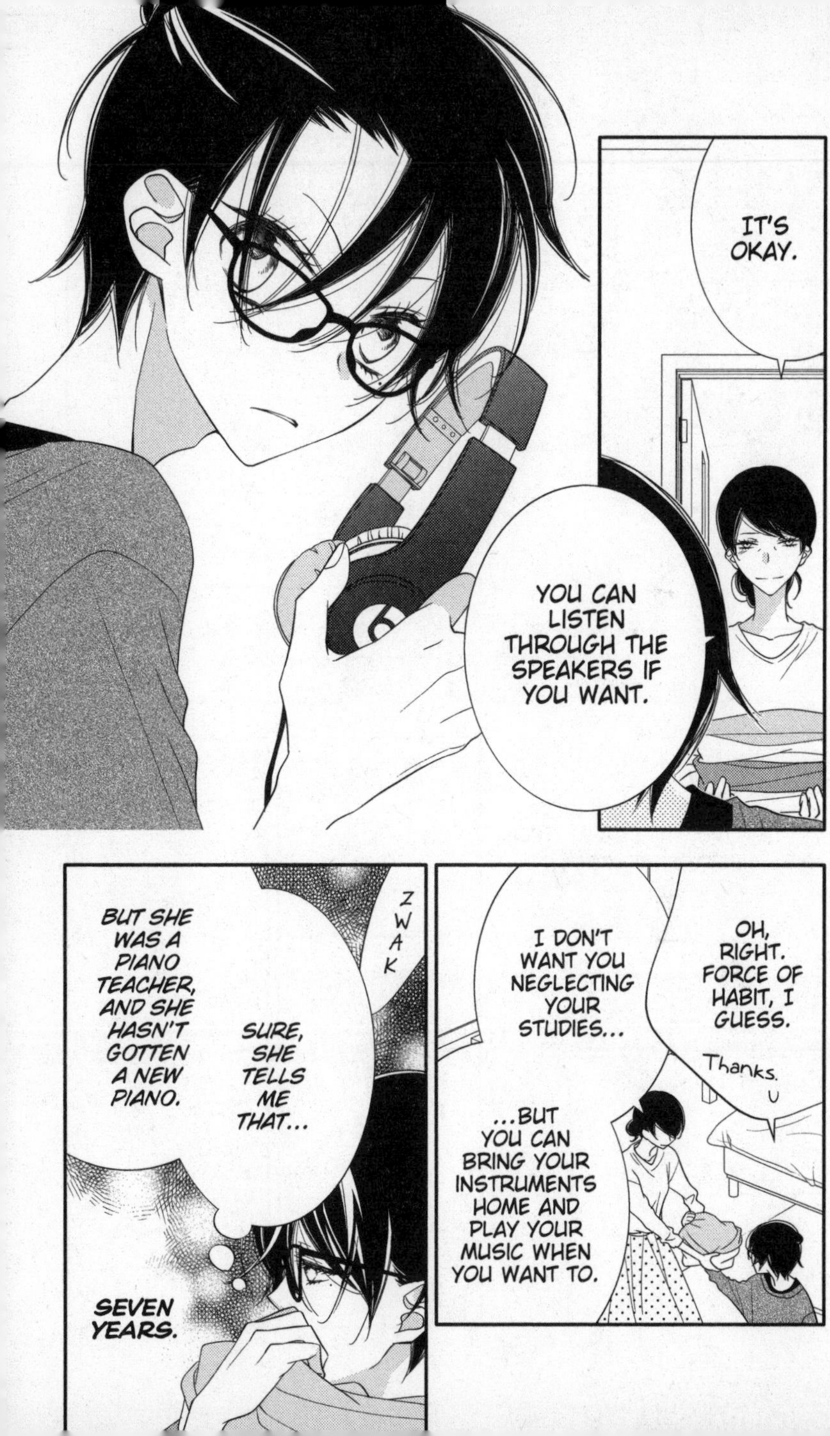
IT'S OKAY.
YOU CAN LISTEN THROUGH THE SPEAKERS IF YOU WANT.
OH, RIGHT. FORCE OF HABIT, I GUESS.
Thanks.
I DON'T WANT YOU NEGLECTING YOUR STUDIES...
...BUT YOU CAN BRING YOUR INSTRUMENTS HOME AND PLAY YOUR MUSIC WHEN YOU WANT TO.
ZWAK
SURE, SHE TELLS ME THAT...
BUT SHE WAS A PIANO TEACHER, AND SHE HASN'T GOTTEN A NEW PIANO.
SEVEN YEARS.

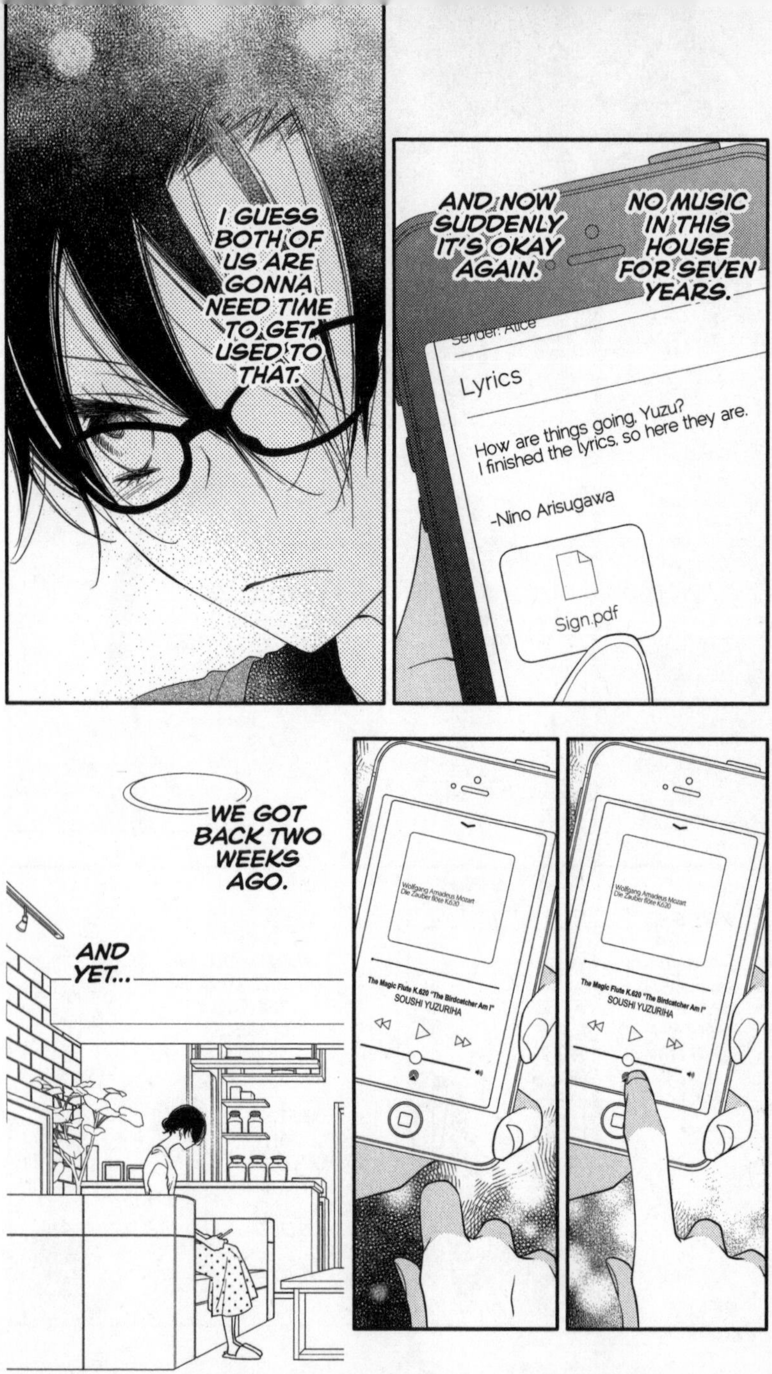
NO MUSIC IN THIS HOUSE FOR SEVEN YEARS.
AND NOW SUDDENLY IT'S OKAY AGAIN.
Lyrics
How are things going, Yuzu? I finished the lyrics, so here they are.
-Nino Arisugawa
Sign.pdf
I GUESS BOTH OF US ARE GONNA NEED TIME TO GET USED TO THAT.
Wolfgang Amadeus Mozart Die Zauber flöte K.620
The Magic Flute K.620 "The Birdcatcher Am I"
SOUSHI YUZURIHA
Wolfgang Amadeus Mozart Die Zauber flöte K.620
The Magic Flute K.620 "The Birdcatcher Am I"
SOUSHI YUZURIHA
WE GOT BACK TWO WEEKS AGO.
AND YET...

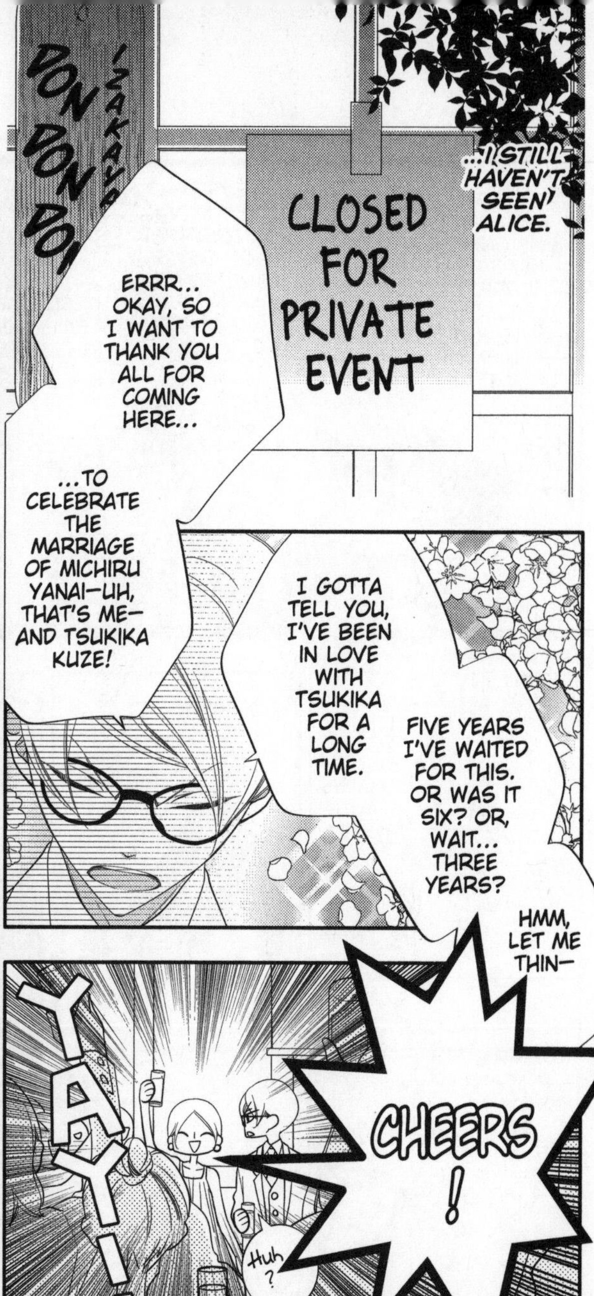
...I STILL HAVEN'T SEEN ALICE.
CLOSED FOR PRIVATE EVENT
IZAKAYA
DON DON DON
ERRR... OKAY, SO I WANT TO THANK YOU ALL FOR COMING HERE...
...TO CELEBRATE THE MARRIAGE OF MICHIRU YANAI—UH, THAT'S ME—AND TSUKIKA KUZE!
I GOTTA TELL YOU, I'VE BEEN IN LOVE WITH TSUKIKA FOR A LONG TIME.
FIVE YEARS I'VE WAITED FOR THIS. OR WAS IT SIX? OR, WAIT... THREE YEARS?
HMM, LET ME THIN—
CHEERS!
YAY!
Huh?

1

Hello and welcome!

Ryoko Fukuyama here.

Thank you for picking up volume 18 of Anonymous Noise. At long last, we've reached the final volume! Wow, this is it...

Kurose is on this volume's cover because it was his turn. I've been experimenting with a new painting style, so drawing this piece felt fresh and fun. I'm so glad it proved to be such a good fit!

This may be the last volume, but writing this column feels the same as always. I really hope you enjoy volume 18!

MY CAT IS NOW TEN YEARS OLD!

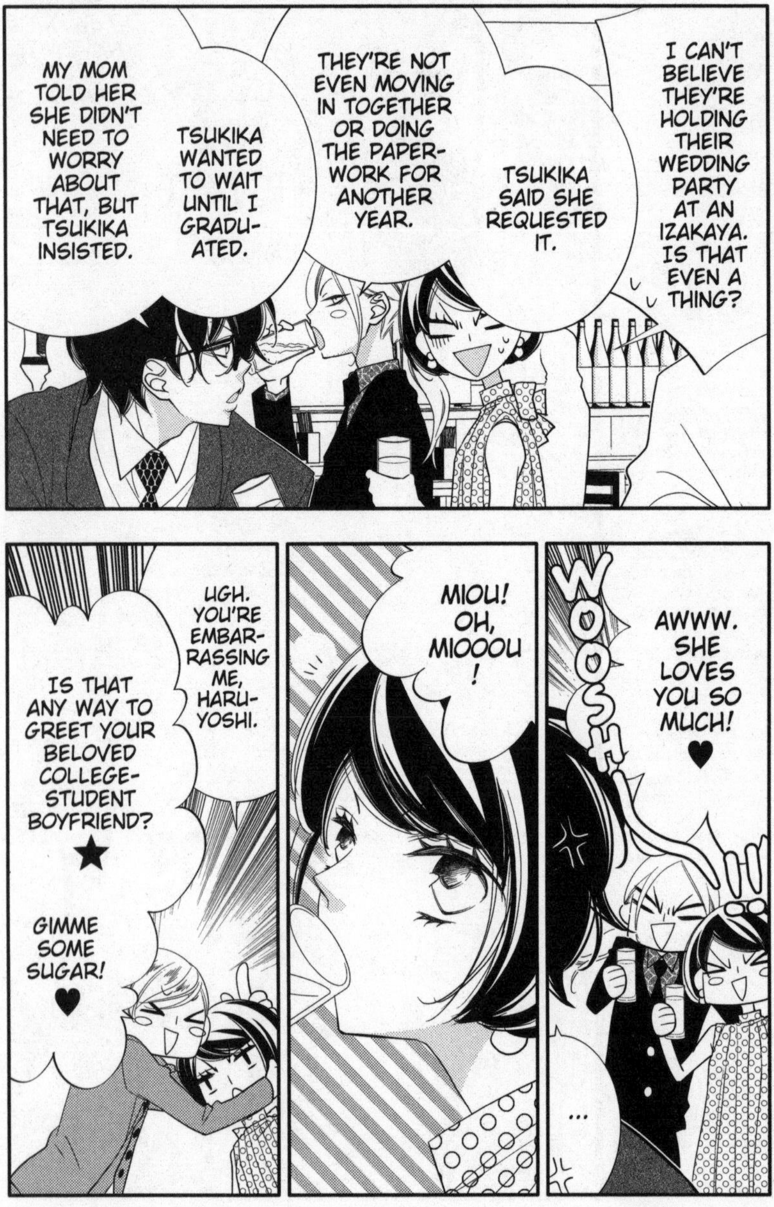
I CAN'T BELIEVE THEY'RE HOLDING THEIR WEDDING PARTY AT AN IZAKAYA. IS THAT EVEN A THING?
TSUKIKA SAID SHE REQUESTED IT.
THEY'RE NOT EVEN MOVING IN TOGETHER OR DOING THE PAPER-WORK FOR ANOTHER YEAR.
TSUKIKA WANTED TO WAIT UNTIL I GRADU-ATED.
MY MOM TOLD HER SHE DIDN'T NEED TO WORRY ABOUT THAT, BUT TSUKIKA INSISTED.
WOOSH!
AWWW. SHE LOVES YOU SO MUCH! ♥
...
MIOU! OH, MIOOOU!
UGH. YOU'RE EMBAR-RASSING ME, HARU-YOSHI.
IS THAT ANY WAY TO GREET YOUR BELOVED COLLEGE-STUDENT BOYFRIEND? ★
GIMME SOME SUGAR! ♥

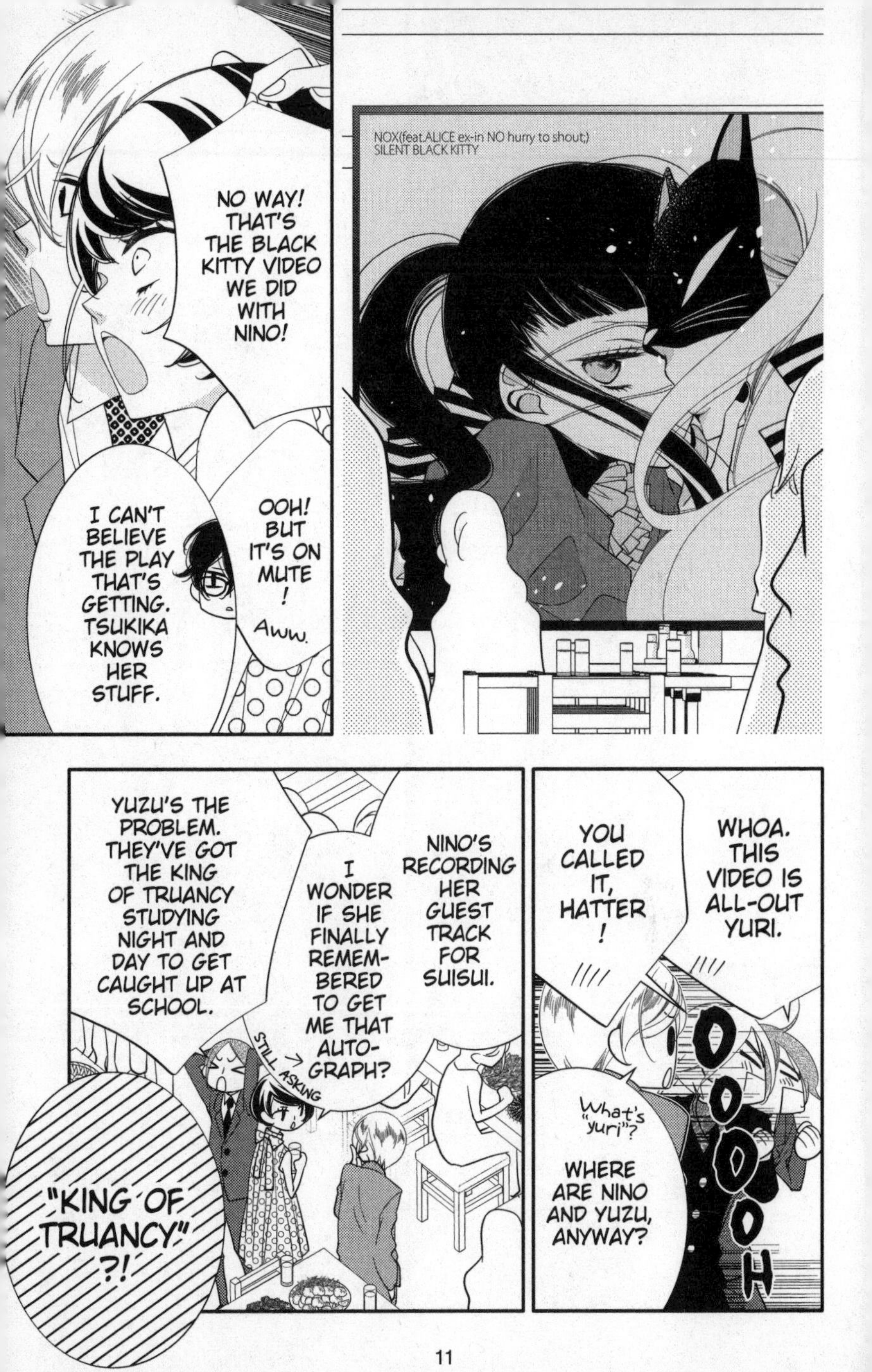
NOX(feat.ALICE ex-in NO hurry to shout,)
SILENT BLACK KITTY
NO WAY! THAT'S THE BLACK KITTY VIDEO WE DID WITH NINO!
OOH! BUT IT'S ON MUTE!
Aww.
I CAN'T BELIEVE THE PLAY THAT'S GETTING. TSUKIKA KNOWS HER STUFF.
WHOA. THIS VIDEO IS ALL-OUT YURI.
YOU CALLED IT, HATTER!
OOOOOH
What's "yuri"?
WHERE ARE NINO AND YUZU, ANYWAY?
NINO'S RECORDING HER GUEST TRACK FOR SUISUI.
I WONDER IF SHE FINALLY REMEMBERED TO GET ME THAT AUTOGRAPH?
STILL ASKING
YUZU'S THE PROBLEM. THEY'VE GOT THE KING OF TRUANCY STUDYING NIGHT AND DAY TO GET CAUGHT UP AT SCHOOL.
"KING OF TRUANCY"?!

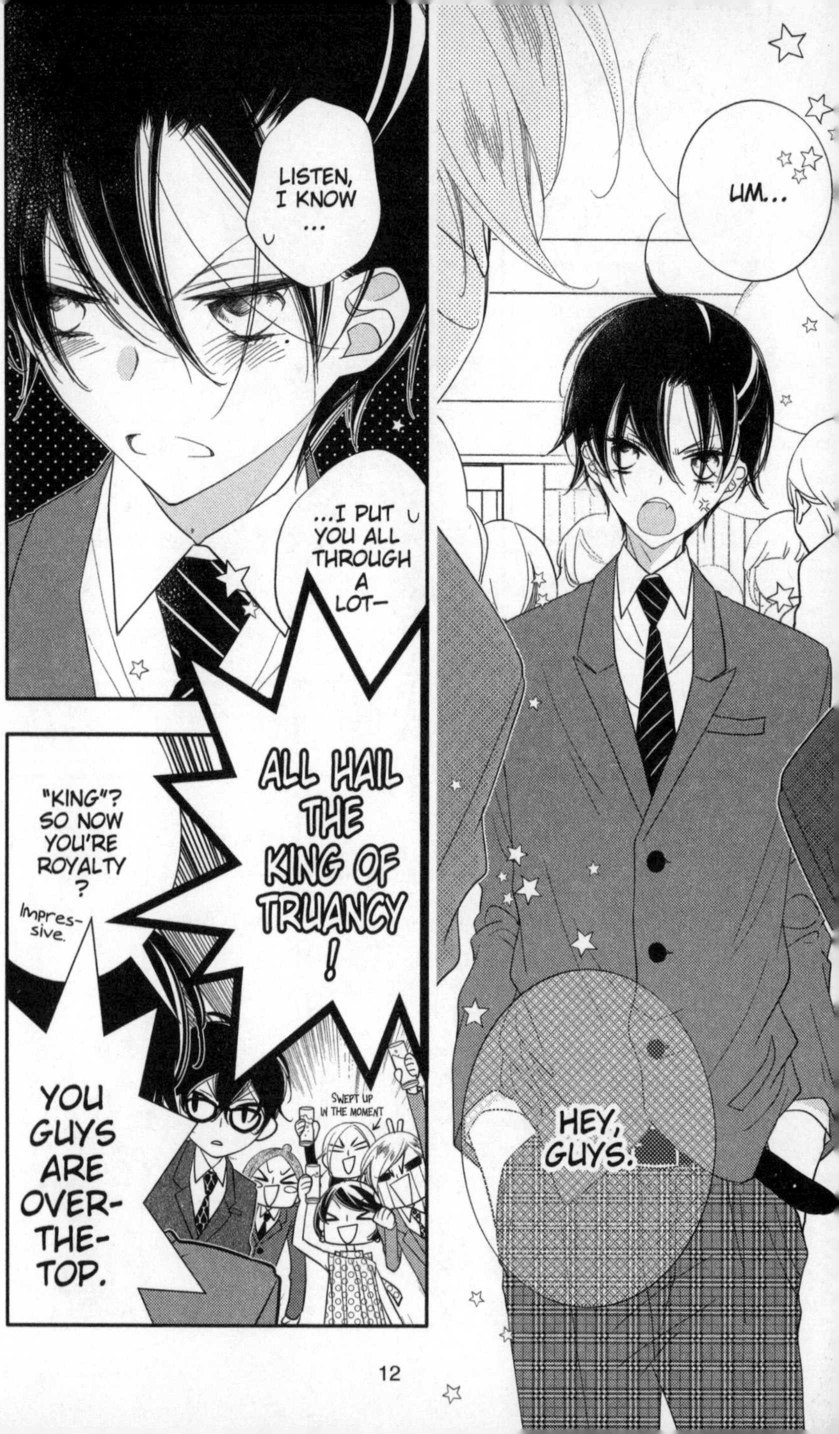
UM...
HEY, GUYS.
LISTEN, I KNOW...
...I PUT YOU ALL THROUGH A LOT—
ALL HAIL THE KING OF TRUANCY!
"KING"? SO NOW YOU'RE ROYALTY?
Impressive.
SWEPT UP IN THE MOMENT
YOU GUYS ARE OVER-THE-TOP.

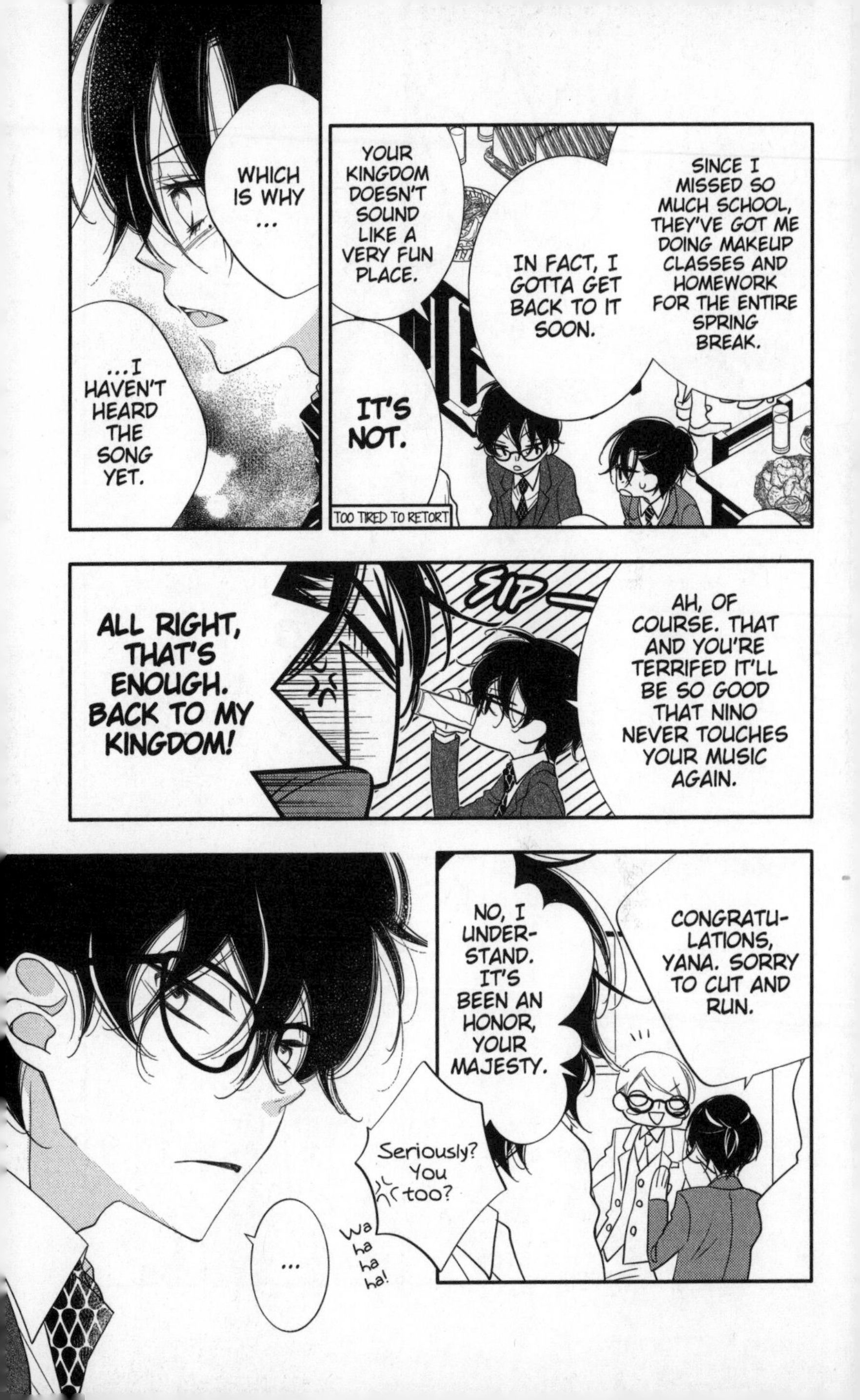
SINCE I MISSED SO MUCH SCHOOL, THEY'VE GOT ME DOING MAKEUP CLASSES AND HOMEWORK FOR THE ENTIRE SPRING BREAK.
IN FACT, I GOTTA GET BACK TO IT SOON.
YOUR KINGDOM DOESN'T SOUND LIKE A VERY FUN PLACE.
IT'S NOT.
TOO TIRED TO RETORT
WHICH IS WHY ...
...I HAVEN'T HEARD THE SONG YET.
AH, OF COURSE. THAT AND YOU'RE TERRIFED IT'LL BE SO GOOD THAT NINO NEVER TOUCHES YOUR MUSIC AGAIN.
SIP
ALL RIGHT, THAT'S ENOUGH. BACK TO MY KINGDOM!
CONGRATULATIONS, YANA. SORRY TO CUT AND RUN.
NO, I UNDERSTAND. IT'S BEEN AN HONOR, YOUR MAJESTY.
Seriously? You too?
Wa ha ha ha!
...

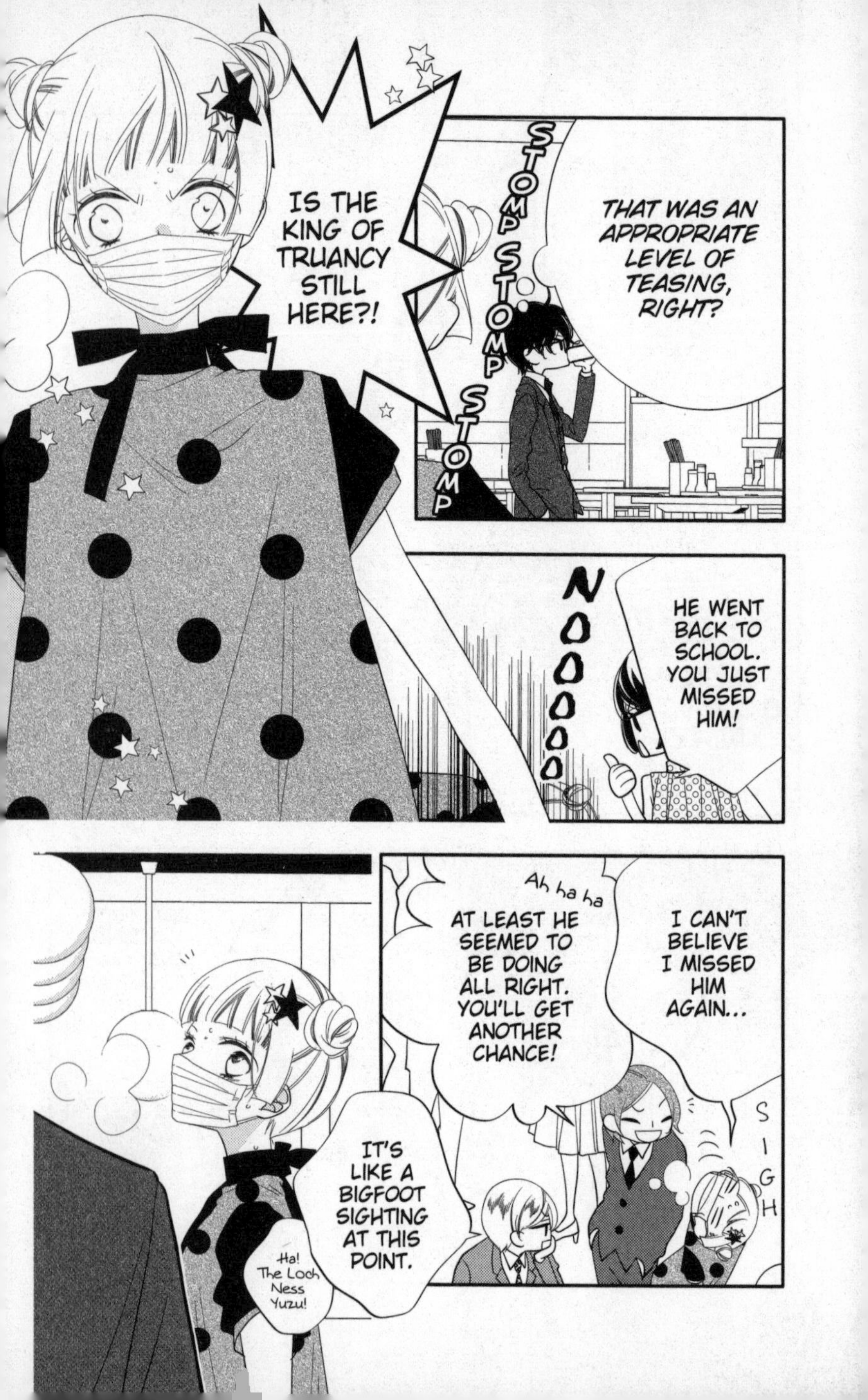

THAT WAS AN APPROPRIATE LEVEL OF TEASING, RIGHT?
STOMP STOMP STOMP STOMP
HE WENT BACK TO SCHOOL. YOU JUST MISSED HIM!
NOOOOOOO
IS THE KING OF TRUANCY STILL HERE?!
I CAN'T BELIEVE I MISSED HIM AGAIN...
SIGH
Ah ha ha
AT LEAST HE SEEMED TO BE DOING ALL RIGHT. YOU'LL GET ANOTHER CHANCE!
IT'S LIKE A BIGFOOT SIGHTING AT THIS POINT.
Ha! The Loch Ness Yuzu!

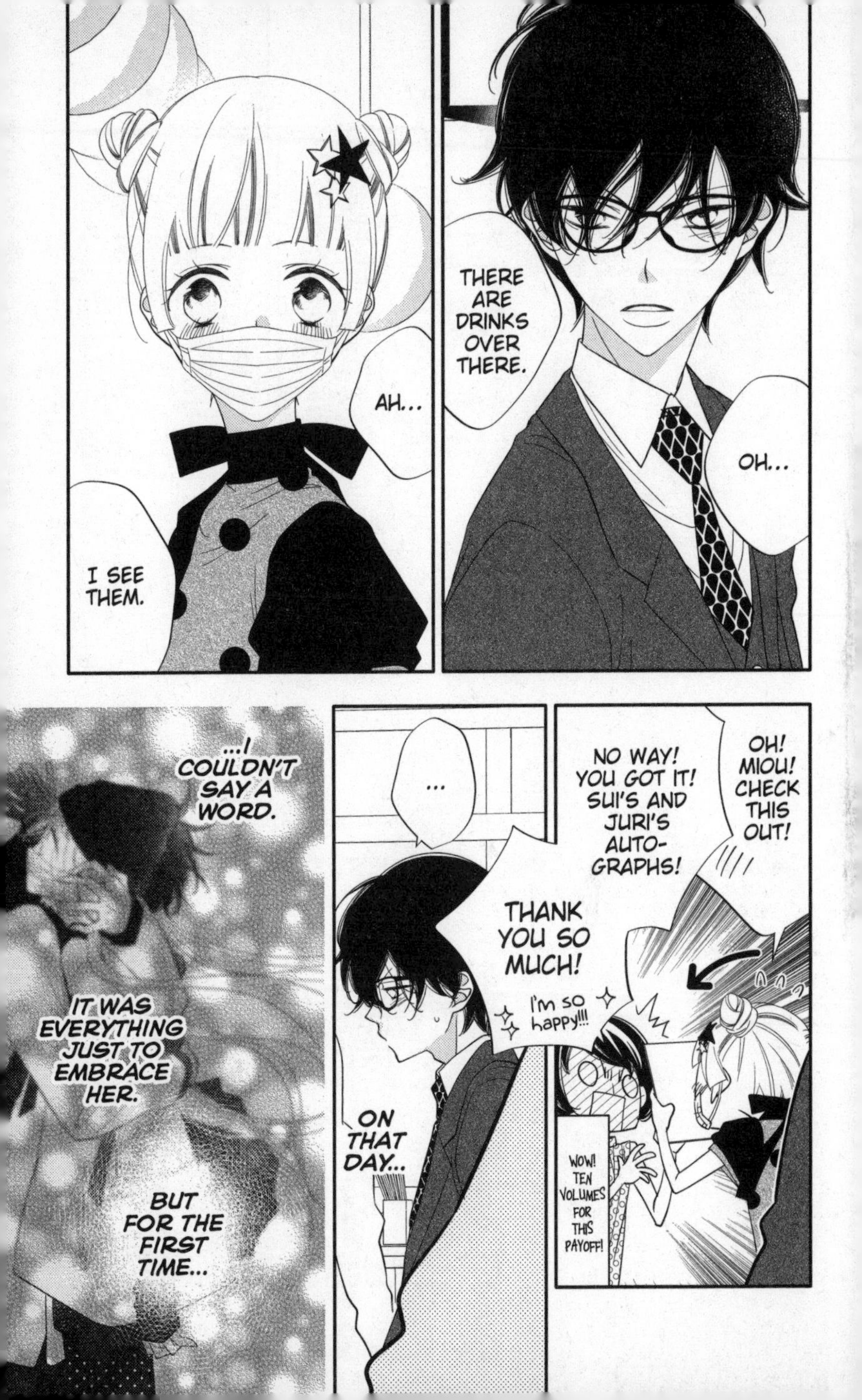
THERE ARE DRINKS OVER THERE.
OH...
AH...
I SEE THEM.
OH! MIOU! CHECK THIS OUT!
NO WAY! YOU GOT IT! SUI'S AND JURI'S AUTO-GRAPHS!
THANK YOU SO MUCH!
I'm so happy!!!
WOW! TEN VOLUMES FOR THIS PAYOFF!
...
ON THAT DAY...
...I COULDN'T SAY A WORD.
IT WAS EVERYTHING JUST TO EMBRACE HER.
BUT FOR THE FIRST TIME...

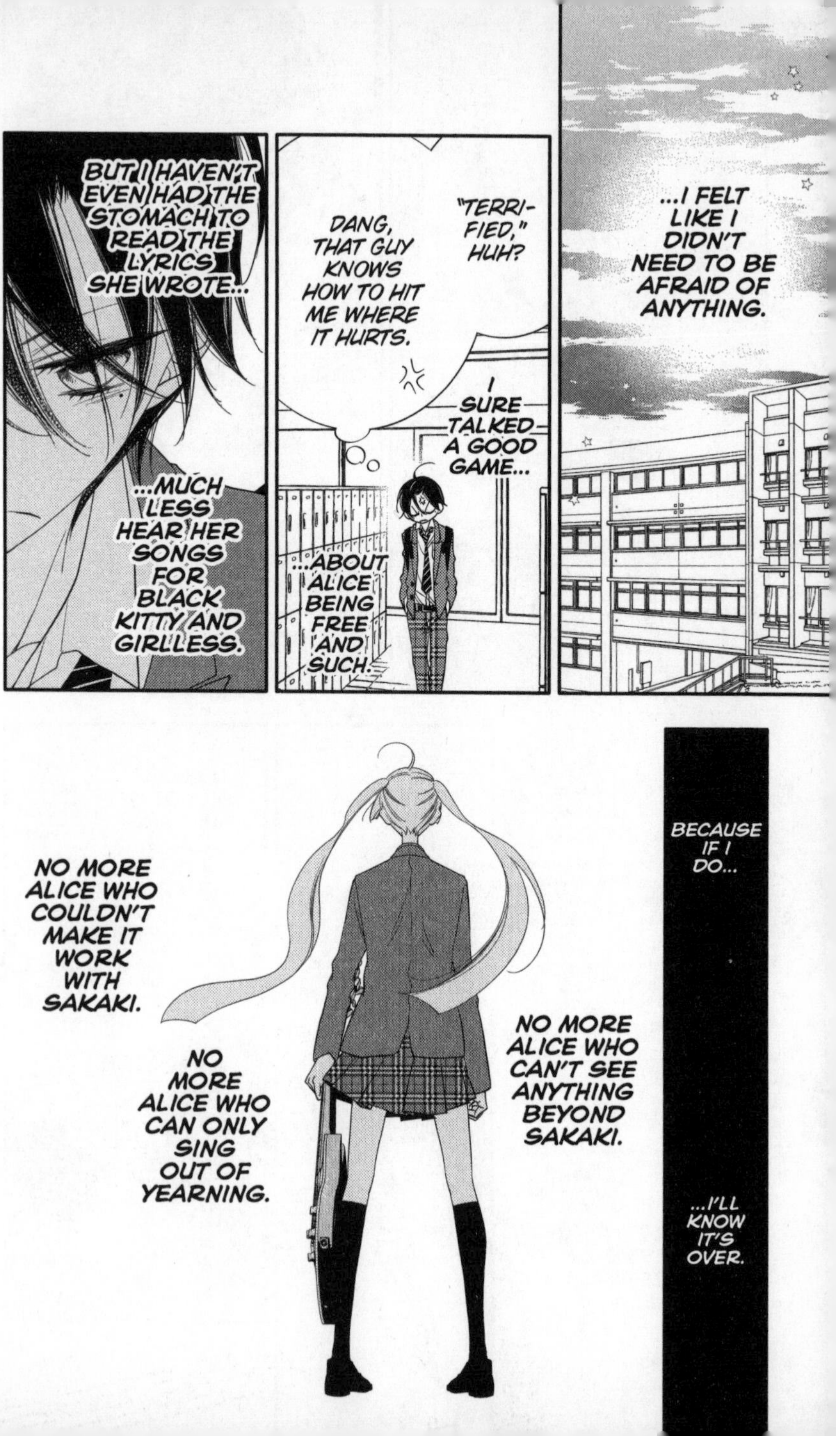
...I FELT LIKE I DIDN'T NEED TO BE AFRAID OF ANYTHING.
"TERRI-FIED," HUH?
DANG, THAT GUY KNOWS HOW TO HIT ME WHERE IT HURTS.
I SURE TALKED A GOOD GAME...
...ABOUT ALICE BEING FREE AND SUCH.
BUT I HAVEN'T EVEN HAD THE STOMACH TO READ THE LYRICS SHE WROTE...
...MUCH LESS HEAR HER SONGS FOR BLACK KITTY AND GIRLLESS.
BECAUSE IF I DO...
...I'LL KNOW IT'S OVER.
NO MORE ALICE WHO CAN'T SEE ANYTHING BEYOND SAKAKI.
NO MORE ALICE WHO COULDN'T MAKE IT WORK WITH SAKAKI.
NO MORE ALICE WHO CAN ONLY SING OUT OF YEARNING.

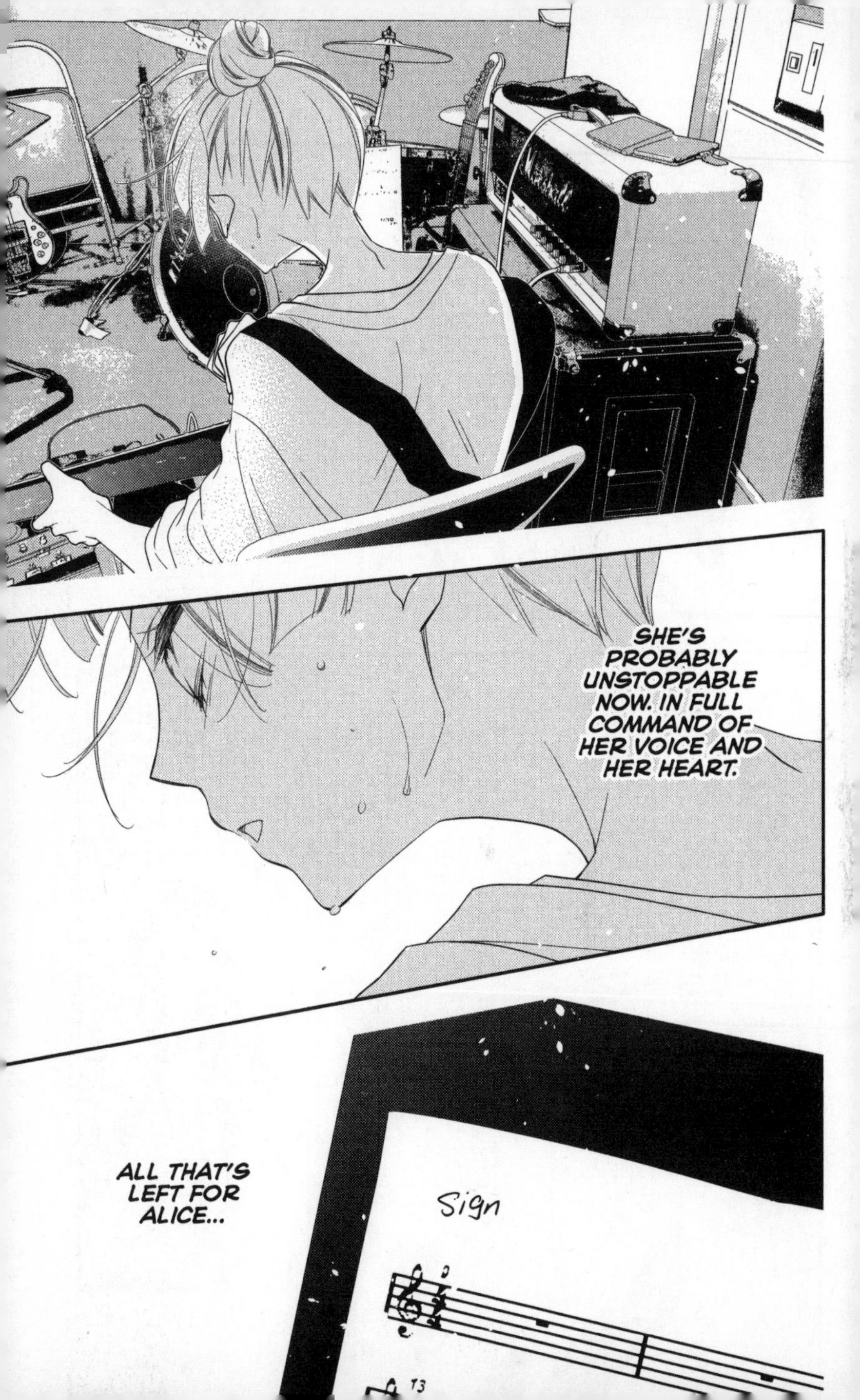
SHE'S PROBABLY UNSTOPPABLE NOW. IN FULL COMMAND OF HER VOICE AND HER HEART.
Sign
ALL THAT'S LEFT FOR ALICE...

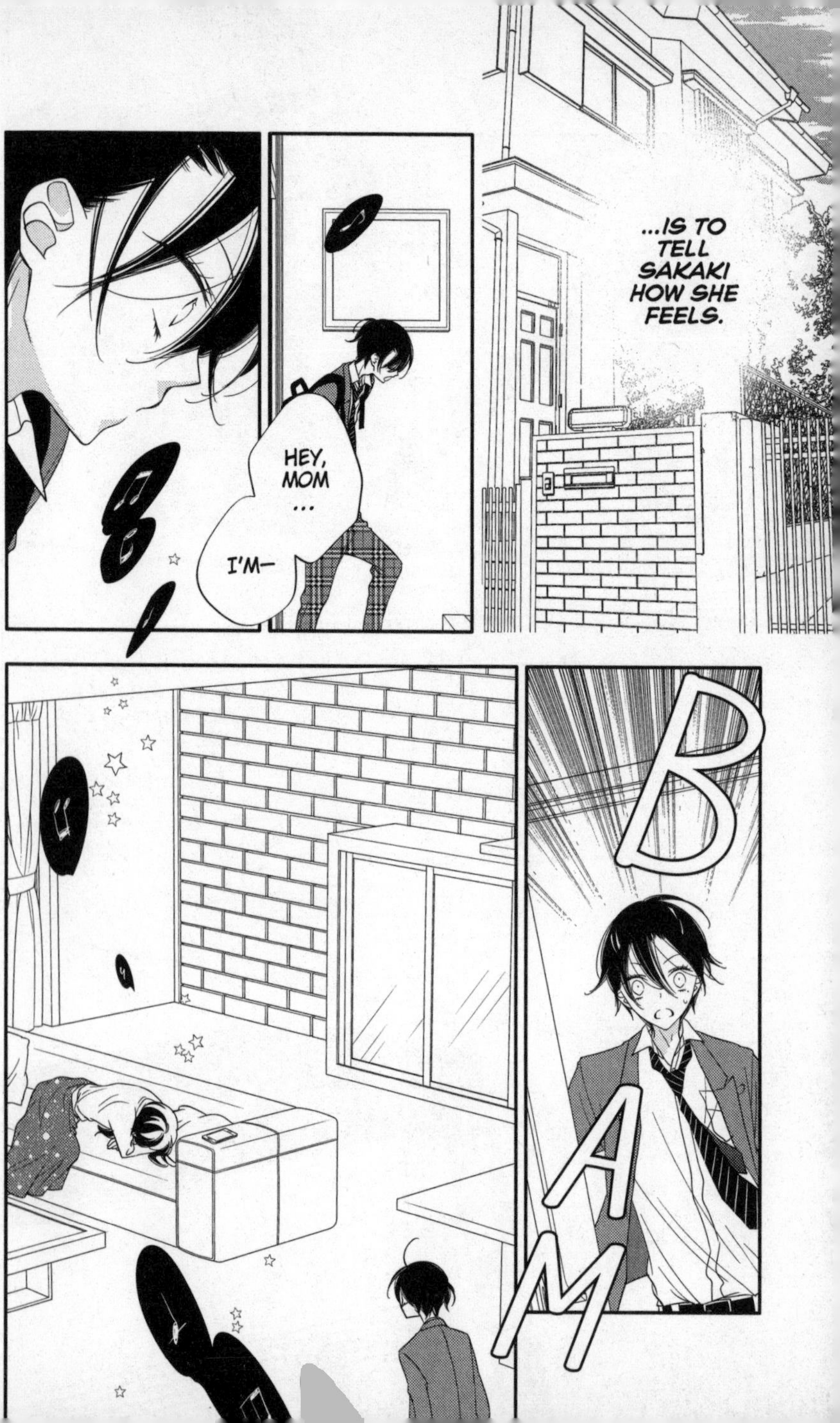
...IS TO TELL SAKAKI HOW SHE FEELS.
HEY, MOM ...
I'M—
BAM

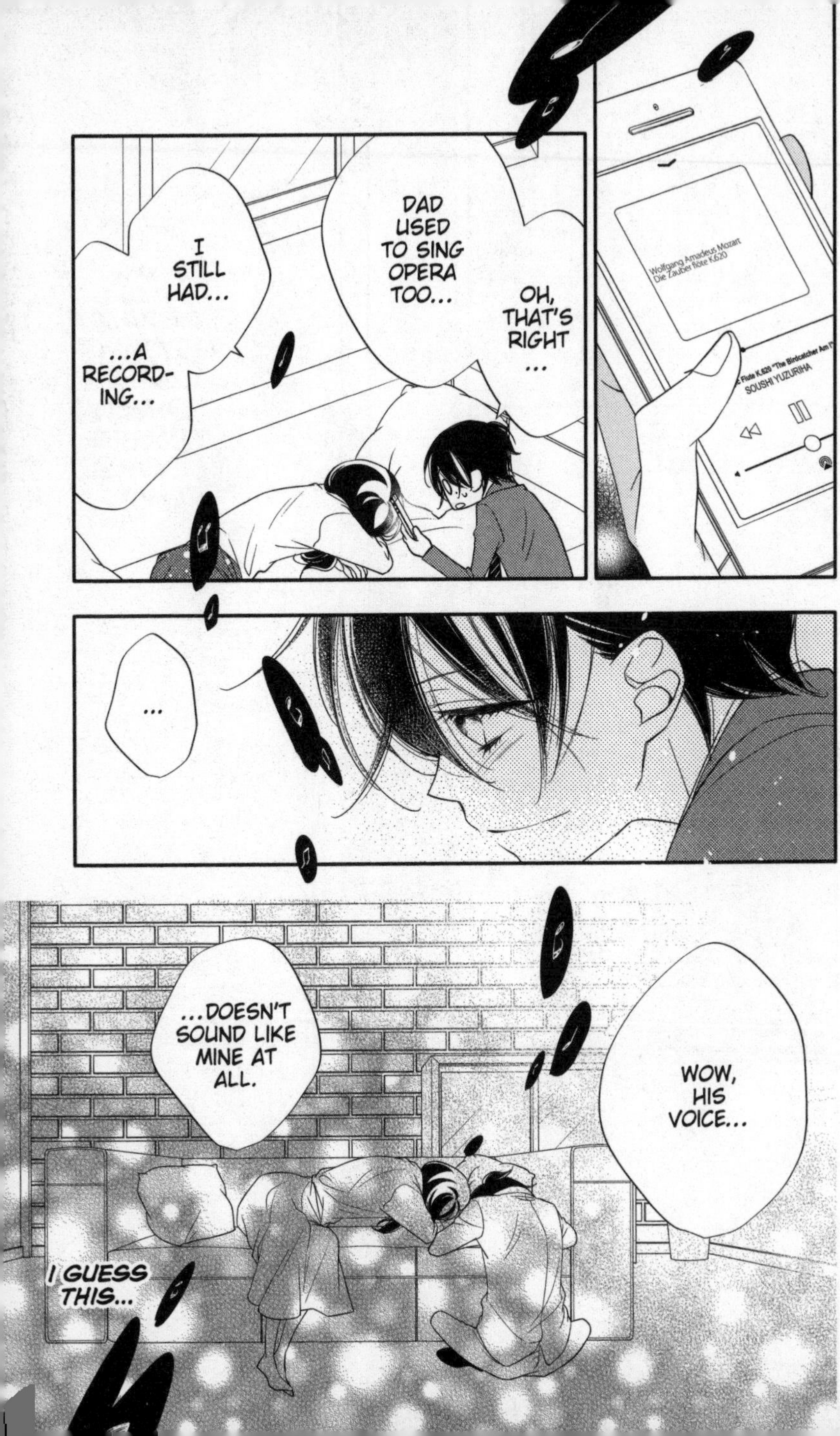
Wolfgang Amadeus Mozart
Die Zauber flöte K.620
Flute K.620 "The Birdcatcher Am I"
SOUSHI YUZURIHA
OH, THAT'S RIGHT...
DAD USED TO SING OPERA TOO...
I STILL HAD...
...A RECORDING...
...
WOW, HIS VOICE...
...DOESN'T SOUND LIKE MINE AT ALL.
I GUESS THIS...

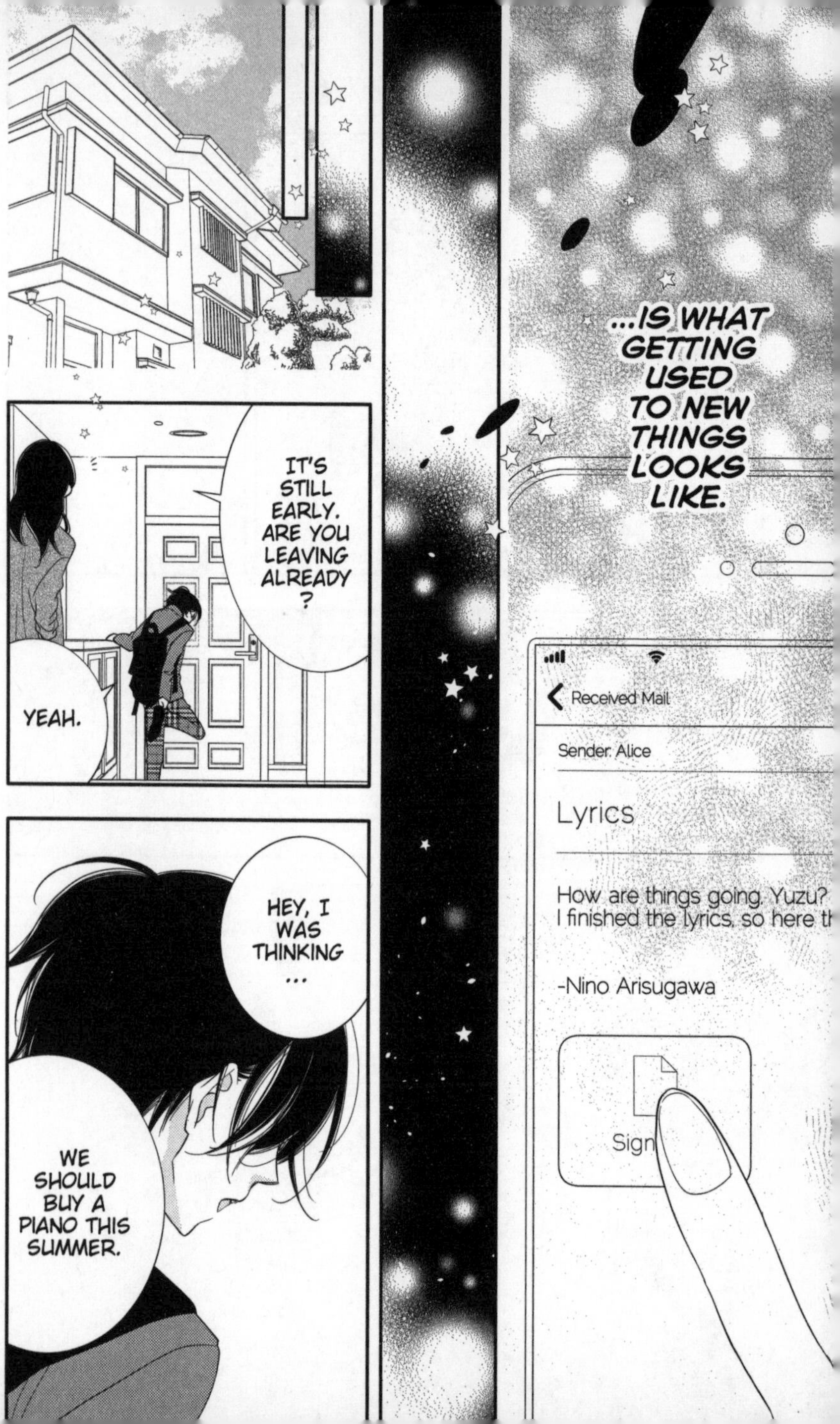
...IS WHAT GETTING USED TO NEW THINGS LOOKS LIKE.
Received Mail
Sender: Alice
Lyrics
How are things going, Yuzu?
I finished the lyrics, so here
-Nino Arisugawa
IT'S STILL EARLY. ARE YOU LEAVING ALREADY?
YEAH.
HEY, I WAS THINKING...
WE SHOULD BUY A PIANO THIS SUMMER.

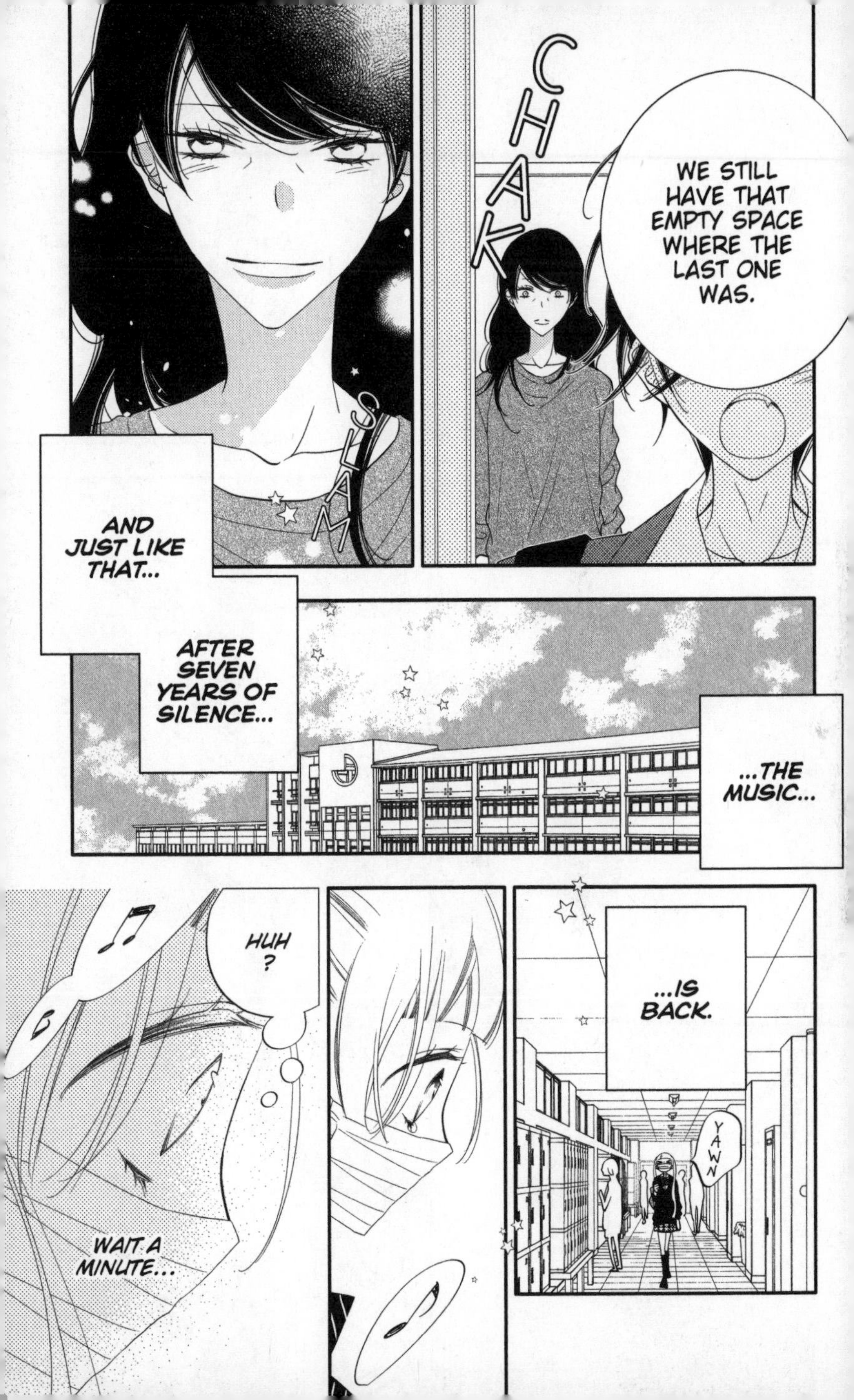
WE STILL HAVE THAT EMPTY SPACE WHERE THE LAST ONE WAS.
CHAK
SLAM
AND JUST LIKE THAT...
AFTER SEVEN YEARS OF SILENCE...
...THE MUSIC...
...IS BACK.
YAWN
HUH?
WAIT A MINUTE...

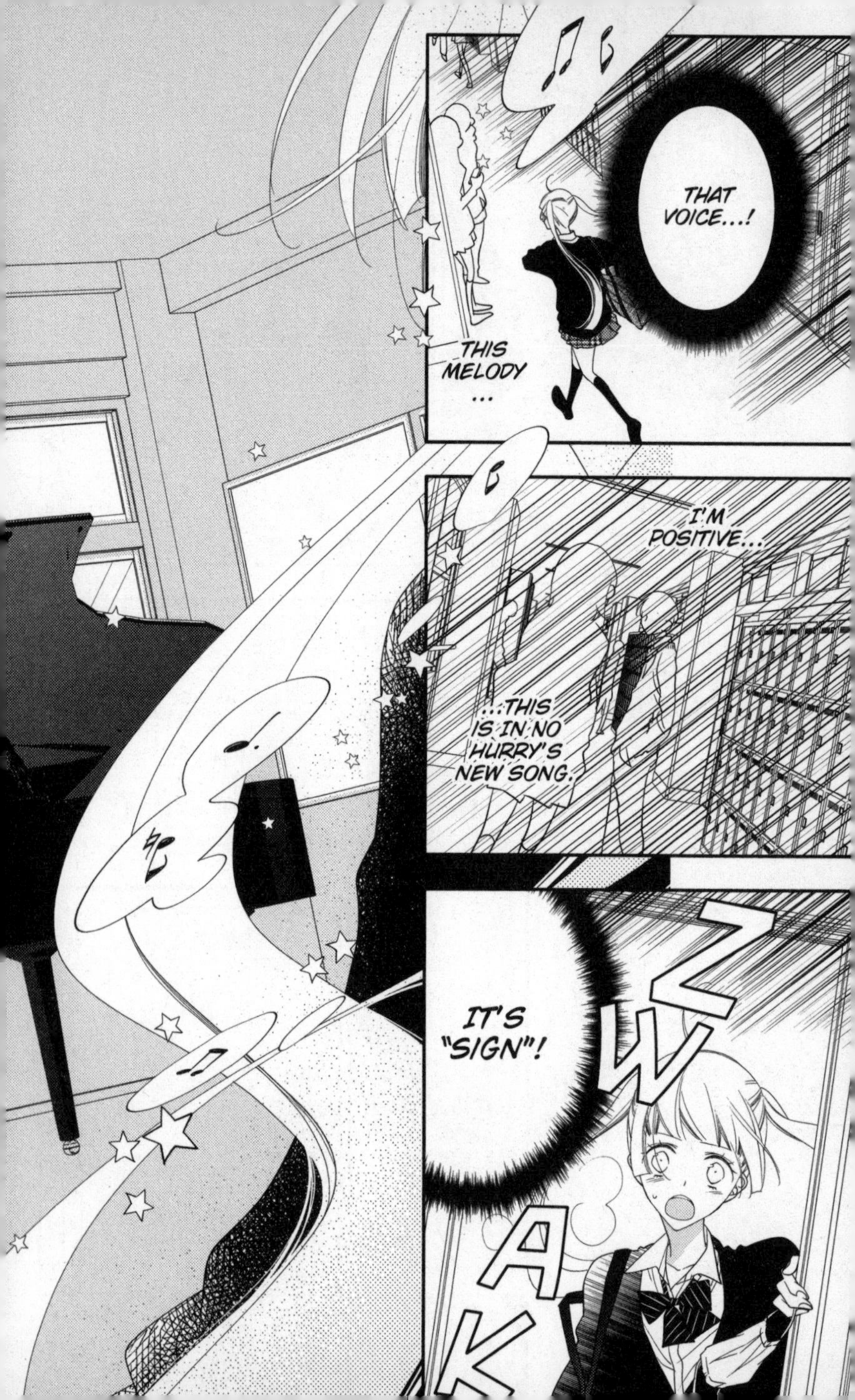
THAT VOICE...!
THIS MELODY ...
I'M POSITIVE...
...THIS IS IN NO HURRY'S NEW SONG.
ZWAK
IT'S "SIGN"!

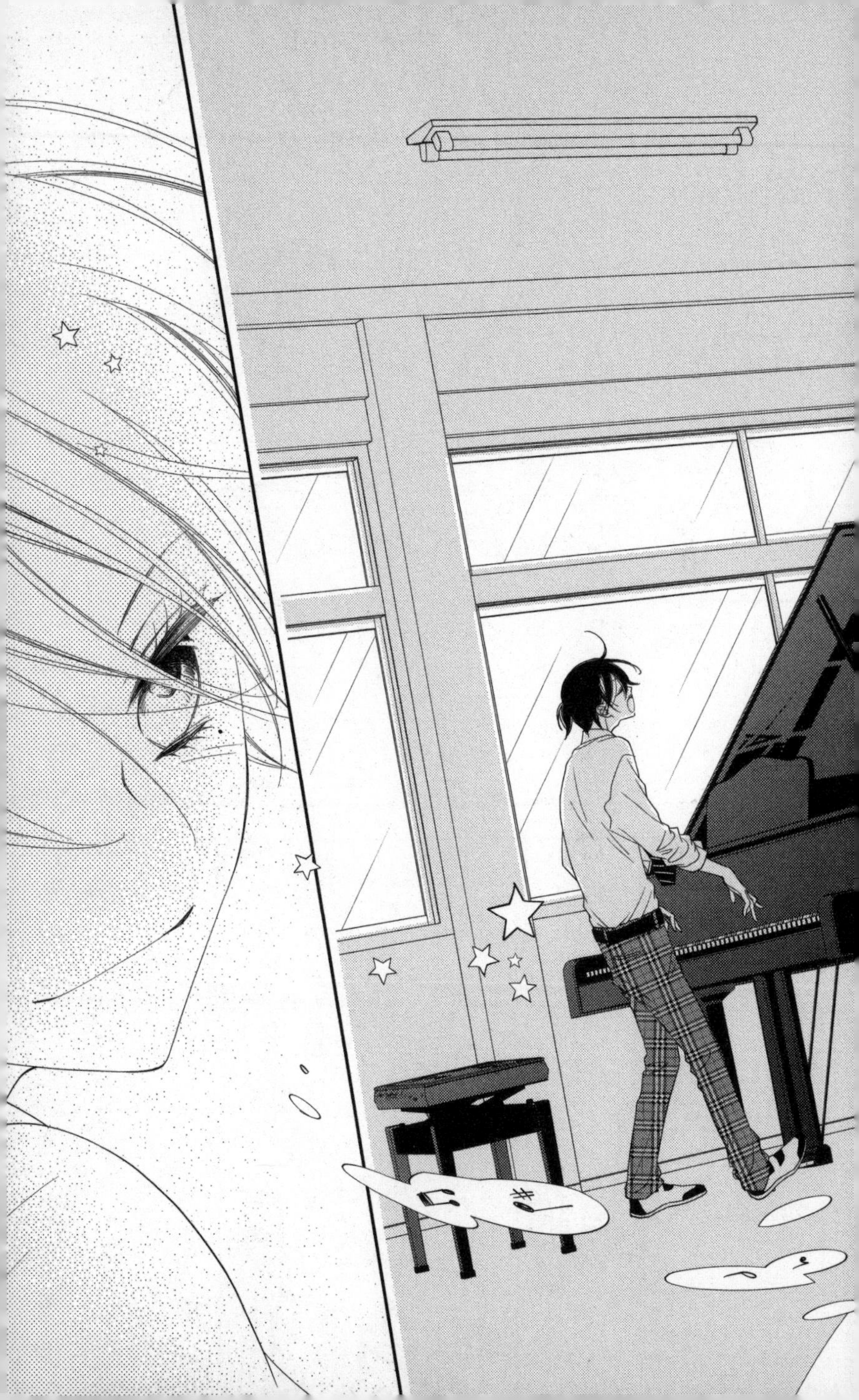

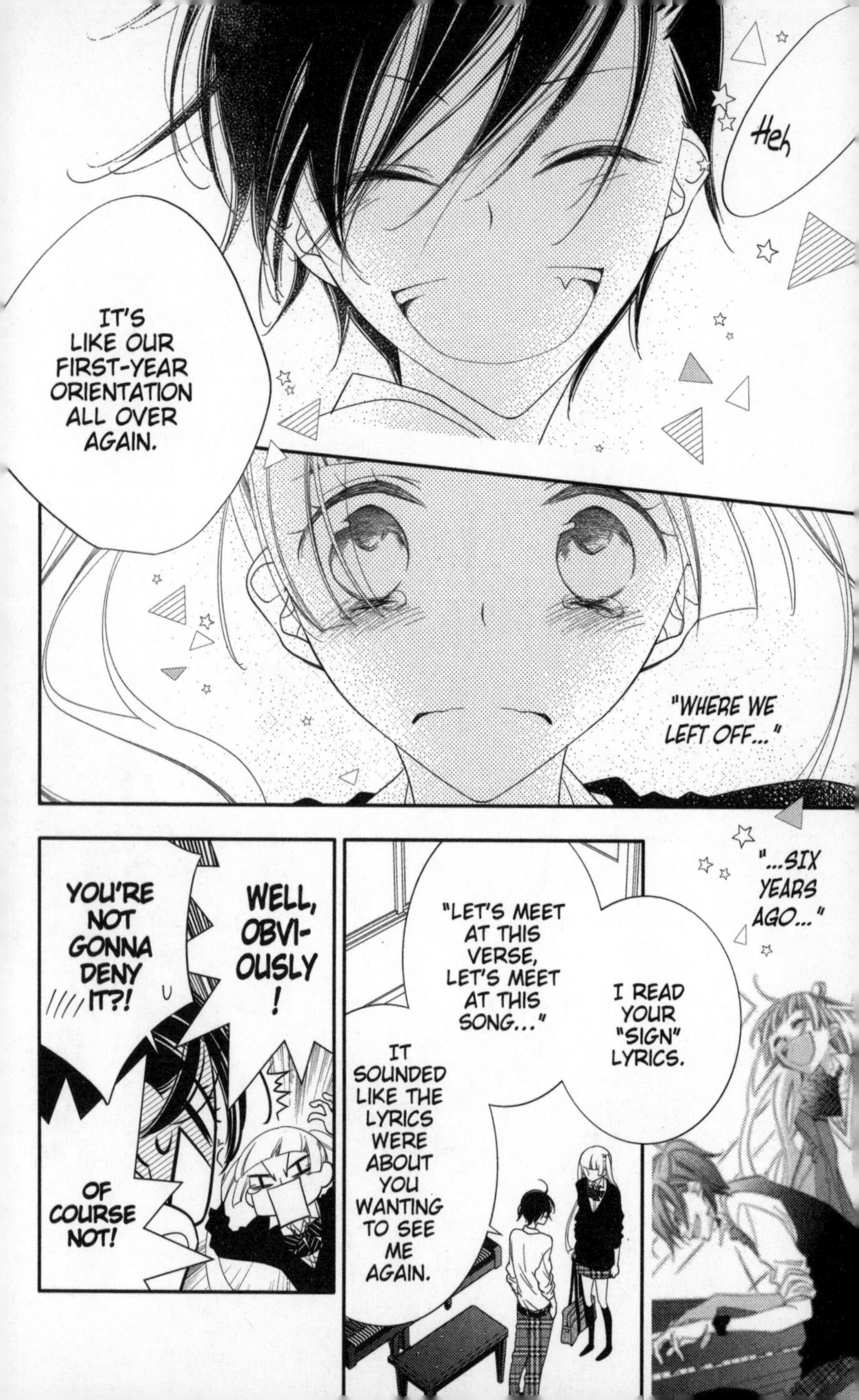
Heh
IT'S LIKE OUR FIRST-YEAR ORIENTATION ALL OVER AGAIN.
"WHERE WE LEFT OFF..."
"...SIX YEARS AGO..."
I READ YOUR "SIGN" LYRICS.
"LET'S MEET AT THIS VERSE, LET'S MEET AT THIS SONG..."
IT SOUNDED LIKE THE LYRICS WERE ABOUT YOU WANTING TO SEE ME AGAIN.
WELL, OBVI-OUSLY!
YOU'RE NOT GONNA DENY IT?!
OF COURSE NOT!

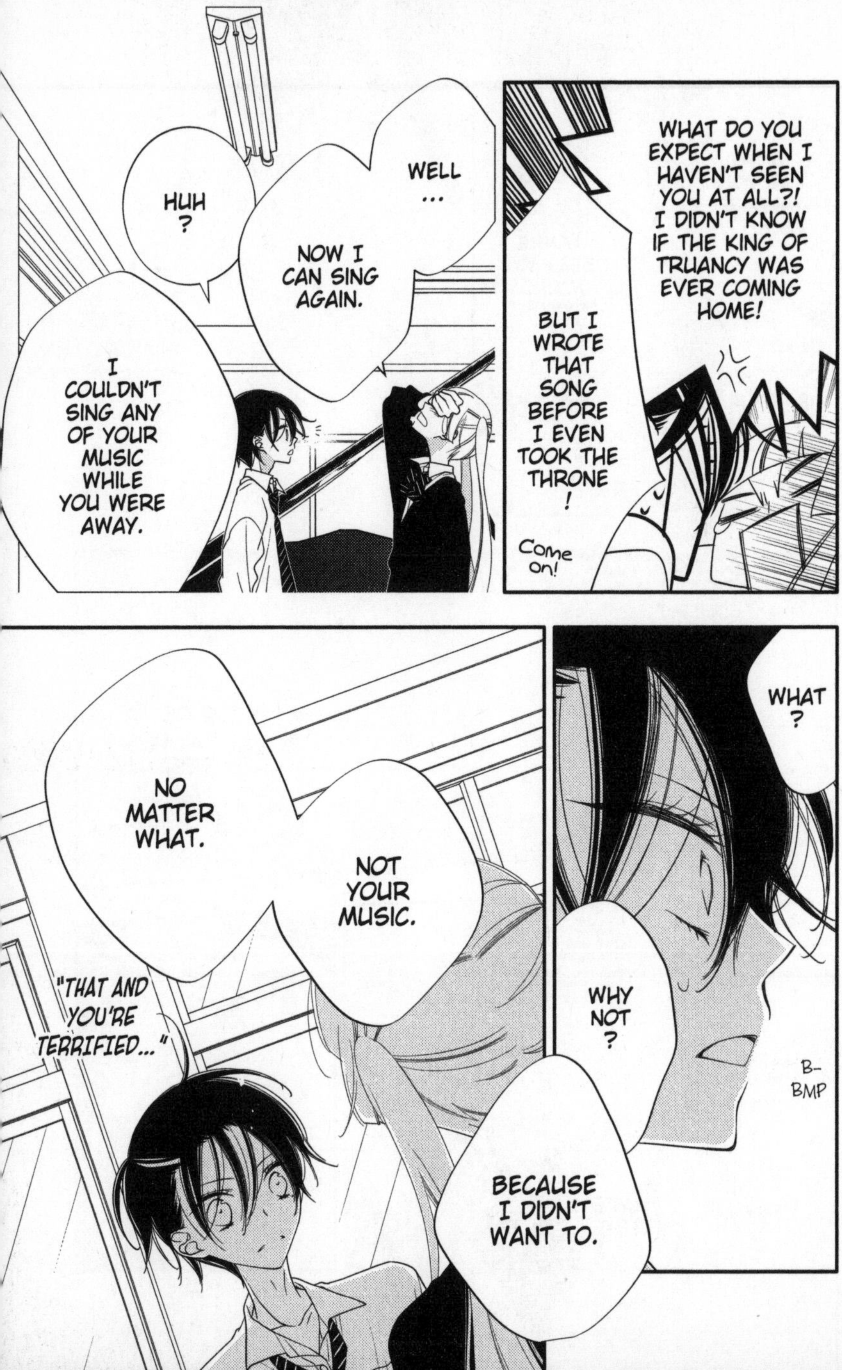
WHAT DO YOU EXPECT WHEN I HAVEN'T SEEN YOU AT ALL?! I DIDN'T KNOW IF THE KING OF TRUANCY WAS EVER COMING HOME!
BUT I WROTE THAT SONG BEFORE I EVEN TOOK THE THRONE!
Come on!
WELL...
NOW I CAN SING AGAIN.
HUH?
I COULDN'T SING ANY OF YOUR MUSIC WHILE YOU WERE AWAY.
WHAT?
WHY NOT?
B-BMP
BECAUSE I DIDN'T WANT TO.
NOT YOUR MUSIC.
NO MATTER WHAT.
"THAT AND YOU'RE TERRIFIED..."

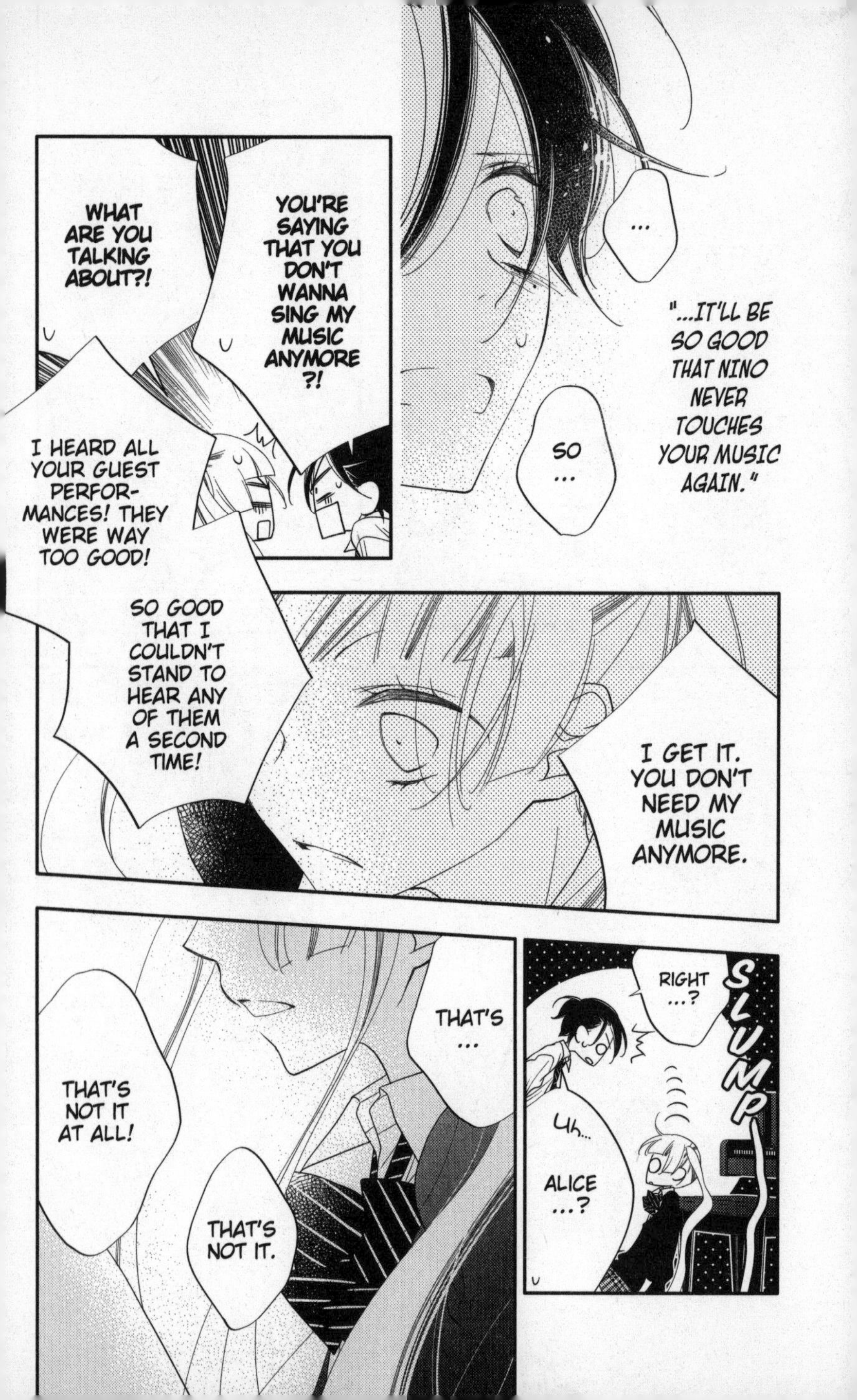
...
"...IT'LL BE SO GOOD THAT NINO NEVER TOUCHES YOUR MUSIC AGAIN."
SO ...
YOU'RE SAYING THAT YOU DON'T WANNA SING MY MUSIC ANYMORE ?!
WHAT ARE YOU TALKING ABOUT?!
I HEARD ALL YOUR GUEST PERFOR-MANCES! THEY WERE WAY TOO GOOD!
SO GOOD THAT I COULDN'T STAND TO HEAR ANY OF THEM A SECOND TIME!
I GET IT. YOU DON'T NEED MY MUSIC ANYMORE.
RIGHT ...?
SLUMP
Uh...
ALICE ...?
THAT'S ...
THAT'S NOT IT AT ALL!
THAT'S NOT IT.

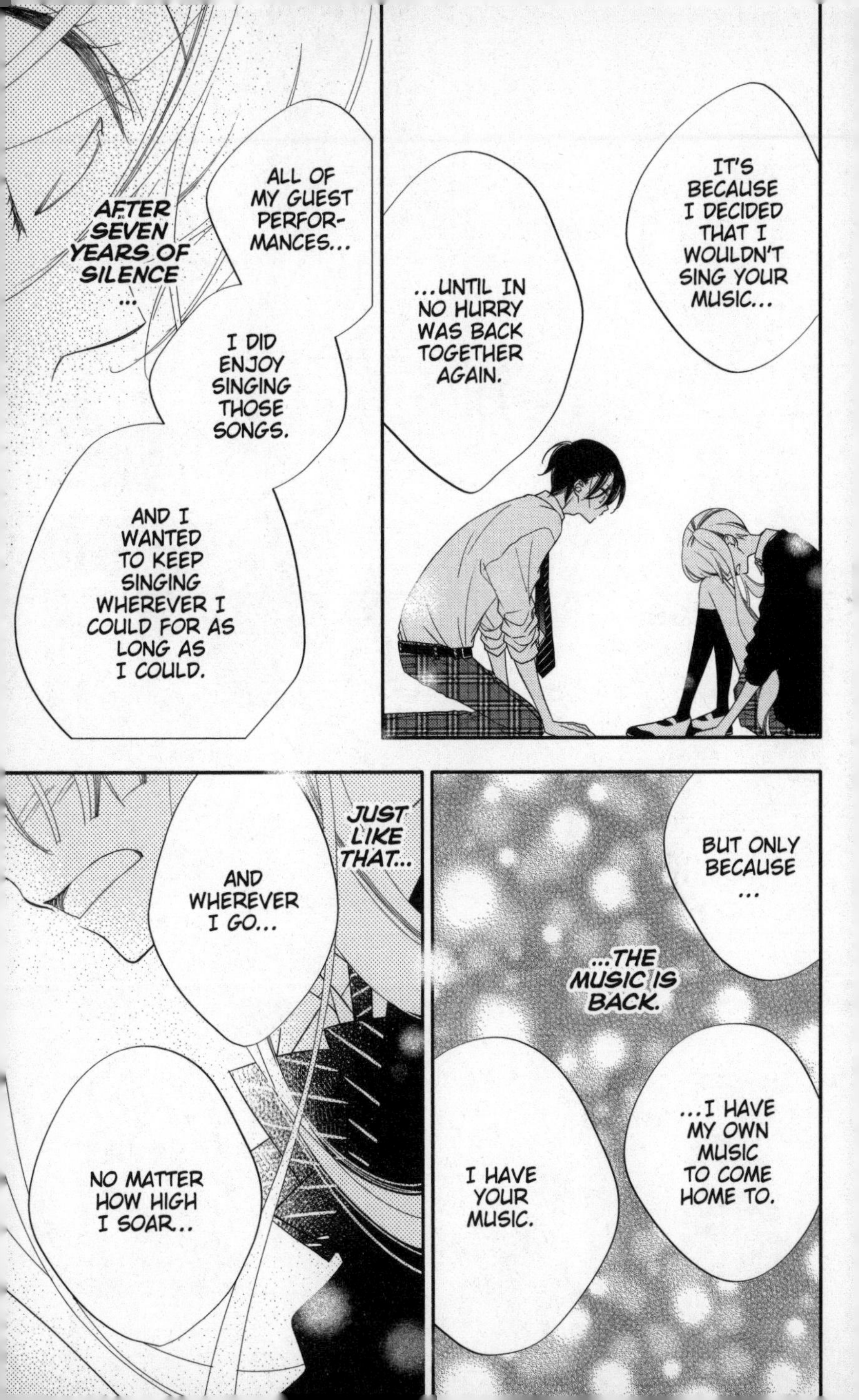
IT'S BECAUSE I DECIDED THAT I WOULDN'T SING YOUR MUSIC...
...UNTIL IN NO HURRY WAS BACK TOGETHER AGAIN.
ALL OF MY GUEST PERFORMANCES...
AFTER SEVEN YEARS OF SILENCE...
I DID ENJOY SINGING THOSE SONGS.
AND I WANTED TO KEEP SINGING WHEREVER I COULD FOR AS LONG AS I COULD.
BUT ONLY BECAUSE...
...THE MUSIC IS BACK.
...I HAVE MY OWN MUSIC TO COME HOME TO.
I HAVE YOUR MUSIC.
JUST LIKE THAT...
AND WHEREVER I GO...
NO MATTER HOW HIGH I SOAR...

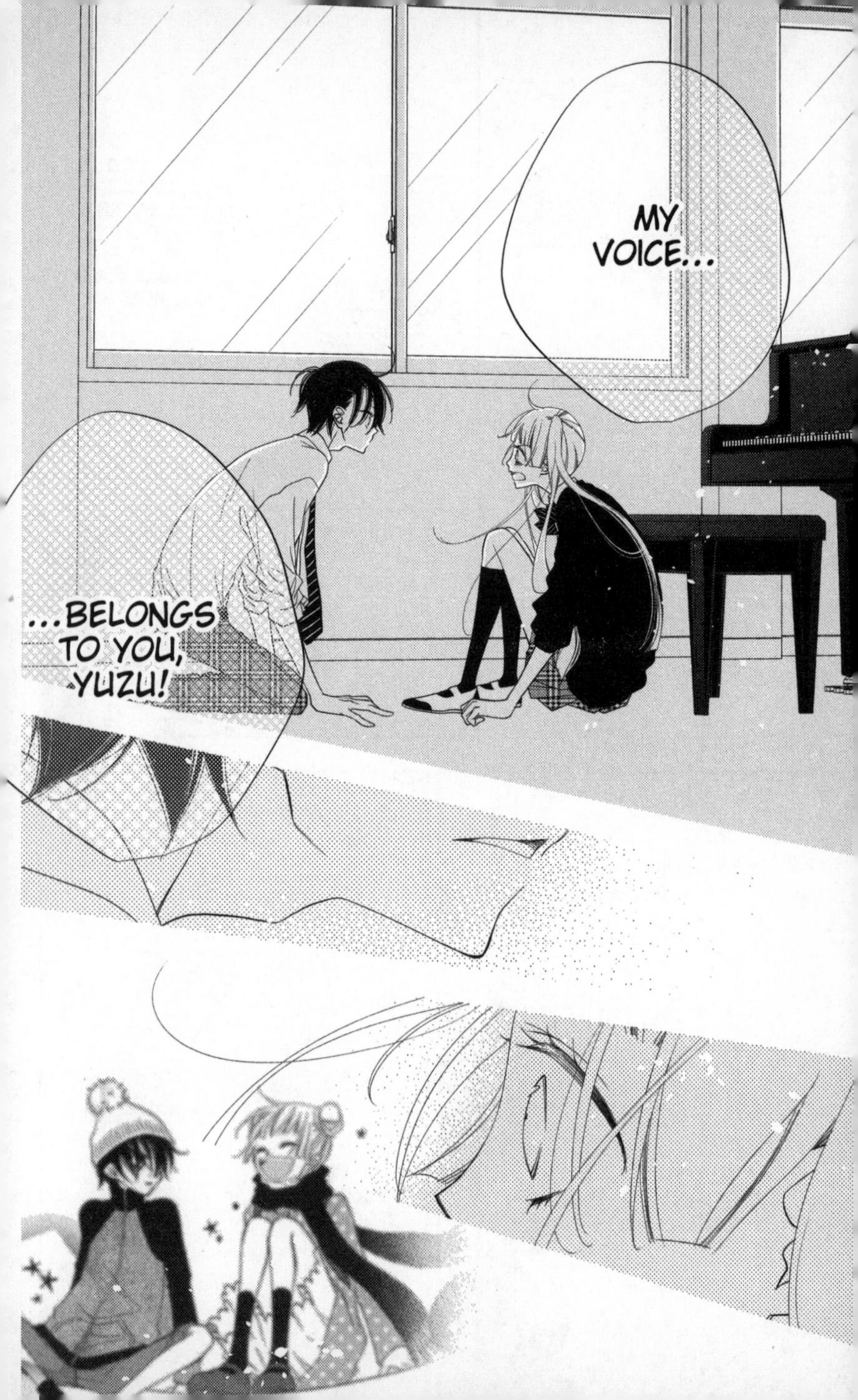
MY VOICE...
...BELONGS TO YOU, YUZU!

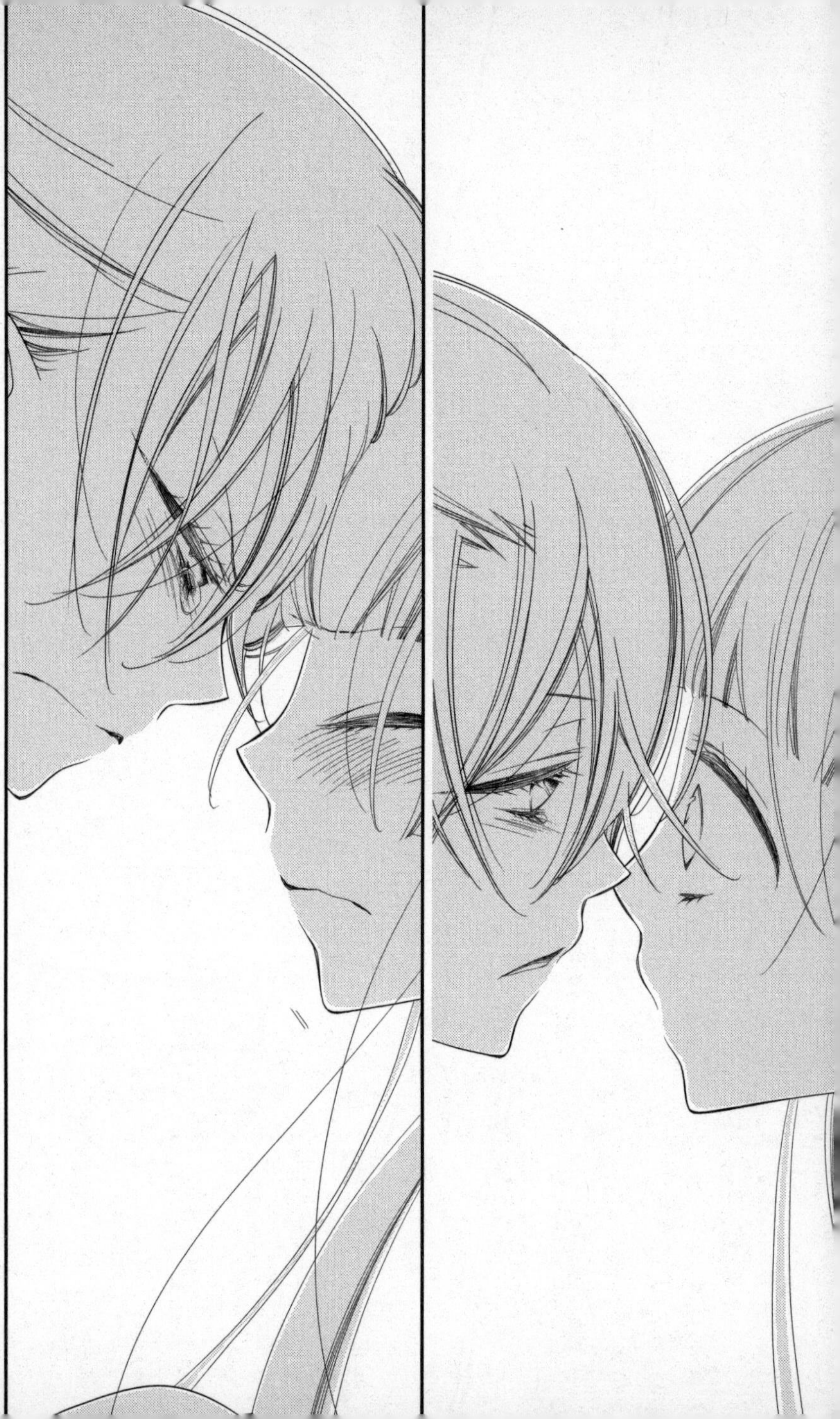

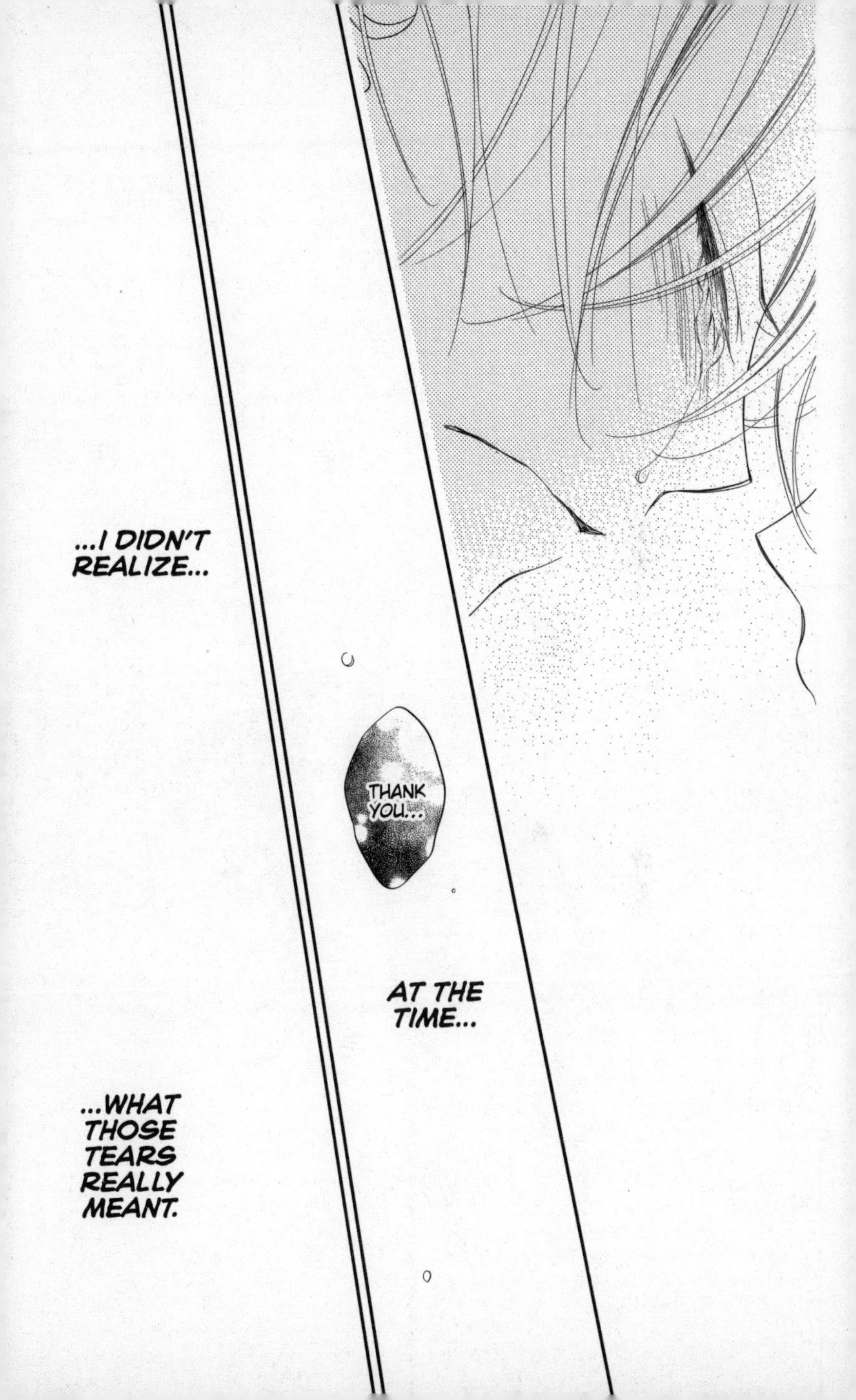
THANK YOU...
AT THE TIME...
...I DIDN'T REALIZE...
...WHAT THOSE TEARS REALLY MEANT.

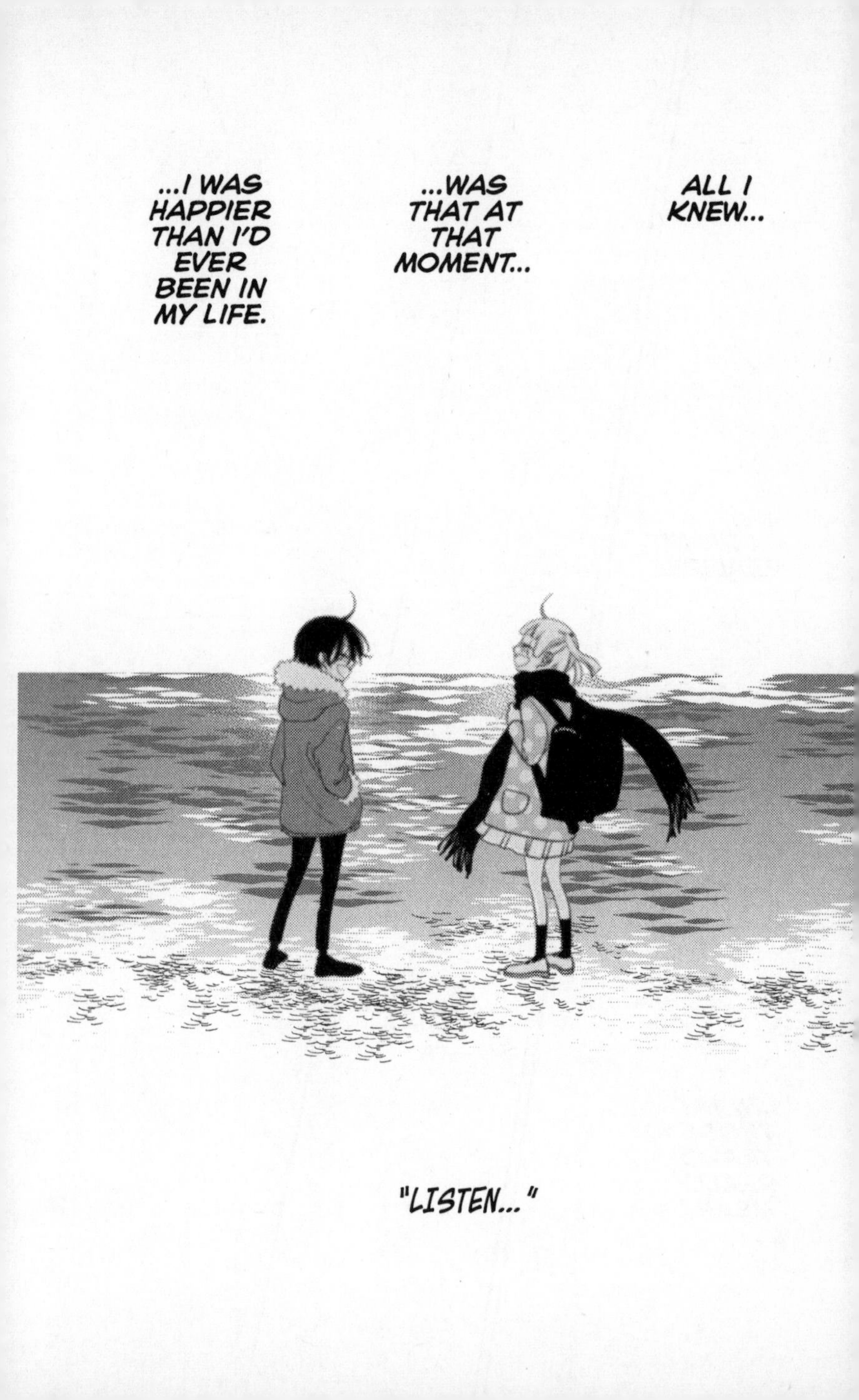
ALL I KNEW...
...WAS THAT AT THAT MOMENT...
...I WAS HAPPIER THAN I'D EVER BEEN IN MY LIFE.
"LISTEN..."

"I FOUND MY VOICE."

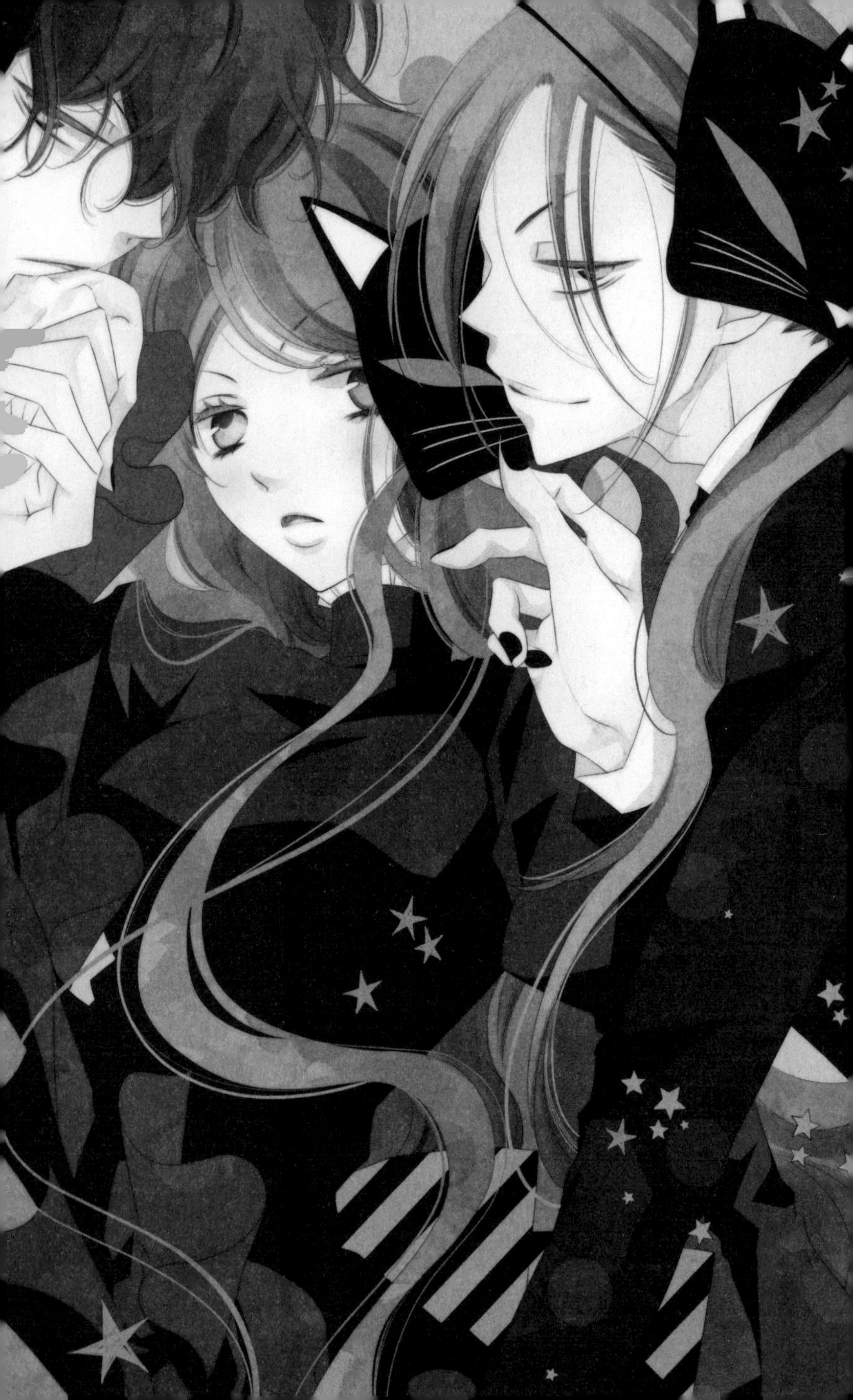

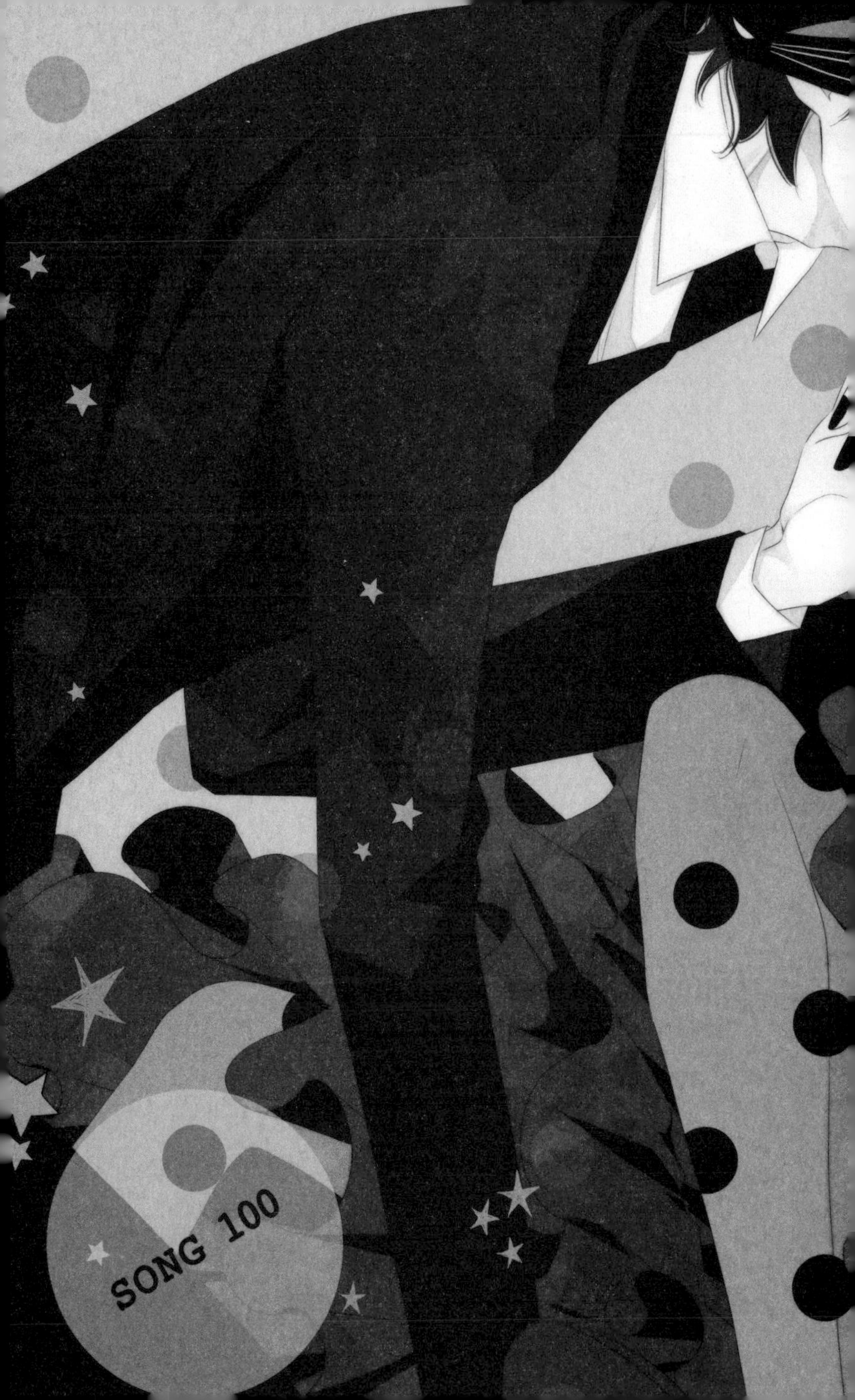
SONG 100

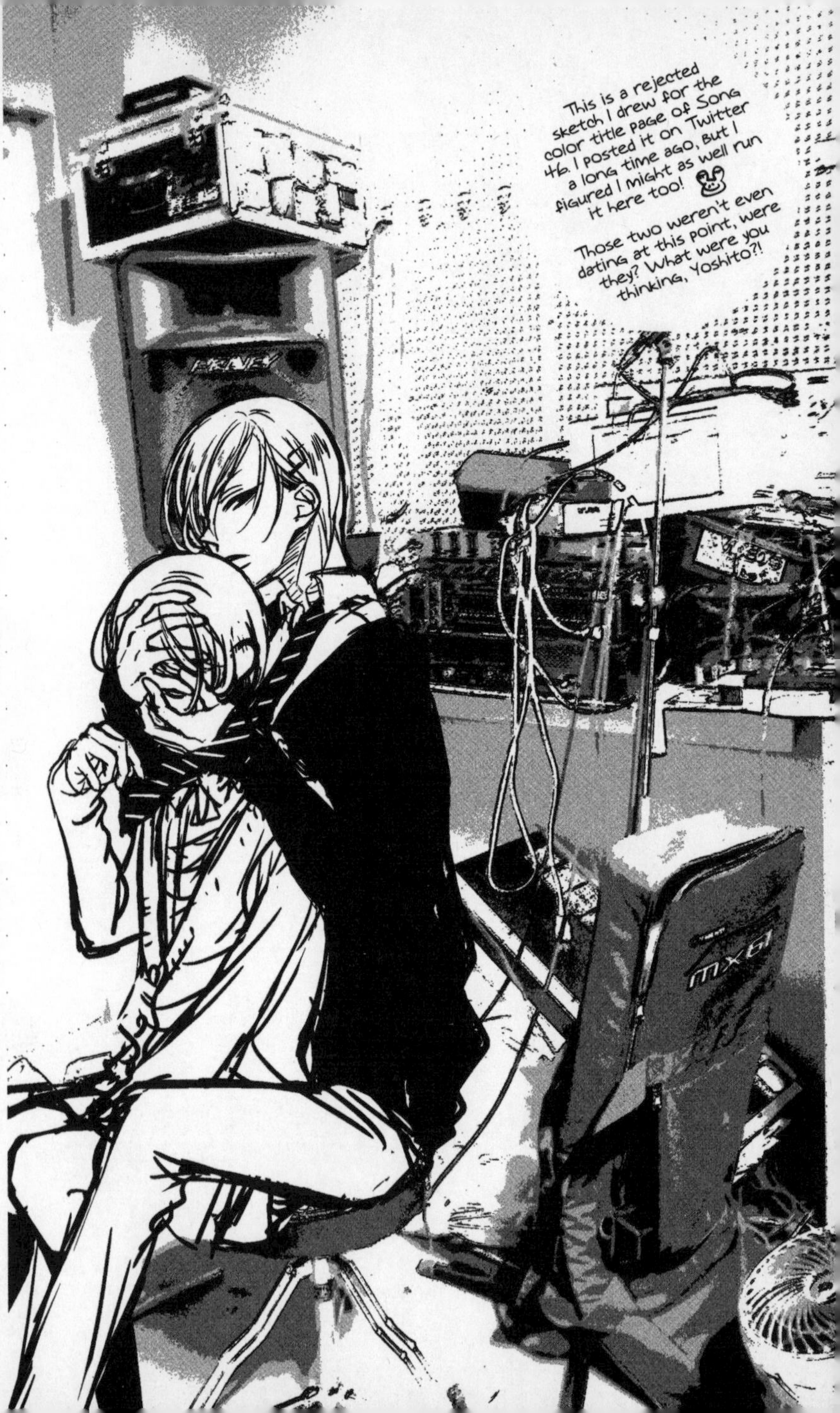
This is a rejected sketch I drew for the color title page of Song 46. I posted it on Twitter a long time ago, but I figured I might as well run it here too!
Those two weren't even dating at this point, were they? What were you thinking, Yoshito?!

ROCK HORIZON 20XX SCHEDULE ANNOUNCED!

HORIZON STAGE	SUNSET STAGE	GROUND STAGE	FLI[...] STA[...]
10:30~ GUMMI	10:30~ I CAN'T REMEMBER	11:05~ DONKVI IST	

HORIZON STAGE

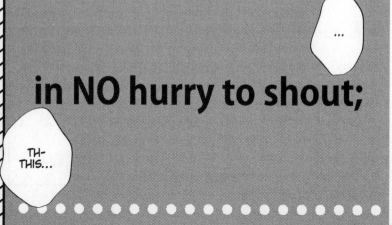

in NO hurry to shout;

...

TH-
THIS...

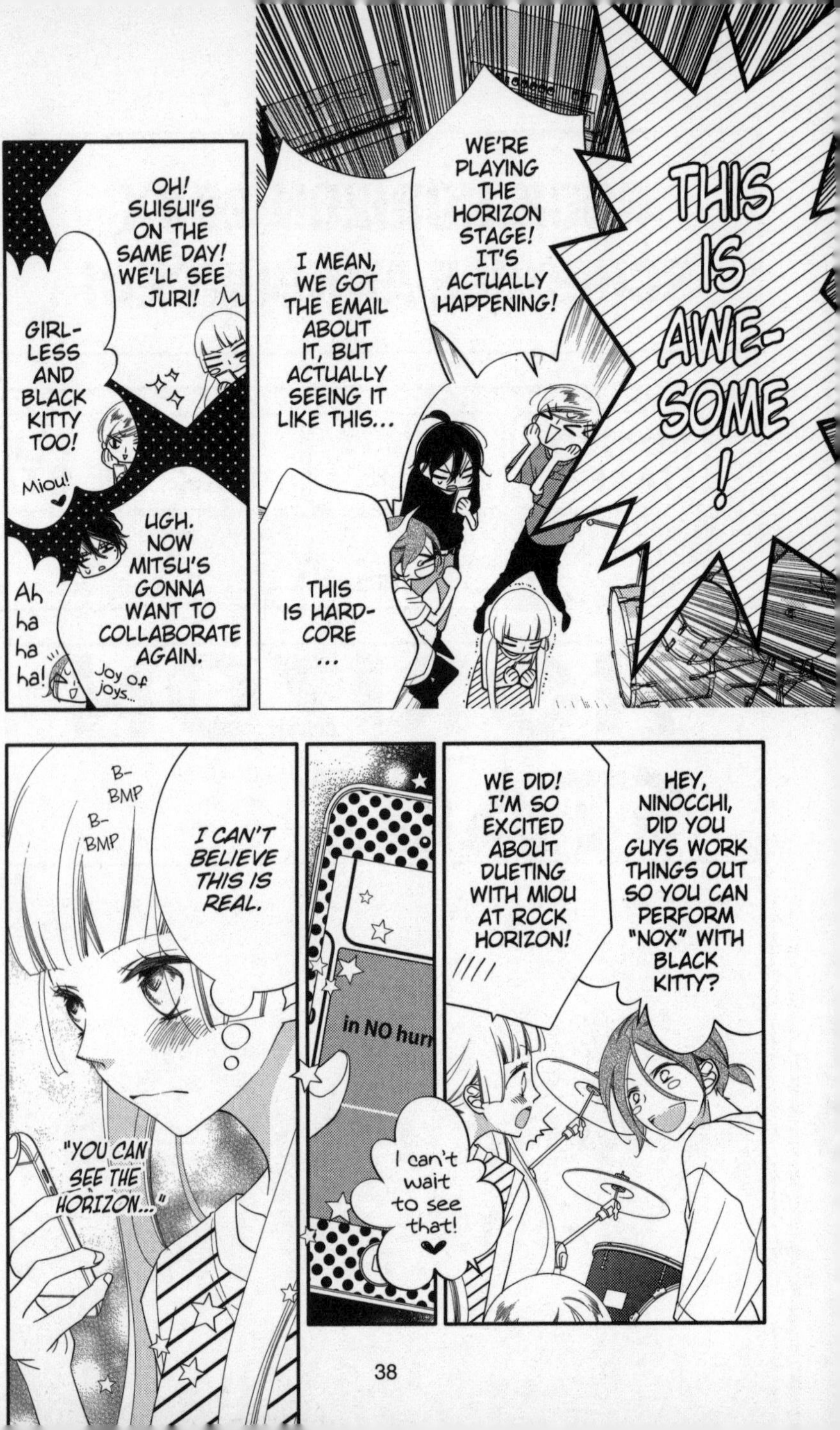
THIS IS AWE-SOME!
WE'RE PLAYING THE HORIZON STAGE! IT'S ACTUALLY HAPPENING!
I MEAN, WE GOT THE EMAIL ABOUT IT, BUT ACTUALLY SEEING IT LIKE THIS...
THIS IS HARD-CORE...
OH! SUISUI'S ON THE SAME DAY! WE'LL SEE JURI!
GIRL-LESS AND BLACK KITTY TOO!
Miou! ♥
UGH. NOW MITSU'S GONNA WANT TO COLLABORATE AGAIN.
Ah ha ha ha!
Joy of joys...
HEY, NINOCCHI, DID YOU GUYS WORK THINGS OUT SO YOU CAN PERFORM "NOX" WITH BLACK KITTY?
WE DID! I'M SO EXCITED ABOUT DUETING WITH MIOU AT ROCK HORIZON!
I can't wait to see that! ♥
B-BMP
B-BMP
I CAN'T BELIEVE THIS IS REAL.
"YOU CAN SEE THE HORIZON..."

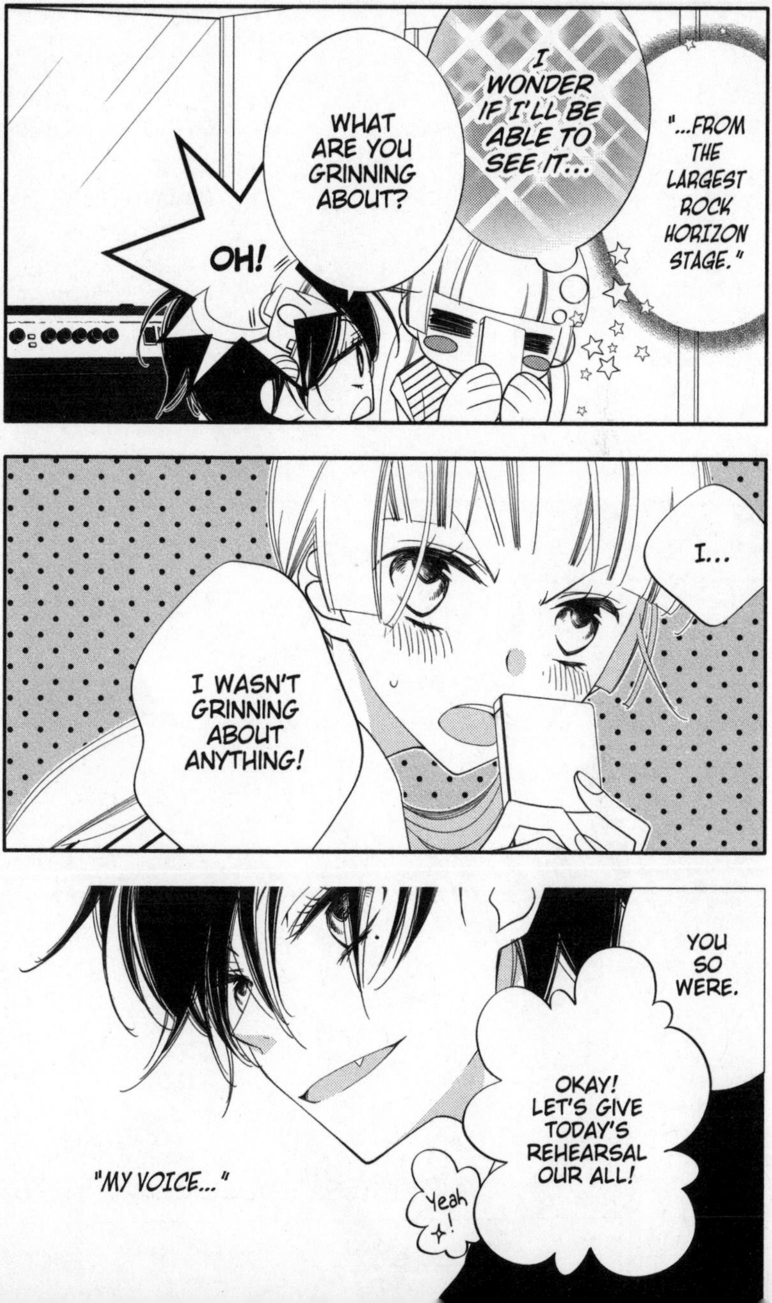
"...FROM THE LARGEST ROCK HORIZON STAGE."
I WONDER IF I'LL BE ABLE TO SEE IT...
WHAT ARE YOU GRINNING ABOUT?
OH!
I...
I WASN'T GRINNING ABOUT ANYTHING!
YOU SO WERE.
OKAY! LET'S GIVE TODAY'S REHEARSAL OUR ALL!
Yeah!
"MY VOICE..."

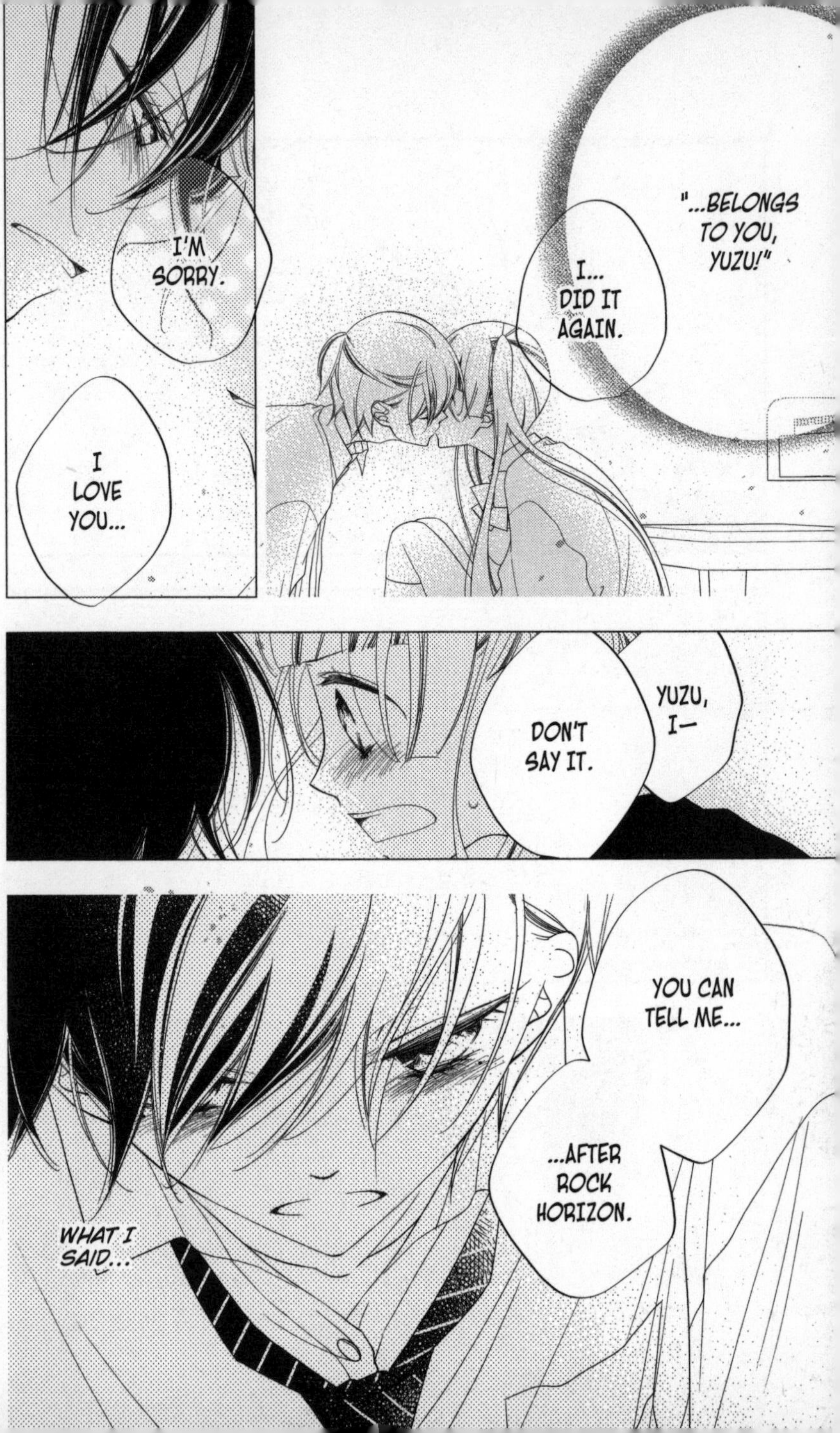
"...BELONGS TO YOU, YUZU!"
I... DID IT AGAIN.
I'M SORRY.
I LOVE YOU...
YUZU, I—
DON'T SAY IT.
YOU CAN TELL ME...
...AFTER ROCK HORIZON.
WHAT I SAID...

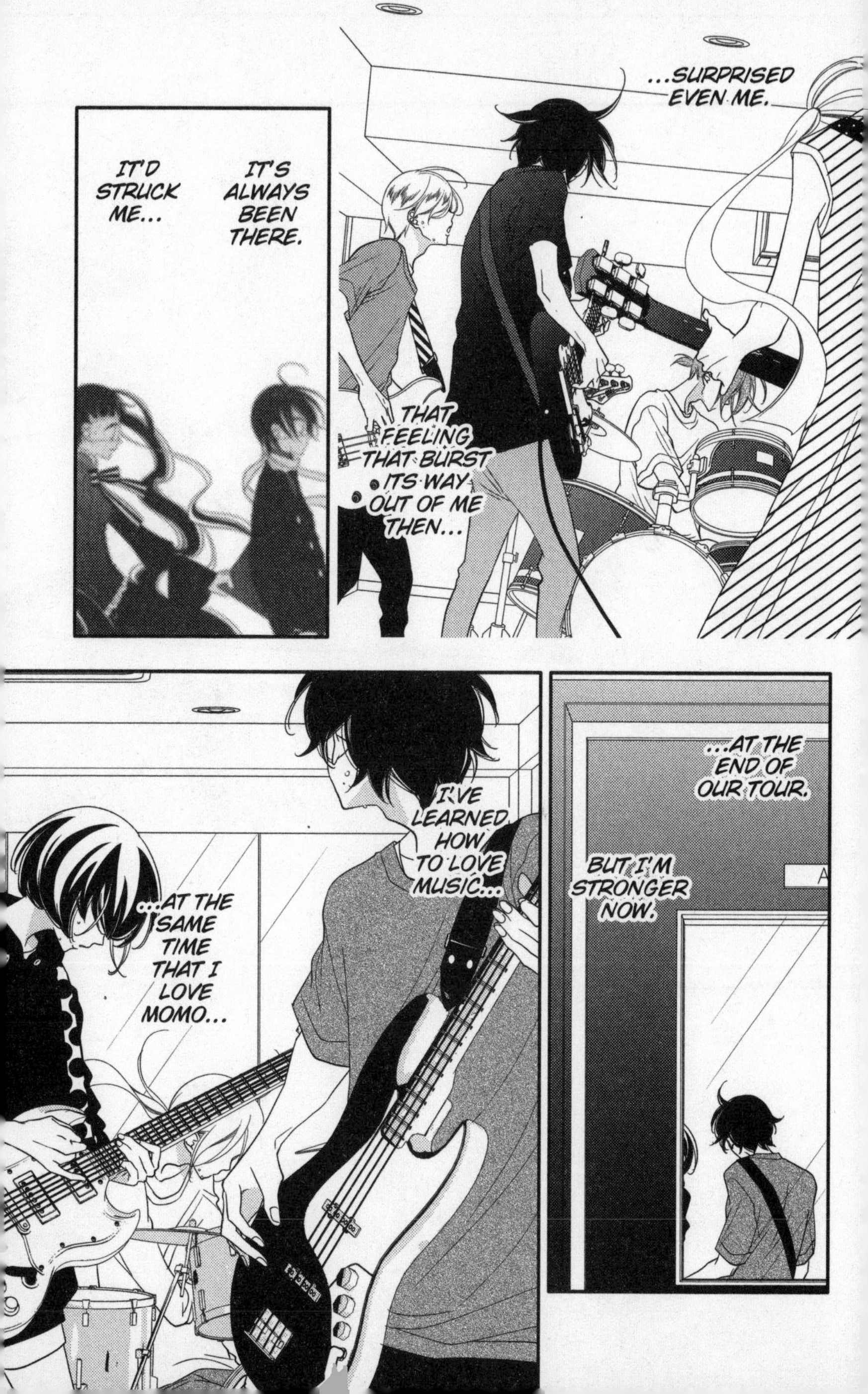
...SURPRISED EVEN ME.
THAT FEELING THAT BURST ITS WAY OUT OF ME THEN...
IT'S ALWAYS BEEN THERE.
IT'D STRUCK ME...
...AT THE END OF OUR TOUR.
BUT I'M STRONGER NOW.
I'VE LEARNED HOW TO LOVE MUSIC...
...AT THE SAME TIME THAT I LOVE MOMO...

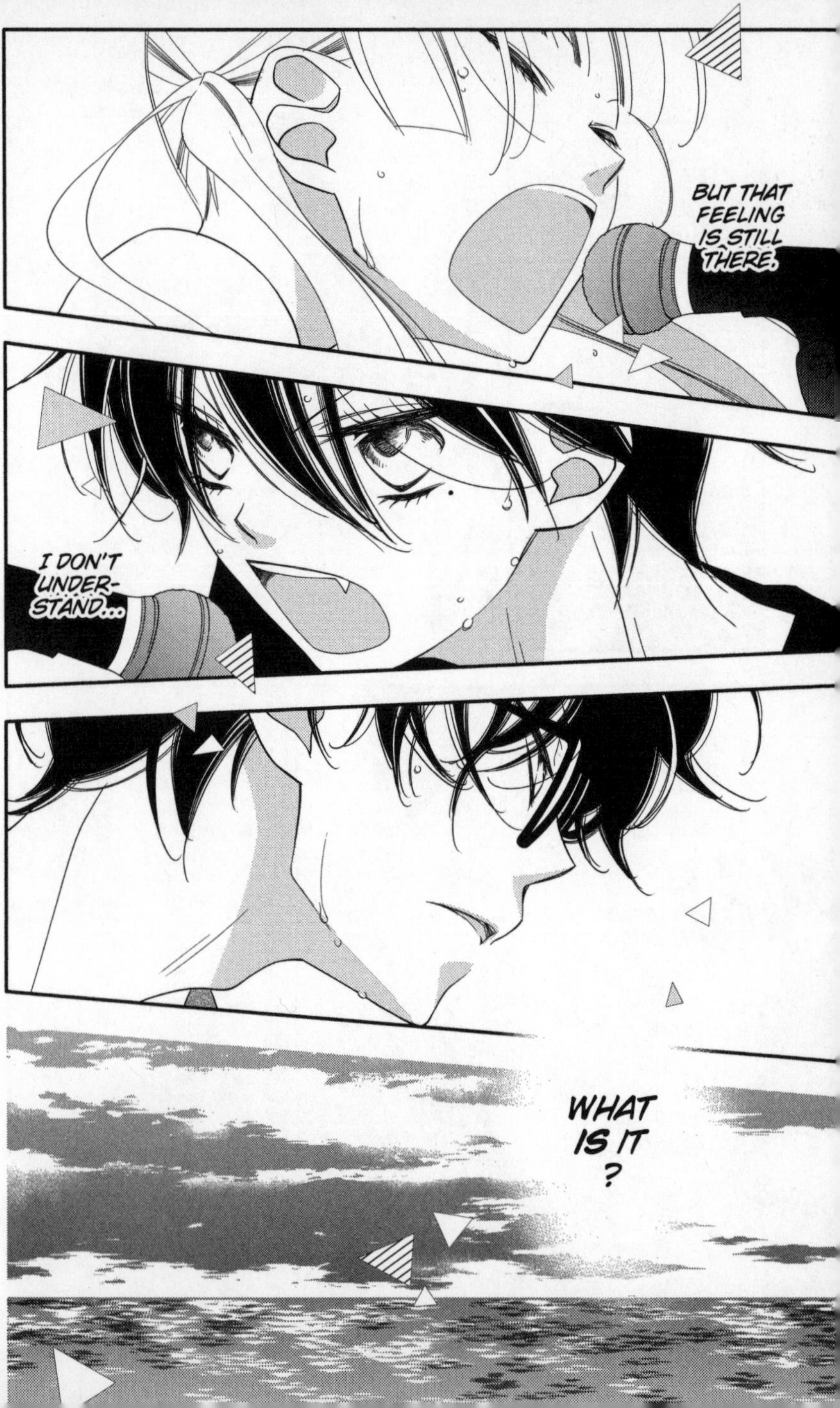
BUT THAT FEELING IS STILL THERE.
I DON'T UNDER-STAND...
WHAT IS IT ?

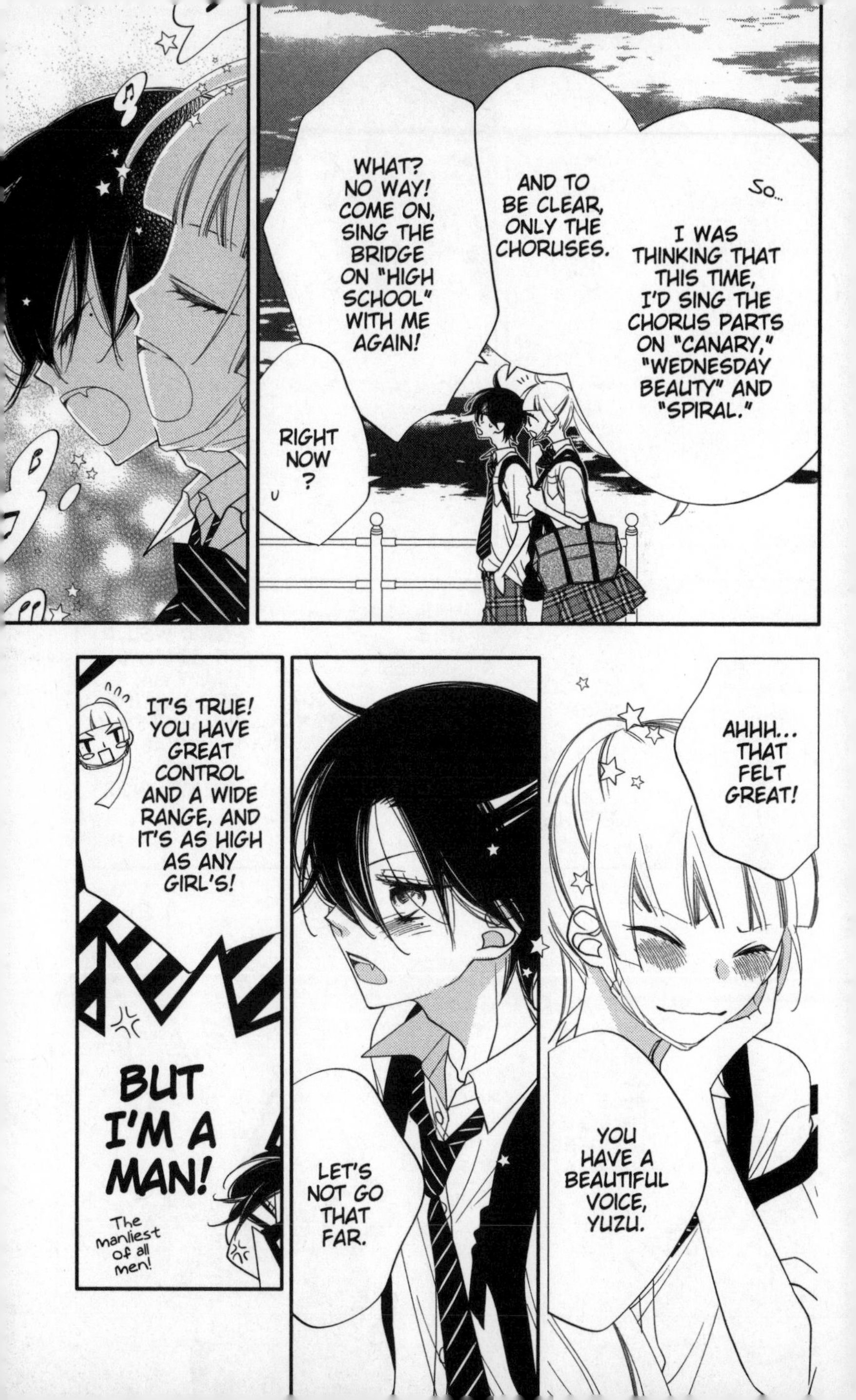
So...
I WAS THINKING THAT THIS TIME, I'D SING THE CHORUS PARTS ON "CANARY," "WEDNESDAY BEAUTY" AND "SPIRAL."
AND TO BE CLEAR, ONLY THE CHORUSES.
WHAT? NO WAY! COME ON, SING THE BRIDGE ON "HIGH SCHOOL" WITH ME AGAIN!
RIGHT NOW?
AHHH... THAT FELT GREAT!
YOU HAVE A BEAUTIFUL VOICE, YUZU.
LET'S NOT GO THAT FAR.
IT'S TRUE! YOU HAVE GREAT CONTROL AND A WIDE RANGE, AND IT'S AS HIGH AS ANY GIRL'S!
BUT I'M A MAN!
The manliest of all men!

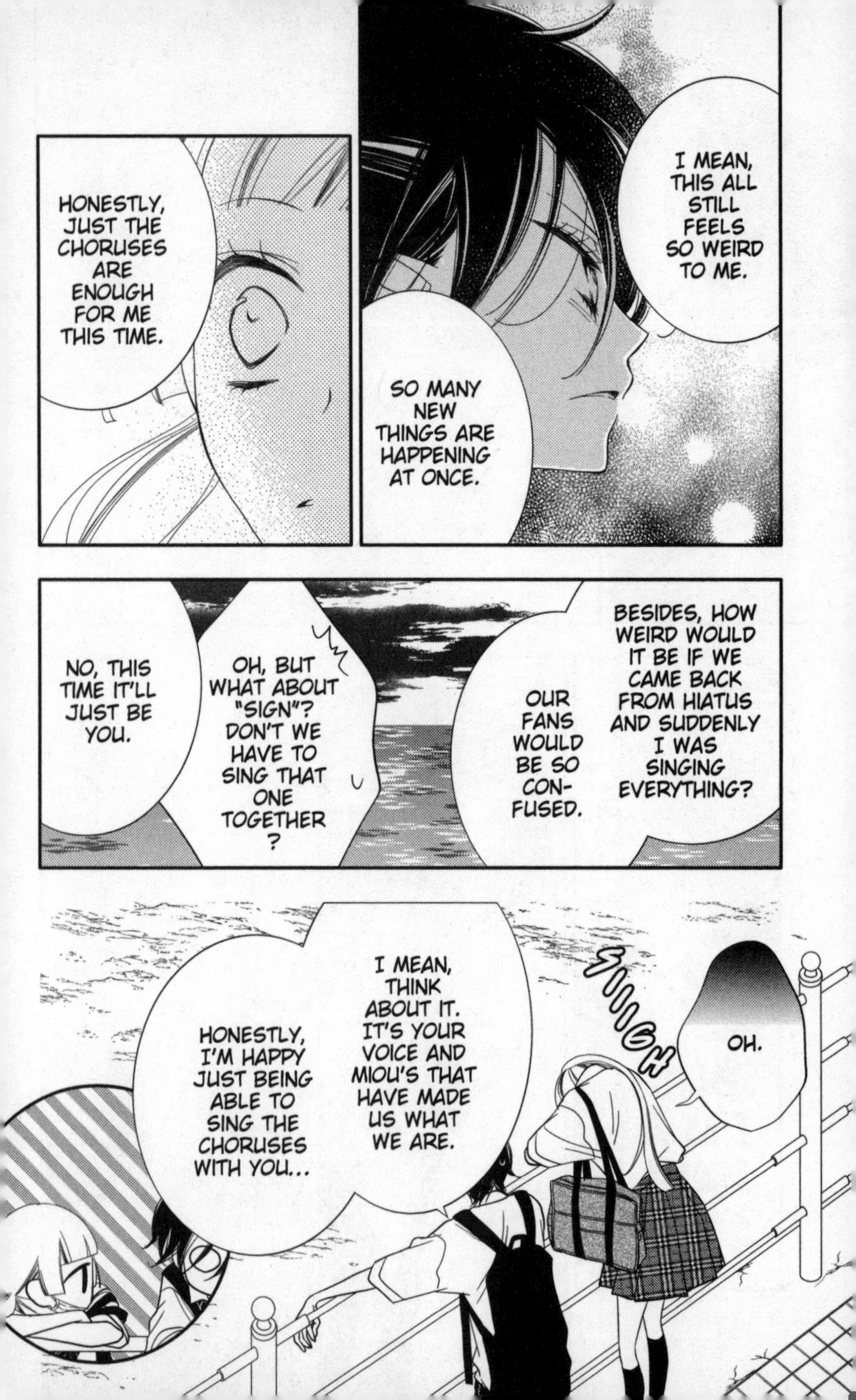
I MEAN, THIS ALL STILL FEELS SO WEIRD TO ME.
SO MANY NEW THINGS ARE HAPPENING AT ONCE.
HONESTLY, JUST THE CHORUSES ARE ENOUGH FOR ME THIS TIME.
BESIDES, HOW WEIRD WOULD IT BE IF WE CAME BACK FROM HIATUS AND SUDDENLY I WAS SINGING EVERYTHING?
OUR FANS WOULD BE SO CON-FUSED.
OH, BUT WHAT ABOUT "SIGN"? DON'T WE HAVE TO SING THAT ONE TOGETHER?
NO, THIS TIME IT'LL JUST BE YOU.
OH.
SIIIGH
I MEAN, THINK ABOUT IT. IT'S YOUR VOICE AND MIOU'S THAT HAVE MADE US WHAT WE ARE.
HONESTLY, I'M HAPPY JUST BEING ABLE TO SING THE CHORUSES WITH YOU...

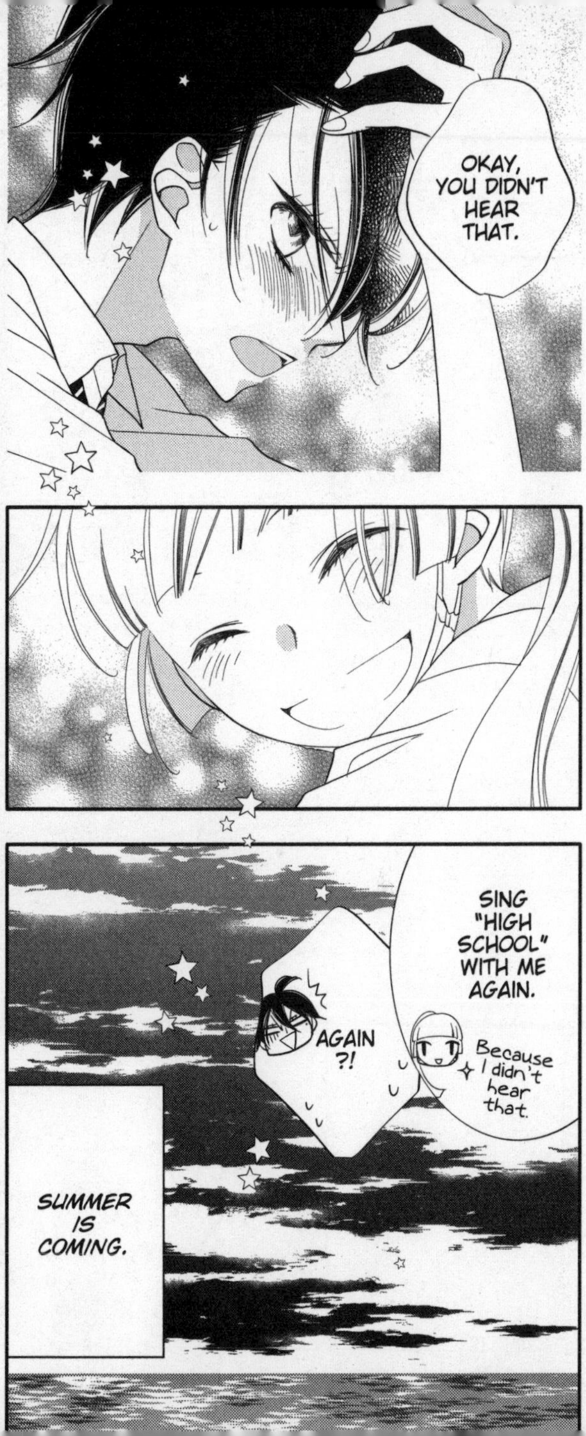
OKAY, YOU DIDN'T HEAR THAT.
SING "HIGH SCHOOL" WITH ME AGAIN.
AGAIN?!
Because I didn't hear that.
SUMMER IS COMING.

2

As I was writing the manuscript for the final chapter, I caught the flu for the first time in my life. At first I thought it was my usual lower-back pain, but it was joint pain from the flu! Ha. My fever topped out at 38°C (100.4°F), so it wasn't a particularly serious case, but having to create manga while dealing with the aforementioned joint pain was quite the ordeal! Anyway, having to get it done under those circumstances left me without any strong sense of "Yeah! I did it! I finished my manga!" at the end. Ha ha. It was only recently, like a month after I submitted it, that it really hit me that it's actually, truly over.

I'M GLAD... REALLY, I AM...

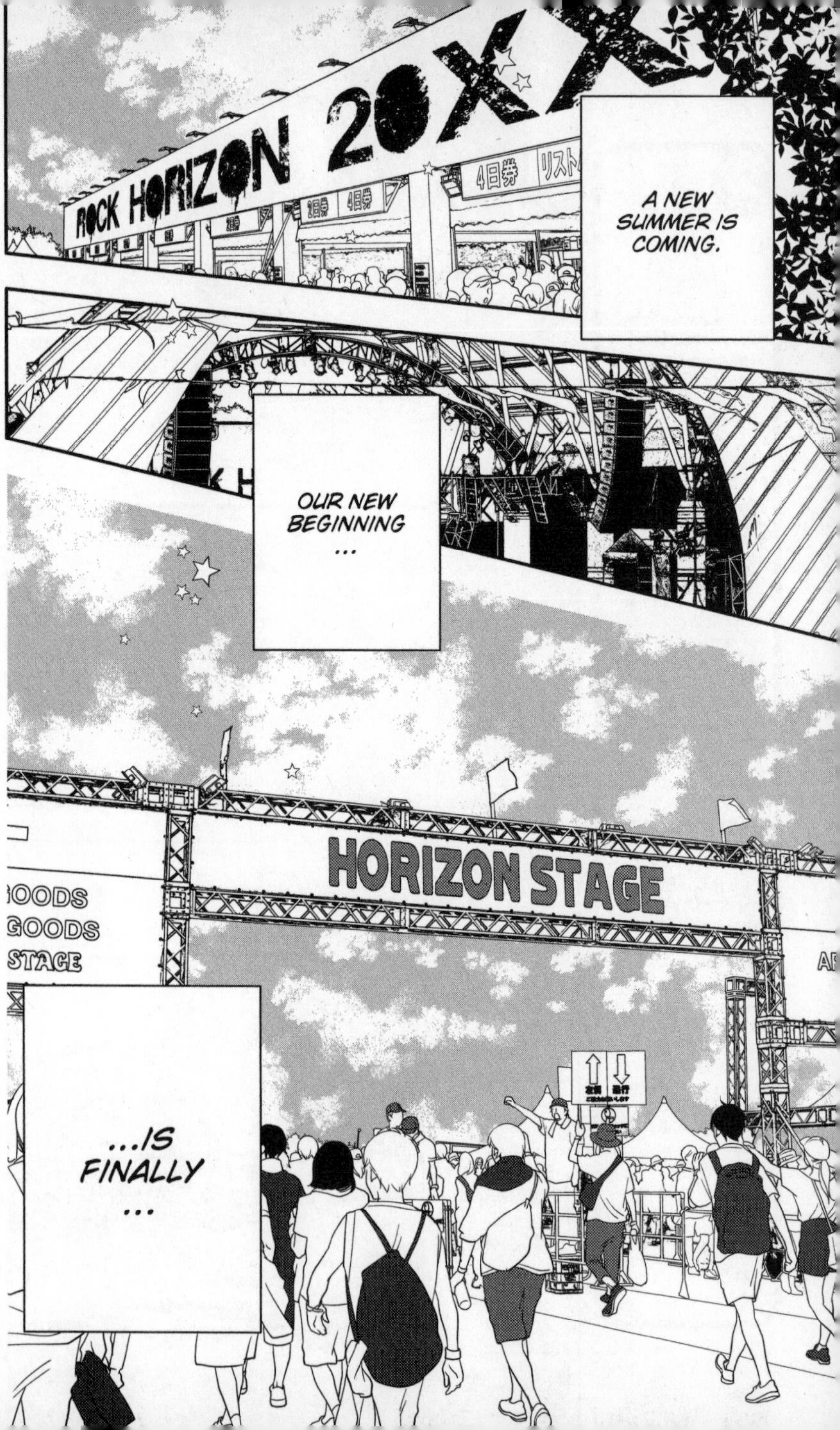
A NEW SUMMER IS COMING.
ROCK HORIZON 20XX
4日券
2日券
4日券
OUR NEW BEGINNING ...
HORIZON STAGE
GOODS
STAGE
...IS FINALLY ...

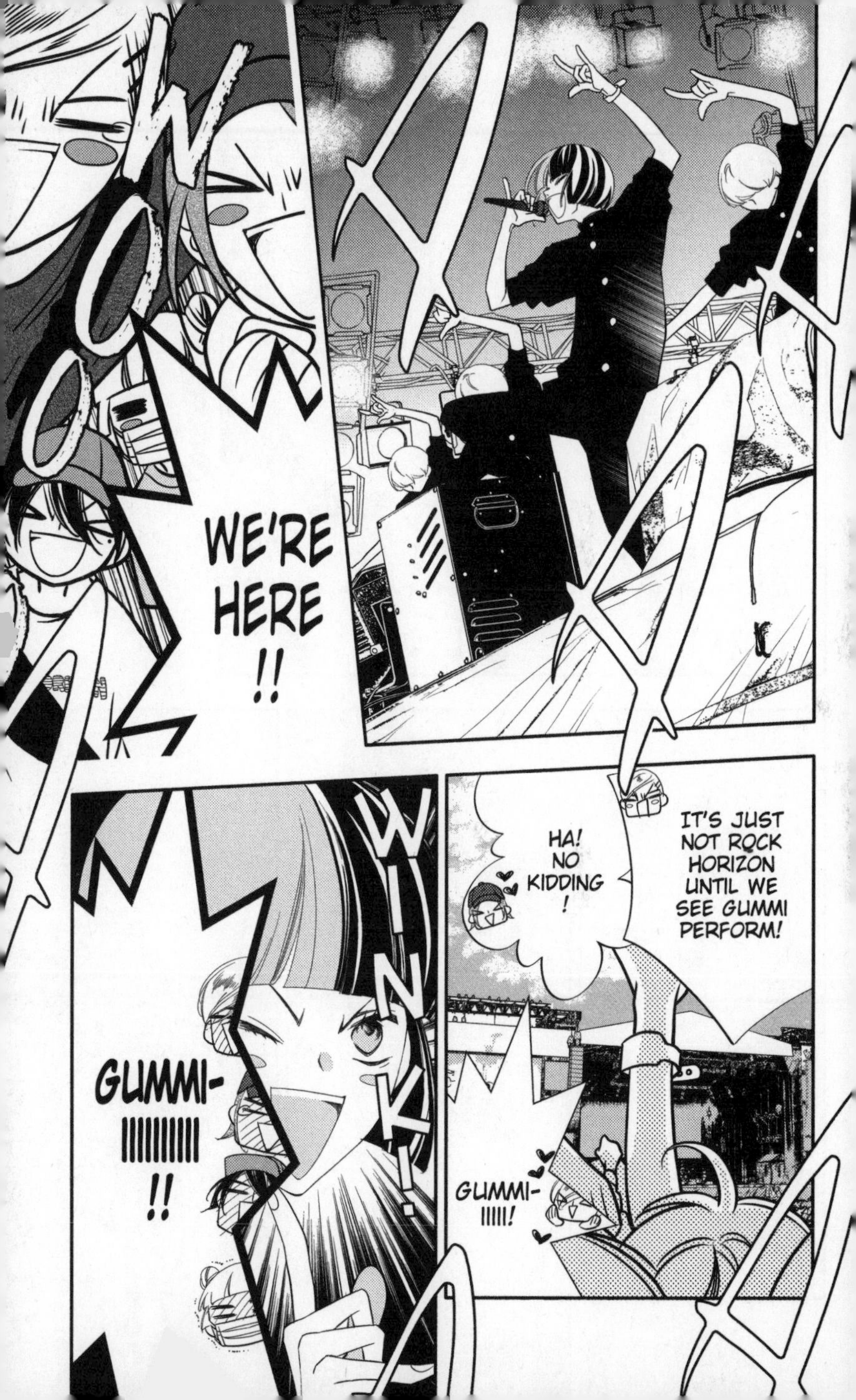
WE'RE HERE!!
IT'S JUST NOT ROCK HORIZON UNTIL WE SEE GUMMI PERFORM!
HA! NO KIDDING!
GUMMI-!!!!!!
WINK!
GUMMI-!!!!!!!!!!!!!!!!

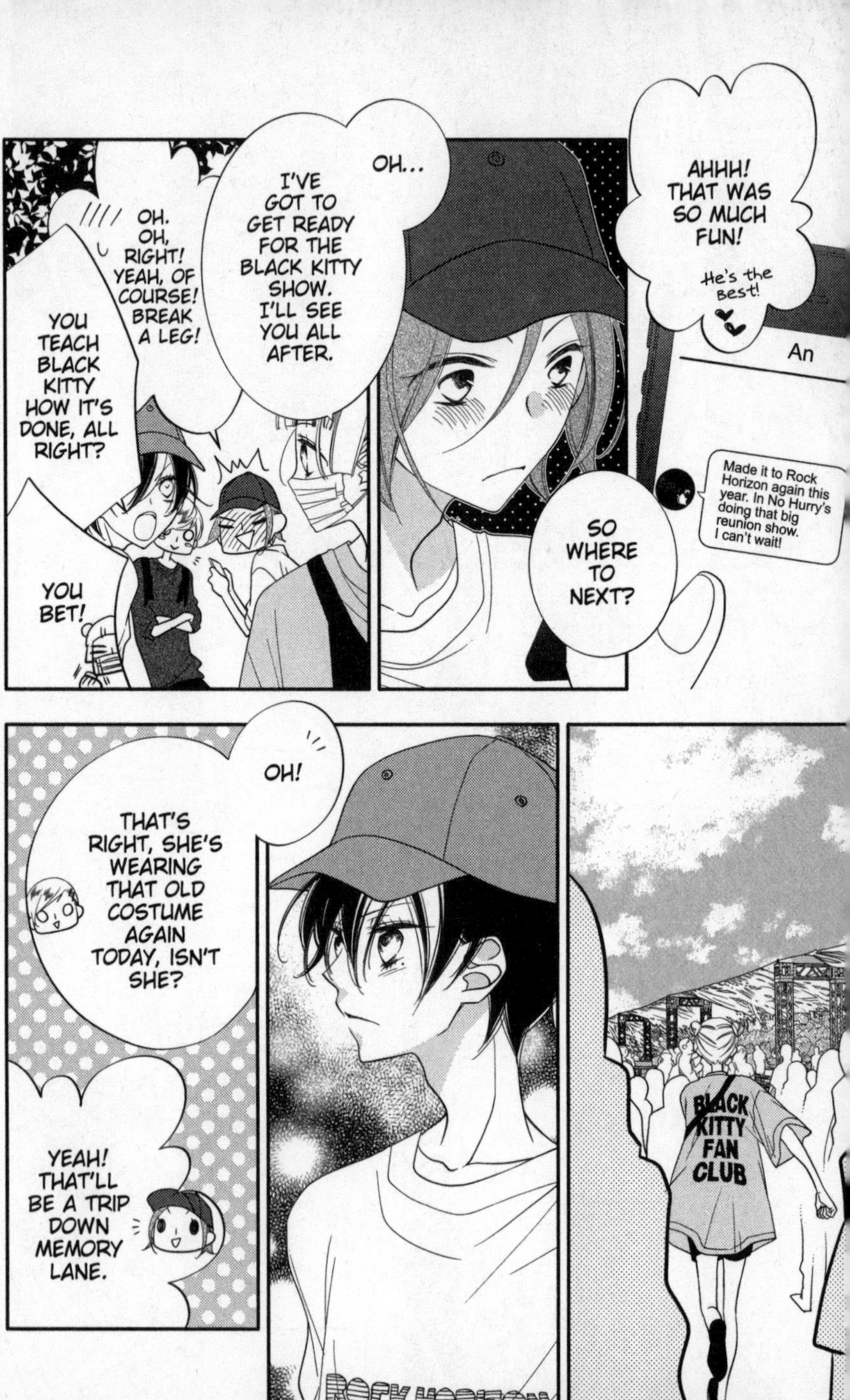
AHHH! THAT WAS SO MUCH FUN!
He's the Best!
An
Made it to Rock Horizon again this year. In No Hurry's doing that big reunion show. I can't wait!
SO WHERE TO NEXT?
OH...
I'VE GOT TO GET READY FOR THE BLACK KITTY SHOW. I'LL SEE YOU ALL AFTER.
OH. OH, RIGHT! YEAH, OF COURSE! BREAK A LEG!
YOU TEACH BLACK KITTY HOW IT'S DONE, ALL RIGHT?
YOU BET!
BLACK KITTY FAN CLUB
OH!
ROCK HORIZON
THAT'S RIGHT, SHE'S WEARING THAT OLD COSTUME AGAIN TODAY, ISN'T SHE?
YEAH! THAT'LL BE A TRIP DOWN MEMORY LANE.

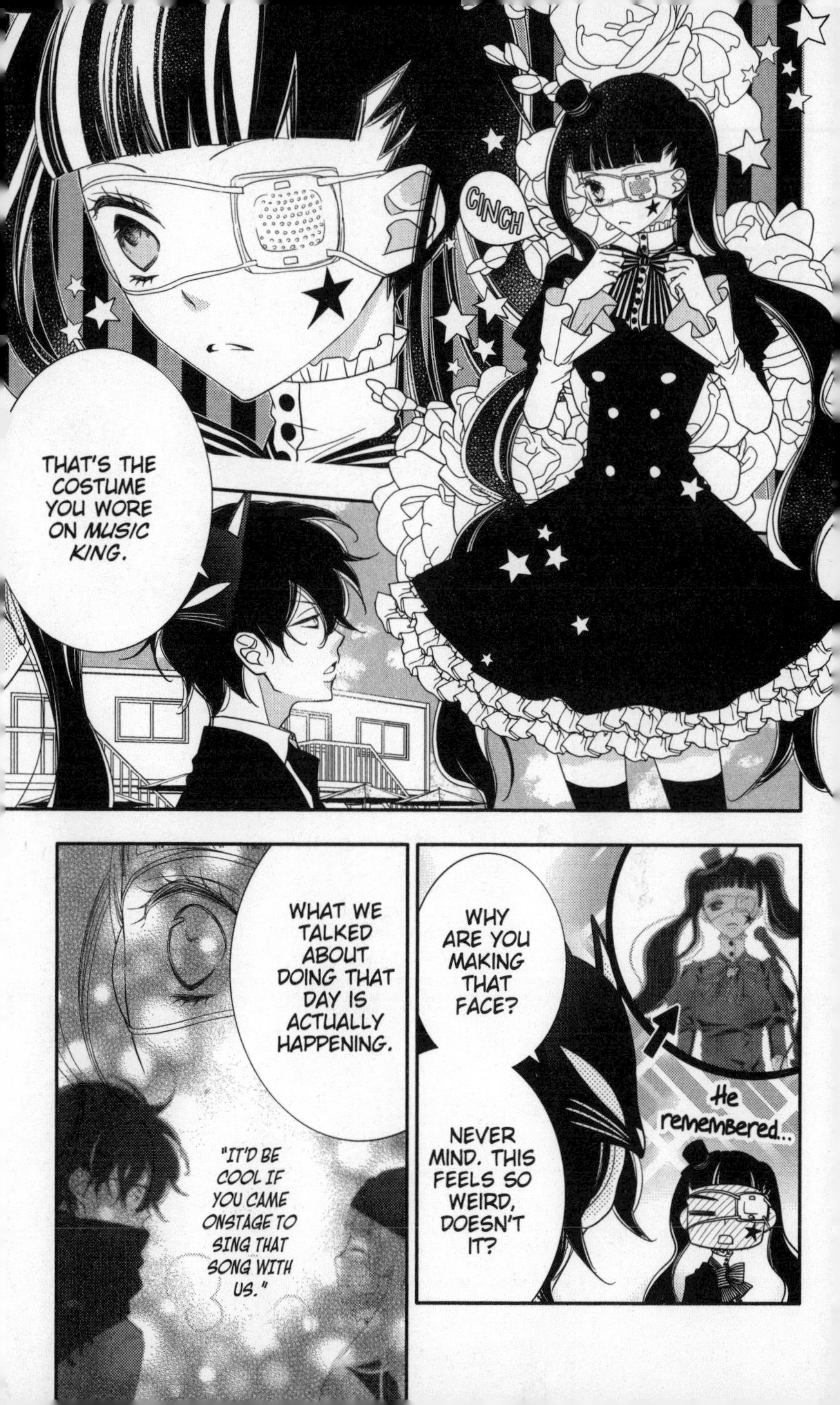

CINCH
THAT'S THE COSTUME YOU WORE ON *MUSIC KING*.
WHY ARE YOU MAKING THAT FACE?
He remembered...
NEVER MIND. THIS FEELS SO WEIRD, DOESN'T IT?
WHAT WE TALKED ABOUT DOING THAT DAY IS ACTUALLY HAPPENING.
"IT'D BE COOL IF YOU CAME ONSTAGE TO SING THAT SONG WITH US."

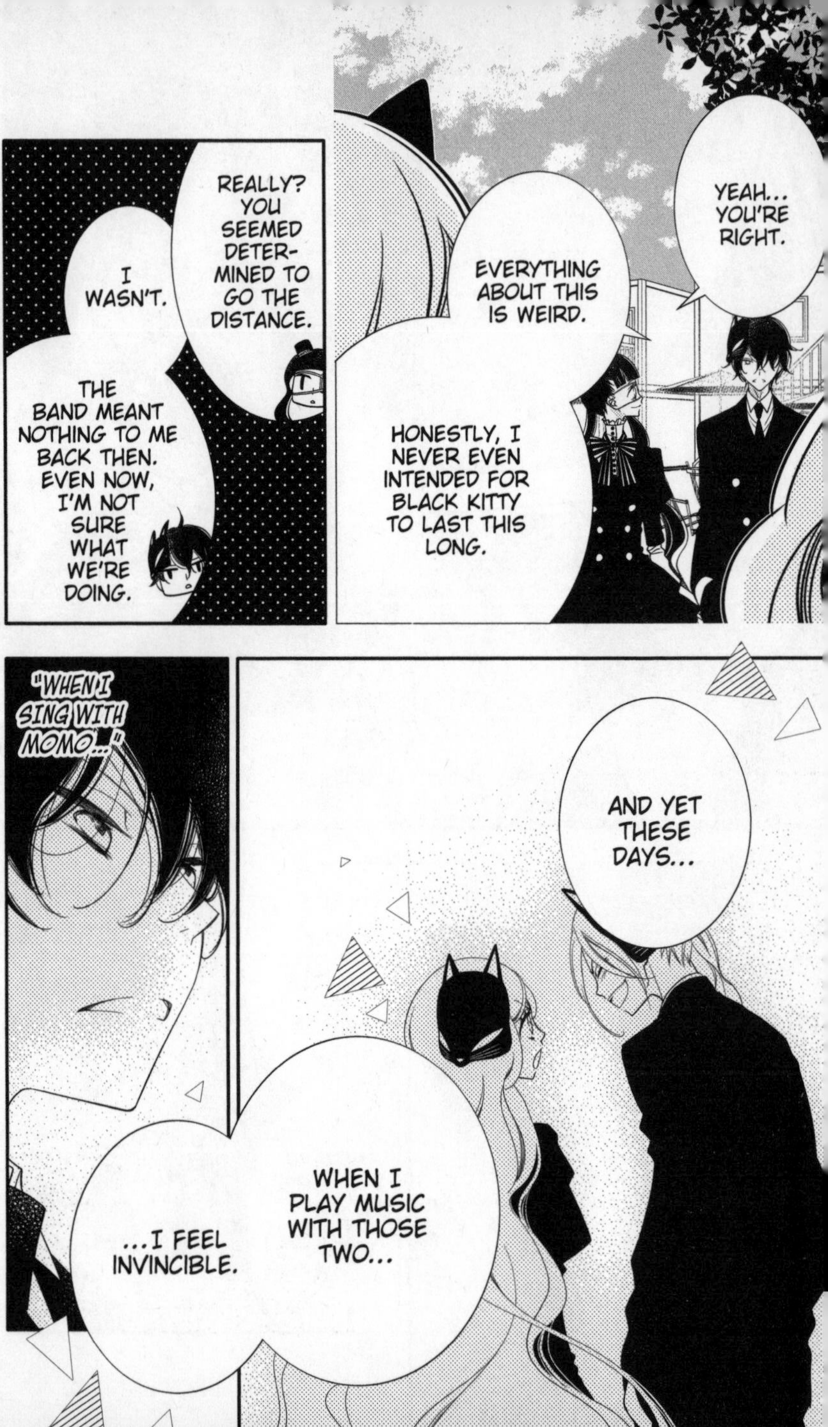
YEAH... YOU'RE RIGHT.
EVERYTHING ABOUT THIS IS WEIRD.
HONESTLY, I NEVER EVEN INTENDED FOR BLACK KITTY TO LAST THIS LONG.
REALLY? YOU SEEMED DETER-MINED TO GO THE DISTANCE.
I WASN'T.
THE BAND MEANT NOTHING TO ME BACK THEN. EVEN NOW, I'M NOT SURE WHAT WE'RE DOING.
AND YET THESE DAYS...
WHEN I PLAY MUSIC WITH THOSE TWO...
...I FEEL INVINCIBLE.
"WHEN I SING WITH MOMO..."

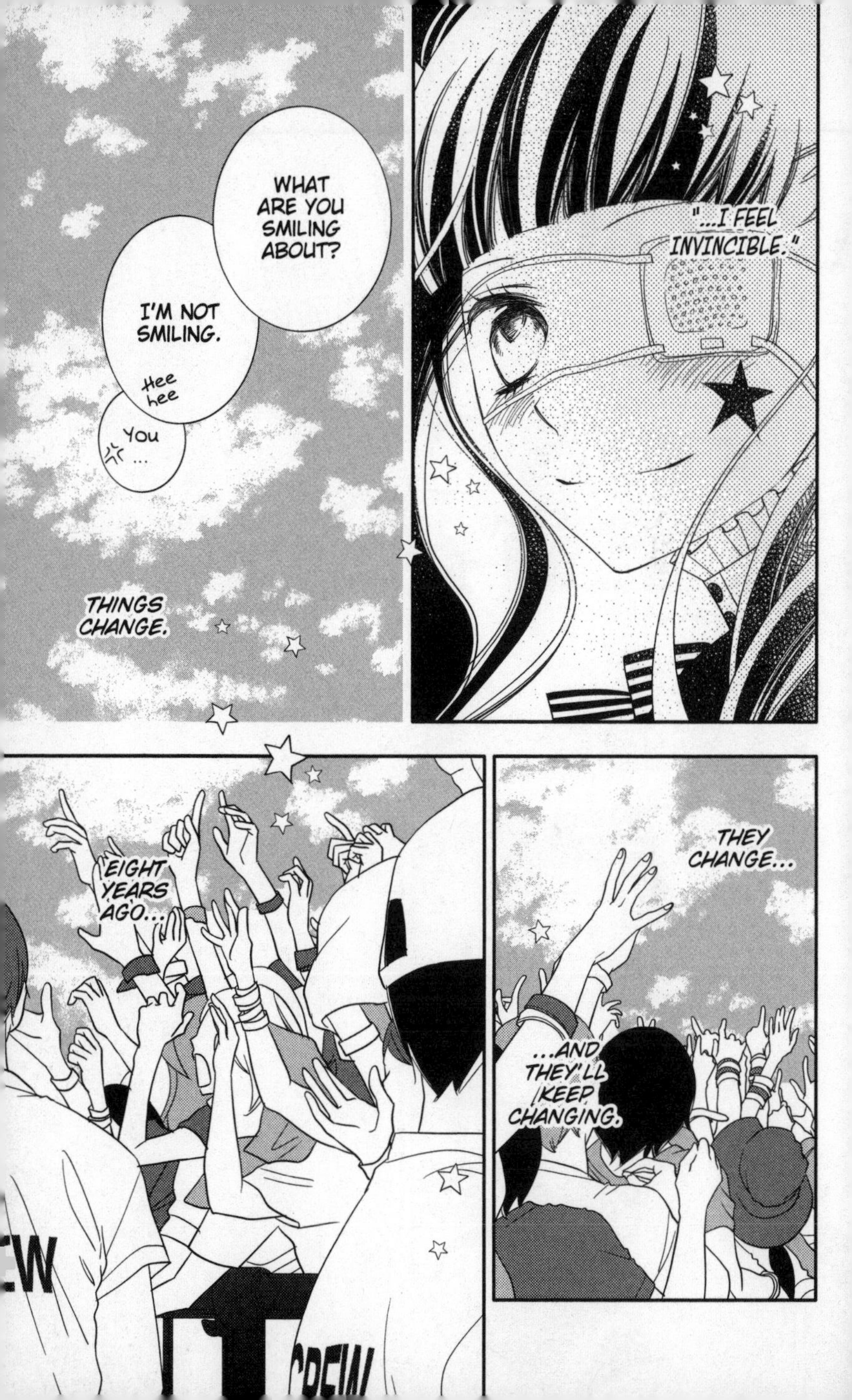
"...I FEEL INVINCIBLE."
WHAT ARE YOU SMILING ABOUT?
I'M NOT SMILING.
Hee hee
You ...
THINGS CHANGE.
THEY CHANGE...
...AND THEY'LL KEEP CHANGING.
EIGHT YEARS AGO...

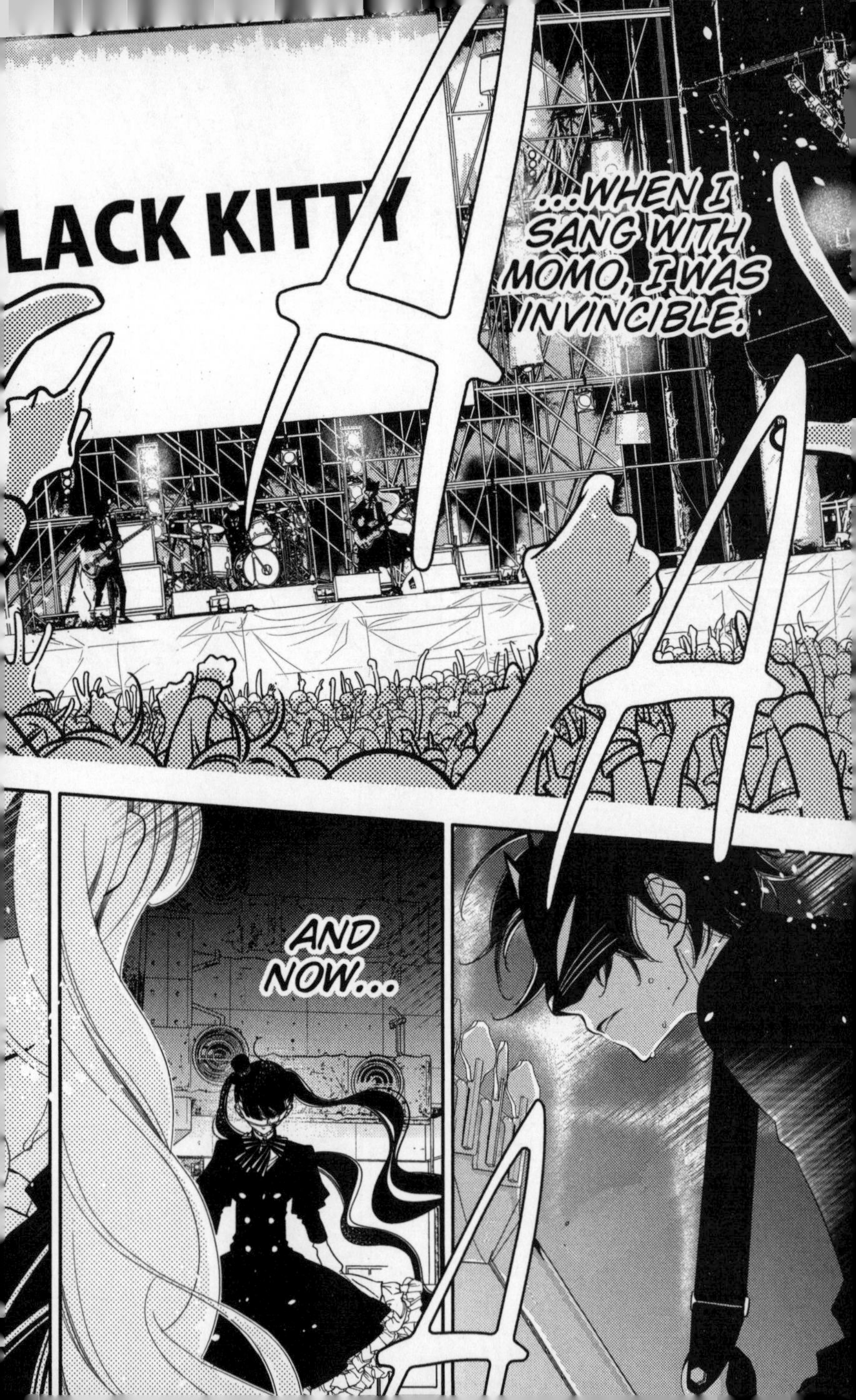
...WHEN I SANG WITH MOMO, I WAS INVINCIBLE.
LACK KITTY
AND NOW...

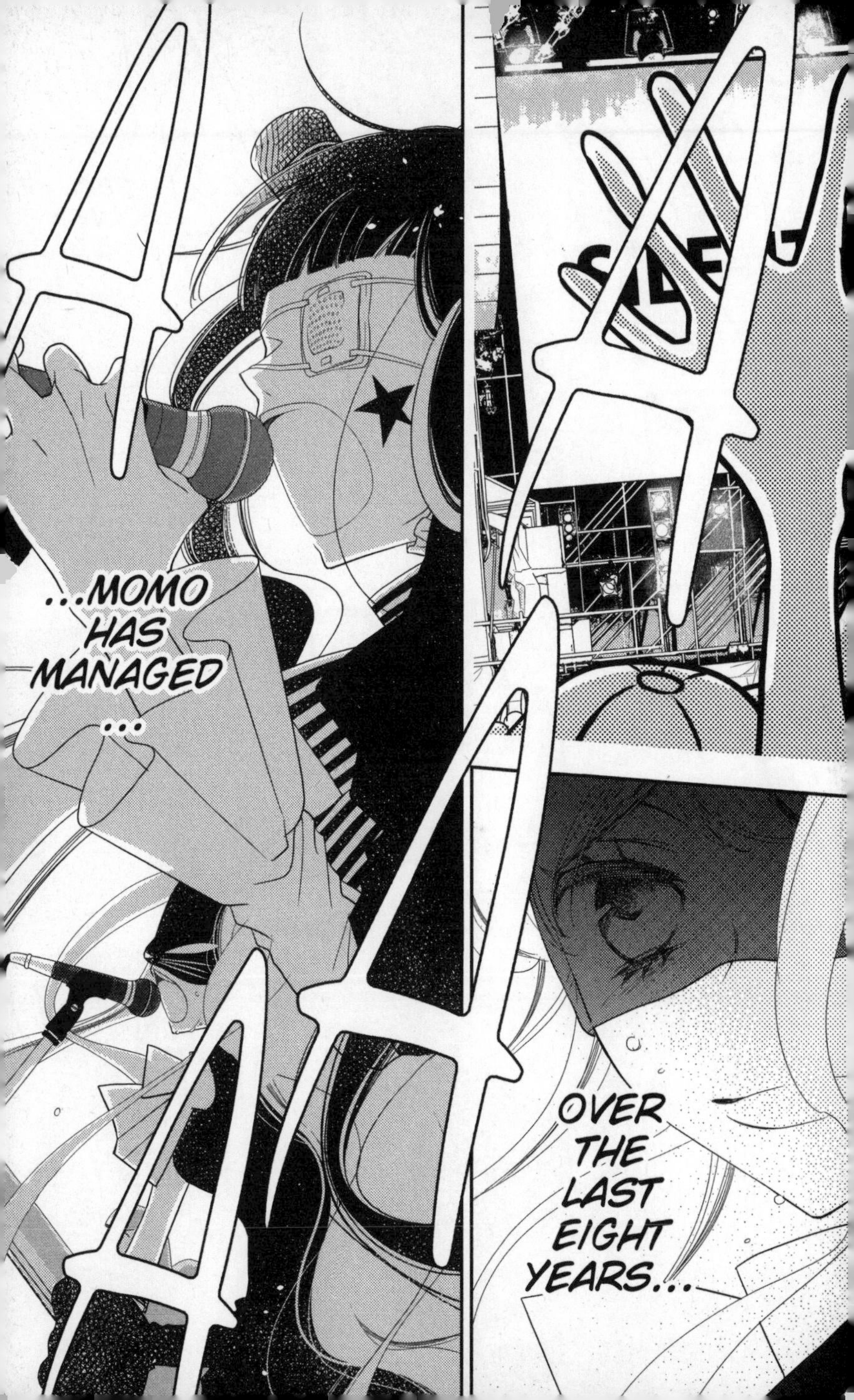
OVER THE LAST EIGHT YEARS...
...MOMO HAS MANAGED...

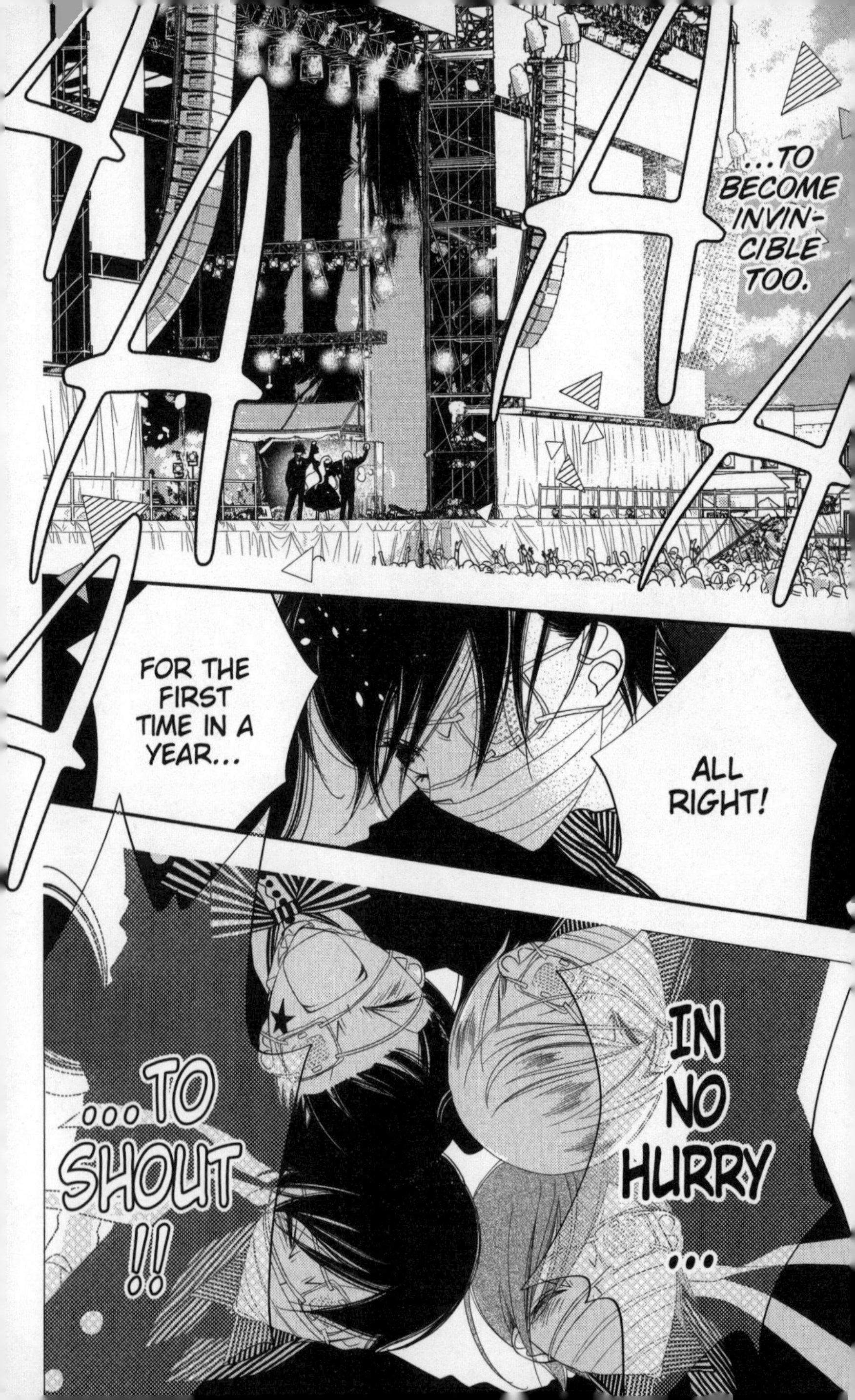
...TO BECOME INVIN-CIBLE TOO.
ALL RIGHT!
FOR THE FIRST TIME IN A YEAR...
IN NO HURRY...
...TO SHOUT!!

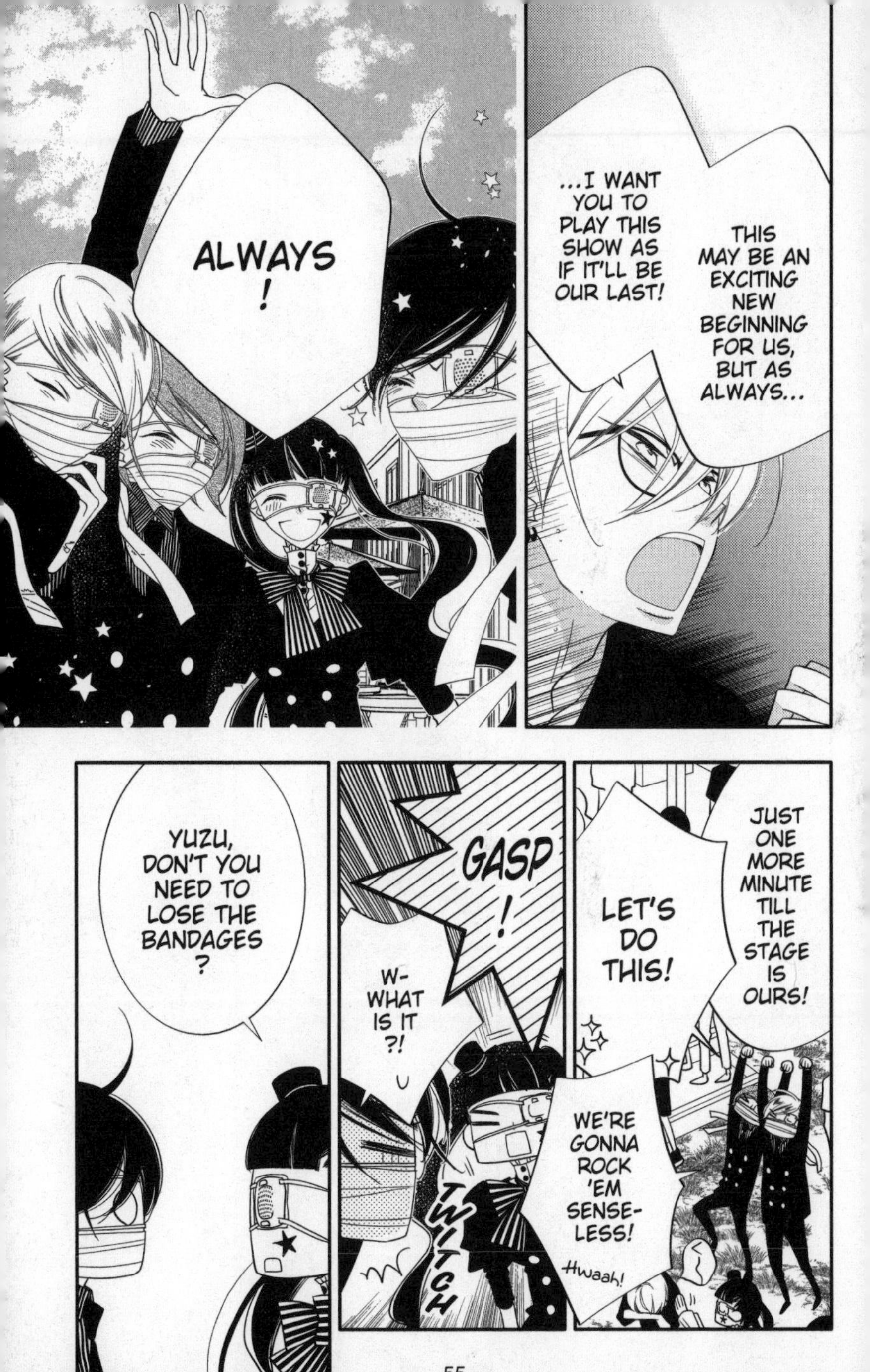
THIS MAY BE AN EXCITING NEW BEGINNING FOR US, BUT AS ALWAYS...
...I WANT YOU TO PLAY THIS SHOW AS IF IT'LL BE OUR LAST!
ALWAYS!
JUST ONE MORE MINUTE TILL THE STAGE IS OURS!
LET'S DO THIS!
WE'RE GONNA ROCK 'EM SENSELESS!
Hwaah!
GASP!
W-WHAT IS IT?!
TWITCH
YUZU, DON'T YOU NEED TO LOSE THE BANDAGES?

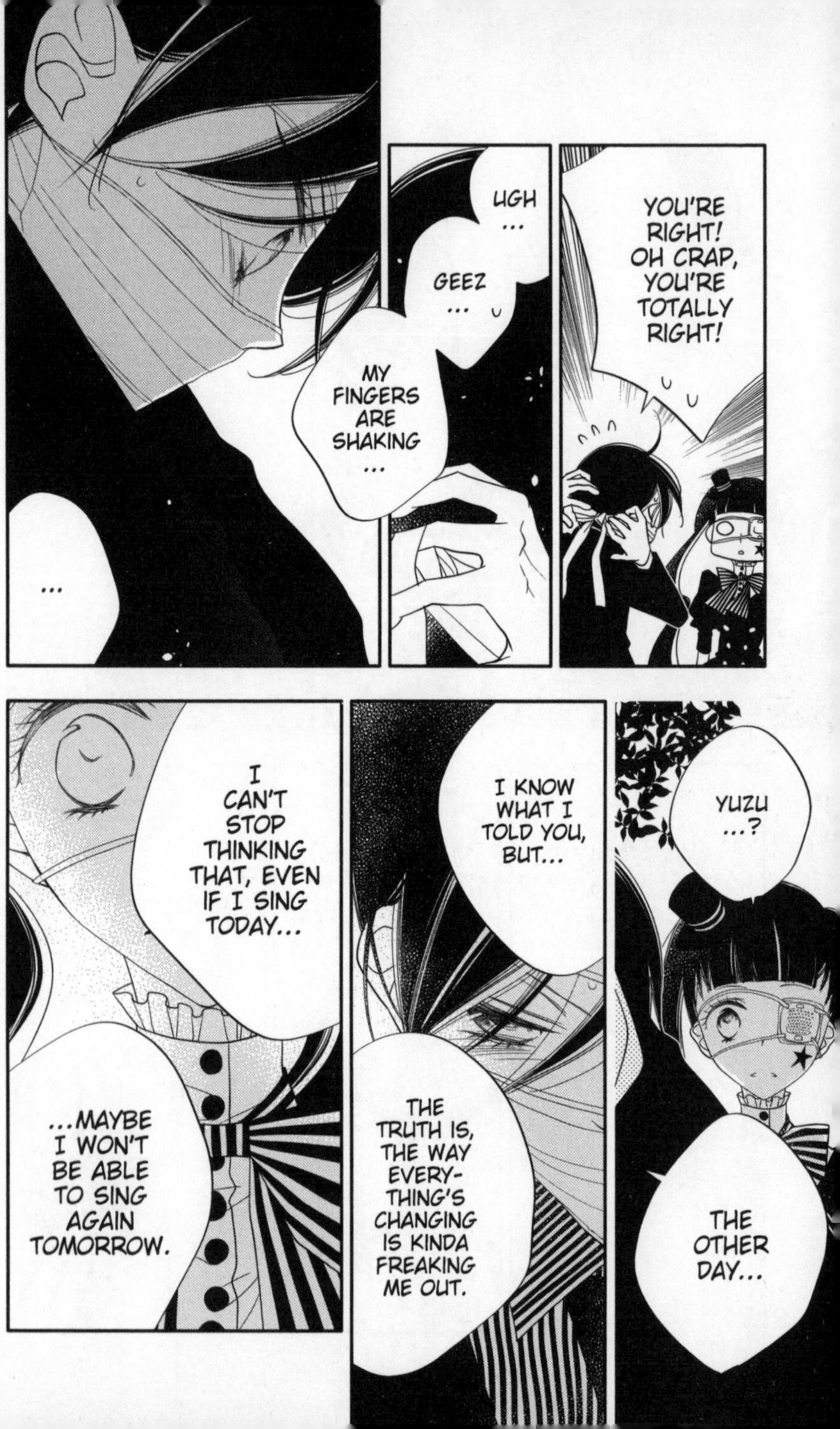
YOU'RE RIGHT! OH CRAP, YOU'RE TOTALLY RIGHT!
UGH ...
GEEZ ...
MY FINGERS ARE SHAKING ...
...
YUZU ...?
THE OTHER DAY...
I KNOW WHAT I TOLD YOU, BUT...
THE TRUTH IS, THE WAY EVERY-THING'S CHANGING IS KINDA FREAKING ME OUT.
I CAN'T STOP THINKING THAT, EVEN IF I SING TODAY...
...MAYBE I WON'T BE ABLE TO SING AGAIN TOMORROW.

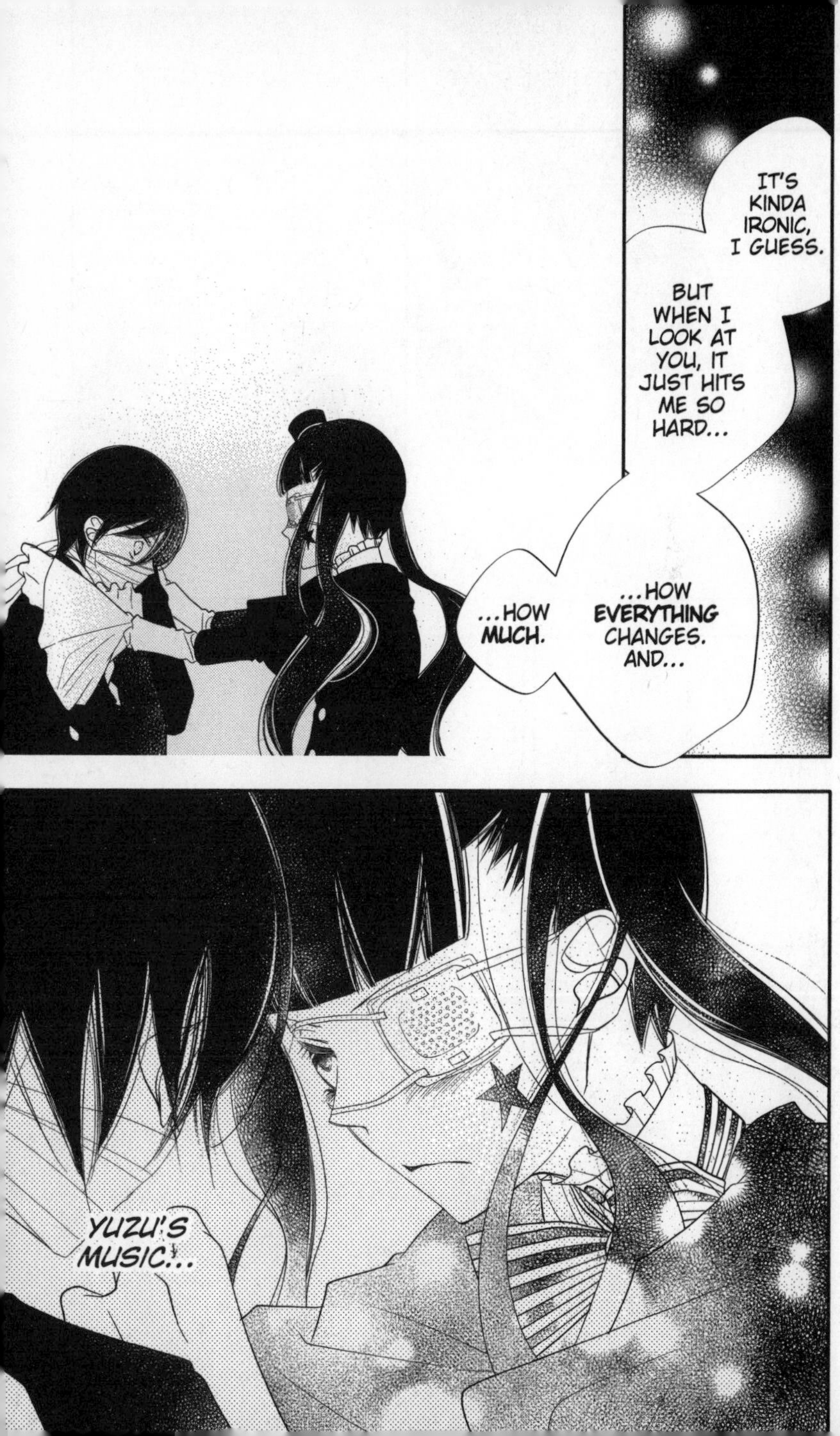
IT'S KINDA IRONIC, I GUESS.
BUT WHEN I LOOK AT YOU, IT JUST HITS ME SO HARD...
...HOW EVERYTHING CHANGES. AND...
...HOW MUCH.
YUZU'S MUSIC...

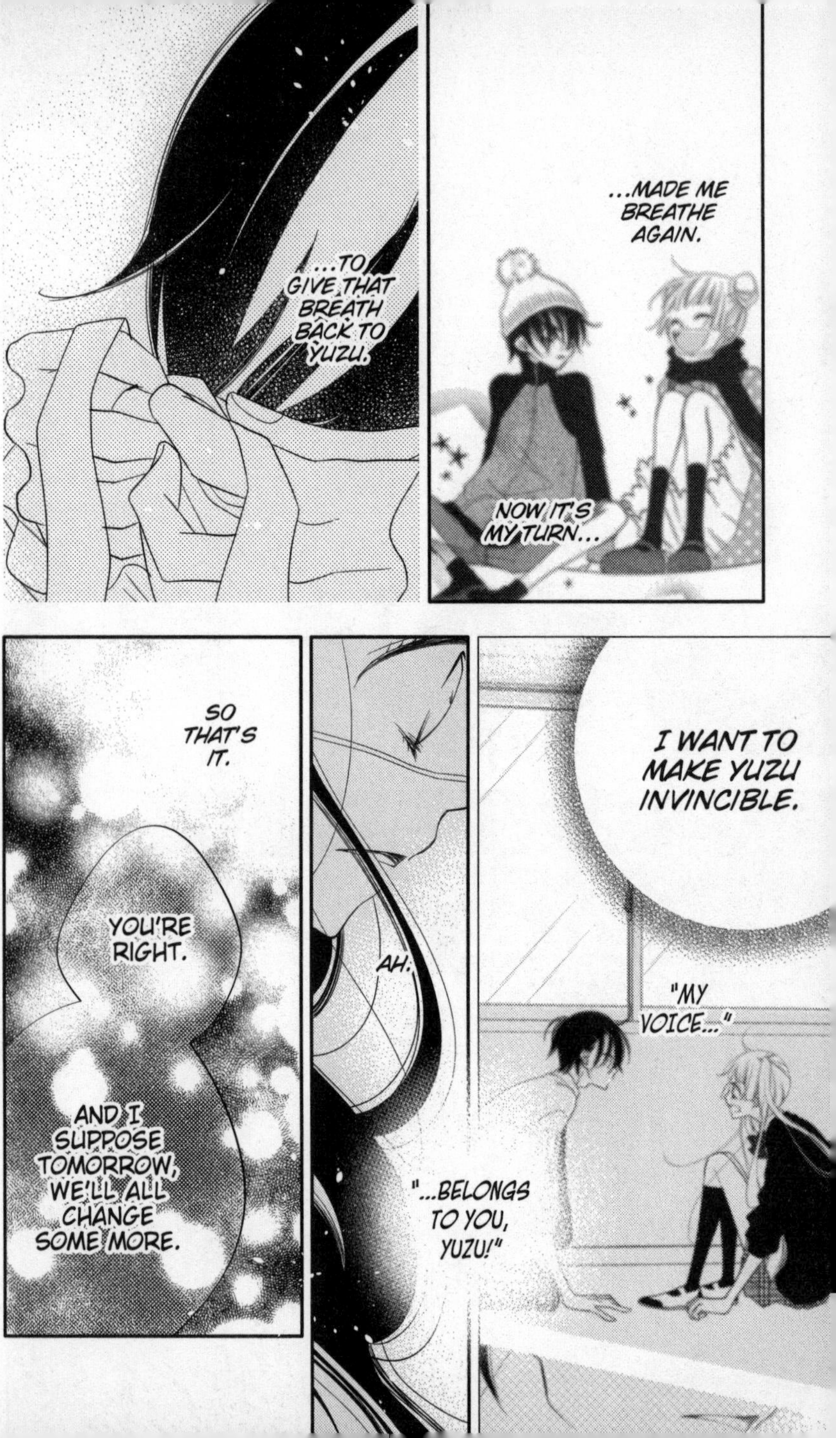

...MADE ME BREATHE AGAIN.
NOW IT'S MY TURN...
...TO GIVE THAT BREATH BACK TO YUZU.
I WANT TO MAKE YUZU INVINCIBLE.
"MY VOICE..."
"...BELONGS TO YOU, YUZU!"
AH.
SO THAT'S IT.
YOU'RE RIGHT.
AND I SUPPOSE TOMORROW, WE'LL ALL CHANGE SOME MORE.

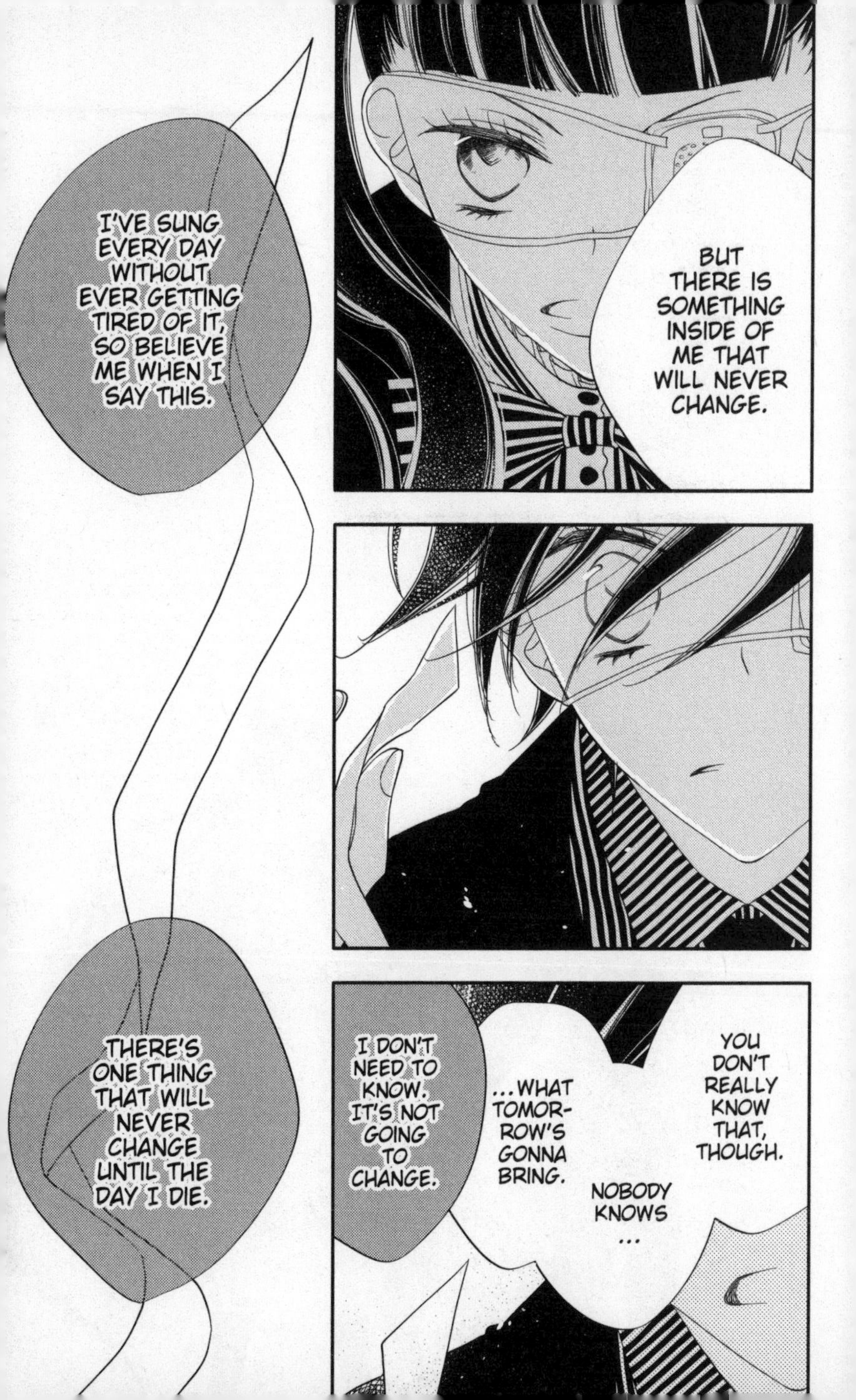
BUT THERE IS SOMETHING INSIDE OF ME THAT WILL NEVER CHANGE.
YOU DON'T REALLY KNOW THAT, THOUGH.
NOBODY KNOWS ...
...WHAT TOMORROW'S GONNA BRING.
I DON'T NEED TO KNOW. IT'S NOT GOING TO CHANGE.
I'VE SUNG EVERY DAY WITHOUT EVER GETTING TIRED OF IT, SO BELIEVE ME WHEN I SAY THIS.
THERE'S ONE THING THAT WILL NEVER CHANGE UNTIL THE DAY I DIE.

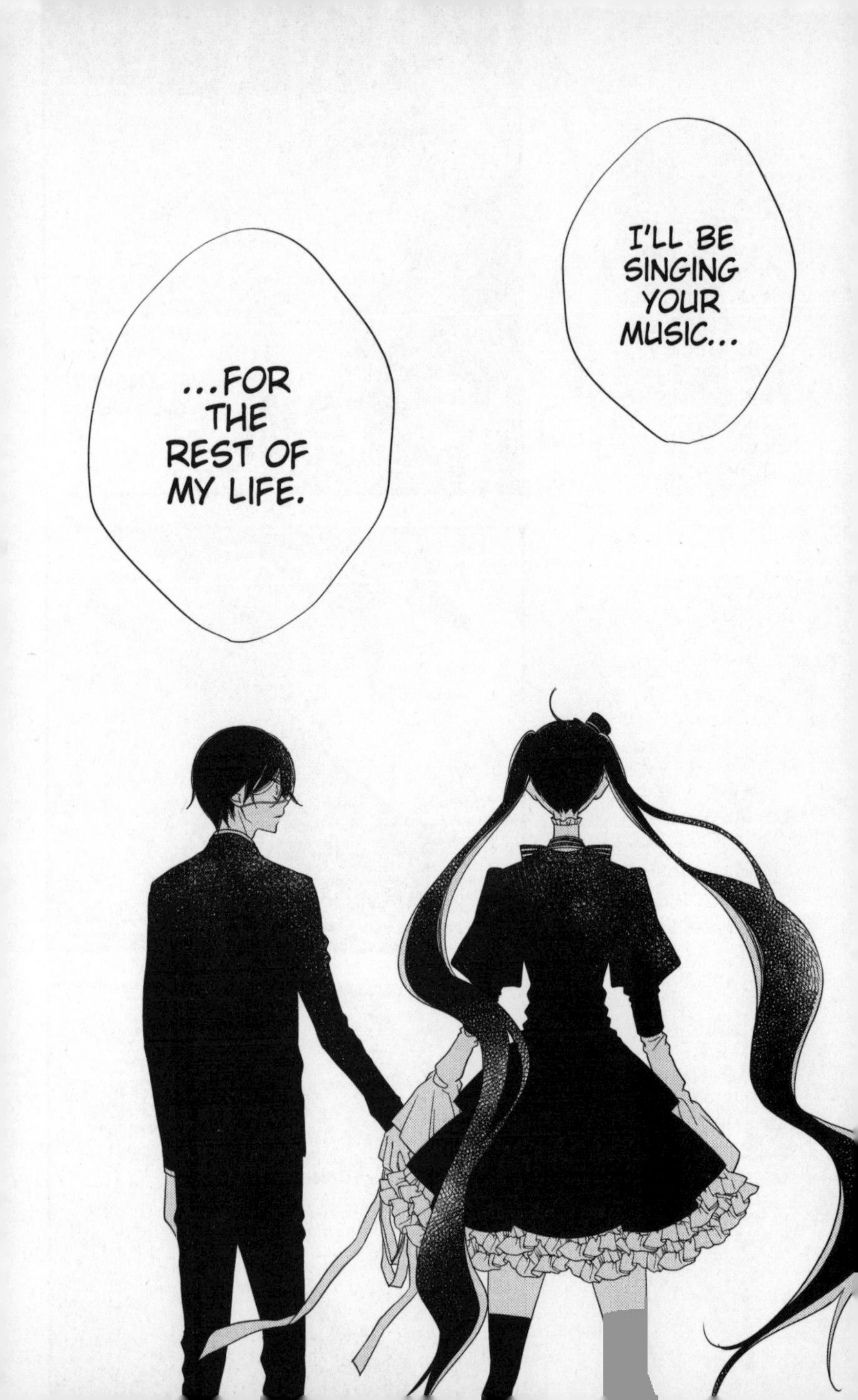
I'LL BE SINGING YOUR MUSIC...
...FOR THE REST OF MY LIFE.

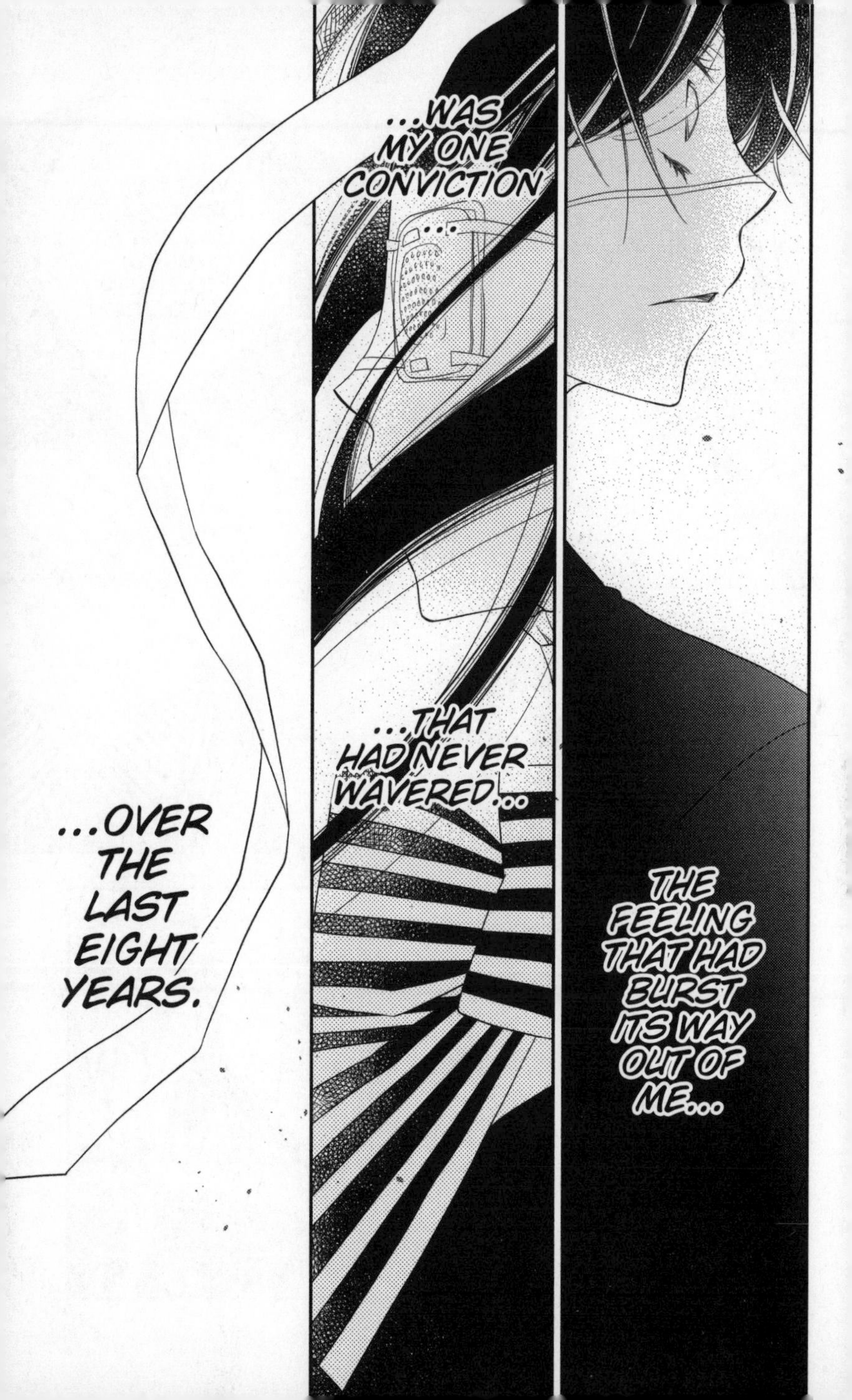
THE FEELING THAT HAD BURST ITS WAY OUT OF ME...
...WAS MY ONE CONVICTION...
...THAT HAD NEVER WAVERED...
...OVER THE LAST EIGHT YEARS.

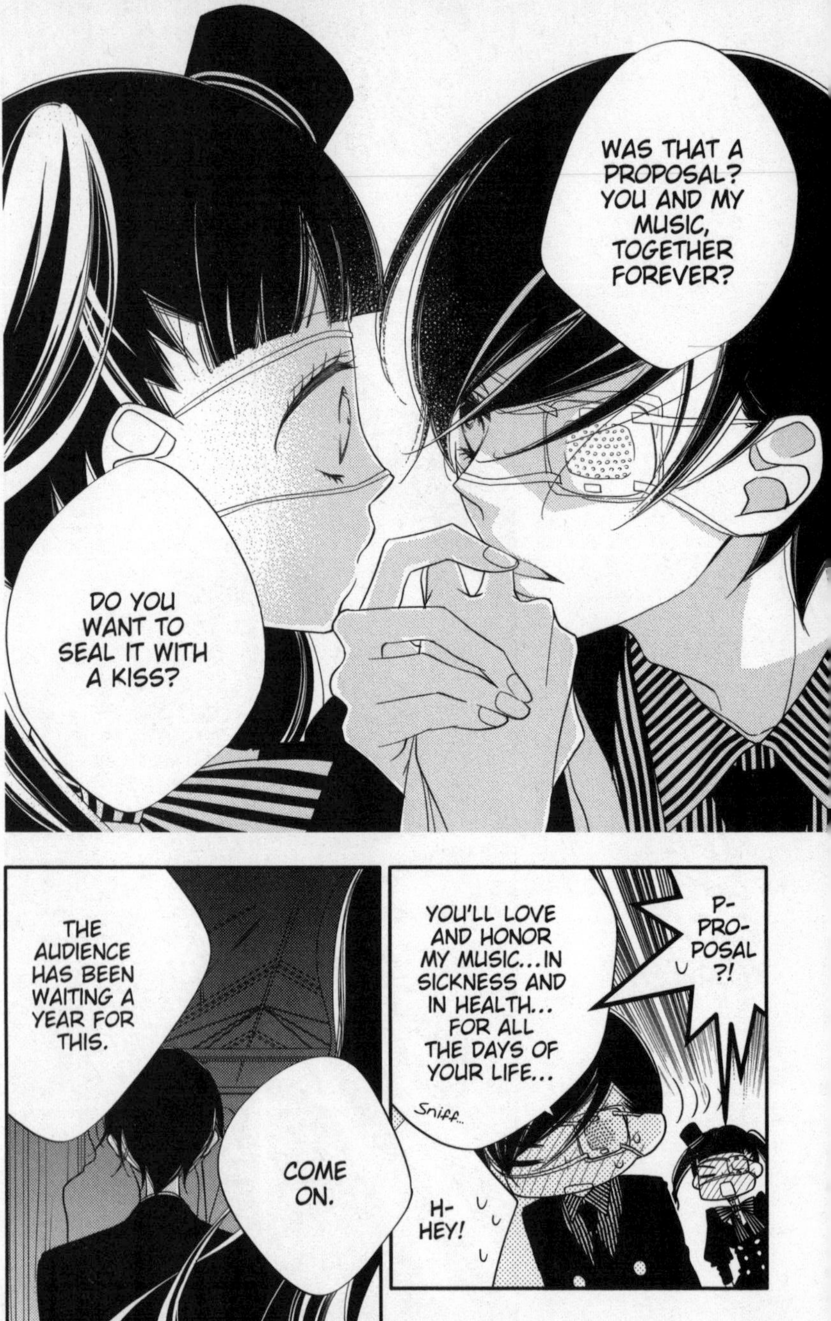
WAS THAT A PROPOSAL? YOU AND MY MUSIC, TOGETHER FOREVER?
DO YOU WANT TO SEAL IT WITH A KISS?
P-PRO-POSAL?!
YOU'LL LOVE AND HONOR MY MUSIC...IN SICKNESS AND IN HEALTH... FOR ALL THE DAYS OF YOUR LIFE...
Sniff...
H-HEY!
THE AUDIENCE HAS BEEN WAITING A YEAR FOR THIS.
COME ON.

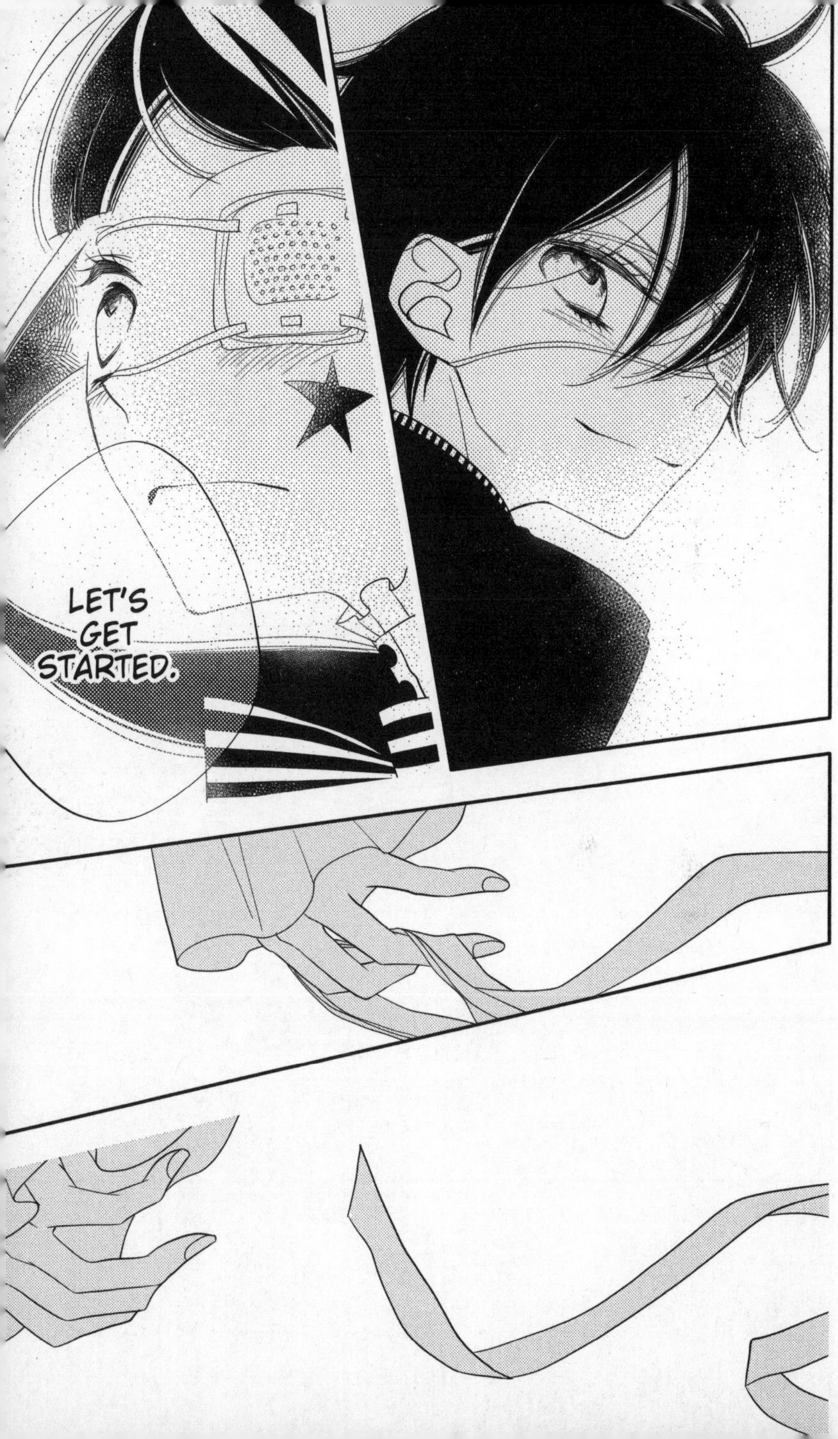
LET'S GET STARTED.

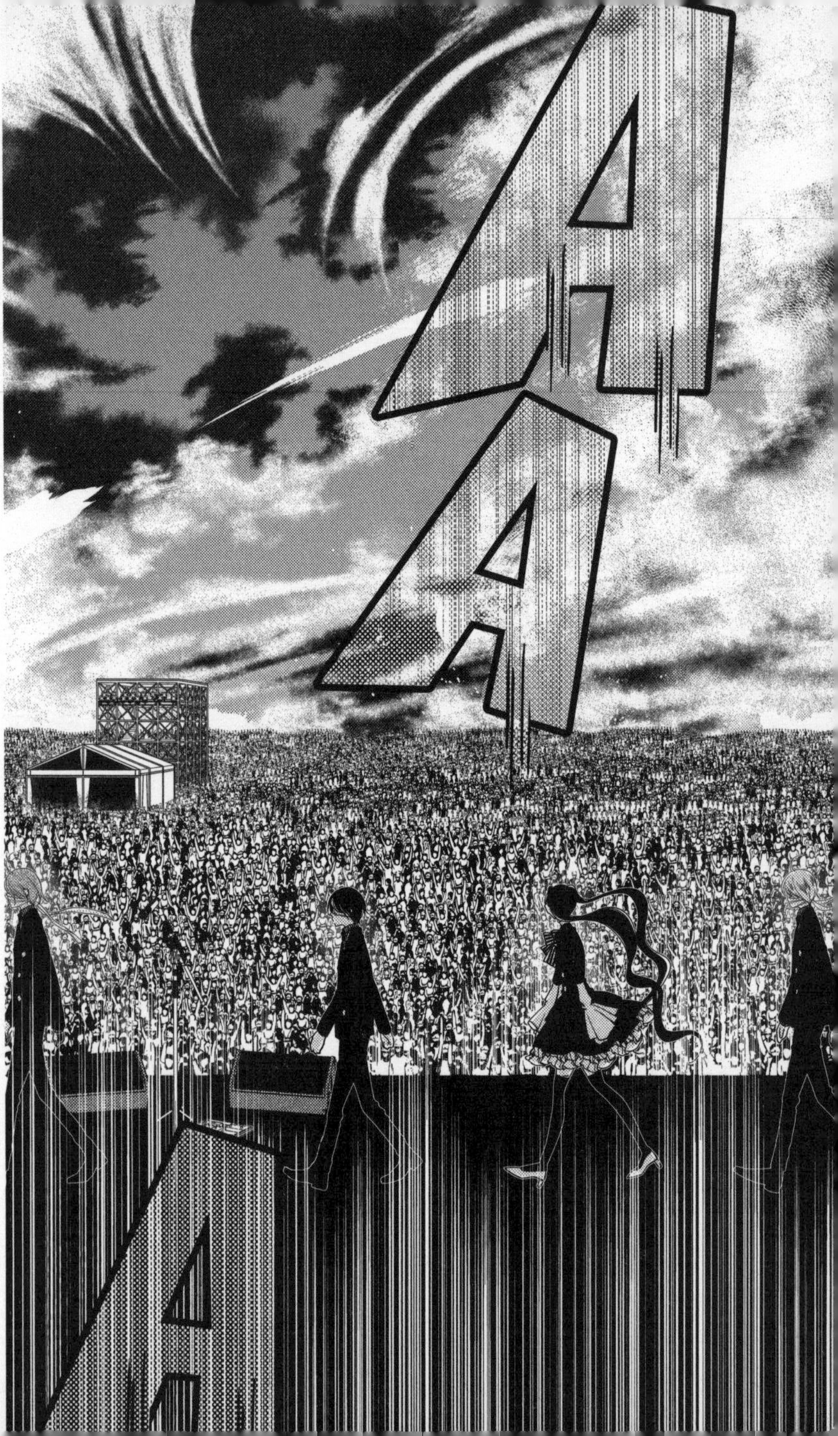
AAA

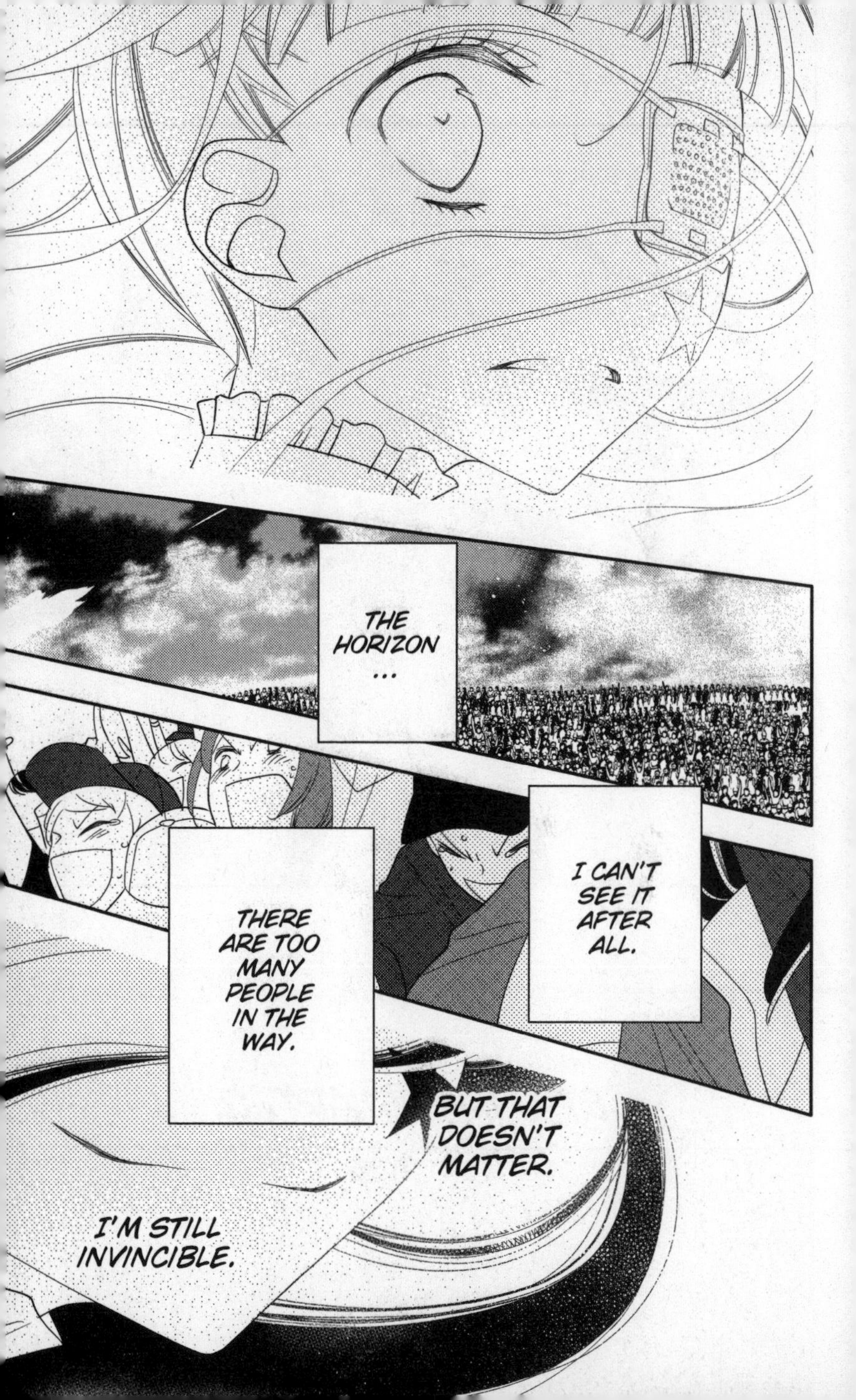
THE HORIZON...
I CAN'T SEE IT AFTER ALL.
THERE ARE TOO MANY PEOPLE IN THE WAY.
BUT THAT DOESN'T MATTER.
I'M STILL INVINCIBLE.

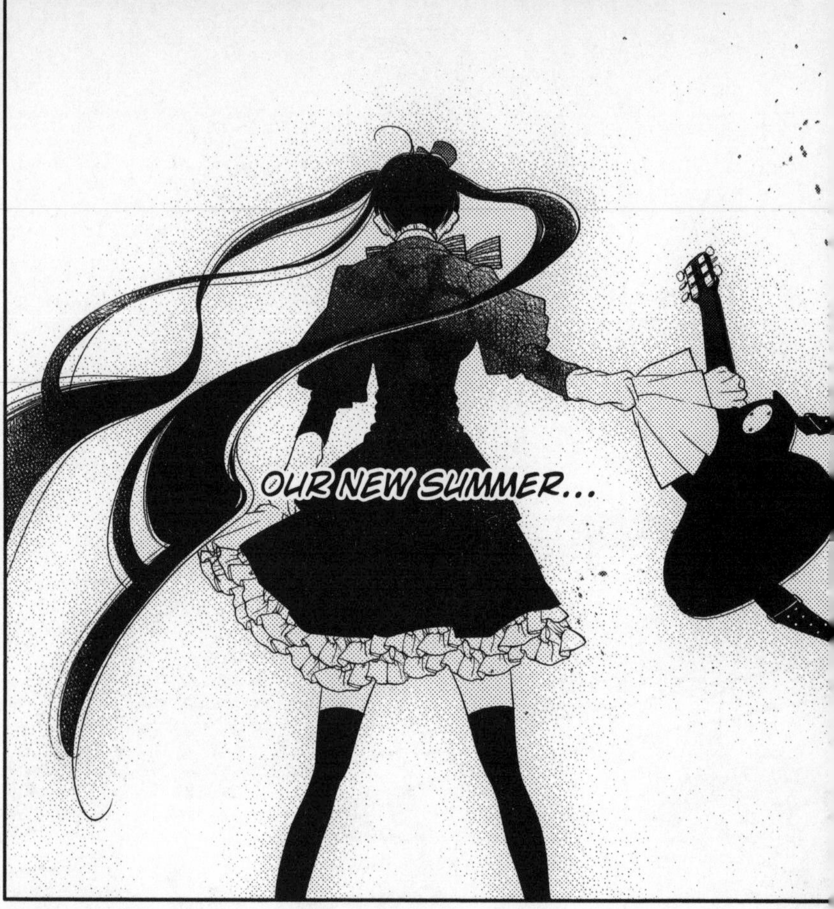
OUR NEW SUMMER...

LET'S GET STARTED.

SONG 101

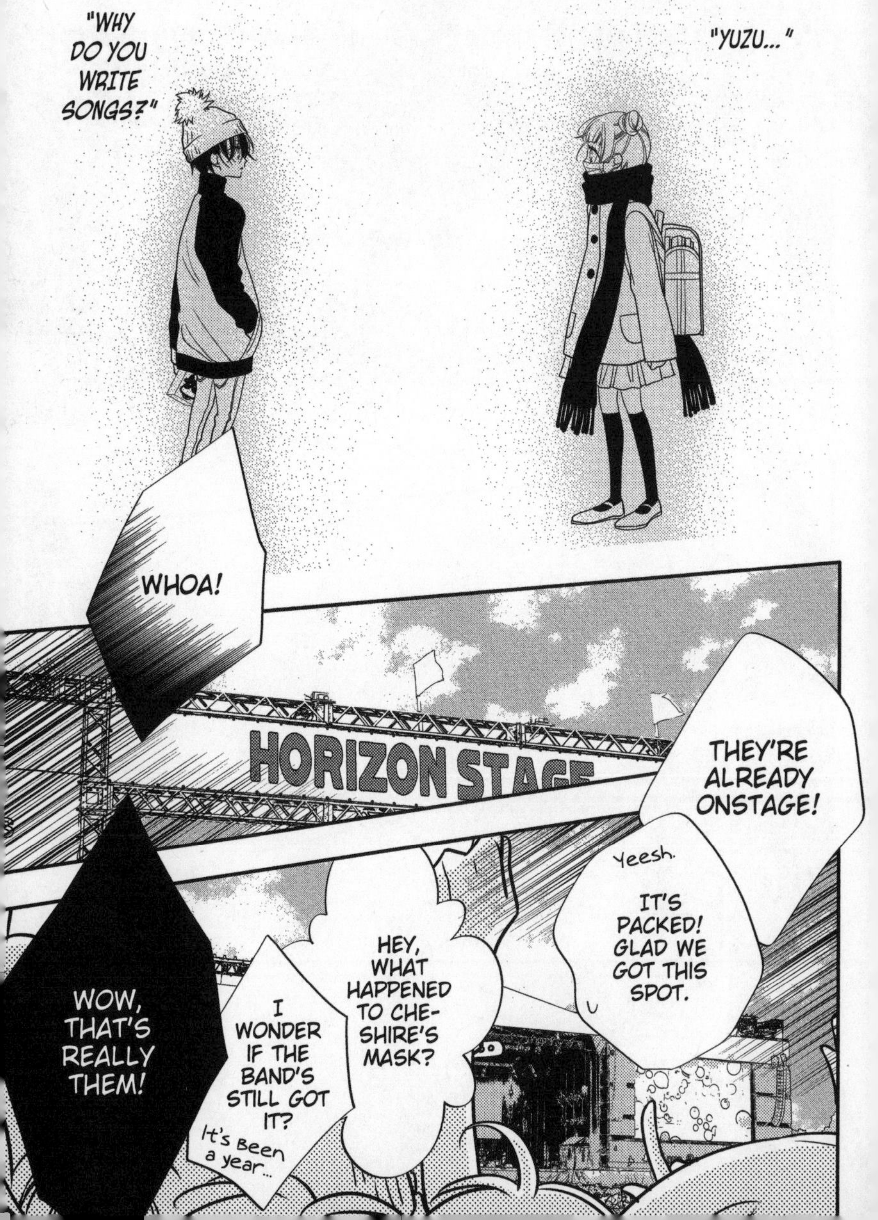

"YUZU..."
"WHY DO YOU WRITE SONGS?"
WHOA!
HORIZON STAGE
THEY'RE ALREADY ONSTAGE!
Yeesh.
IT'S PACKED! GLAD WE GOT THIS SPOT.
HEY, WHAT HAPPENED TO CHE-SHIRE'S MASK?
I WONDER IF THE BAND'S STILL GOT IT?
It's Been a year...
WOW, THAT'S REALLY THEM!

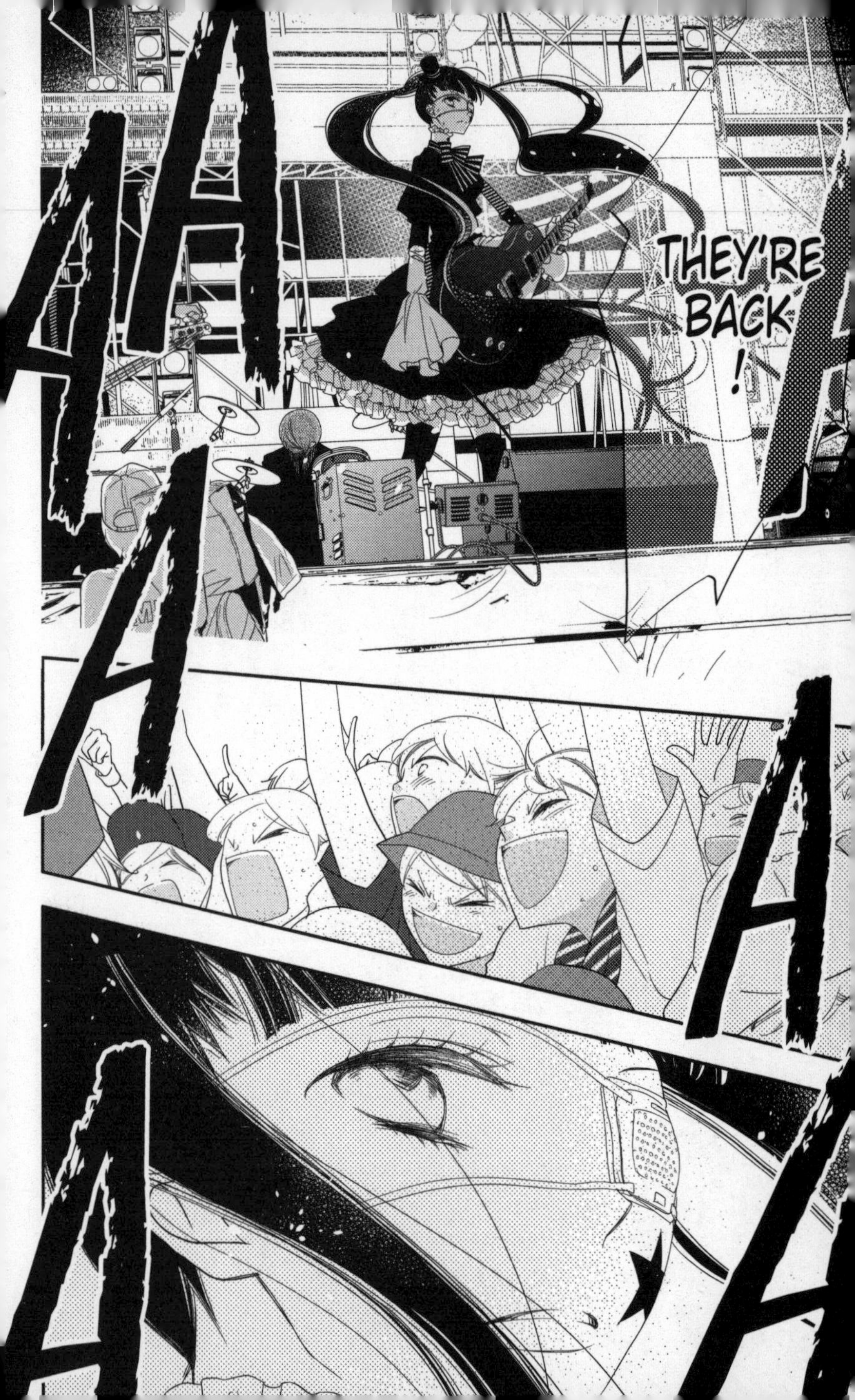
THEY'RE BACK!
AAAAAA

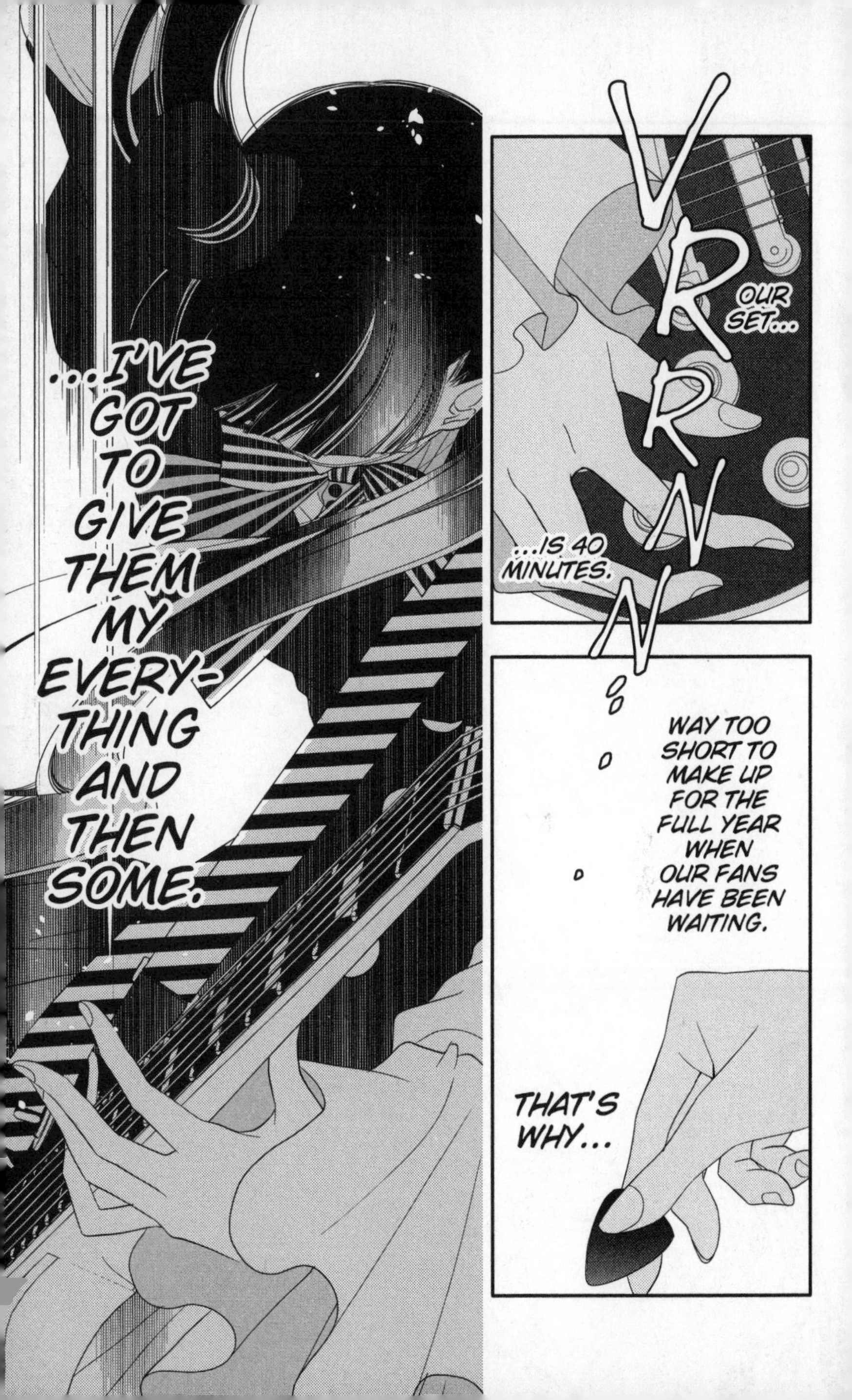
VRRNN
OUR SET...
...IS 40 MINUTES.
WAY TOO SHORT TO MAKE UP FOR THE FULL YEAR WHEN OUR FANS HAVE BEEN WAITING.
THAT'S WHY...
...I'VE GOT TO GIVE THEM MY EVERYTHING AND THEN SOME.

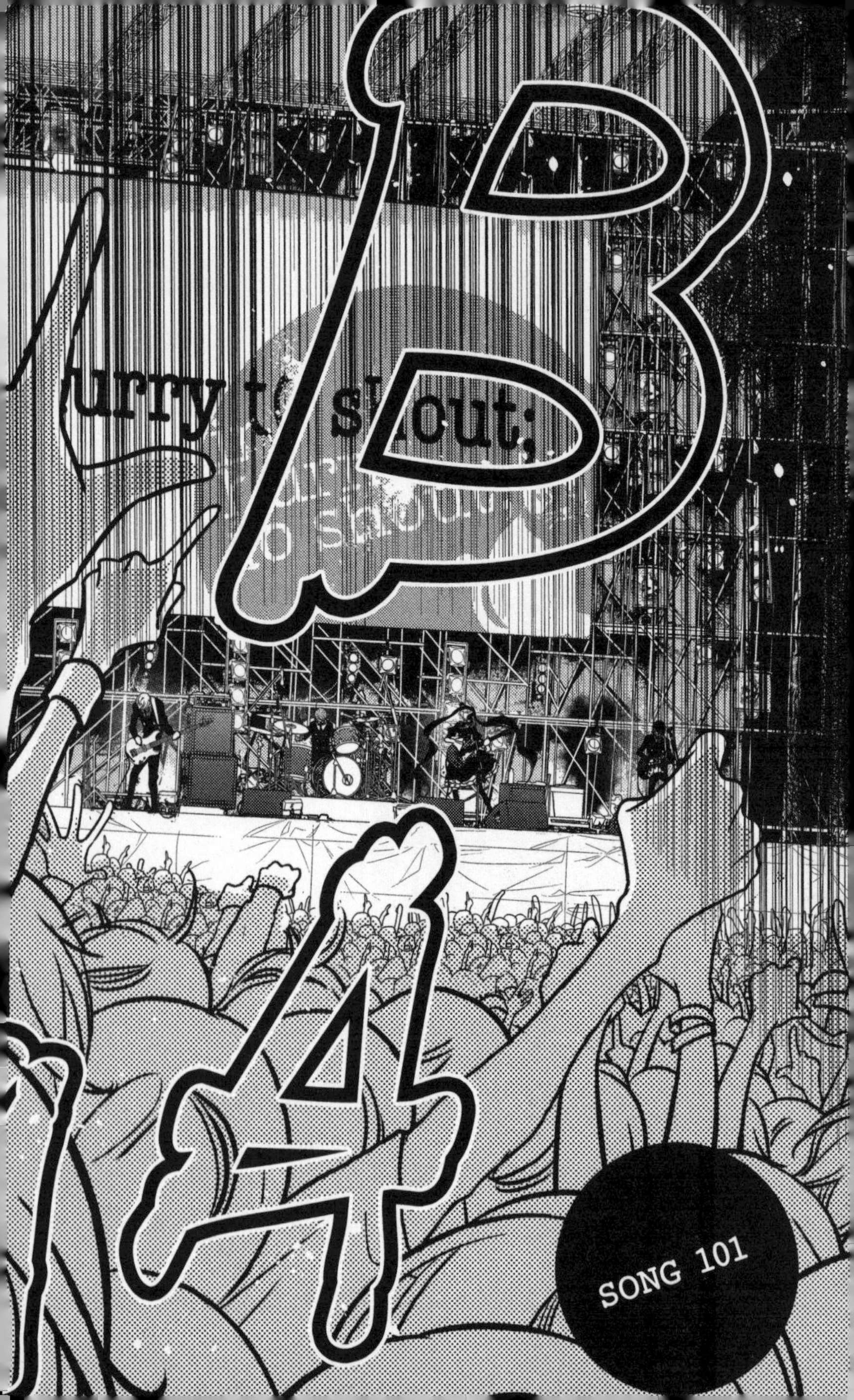
SONG 101

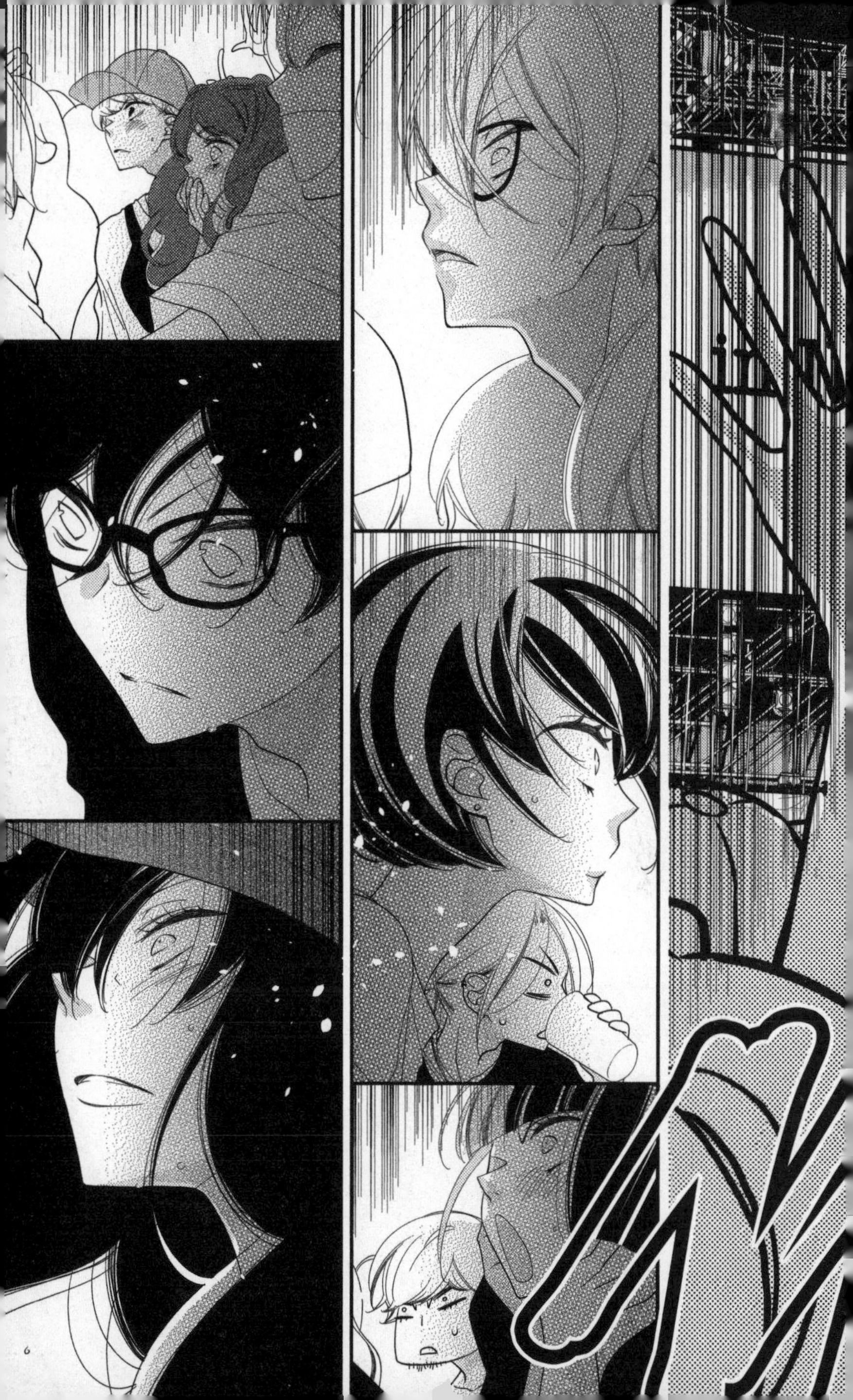

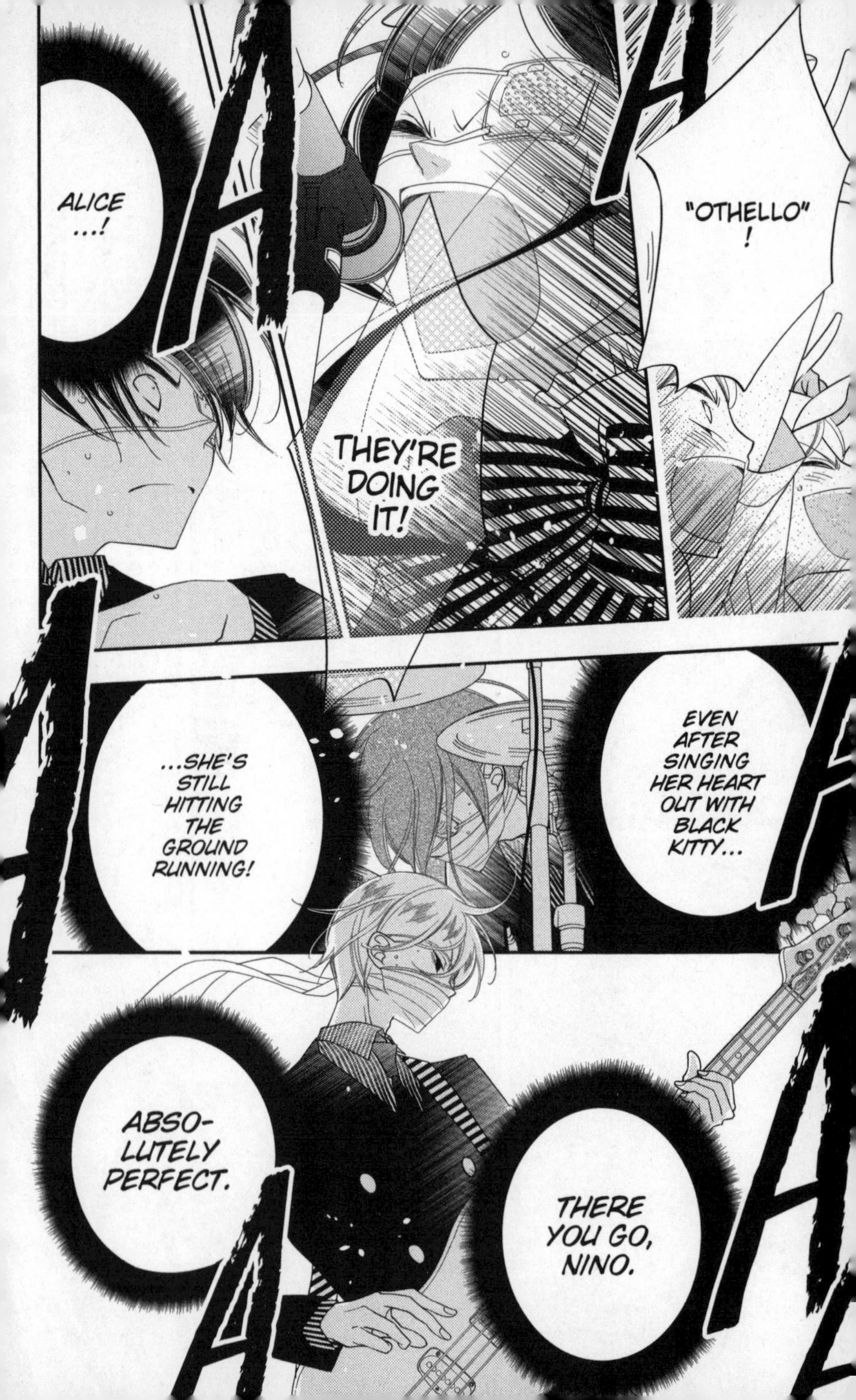
"OTHELLO" !
THEY'RE DOING IT!
ALICE ...!
EVEN AFTER SINGING HER HEART OUT WITH BLACK KITTY...
...SHE'S STILL HITTING THE GROUND RUNNING!
THERE YOU GO, NINO.
ABSO-LUTELY PERFECT.

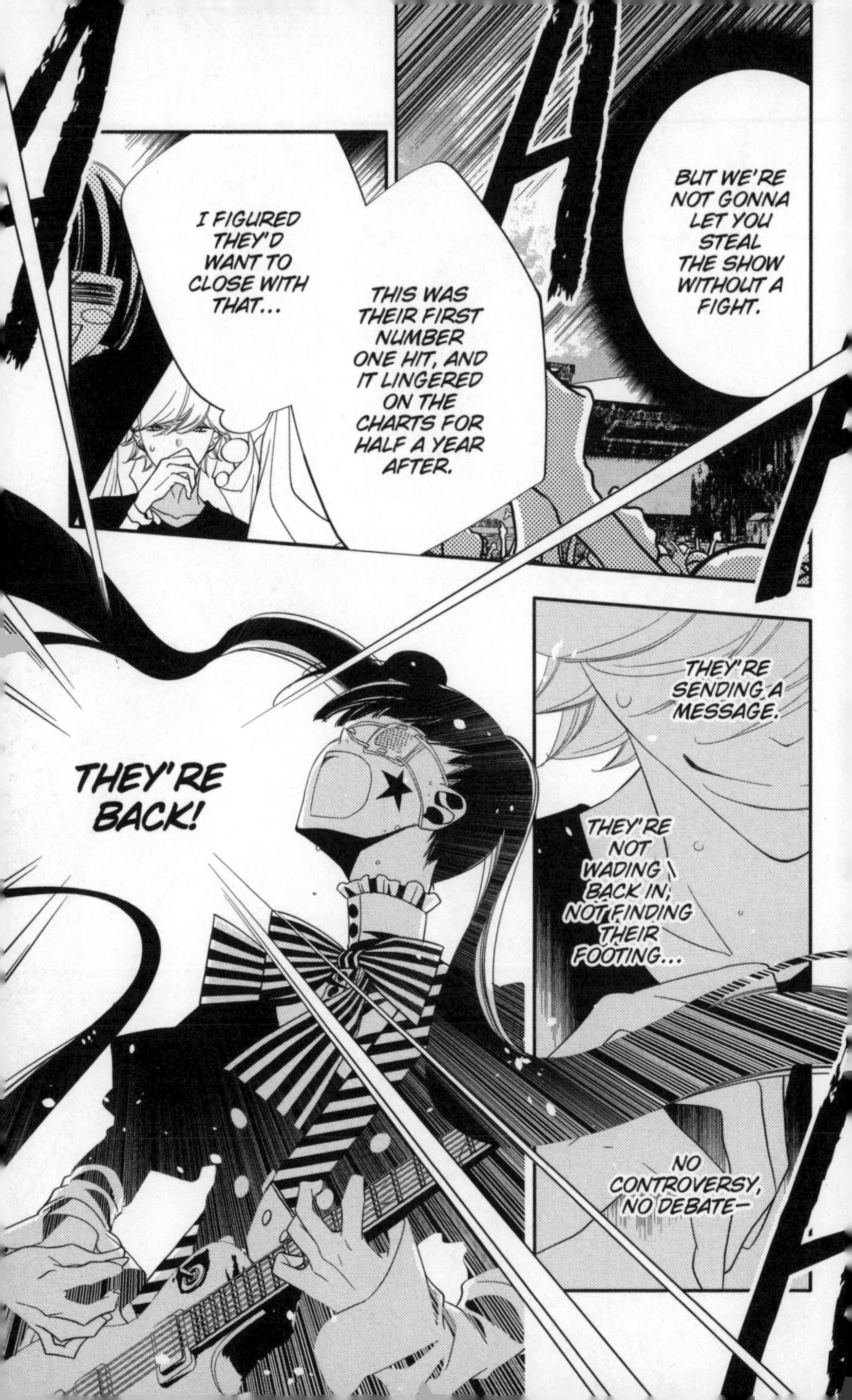
BUT WE'RE NOT GONNA LET YOU STEAL THE SHOW WITHOUT A FIGHT.
I FIGURED THEY'D WANT TO CLOSE WITH THAT...
THIS WAS THEIR FIRST NUMBER ONE HIT, AND IT LINGERED ON THE CHARTS FOR HALF A YEAR AFTER.
THEY'RE SENDING A MESSAGE.
THEY'RE NOT WADING BACK IN, NOT FINDING THEIR FOOTING...
NO CONTROVERSY, NO DEBATE—
THEY'RE BACK!

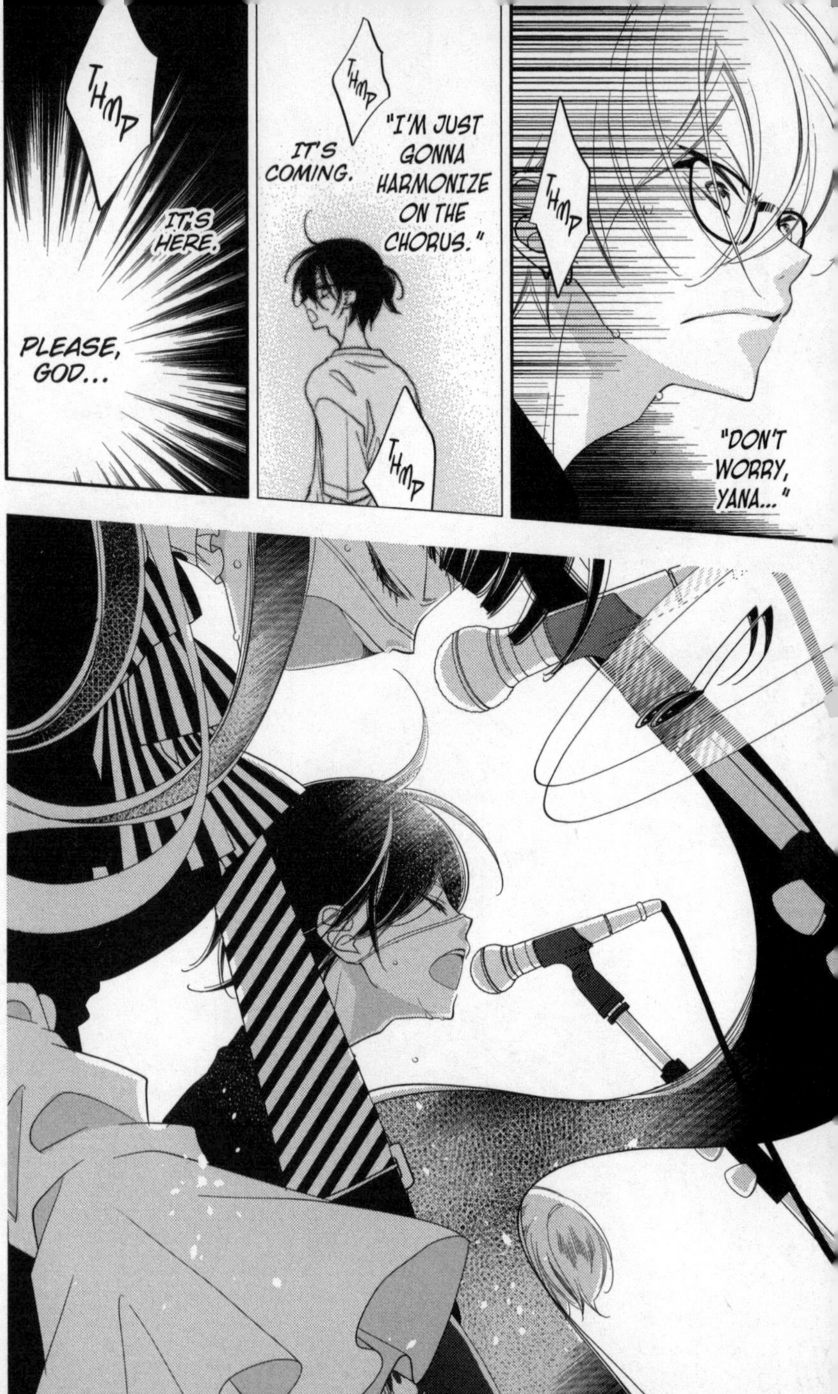
THMP
"DON'T WORRY, YANA..."
THMP
"I'M JUST GONNA HARMONIZE ON THE CHORUS."
IT'S COMING.
THMP
THMP
IT'S HERE.
PLEASE, GOD...

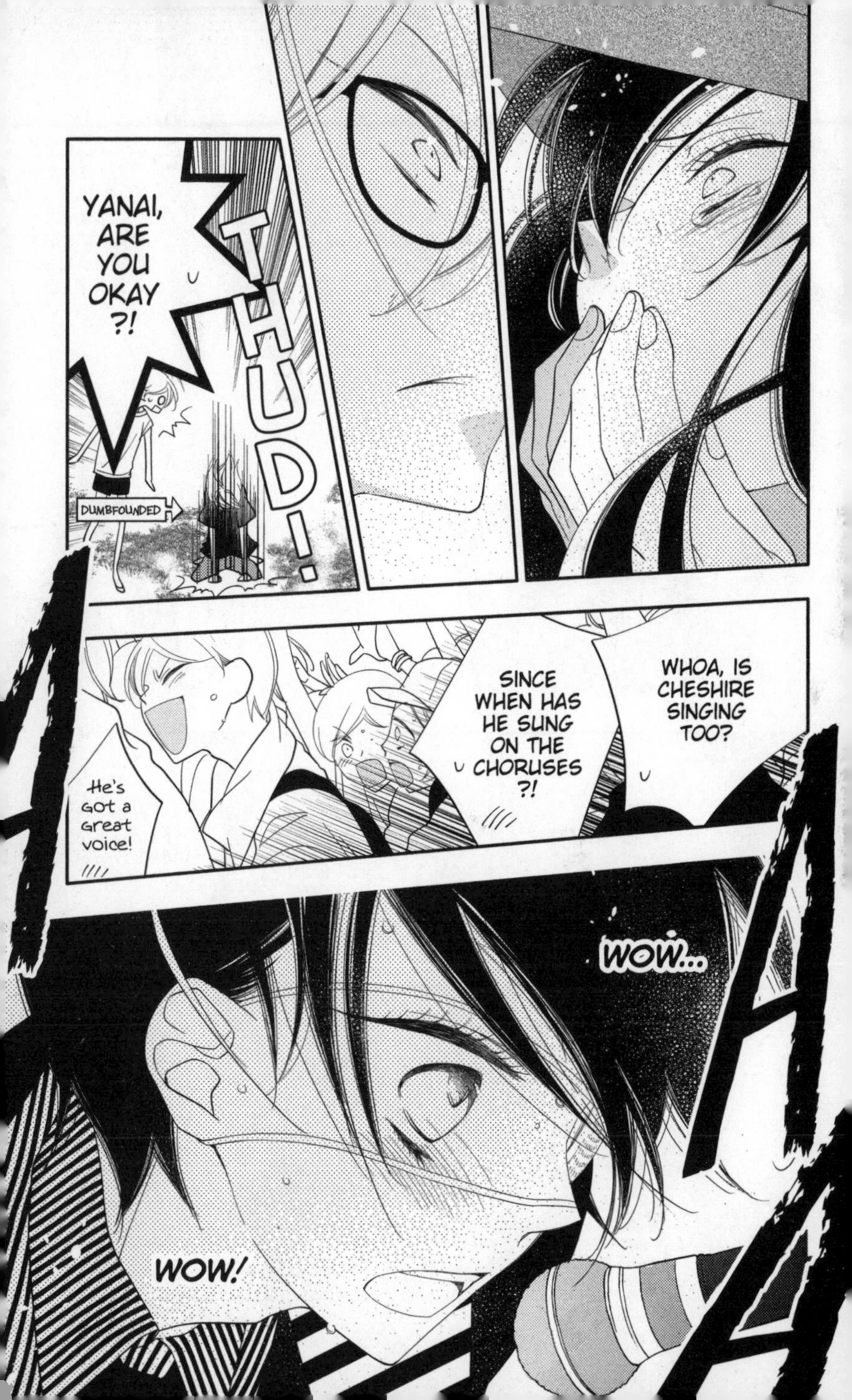
THUD!!
YANAI, ARE YOU OKAY ?!
DUMBFOUNDED
WHOA, IS CHESHIRE SINGING TOO?
SINCE WHEN HAS HE SUNG ON THE CHORUSES ?!
He's got a great voice!
WOW...
WOW!

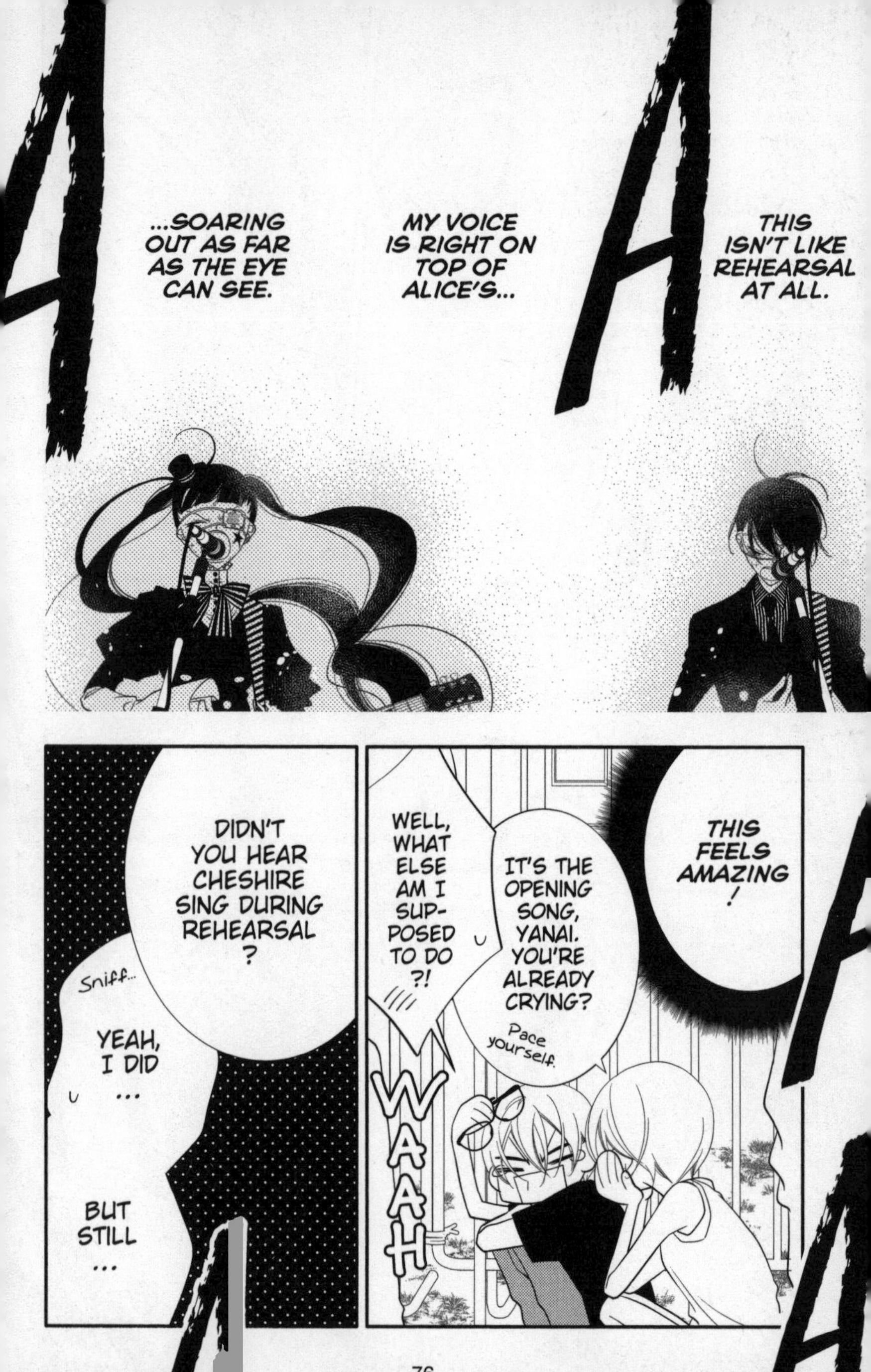
AAA
THIS ISN'T LIKE REHEARSAL AT ALL.
MY VOICE IS RIGHT ON TOP OF ALICE'S...
...SOARING OUT AS FAR AS THE EYE CAN SEE.
THIS FEELS AMAZING!
IT'S THE OPENING SONG, YANAI. YOU'RE ALREADY CRYING?
Pace yourself.
WELL, WHAT ELSE AM I SUP-POSED TO DO?!
WAAAH
DIDN'T YOU HEAR CHESHIRE SING DURING REHEARSAL?
Sniff...
YEAH, I DID...
BUT STILL...

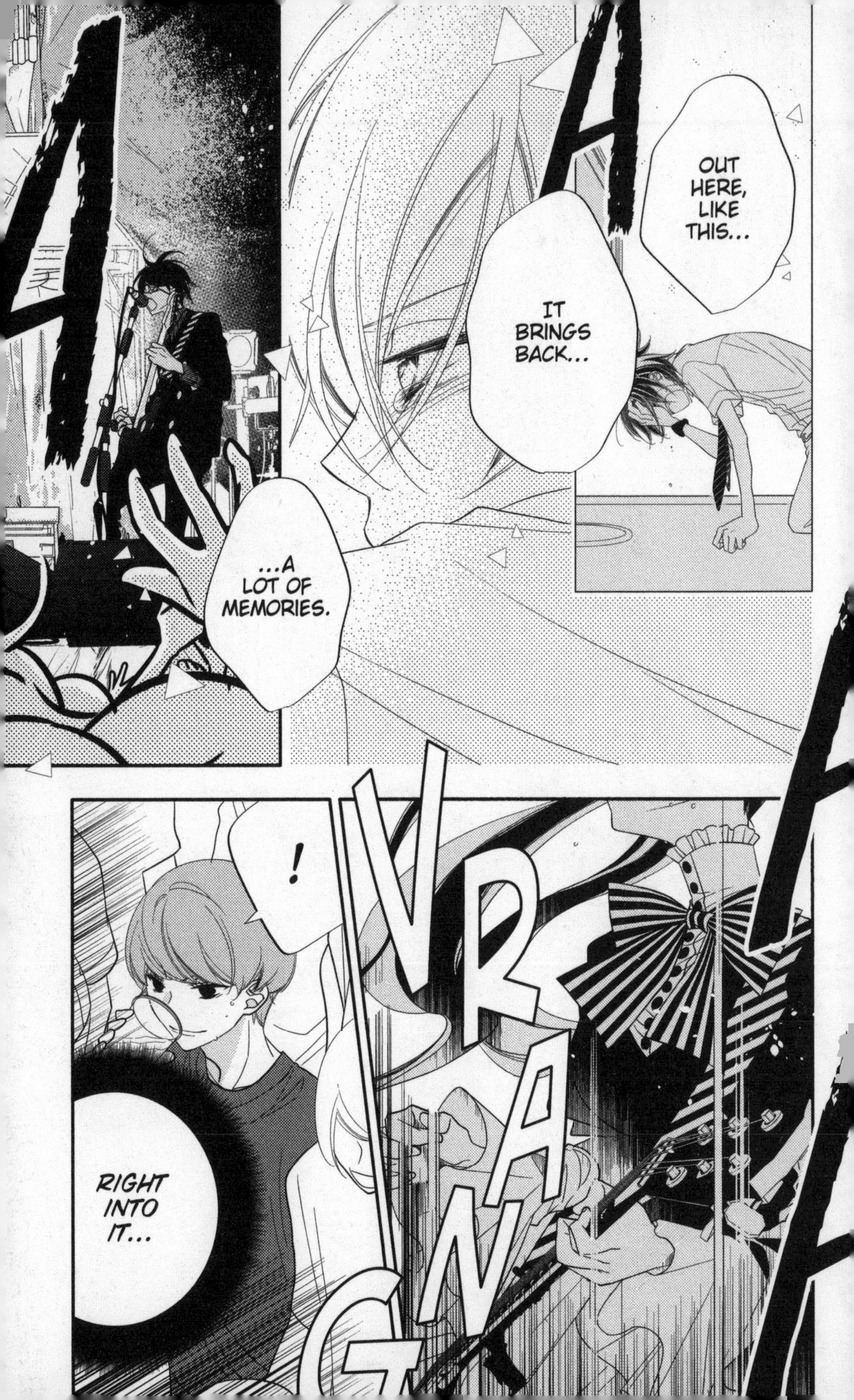
OUT HERE, LIKE THIS...
IT BRINGS BACK...
...A LOT OF MEMORIES.
!
RIGHT INTO IT...

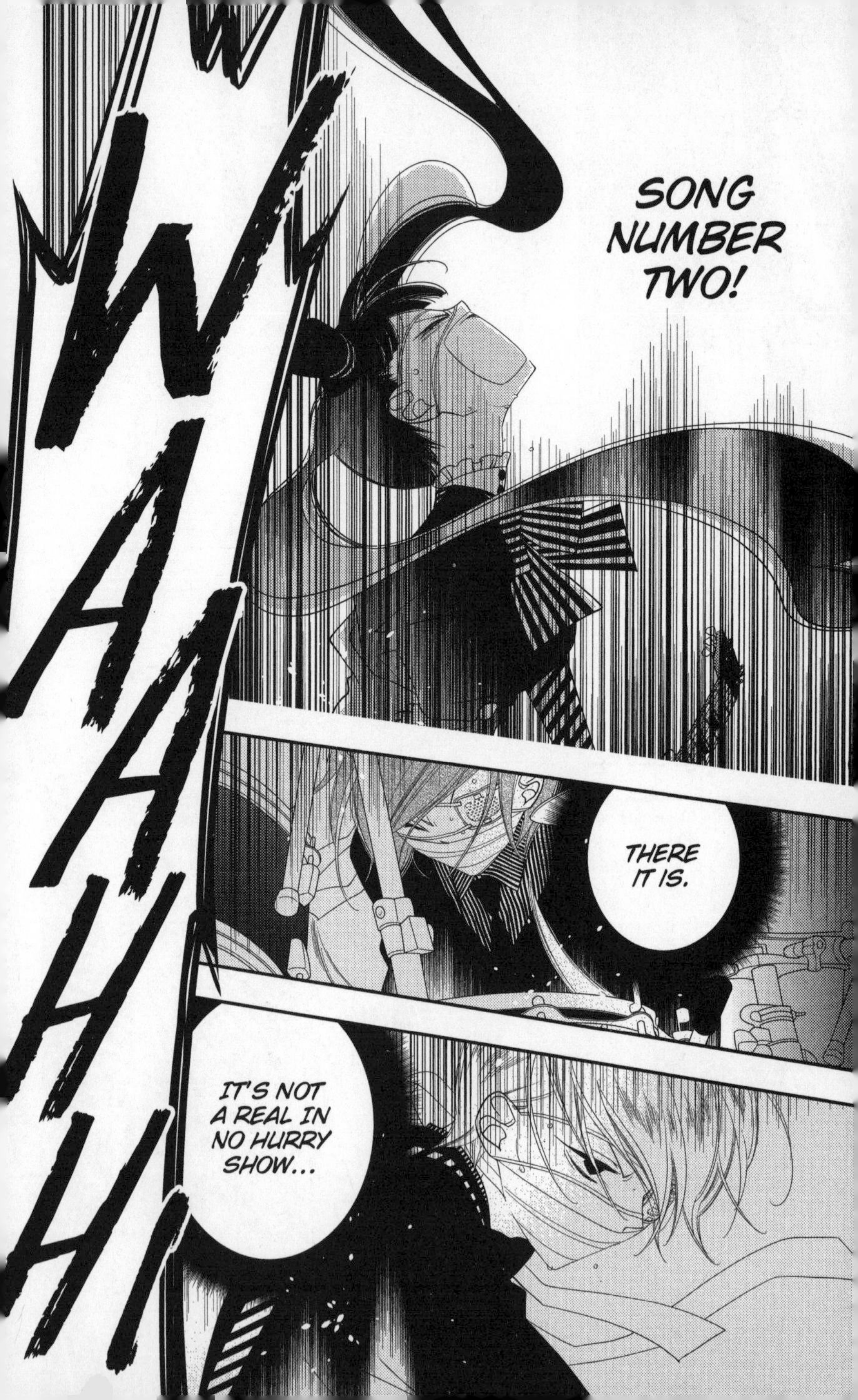
SONG NUMBER TWO!
THERE IT IS.
IT'S NOT A REAL IN NO HURRY SHOW...

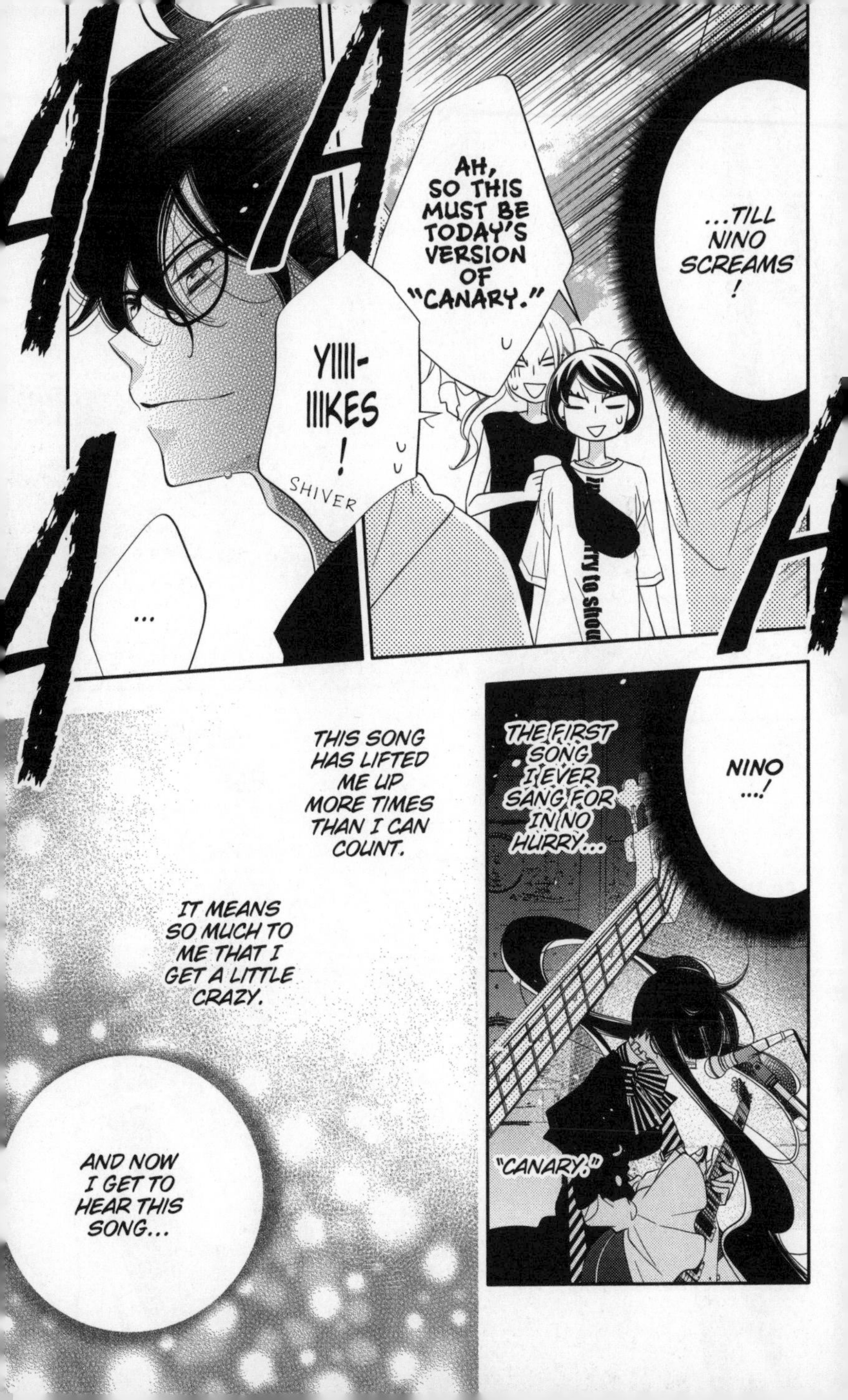
...TILL NINO SCREAMS!
AH, SO THIS MUST BE TODAY'S VERSION OF "CANARY."
YIIII-IIIIKES!
SHIVER
...
NINO...!
THE FIRST SONG I EVER SANG FOR IN NO HURRY...
"CANARY."
THIS SONG HAS LIFTED ME UP MORE TIMES THAN I CAN COUNT.
IT MEANS SO MUCH TO ME THAT I GET A LITTLE CRAZY.
AND NOW I GET TO HEAR THIS SONG...

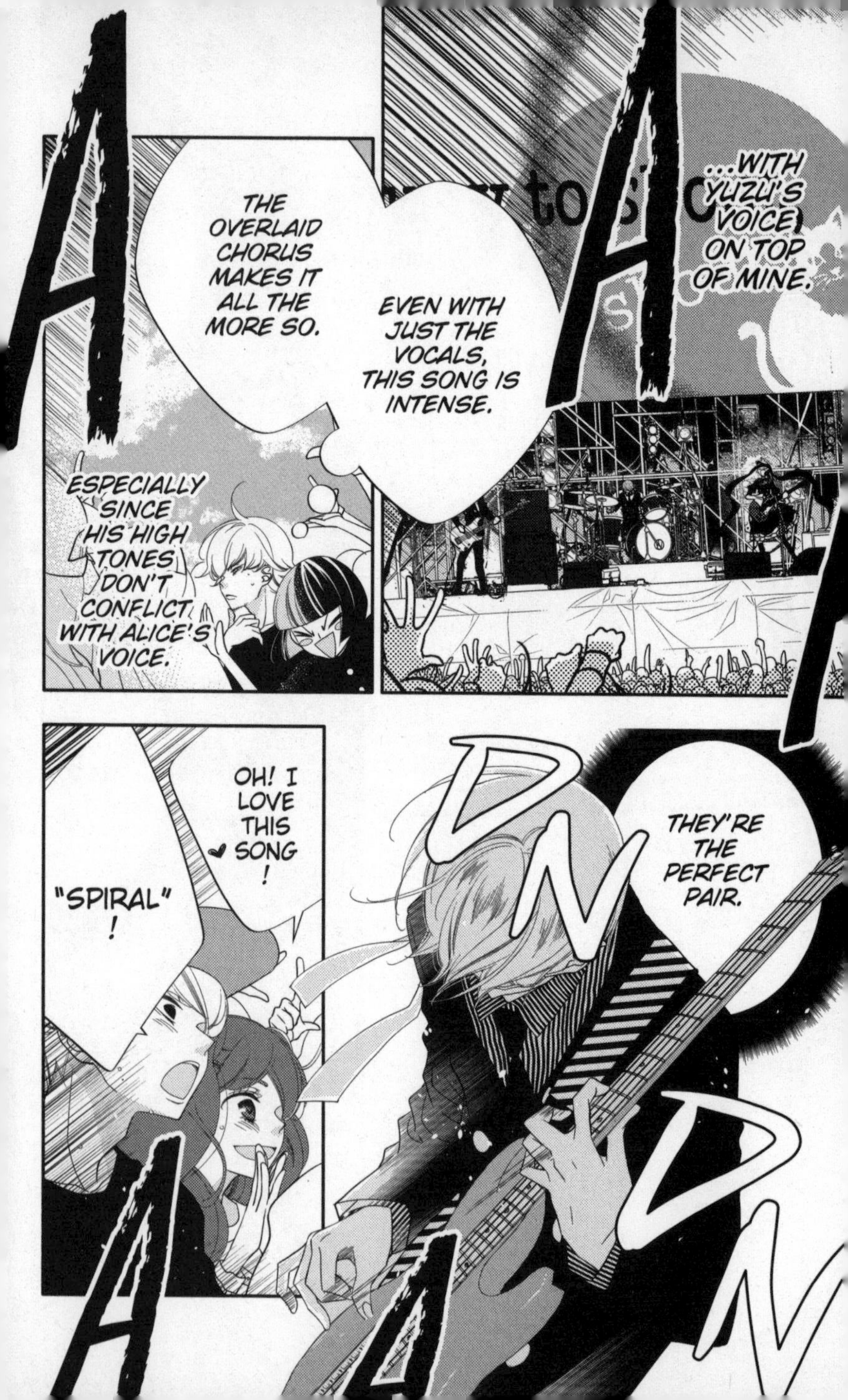
...WITH YUZU'S VOICE ON TOP OF MINE.
EVEN WITH JUST THE VOCALS, THIS SONG IS INTENSE.
THE OVERLAID CHORUS MAKES IT ALL THE MORE SO.
ESPECIALLY SINCE HIS HIGH TONES DON'T CONFLICT WITH ALICE'S VOICE.
THEY'RE THE PERFECT PAIR.
OH! I LOVE THIS SONG♥!
"SPIRAL"!

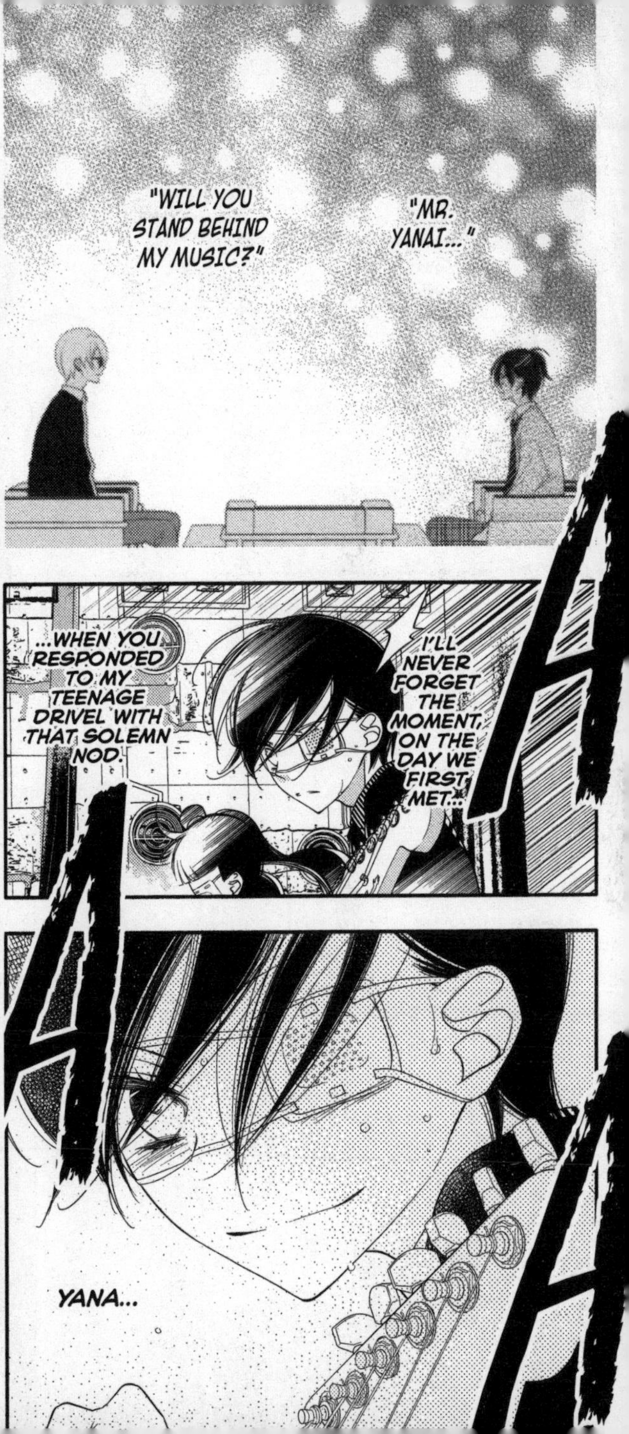
"MR. YANAI..."
"WILL YOU STAND BEHIND MY MUSIC?"
I'LL NEVER FORGET THE MOMENT, ON THE DAY WE FIRST MET...
...WHEN YOU RESPONDED TO MY TEENAGE DRIVEL WITH THAT SOLEMN NOD.
YANA...

3

Anonymous Noise is the source of so many memories for me! The anime adaption, the film adaptation, and privately, my cat Sora (see volume 5 for details)... It's made many of my dreams come true, inspired many new dreams and taught me lessons about the value of life—those are just some of the reasons this work will be a part of me forever.

I wrote a whole bunch more after that but deleted it. *Ha ha.* Babbling on like that would just be boorish of me. All that really matters is what you feel after you finish reading this. And if even one small part of Anonymous Noise remains with you when all is said and done, nothing would make me happier.

THANK YOU SO MUCH! I LOVE YOU!

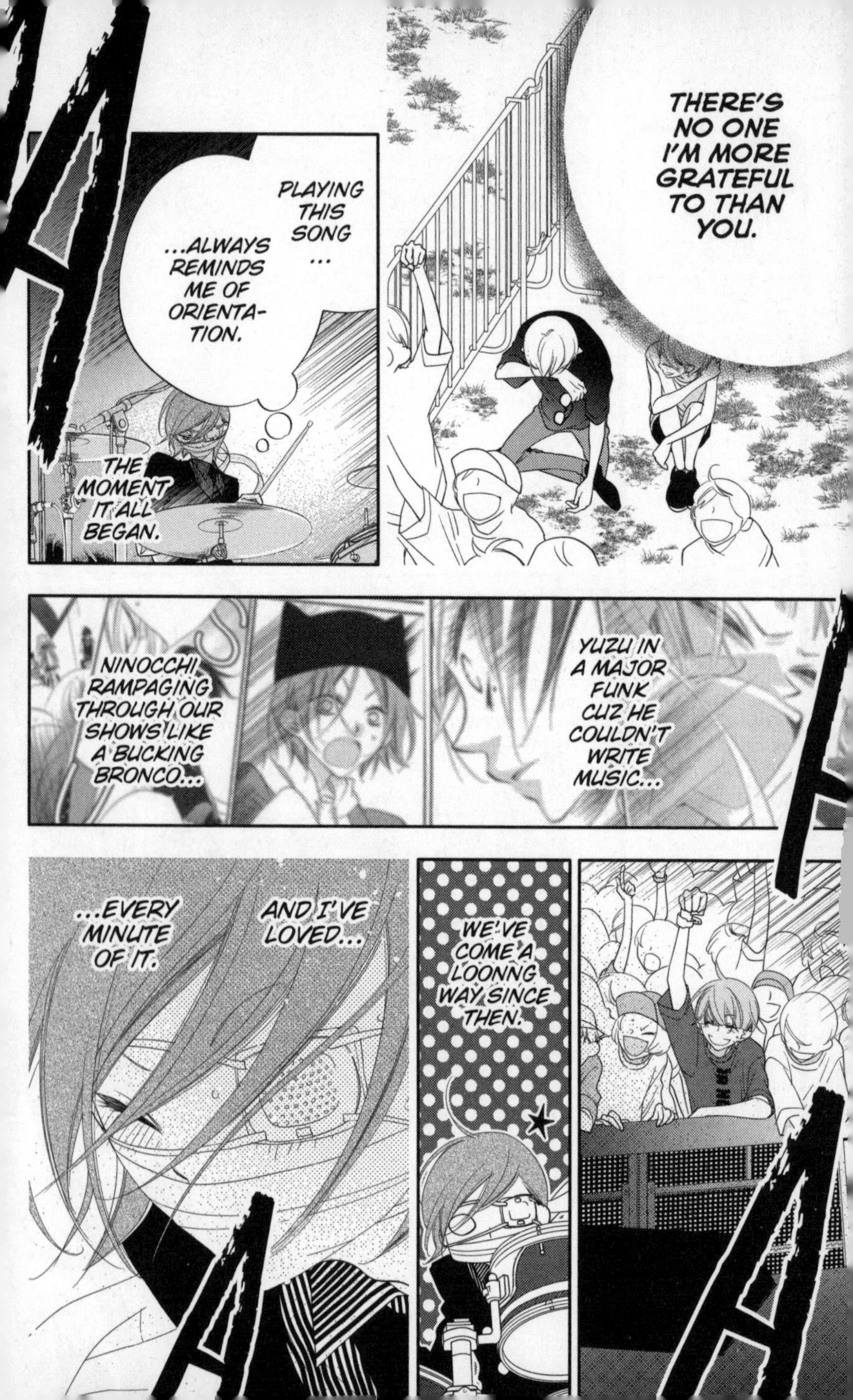
THERE'S NO ONE I'M MORE GRATEFUL TO THAN YOU.
PLAYING THIS SONG ...
...ALWAYS REMINDS ME OF ORIENTATION.
THE MOMENT IT ALL BEGAN.
YUZU IN A MAJOR FUNK CUZ HE COULDN'T WRITE MUSIC...
NINOCCHI RAMPAGING THROUGH OUR SHOWS LIKE A BUCKING BRONCO...
WE'VE COME A LOONNG WAY SINCE THEN.
AND I'VE LOVED...
...EVERY MINUTE OF IT.

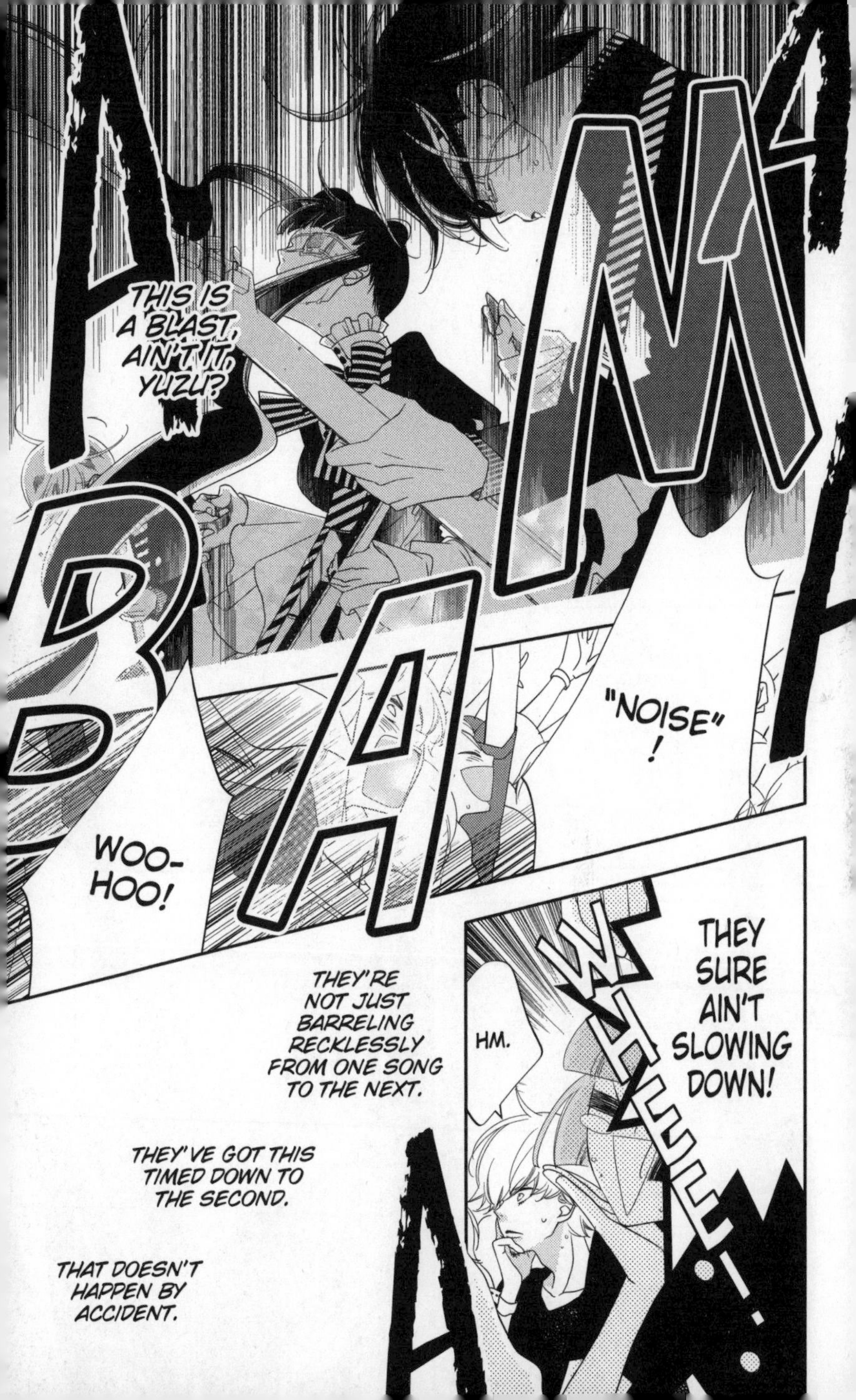
THIS IS A BLAST, AIN'T IT, YUZU?
"NOISE"!
WOO-HOO!
THEY SURE AIN'T SLOWING DOWN!
HM.
THEY'RE NOT JUST BARRELING RECKLESSLY FROM ONE SONG TO THE NEXT.
THEY'VE GOT THIS TIMED DOWN TO THE SECOND.
THAT DOESN'T HAPPEN BY ACCIDENT.

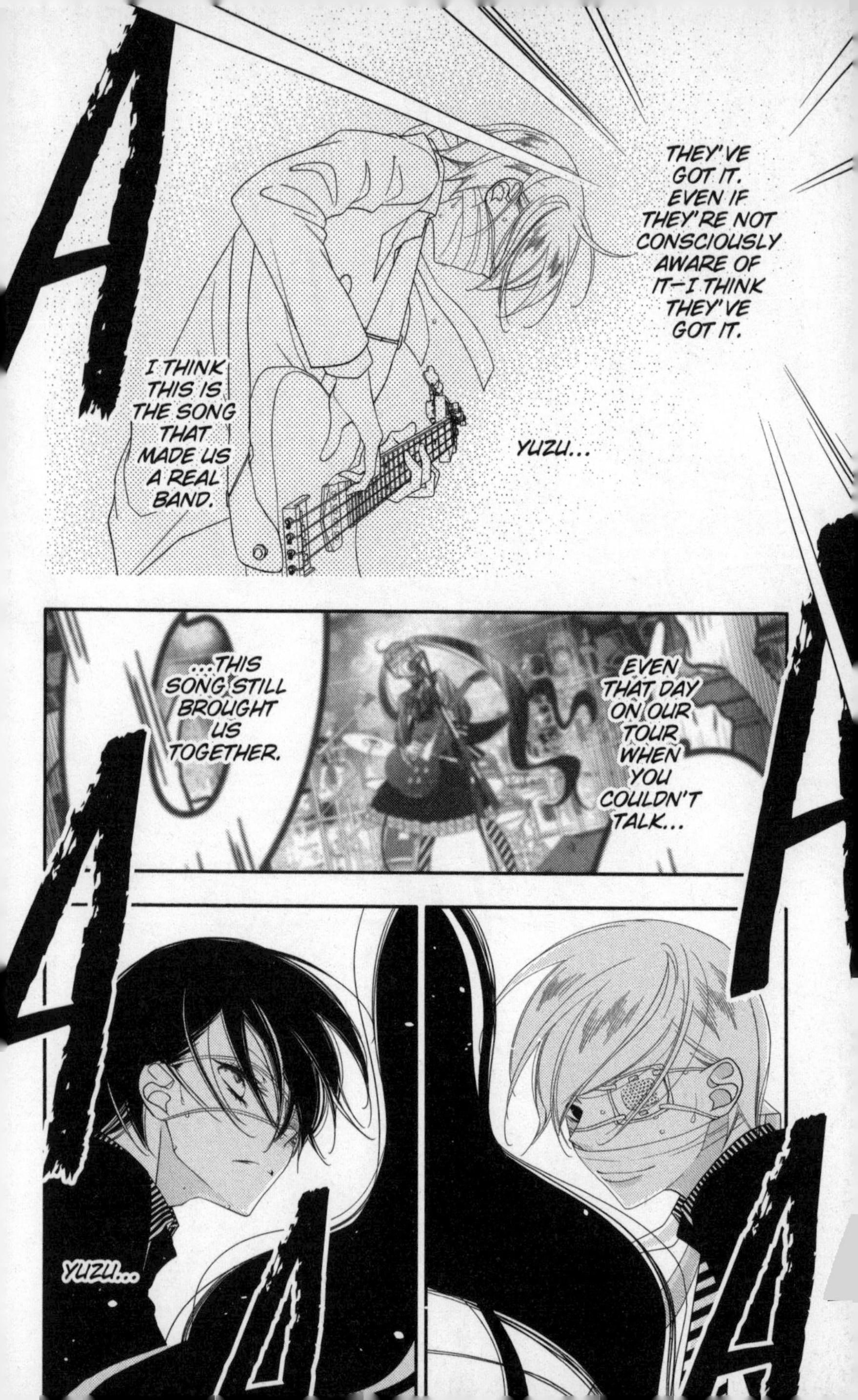
THEY'VE GOT IT. EVEN IF THEY'RE NOT CONSCIOUSLY AWARE OF IT—I THINK THEY'VE GOT IT.
I THINK THIS IS THE SONG THAT MADE US A REAL BAND.
YUZU...
EVEN THAT DAY ON OUR TOUR WHEN YOU COULDN'T TALK...
...THIS SONG STILL BROUGHT US TOGETHER.
YUZU...

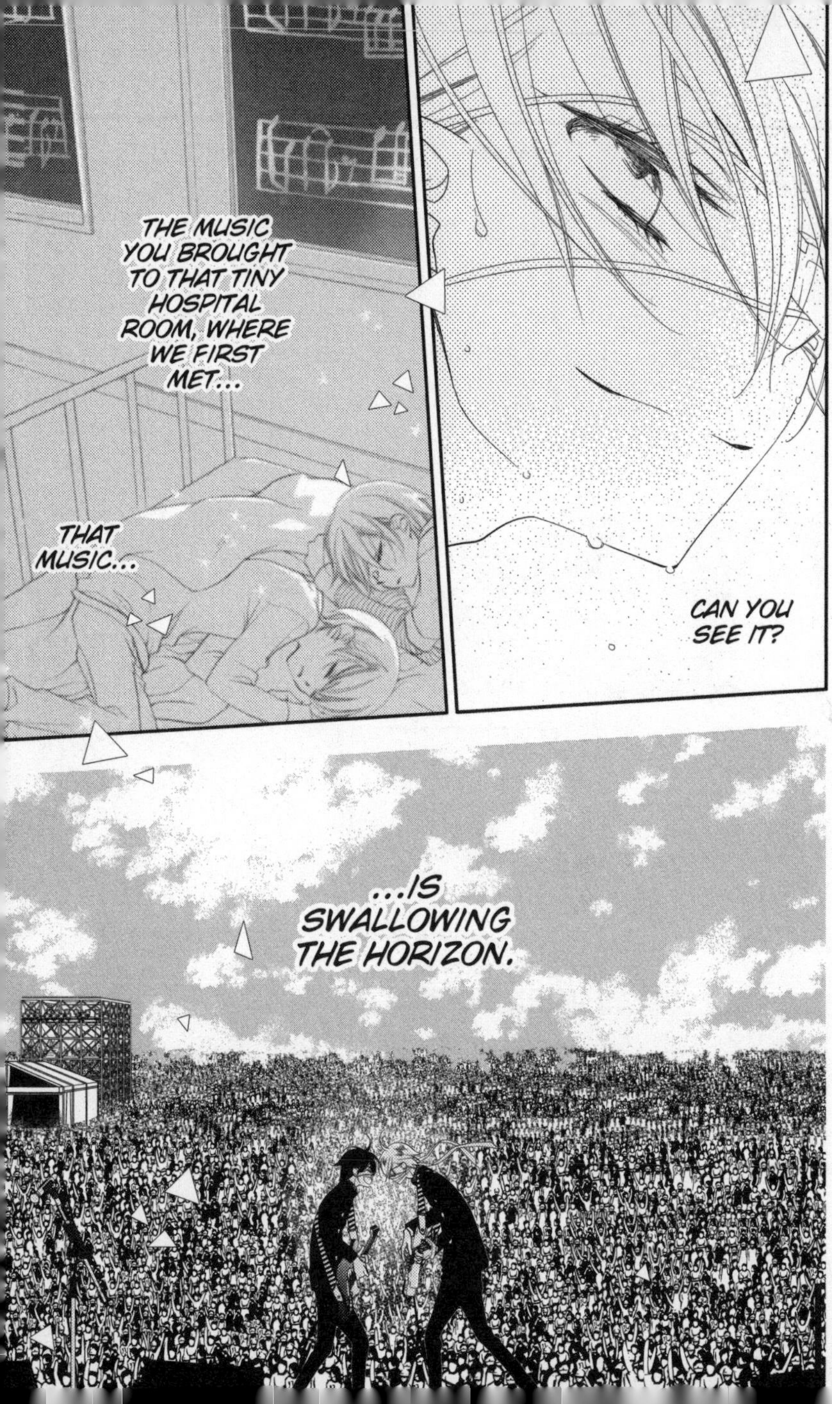
CAN YOU SEE IT?
THE MUSIC YOU BROUGHT TO THAT TINY HOSPITAL ROOM, WHERE WE FIRST MET...
THAT MUSIC...
...IS SWALLOWING THE HORIZON.

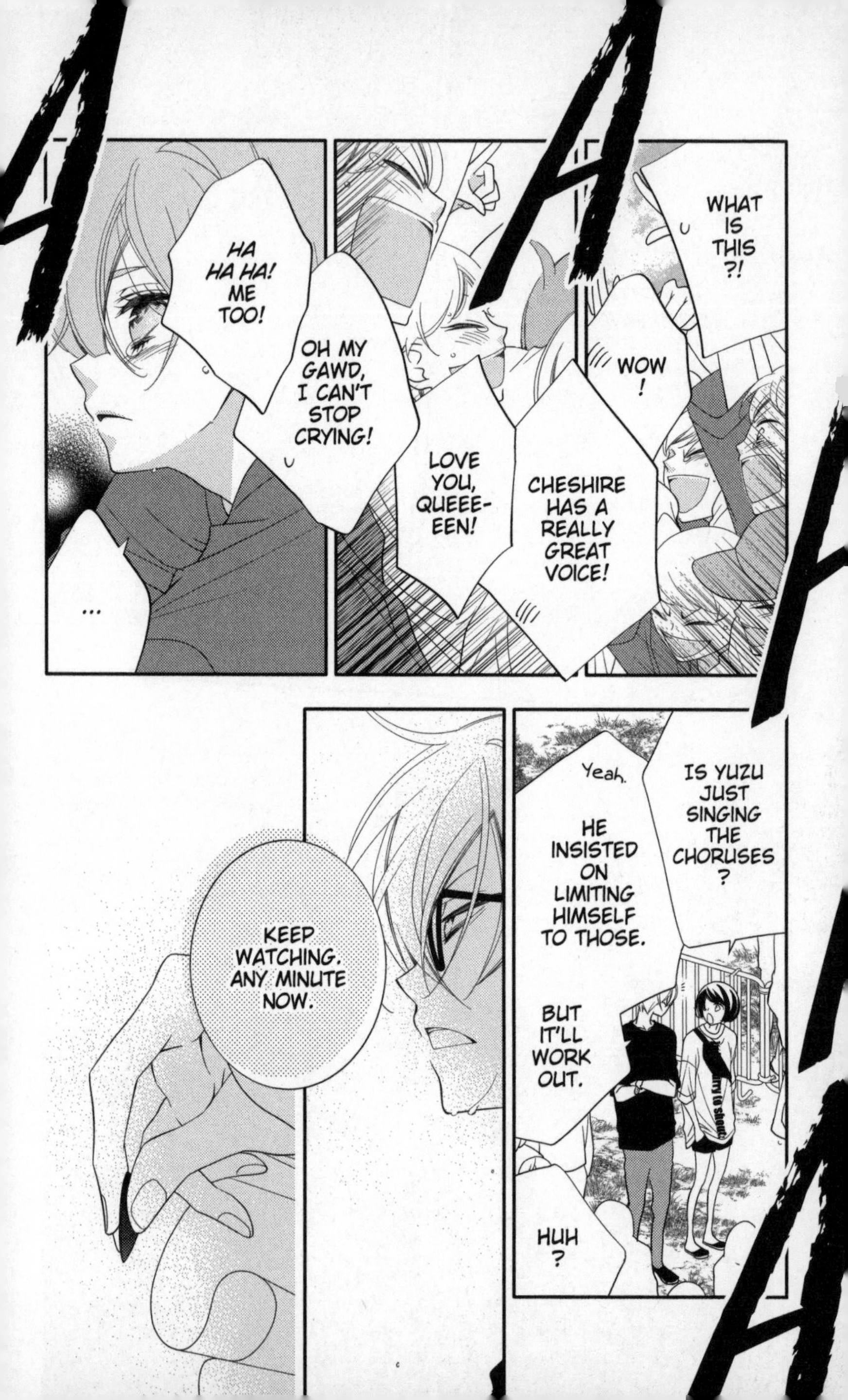
WHAT IS THIS ?!
WOW !
CHESHIRE HAS A REALLY GREAT VOICE!
LOVE YOU, QUEEEEEN!
OH MY GAWD, I CAN'T STOP CRYING!
HA HA HA! ME TOO!
...
IS YUZU JUST SINGING THE CHORUSES ?
Yeah.
HE INSISTED ON LIMITING HIMSELF TO THOSE.
BUT IT'LL WORK OUT.
HUH ?
KEEP WATCHING. ANY MINUTE NOW.

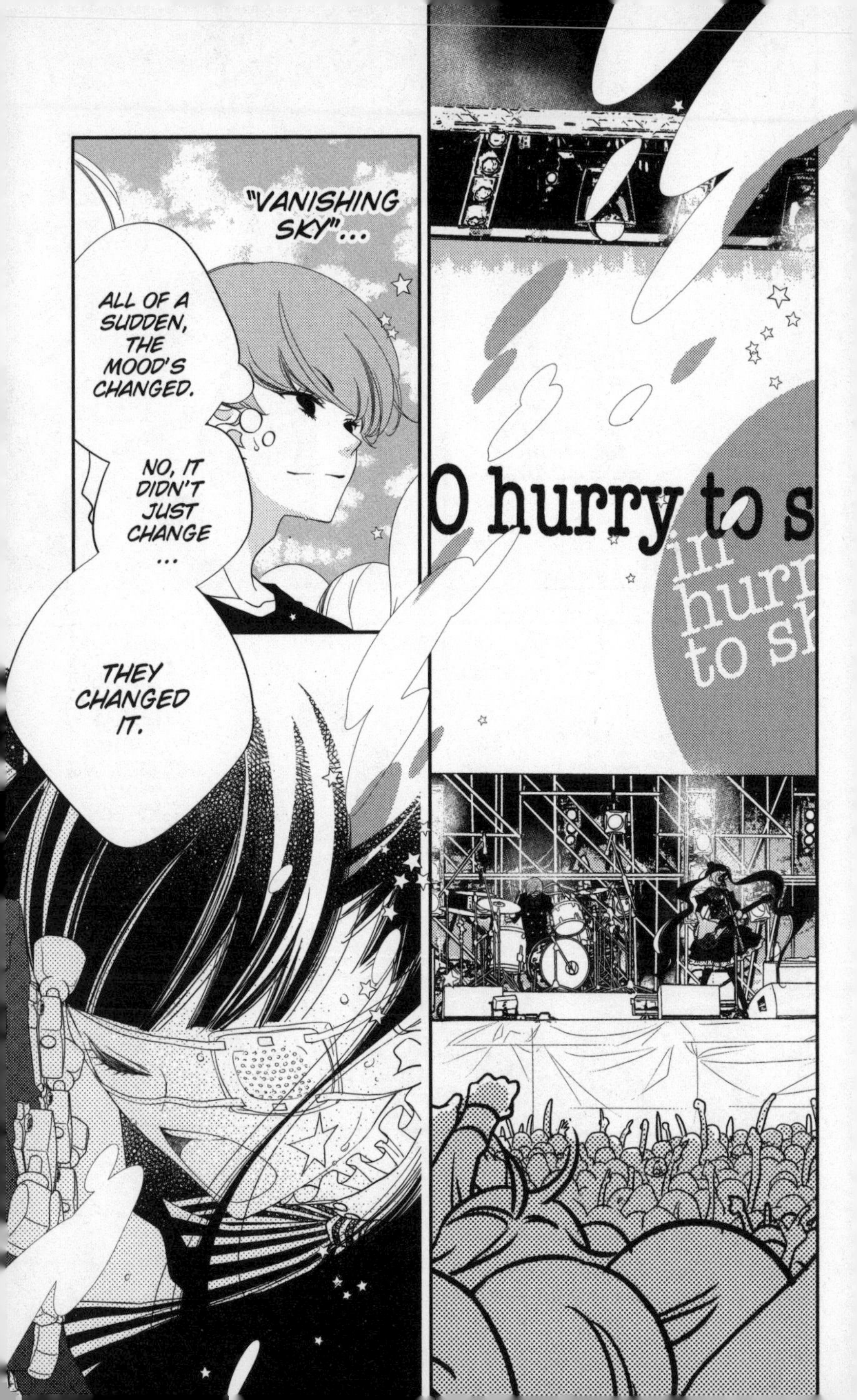
O hurry to s
in
hurr
to sh
"VANISHING SKY"...
ALL OF A SUDDEN, THE MOOD'S CHANGED.
NO, IT DIDN'T JUST CHANGE...
THEY CHANGED IT.

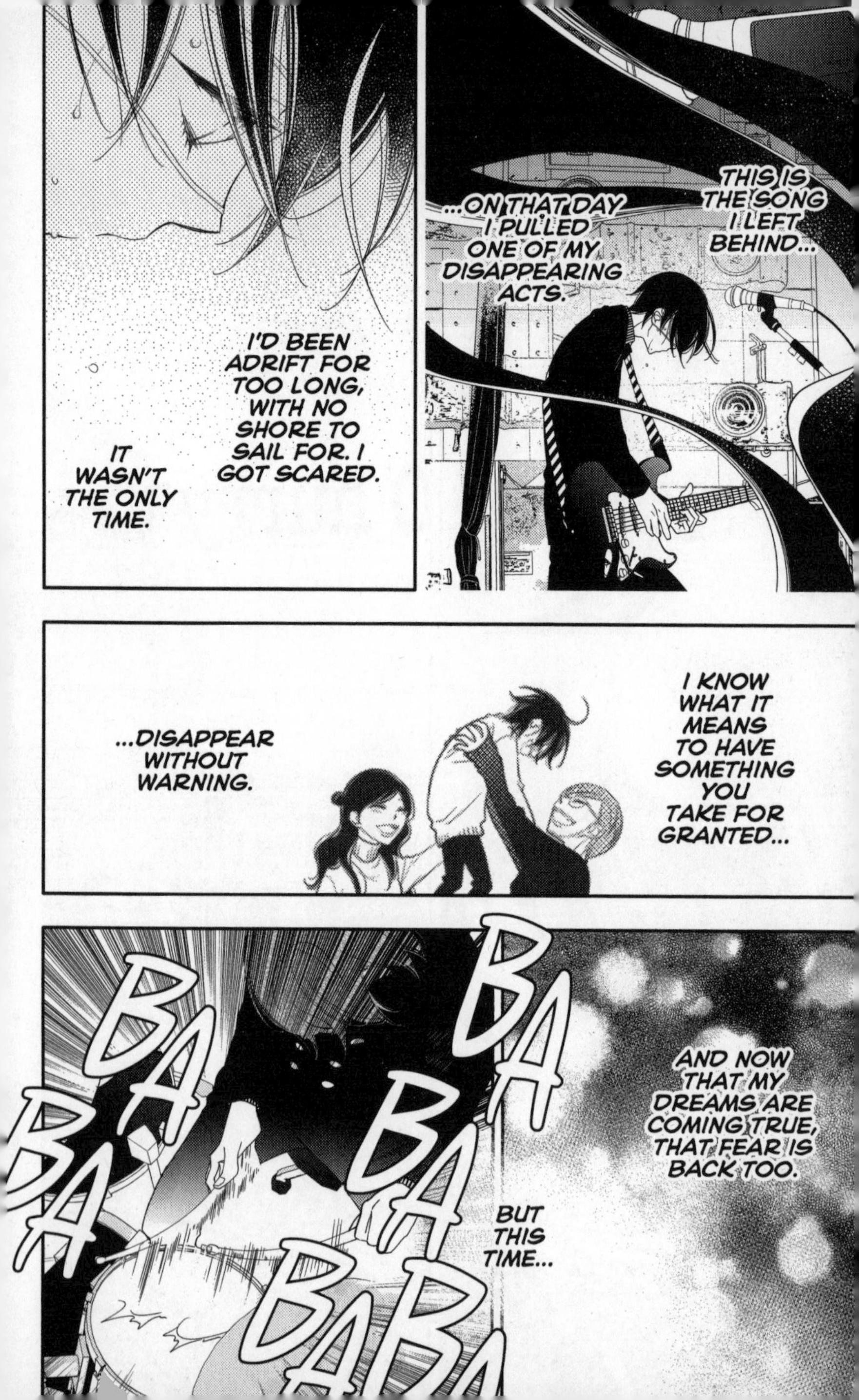
THIS IS THE SONG I LEFT BEHIND...
...ON THAT DAY I PULLED ONE OF MY DISAPPEARING ACTS.
I'D BEEN ADRIFT FOR TOO LONG, WITH NO SHORE TO SAIL FOR. I GOT SCARED.
IT WASN'T THE ONLY TIME.
I KNOW WHAT IT MEANS TO HAVE SOMETHING YOU TAKE FOR GRANTED...
...DISAPPEAR WITHOUT WARNING.
AND NOW THAT MY DREAMS ARE COMING TRUE, THAT FEAR IS BACK TOO.
BA BA BA BABA
BUT THIS TIME...
BA BA BA

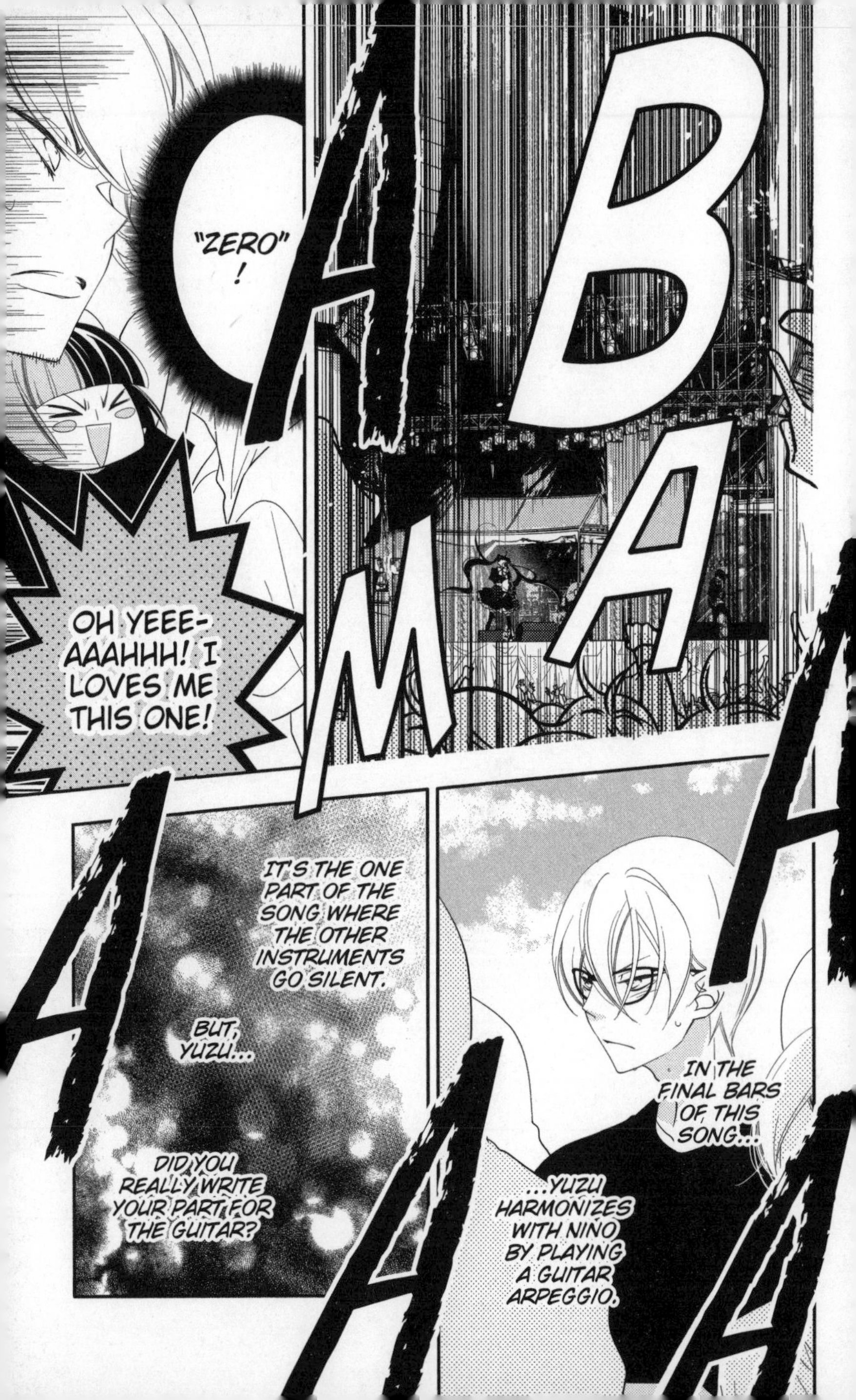
"ZERO" !
OH YEEE-AAAHHH! I LOVES ME THIS ONE!
IN THE FINAL BARS OF THIS SONG...
...YUZU HARMONIZES WITH NINO BY PLAYING A GUITAR ARPEGGIO.
IT'S THE ONE PART OF THE SONG WHERE THE OTHER INSTRUMENTS GO SILENT.
BUT, YUZU...
DID YOU REALLY WRITE YOUR PART FOR THE GUITAR?

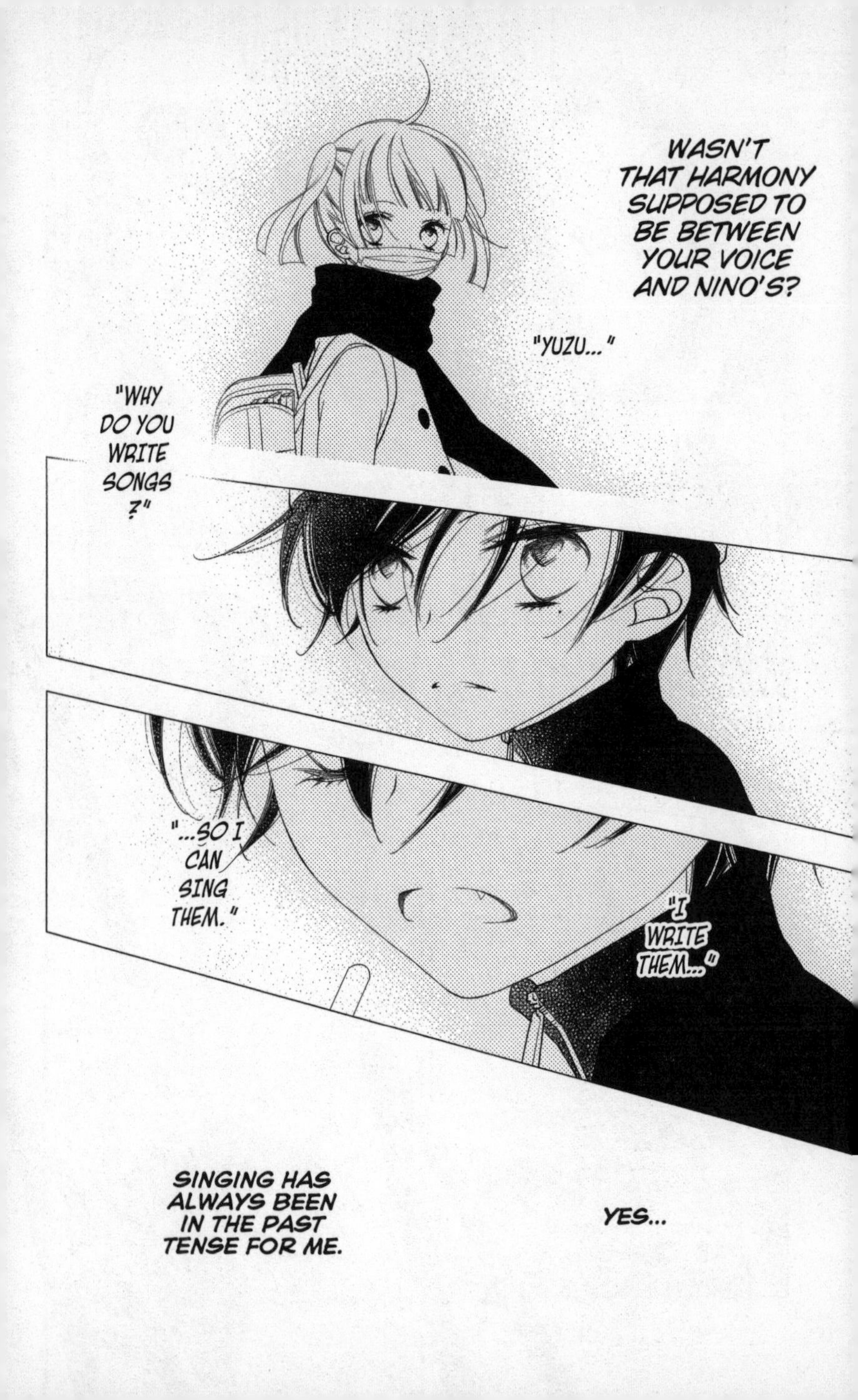
WASN'T THAT HARMONY SUPPOSED TO BE BETWEEN YOUR VOICE AND NINO'S?
"YUZU..."
"WHY DO YOU WRITE SONGS?"
"I WRITE THEM..."
"...SO I CAN SING THEM."
YES...
SINGING HAS ALWAYS BEEN IN THE PAST TENSE FOR ME.

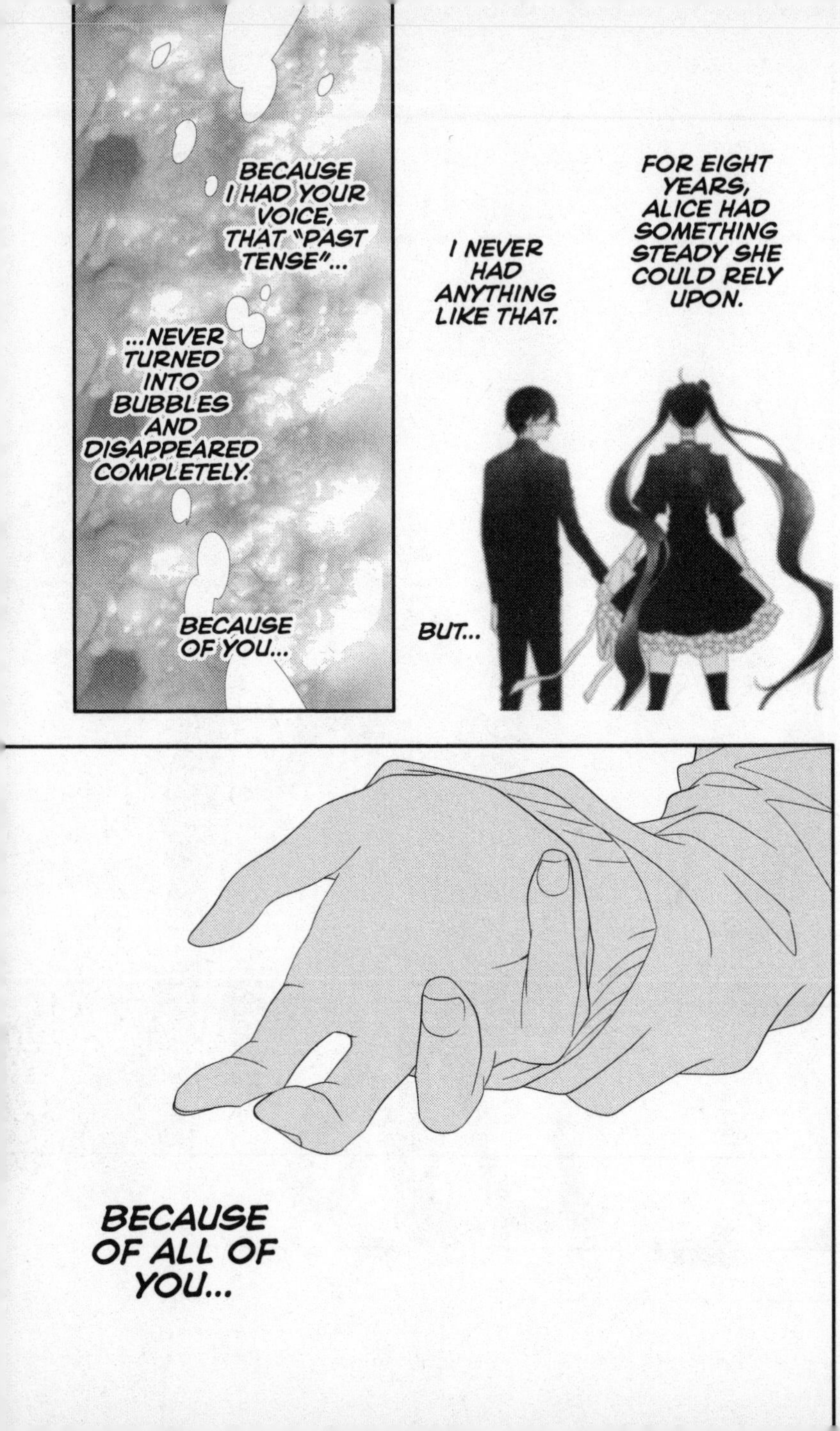
FOR EIGHT YEARS, ALICE HAD SOMETHING STEADY SHE COULD RELY UPON.
I NEVER HAD ANYTHING LIKE THAT.
BUT...
BECAUSE I HAD YOUR VOICE, THAT "PAST TENSE"...
...NEVER TURNED INTO BUBBLES AND DISAPPEARED COMPLETELY.
BECAUSE OF YOU...
BECAUSE OF ALL OF YOU...

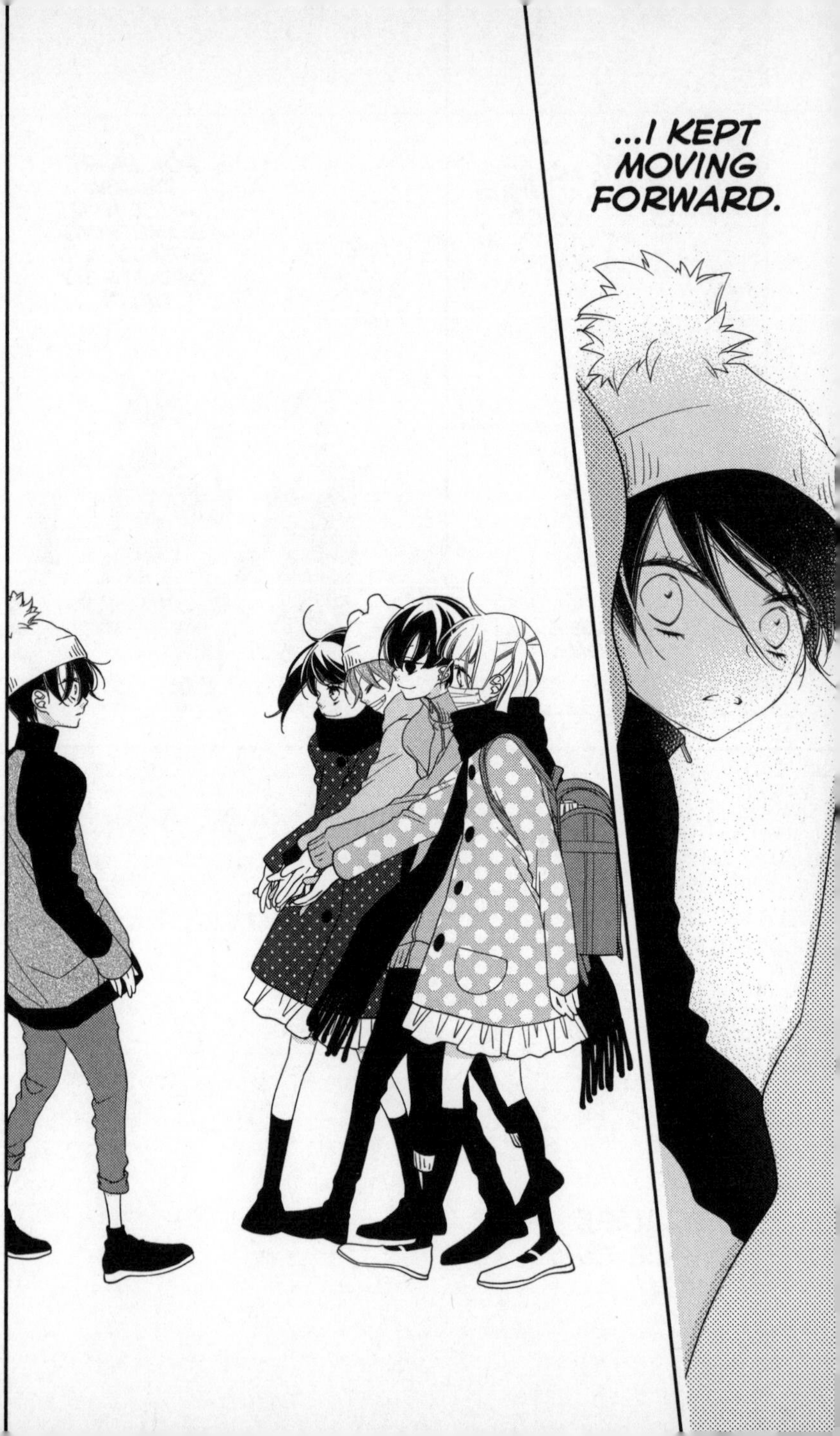
...I KEPT MOVING FORWARD.

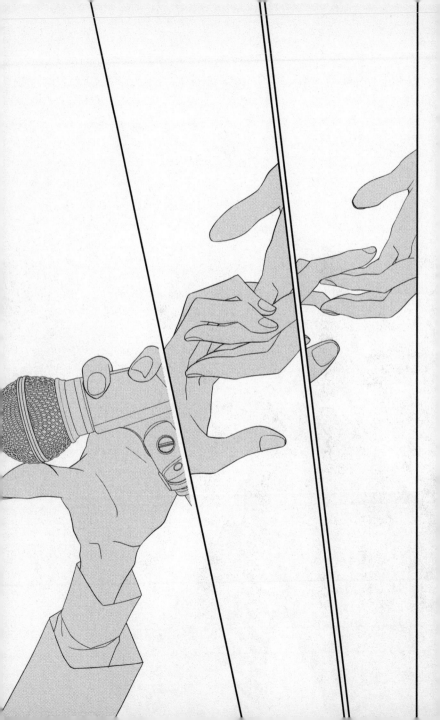

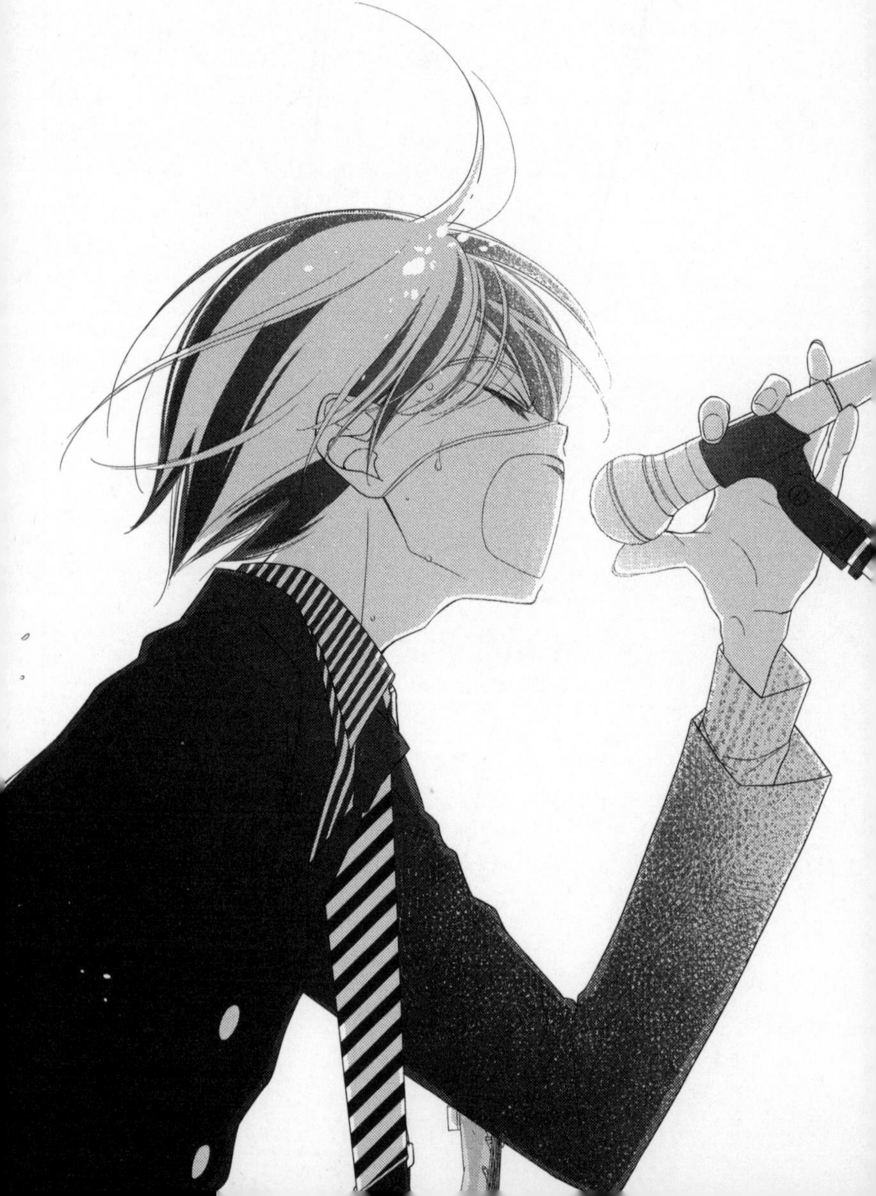

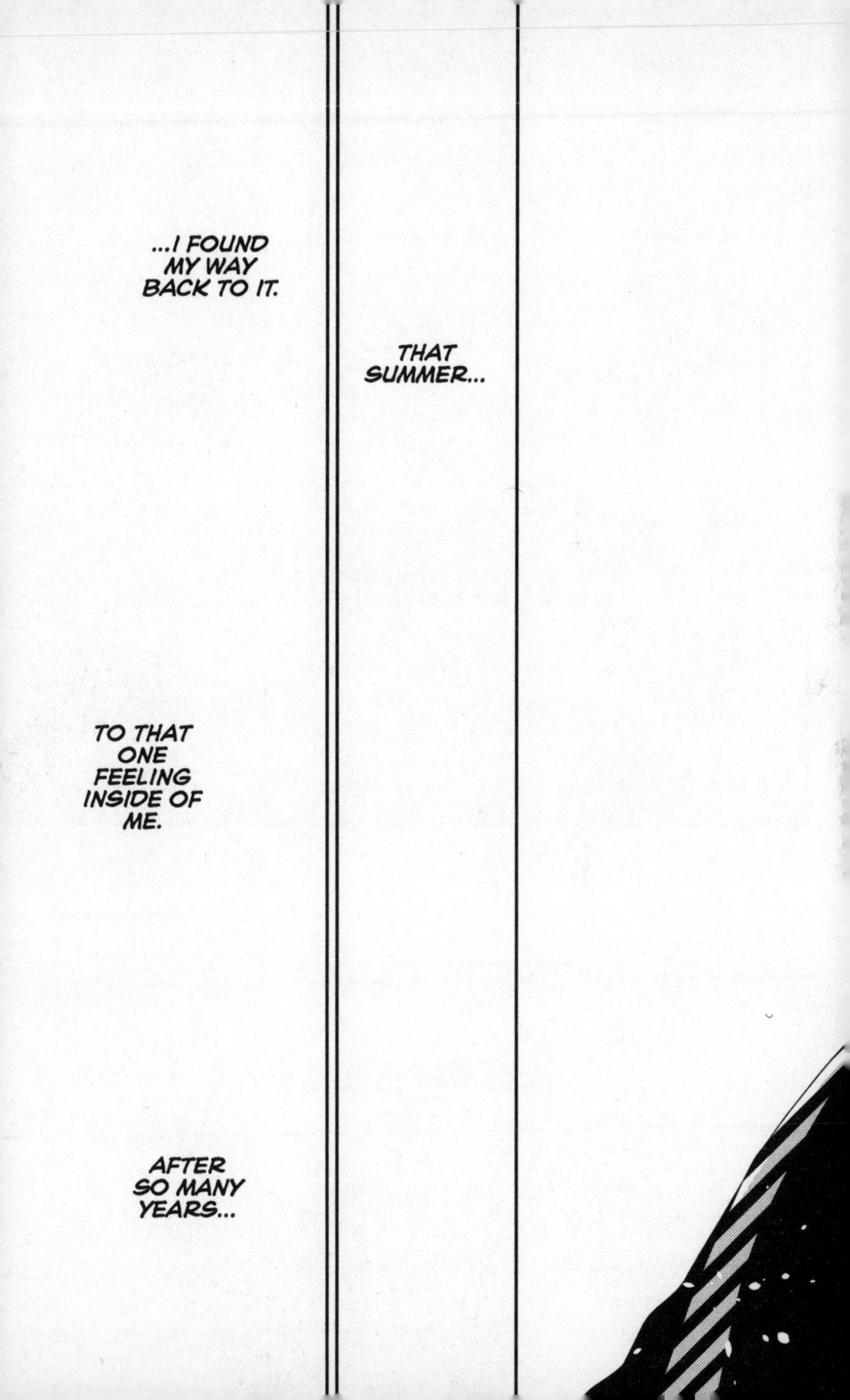
THAT SUMMER...
...I FOUND MY WAY BACK TO IT.
TO THAT ONE FEELING INSIDE OF ME.
AFTER SO MANY YEARS...

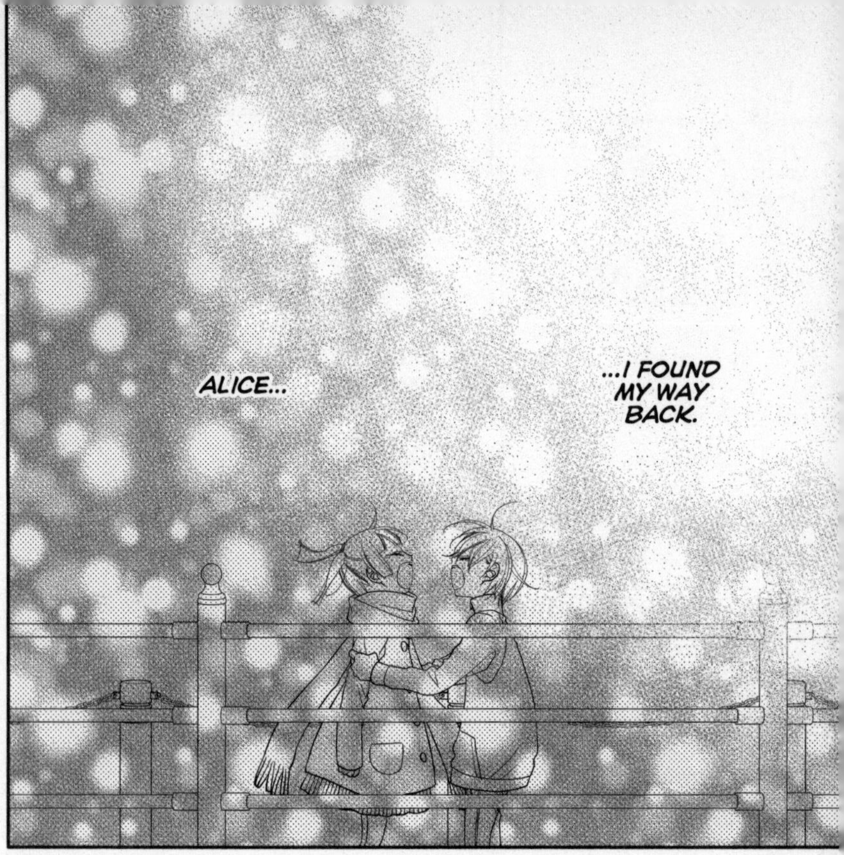
...I FOUND MY WAY BACK.
ALICE...

"...SO I CAN SING THEM."

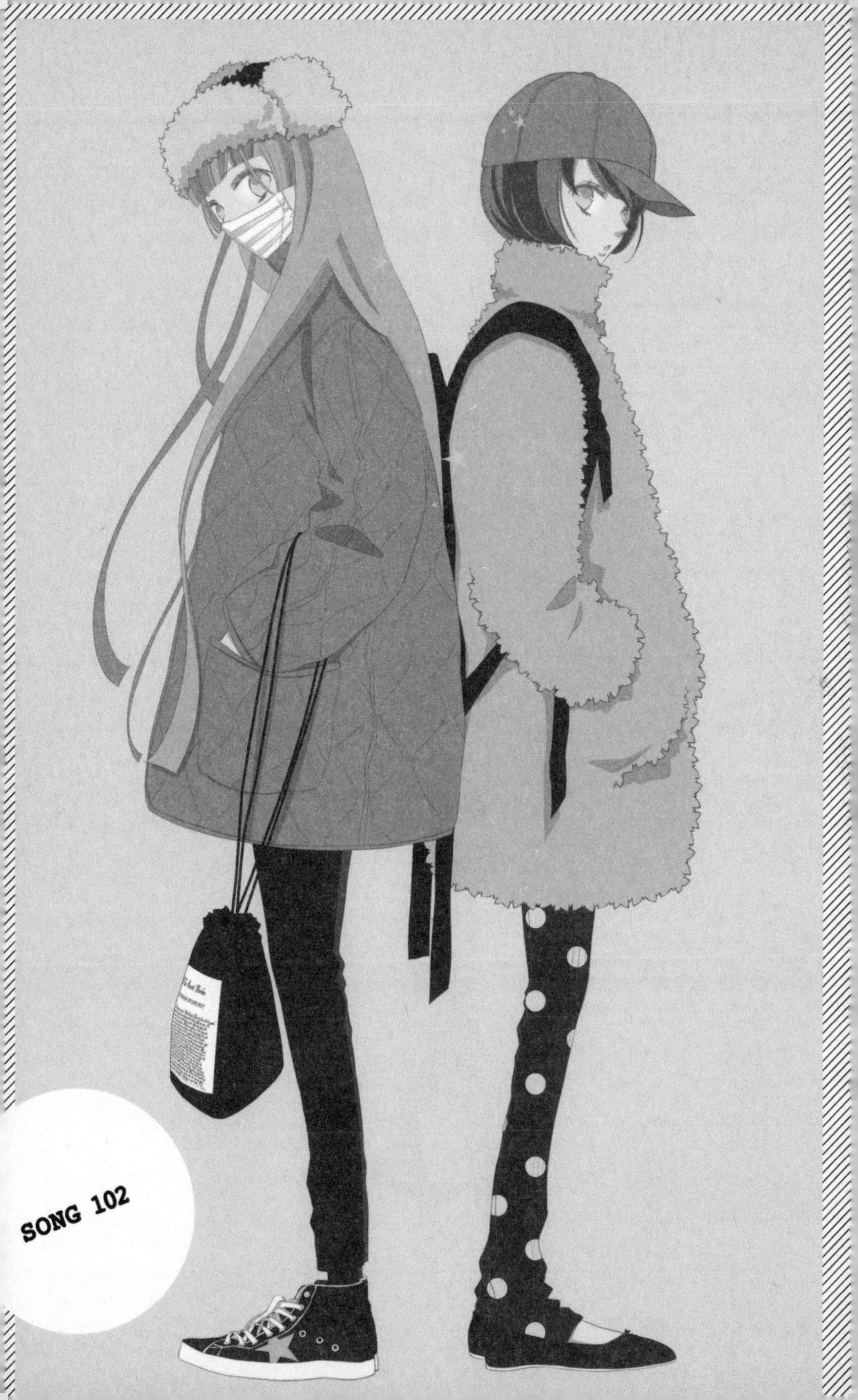
SONG 102

"JUST THE CHORUSES ARE ENOUGH FOR ME THIS TIME."

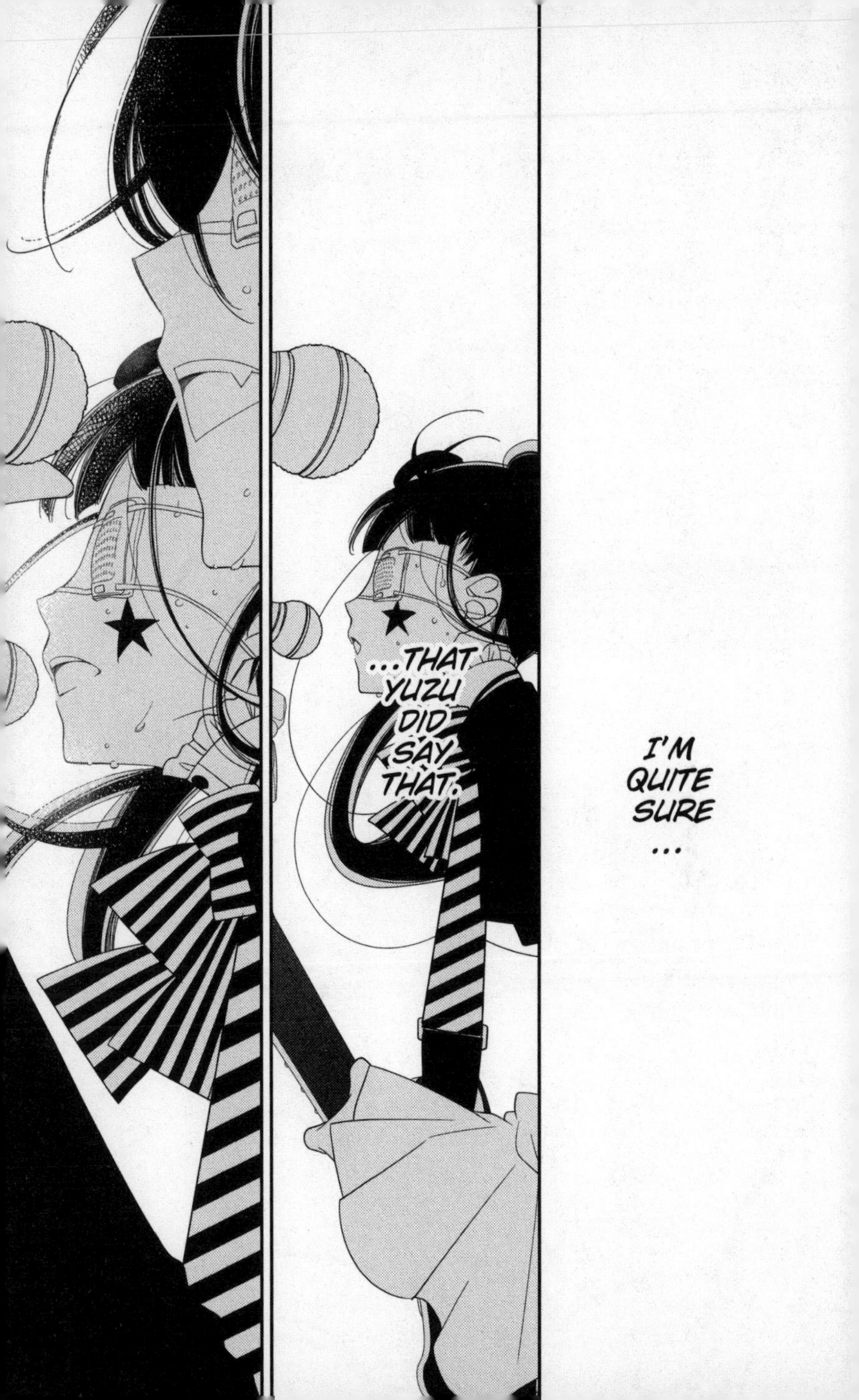
I'M QUITE SURE ...
...THAT YUZU DID SAY THAT.

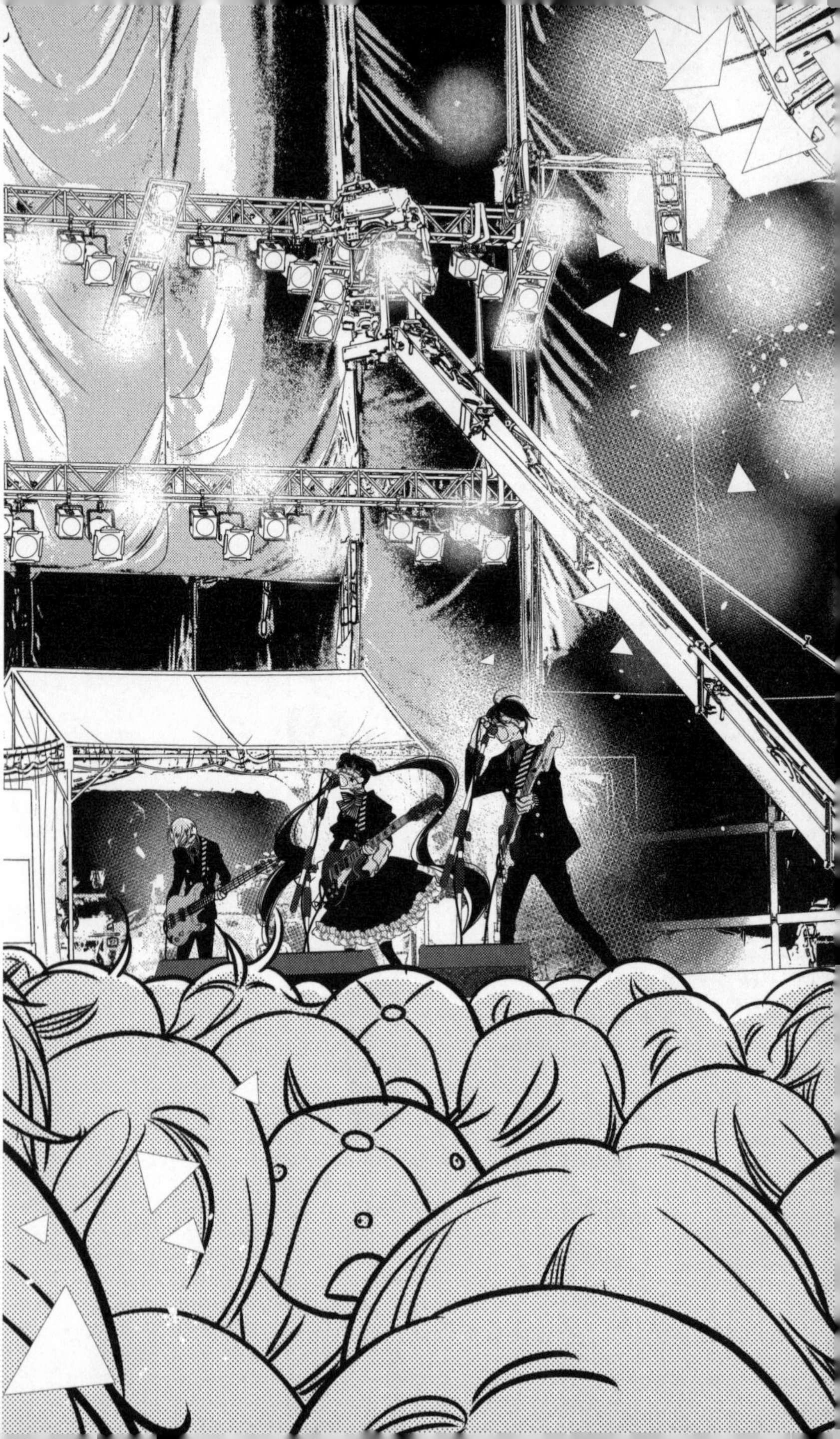

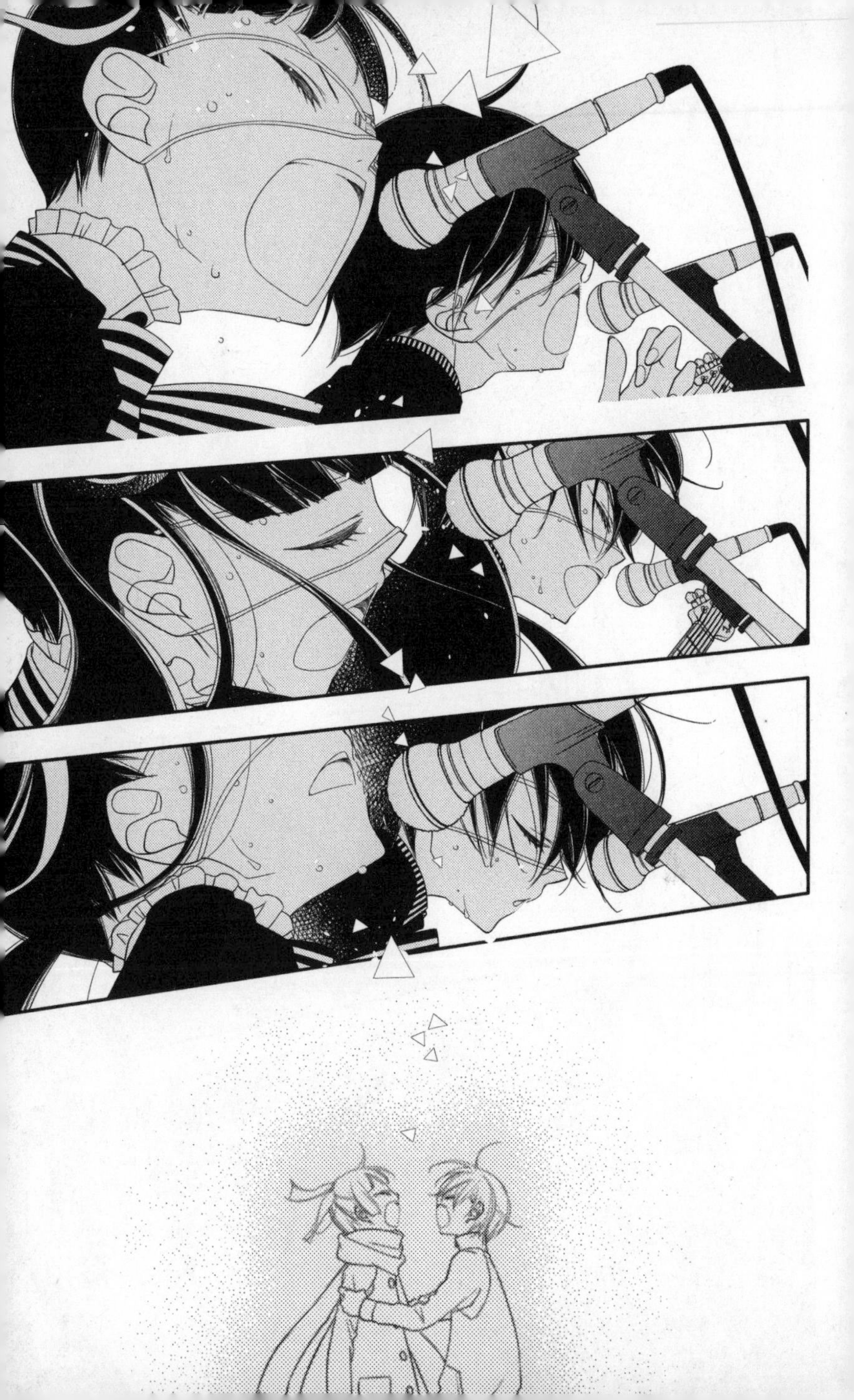

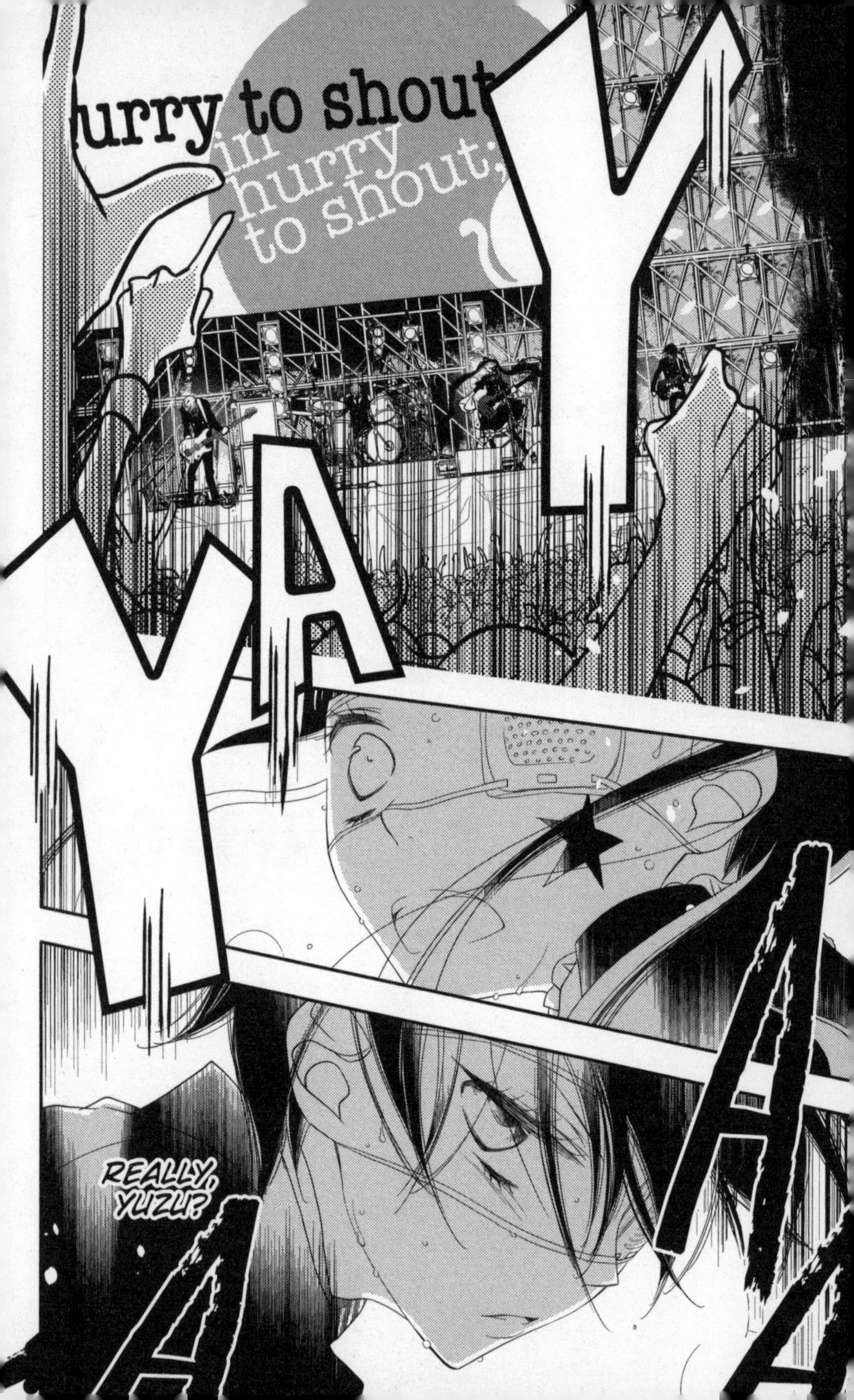
urry to shout
in hurry to shout;
YAYAA
REALLY, YUZU?

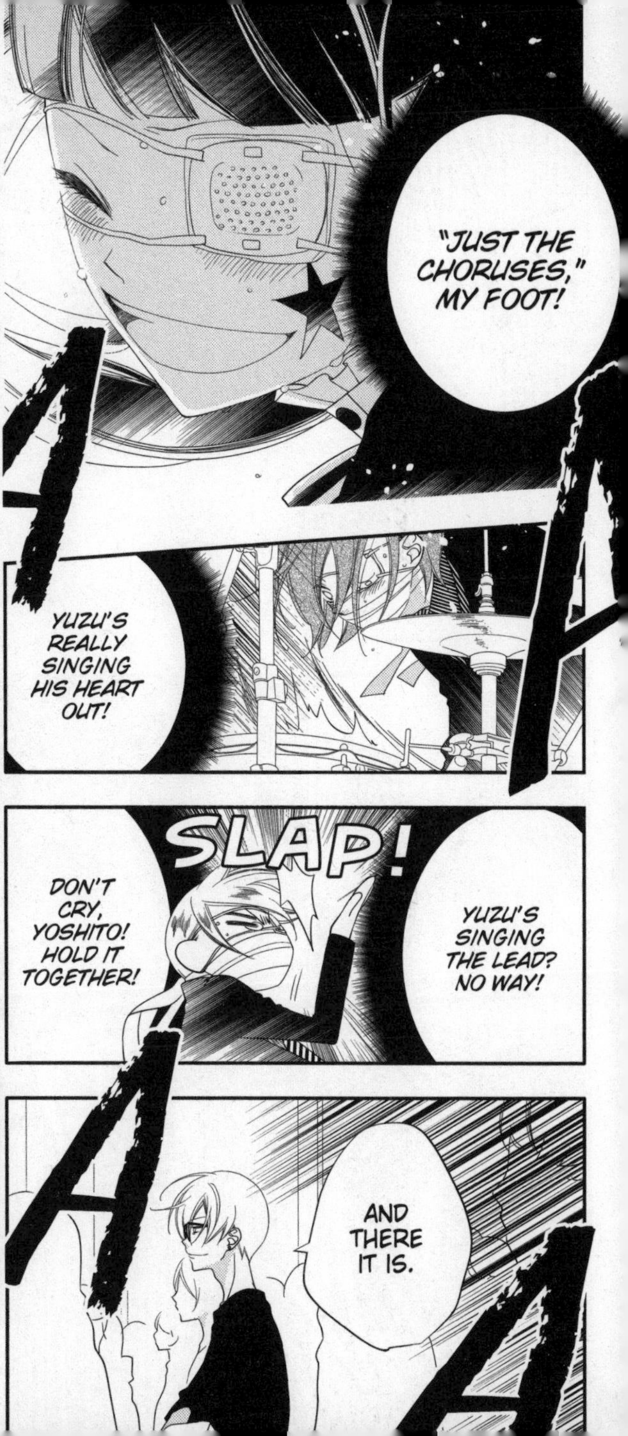
"JUST THE CHORUSES," MY FOOT!
YUZU'S REALLY SINGING HIS HEART OUT!
YUZU'S SINGING THE LEAD? NO WAY!
SLAP!
DON'T CRY, YOSHITO! HOLD IT TOGETHER!
AND THERE IT IS.

4

Well, I guess that makes this my final column! All I have left to say is how overwhelmed with gratitude I am to everyone who stayed with our cast all the way to their journey's end. Thank you. Thank you so much. I pray that we'll meet again in the pages of some future manga.

Until then...!

Ryoko Fukuyama
3/20/19

[SPECIAL THANKS]
MOSAGE
TAKAYUKI NAGASHIMA
IKUMI ISHIGAKI
AYAKA TOKUSHIGE
KENJU NORO
MY FAMILY
MY FRIENDS
AND YOU!!

Ryoko Fukuyama
c/o Anonymous Noise Editor
VIZ Media
P.O. Box 77010
San Francisco, CA 94107

HP http://ryoconet/
@ryocoryocoryoco
https://www.instagram.com/ryocofukuyama/

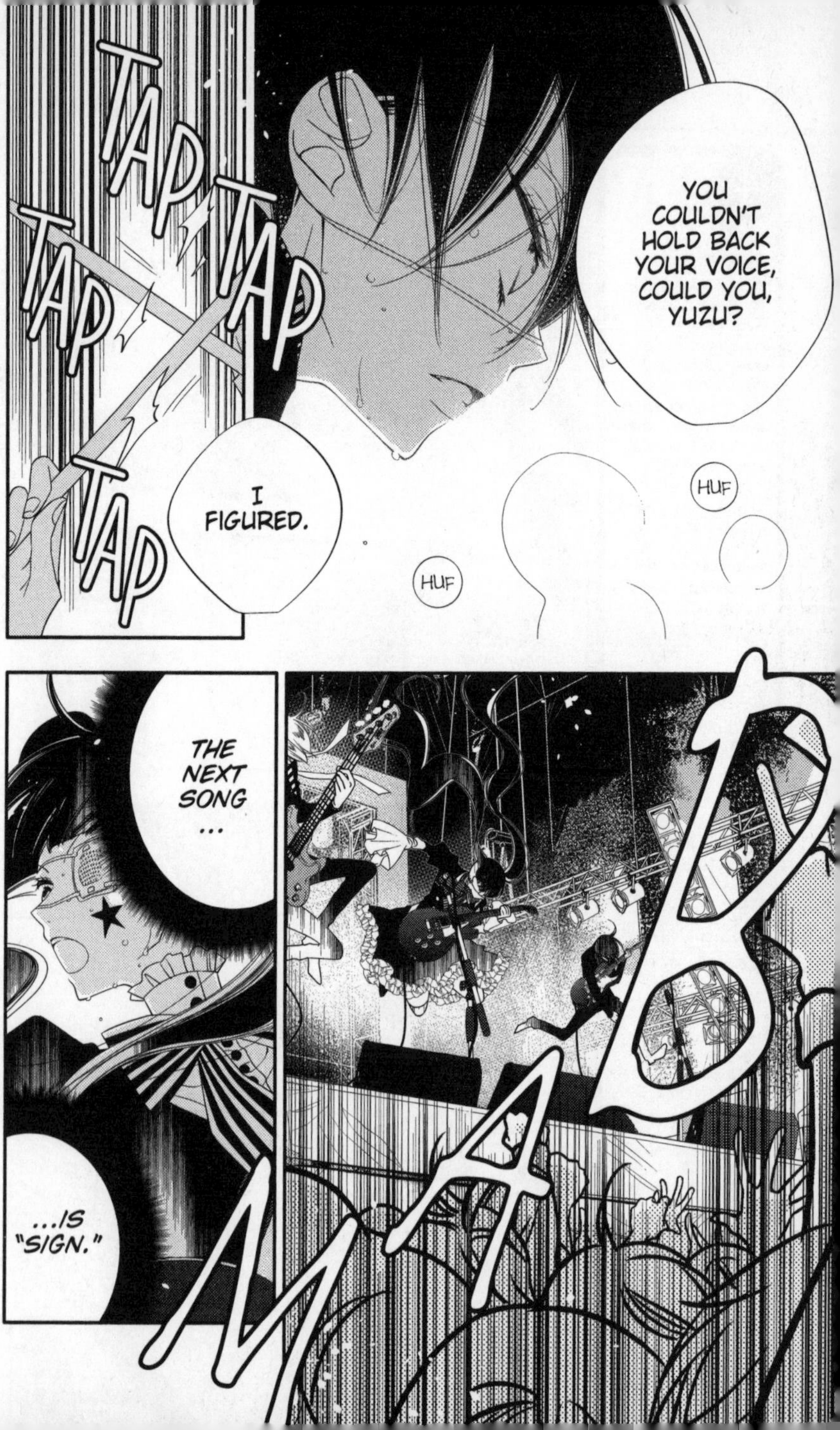
YOU COULDN'T HOLD BACK YOUR VOICE, COULD YOU, YUZU?
HUF
HUF
TAP TAP
TAP TAP
I FIGURED.
BAM
THE NEXT SONG...
...IS "SIGN."

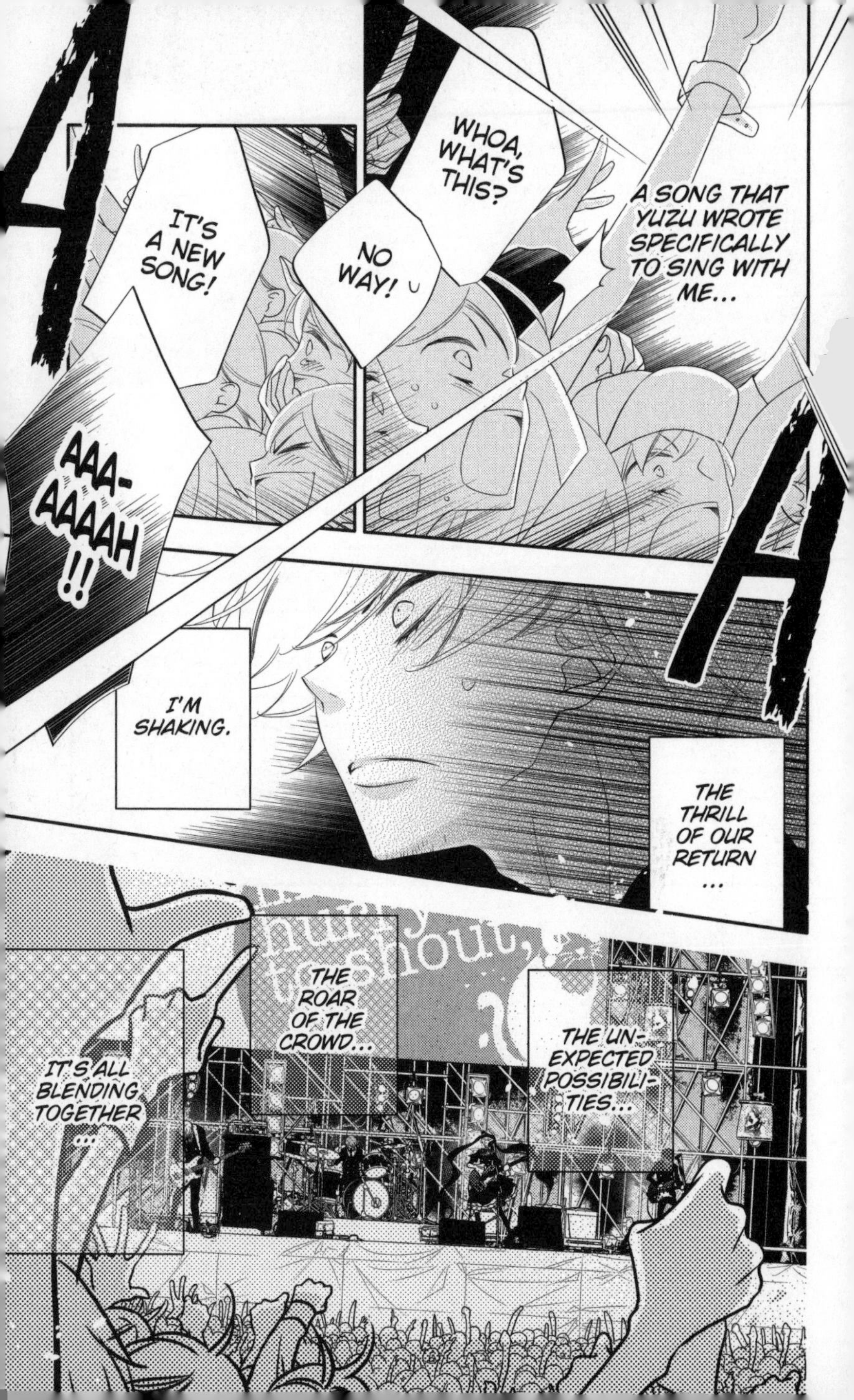
A SONG THAT YUZU WROTE SPECIFICALLY TO SING WITH ME...
WHOA, WHAT'S THIS?
NO WAY!
IT'S A NEW SONG!
AAAAAAAH!!
THE THRILL OF OUR RETURN...
I'M SHAKING.
THE UN-EXPECTED POSSIBILI-TIES...
THE ROAR OF THE CROWD...
IT'S ALL BLENDING TOGETHER...

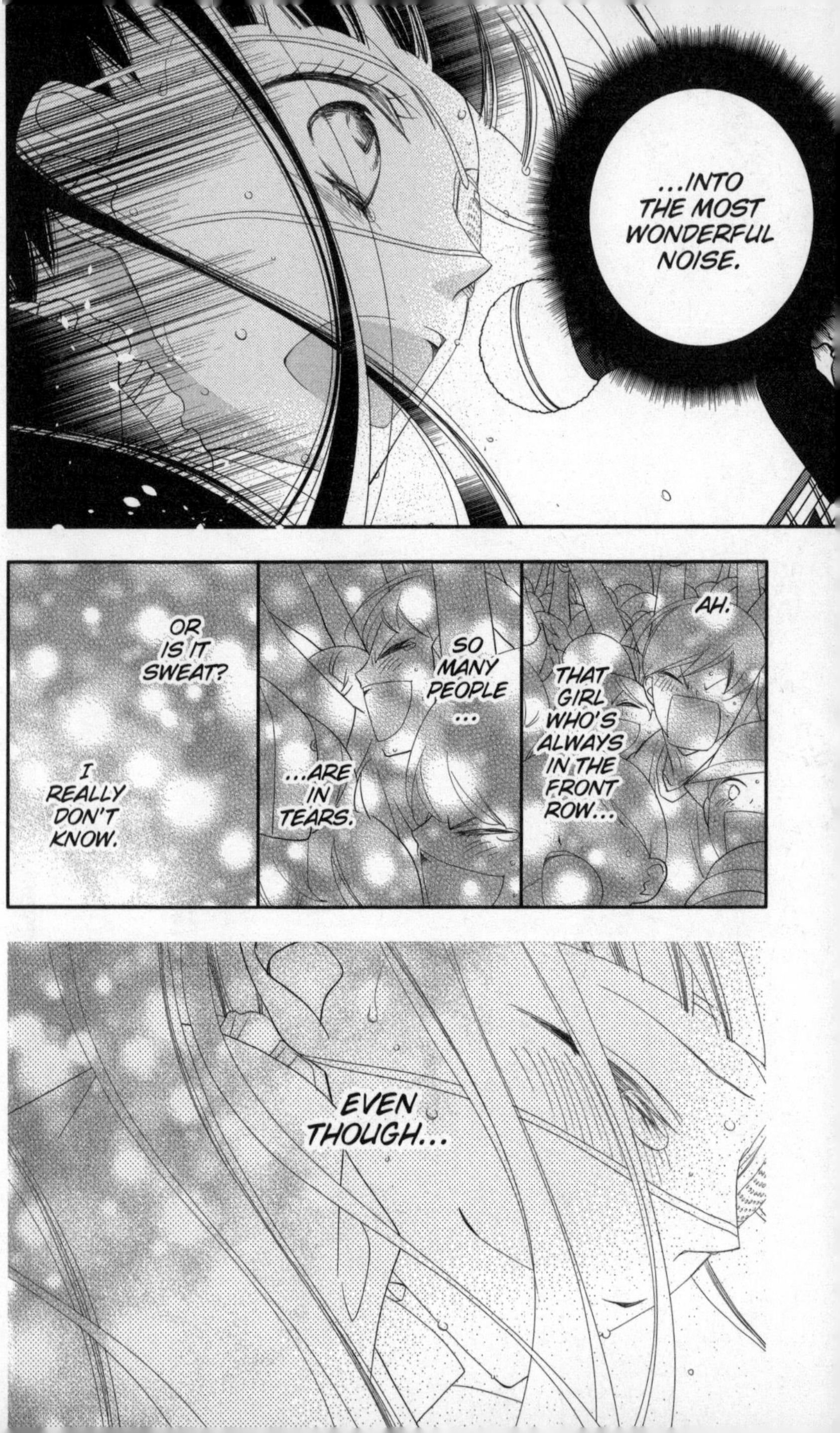
...INTO THE MOST WONDERFUL NOISE.
AH.
THAT GIRL WHO'S ALWAYS IN THE FRONT ROW...
SO MANY PEOPLE ...
...ARE IN TEARS.
OR IS IT SWEAT?
I REALLY DON'T KNOW.
EVEN THOUGH...

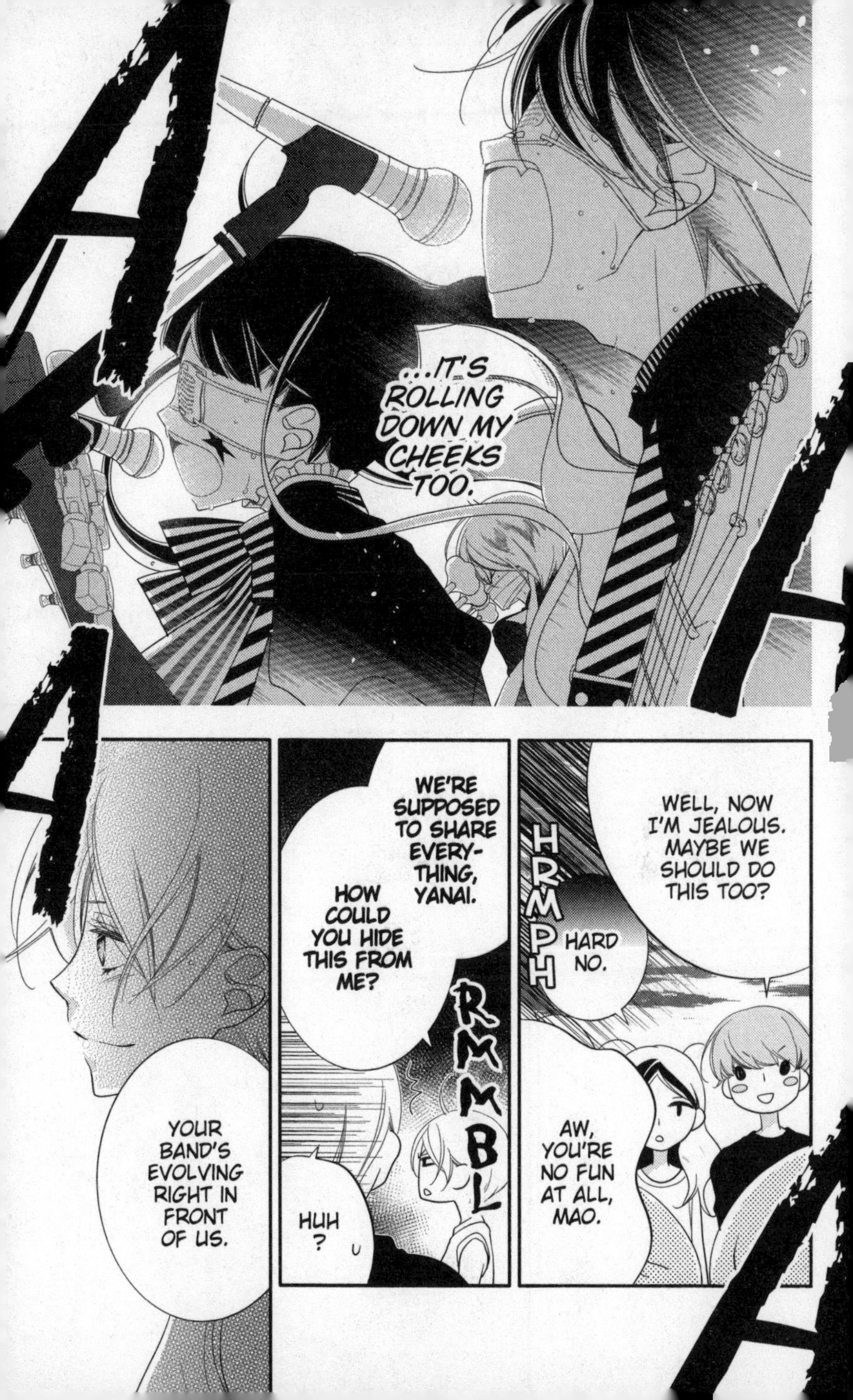
AAAA
...IT'S ROLLING DOWN MY CHEEKS TOO.
WELL, NOW I'M JEALOUS. MAYBE WE SHOULD DO THIS TOO?
HRMPH
HARD NO.
AW, YOU'RE NO FUN AT ALL, MAO.
WE'RE SUPPOSED TO SHARE EVERY-THING, YANAI.
HOW COULD YOU HIDE THIS FROM ME?
RMMBL
HUH?
YOUR BAND'S EVOLVING RIGHT IN FRONT OF US.

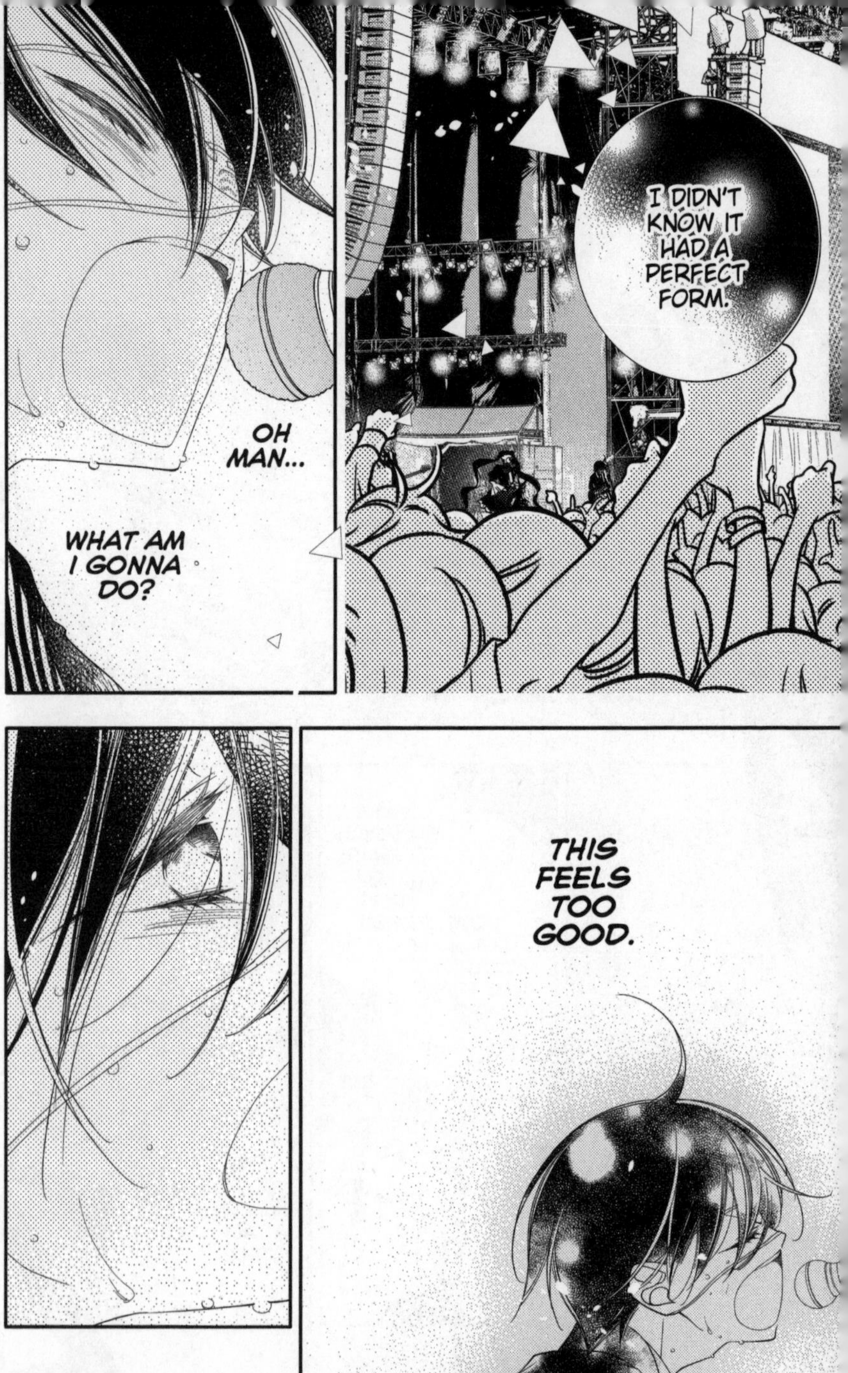
I DIDN'T KNOW IT HAD A PERFECT FORM.
OH MAN...
WHAT AM I GONNA DO?
THIS FEELS TOO GOOD.

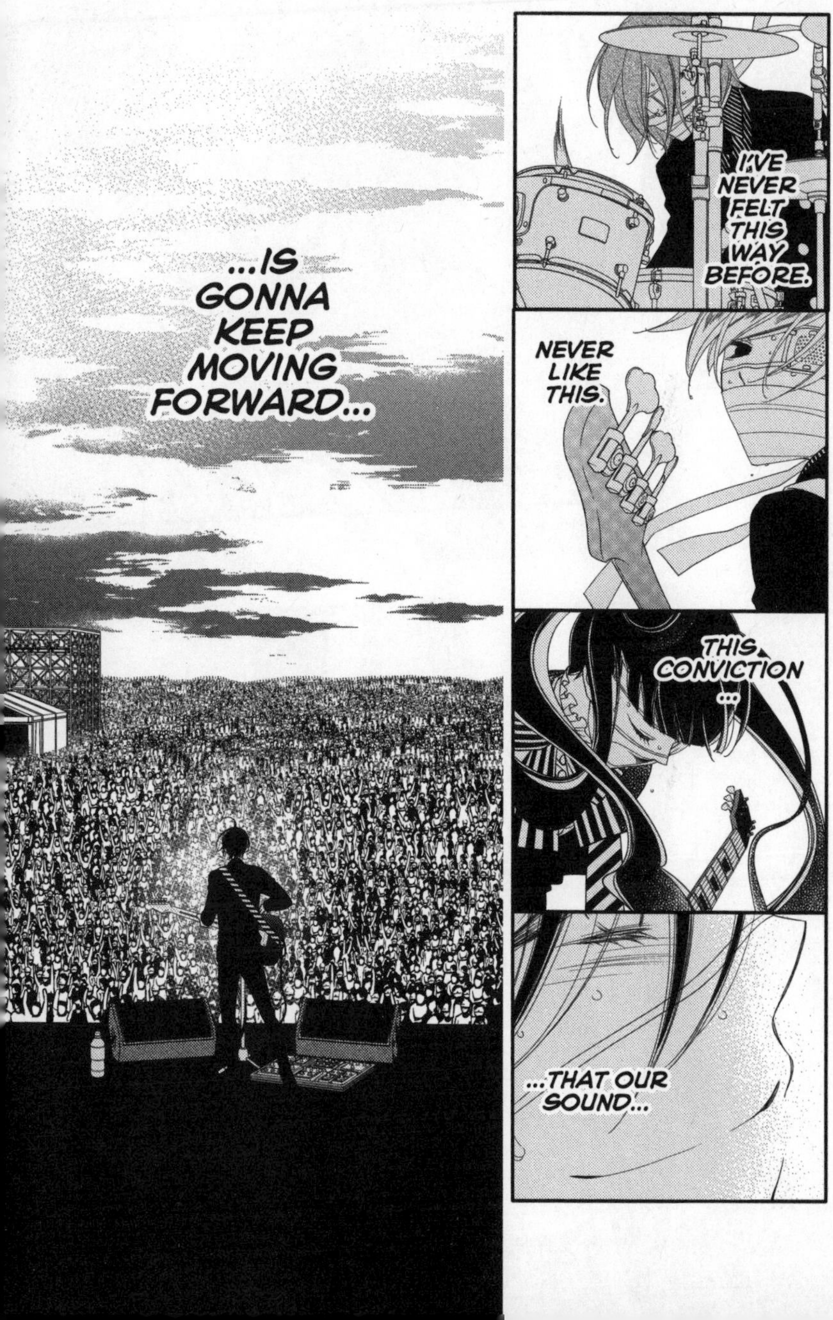
I'VE NEVER FELT THIS WAY BEFORE.
NEVER LIKE THIS.
THIS CONVICTION ...
...THAT OUR SOUND...
...IS GONNA KEEP MOVING FORWARD...

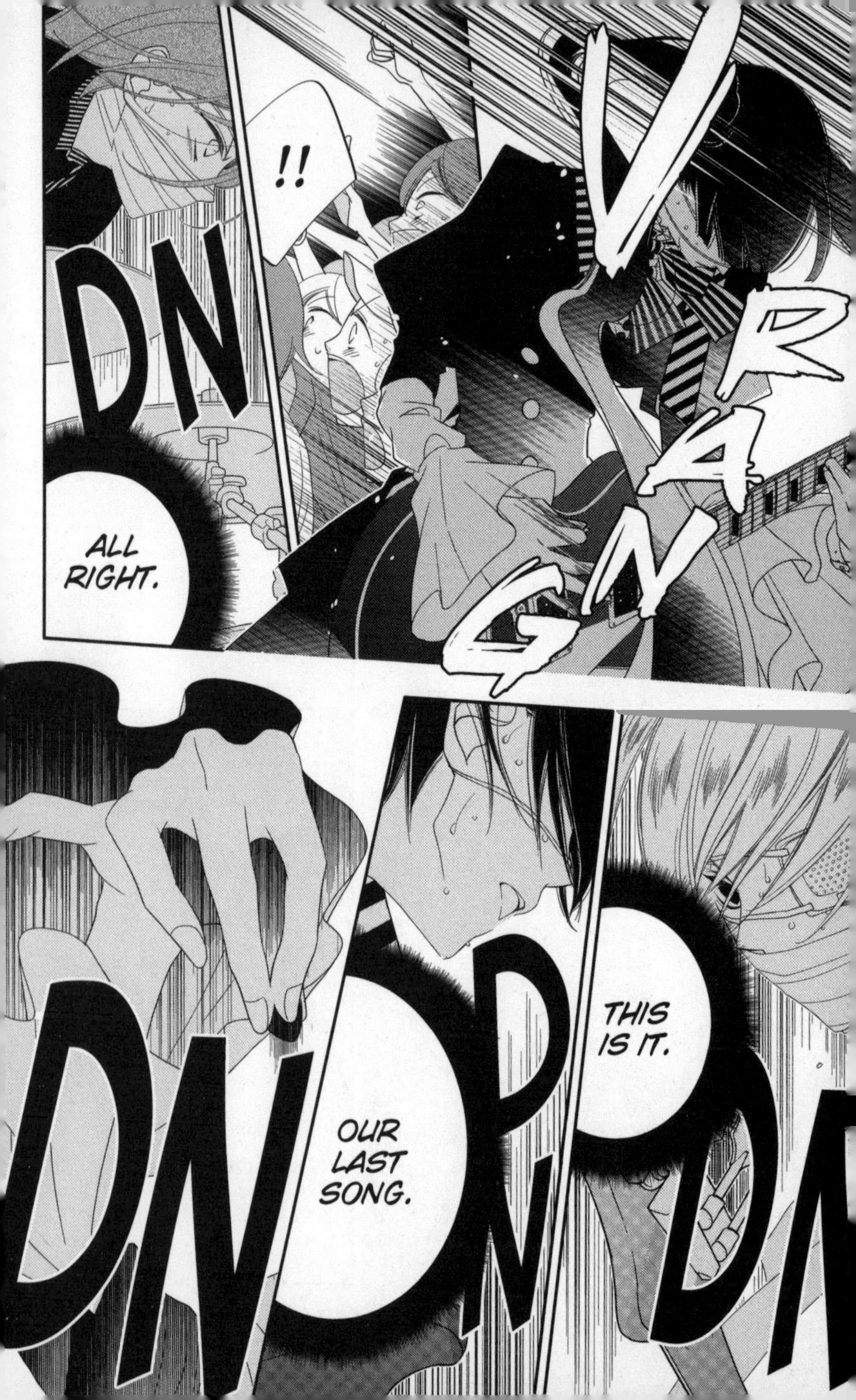
VRANG
!!
DN
ALL RIGHT.
THIS IS IT.
DN
OUR LAST SONG.
DN
DN

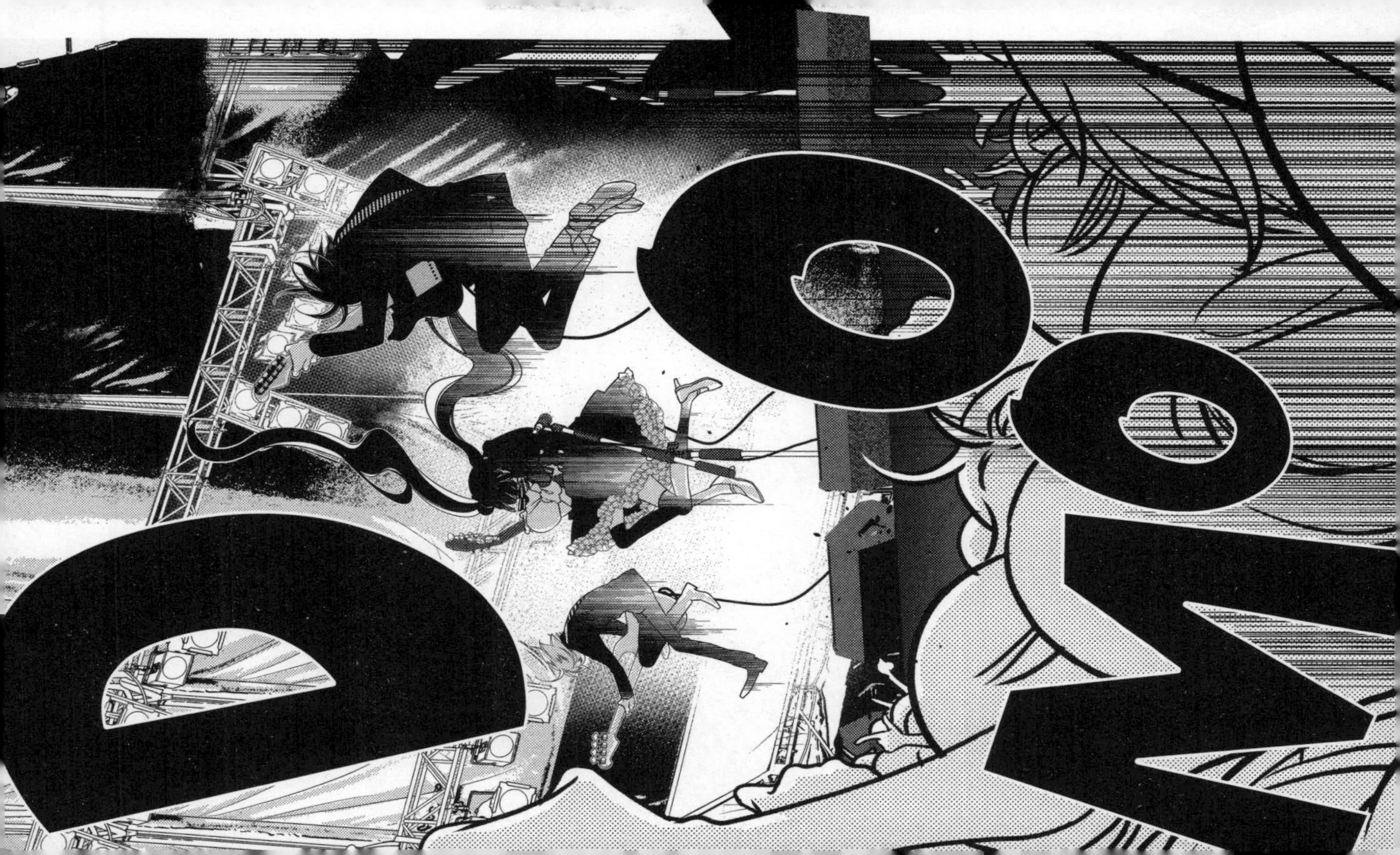
DOOM

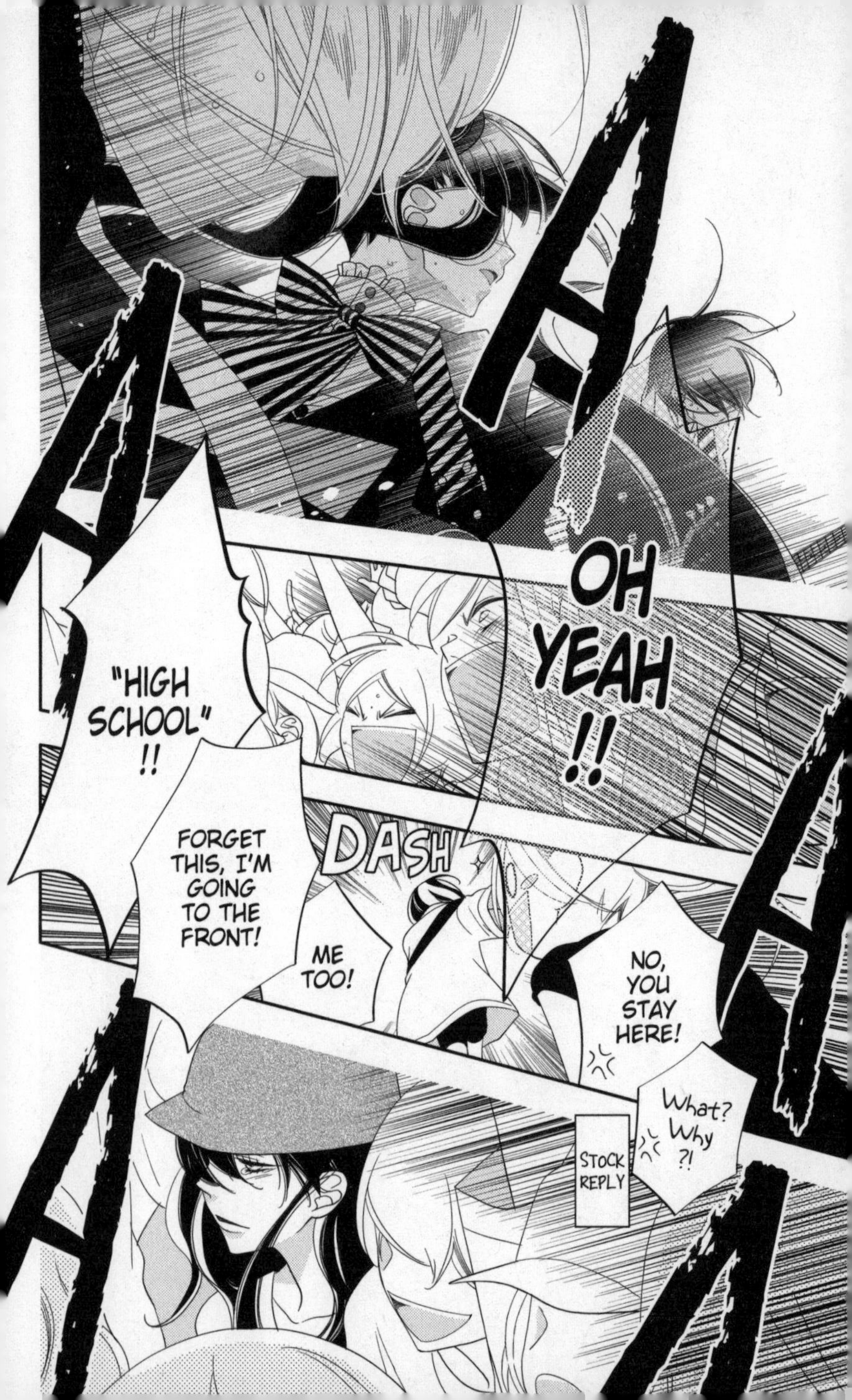
OH YEAH !!
"HIGH SCHOOL" !!
DASH
FORGET THIS, I'M GOING TO THE FRONT!
ME TOO!
NO, YOU STAY HERE!
What? Why ?!
STOCK REPLY

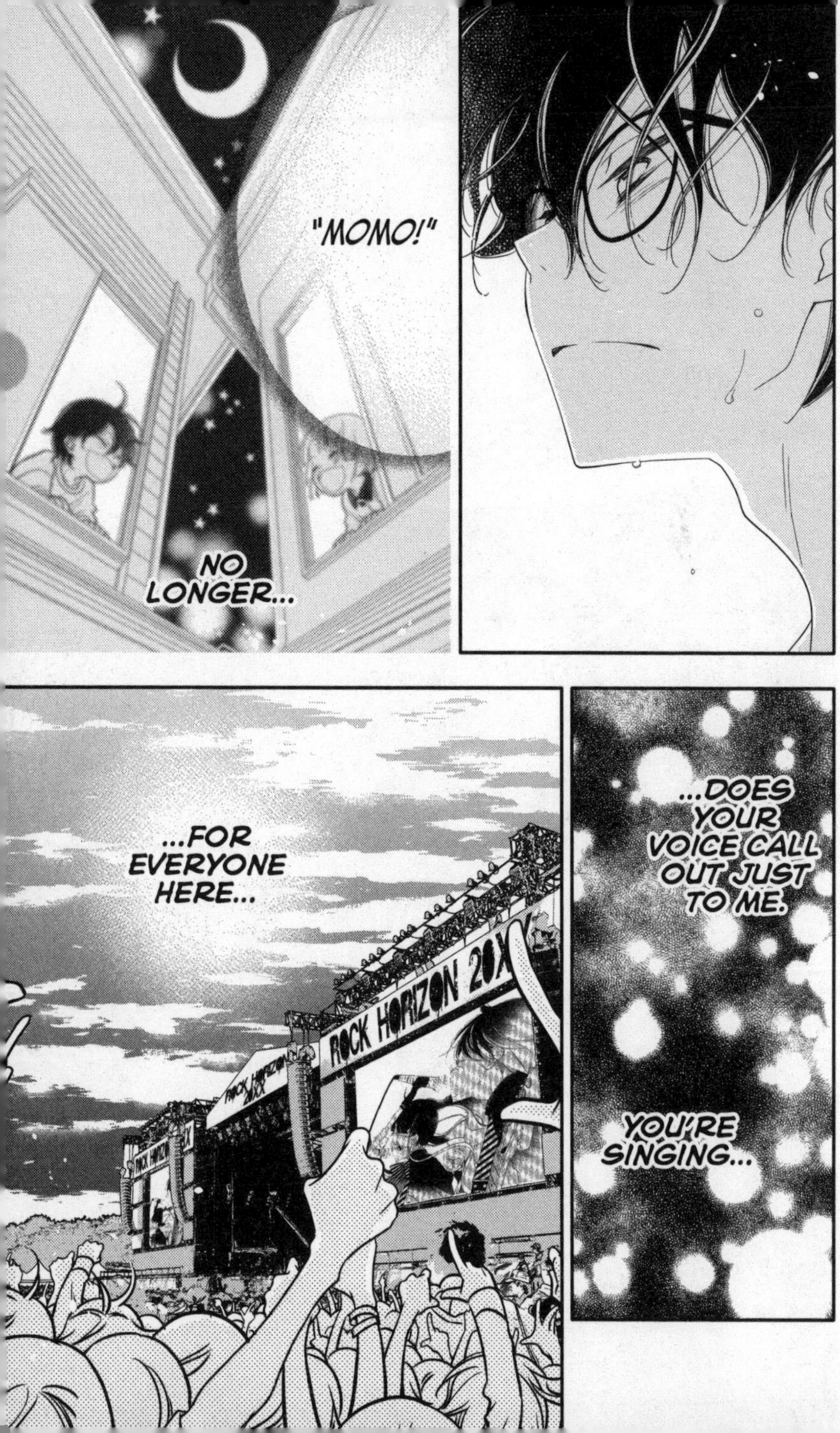
"MOMO!"
NO LONGER...
...DOES YOUR VOICE CALL OUT JUST TO ME.
YOU'RE SINGING...
...FOR EVERYONE HERE...
ROCK HORIZON 20X
ROCK HORIZON 20XX

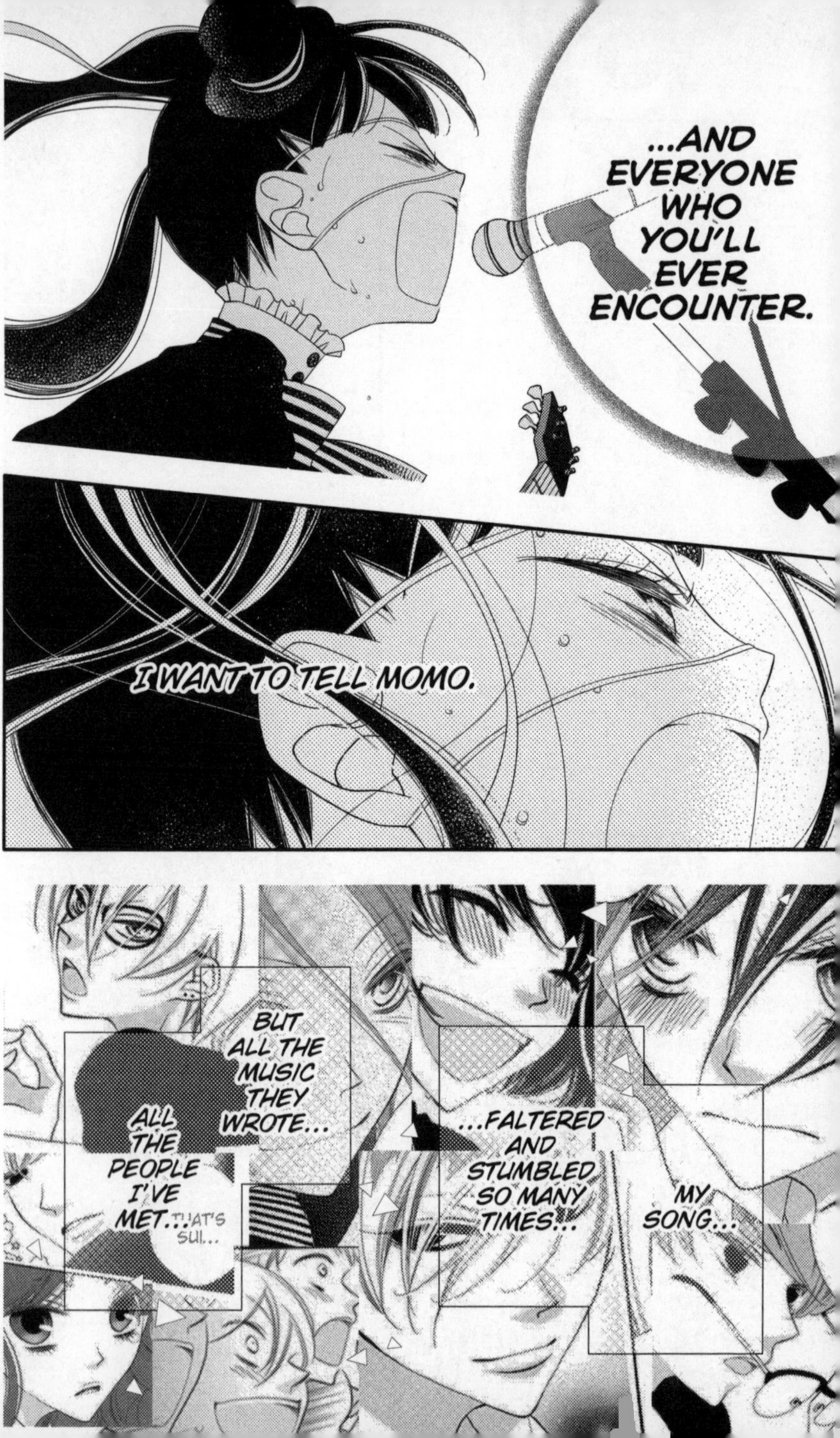
...AND EVERYONE WHO YOU'LL EVER ENCOUNTER.
I WANT TO TELL MOMO.
MY SONG...
...FALTERED AND STUMBLED SO MANY TIMES...
BUT ALL THE MUSIC THEY WROTE...
ALL THE PEOPLE I'VE MET...
THAT'S SUI...

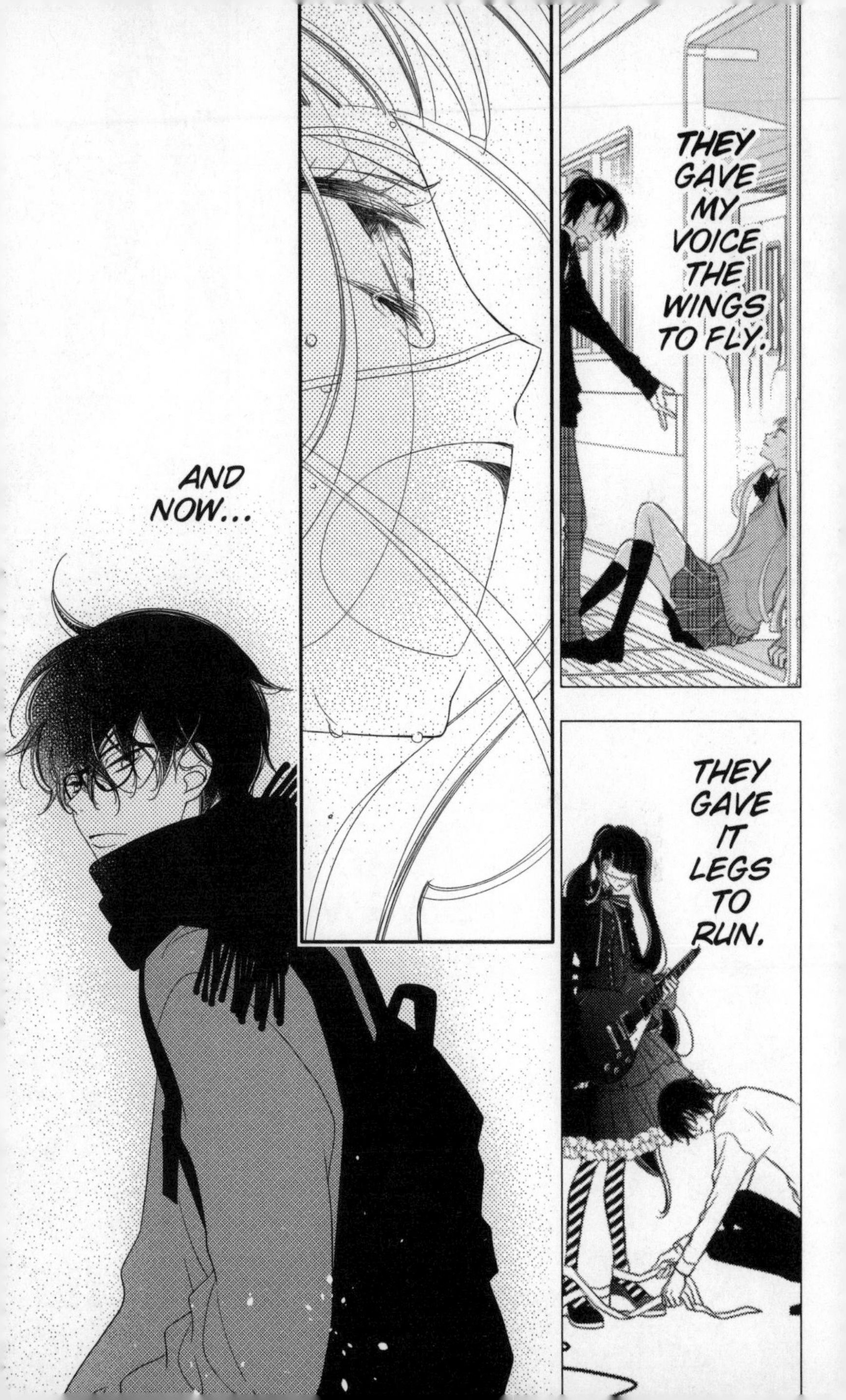
THEY GAVE MY VOICE THE WINGS TO FLY.
THEY GAVE IT LEGS TO RUN.
AND NOW...

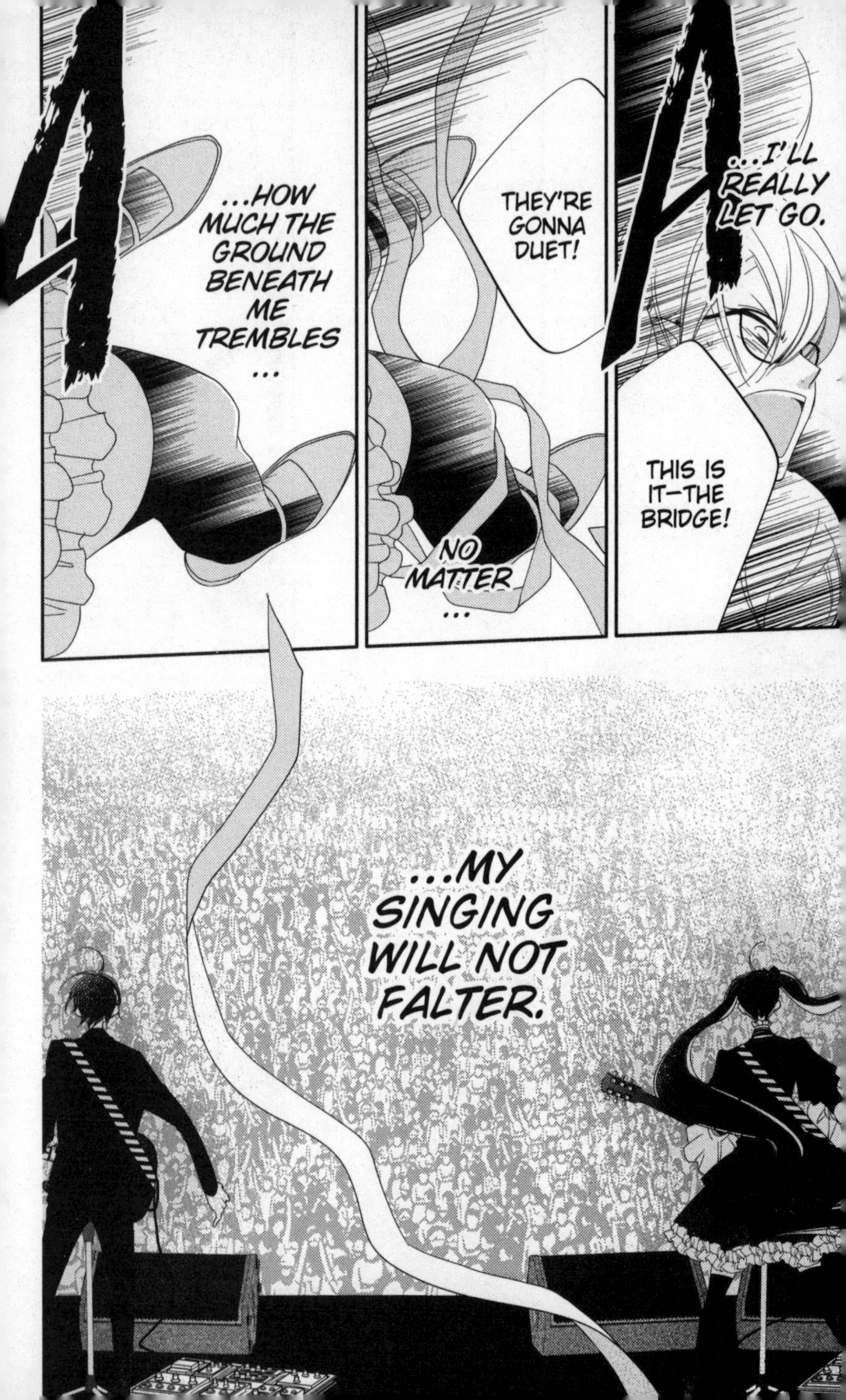
...I'LL REALLY LET GO.
THIS IS IT—THE BRIDGE!
THEY'RE GONNA DUET!
NO MATTER...
...HOW MUCH THE GROUND BENEATH ME TREMBLES...
...MY SINGING WILL NOT FALTER.

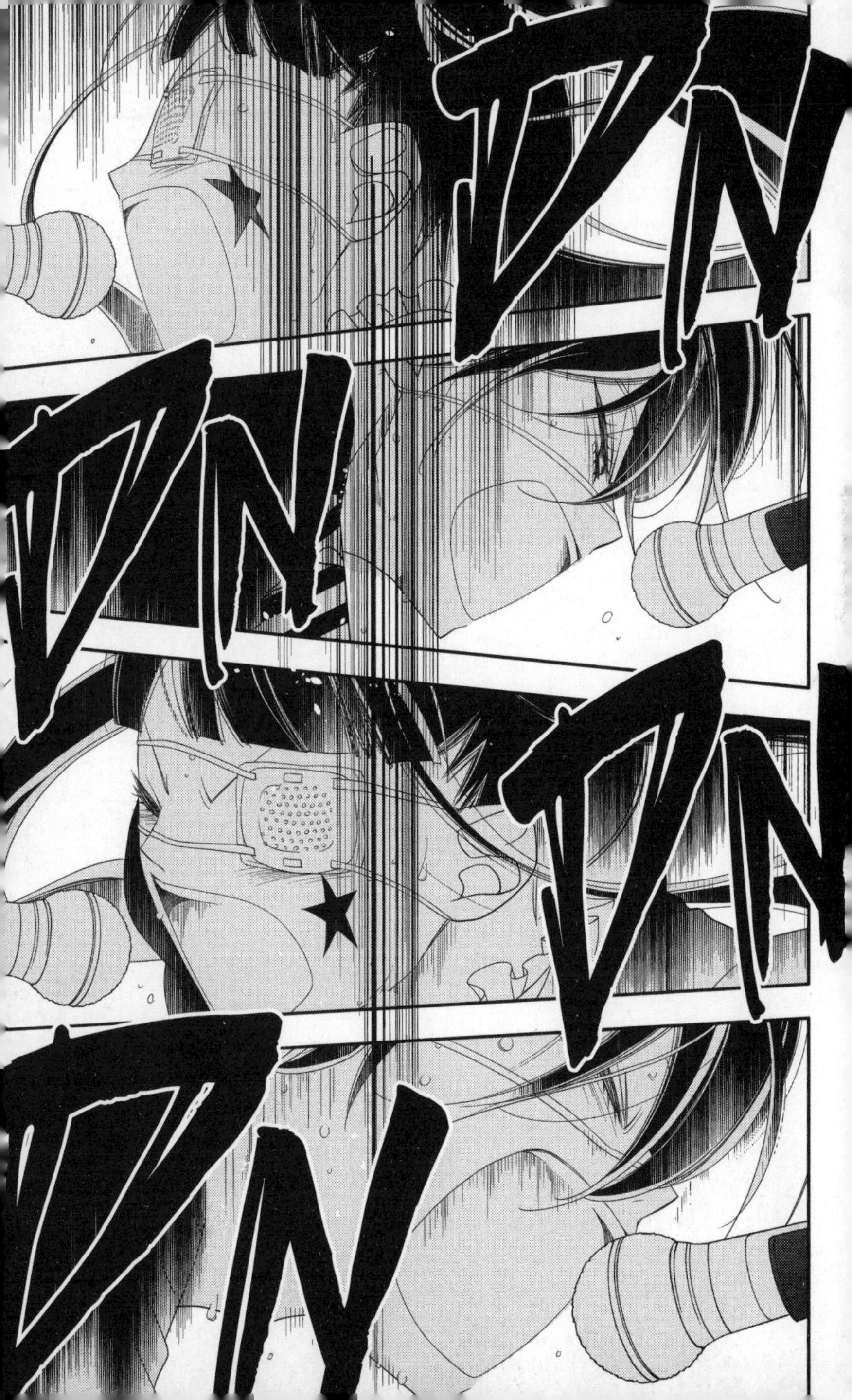
DN
DN
DN
DN

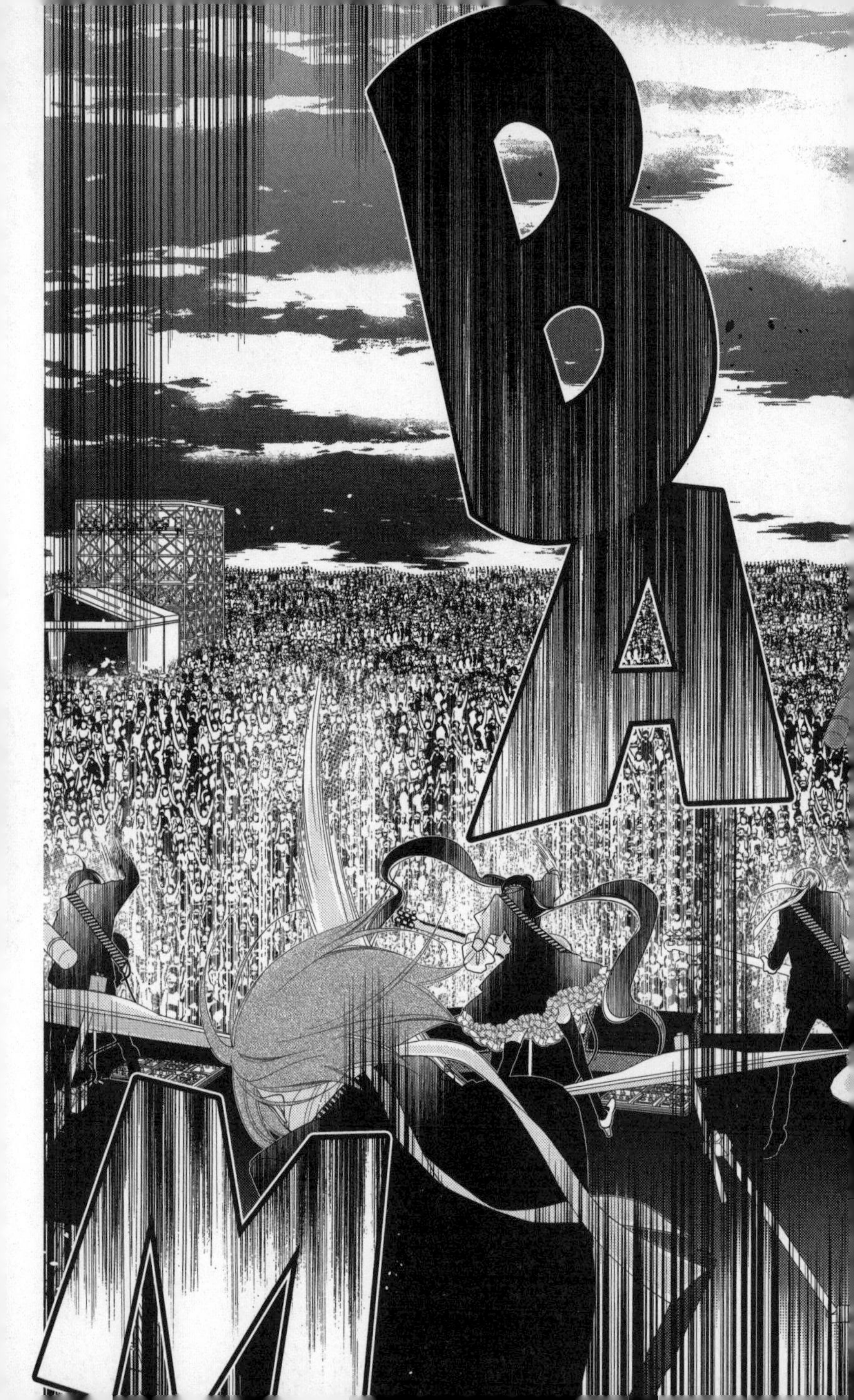
BAM

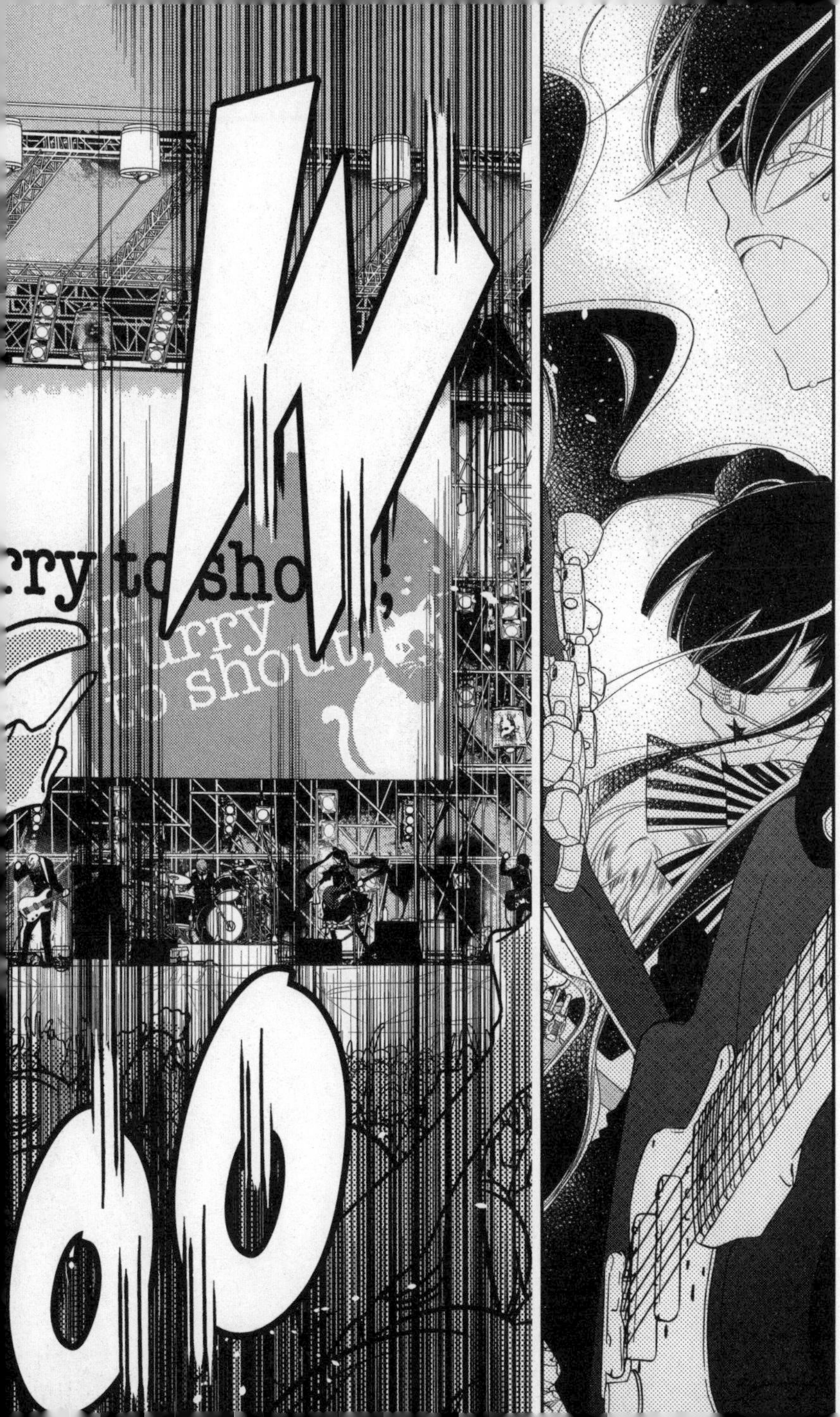

WOO
rry to sho
urry
o shout,

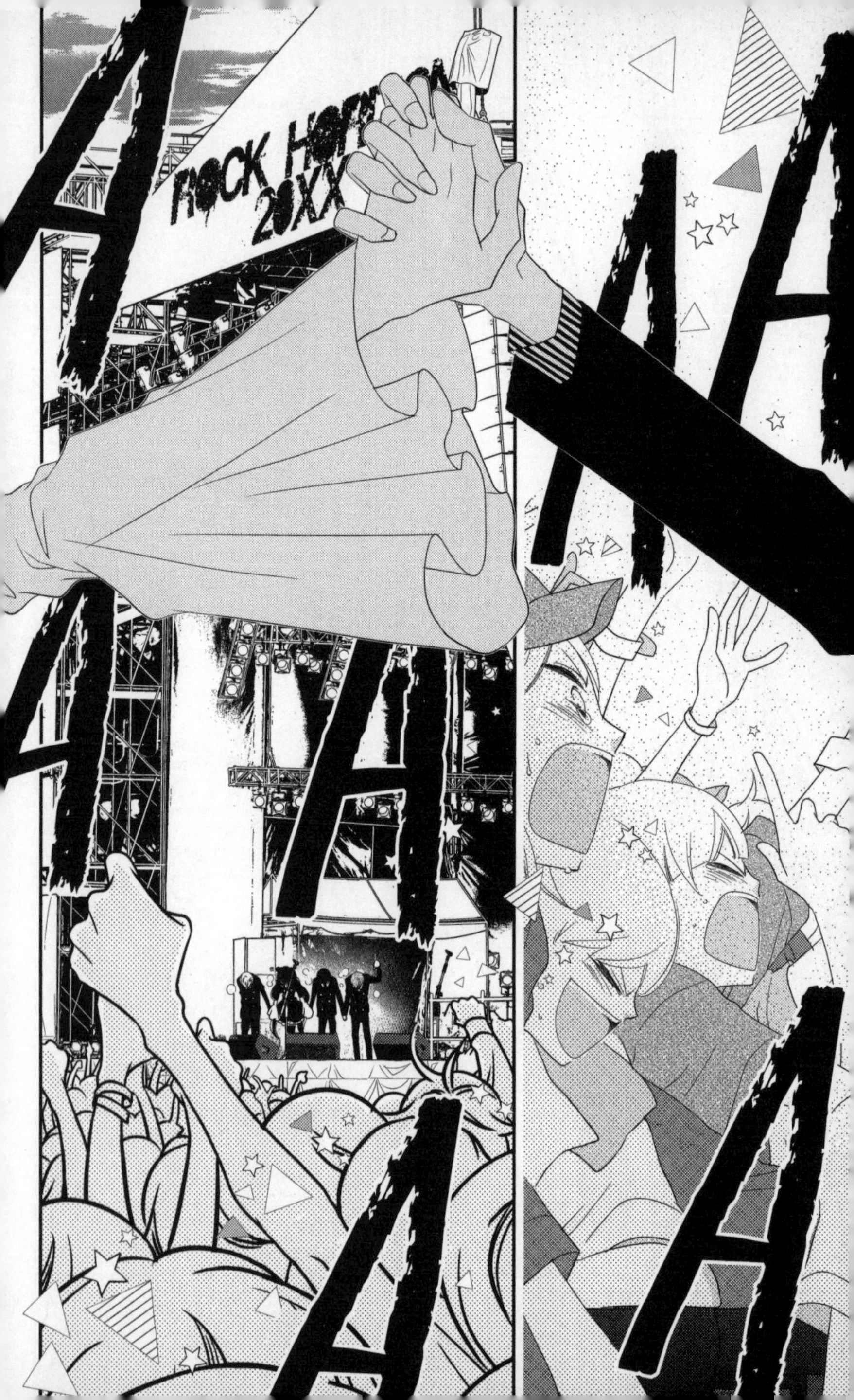
AAAA
ROCK HOR
20XX
AAAAA

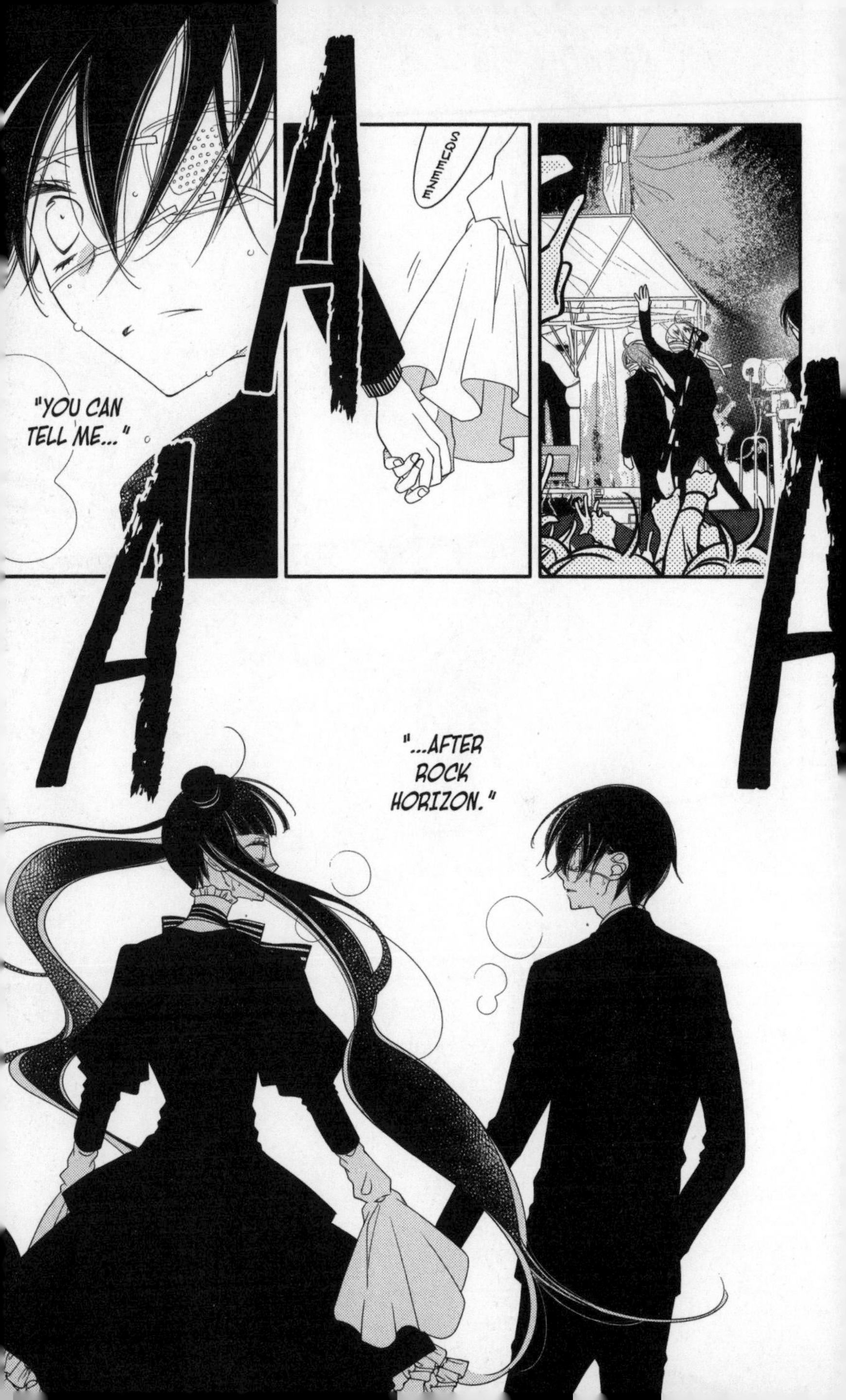
SQUEEEE
"YOU CAN TELL ME..."
"...AFTER ROCK HORIZON."

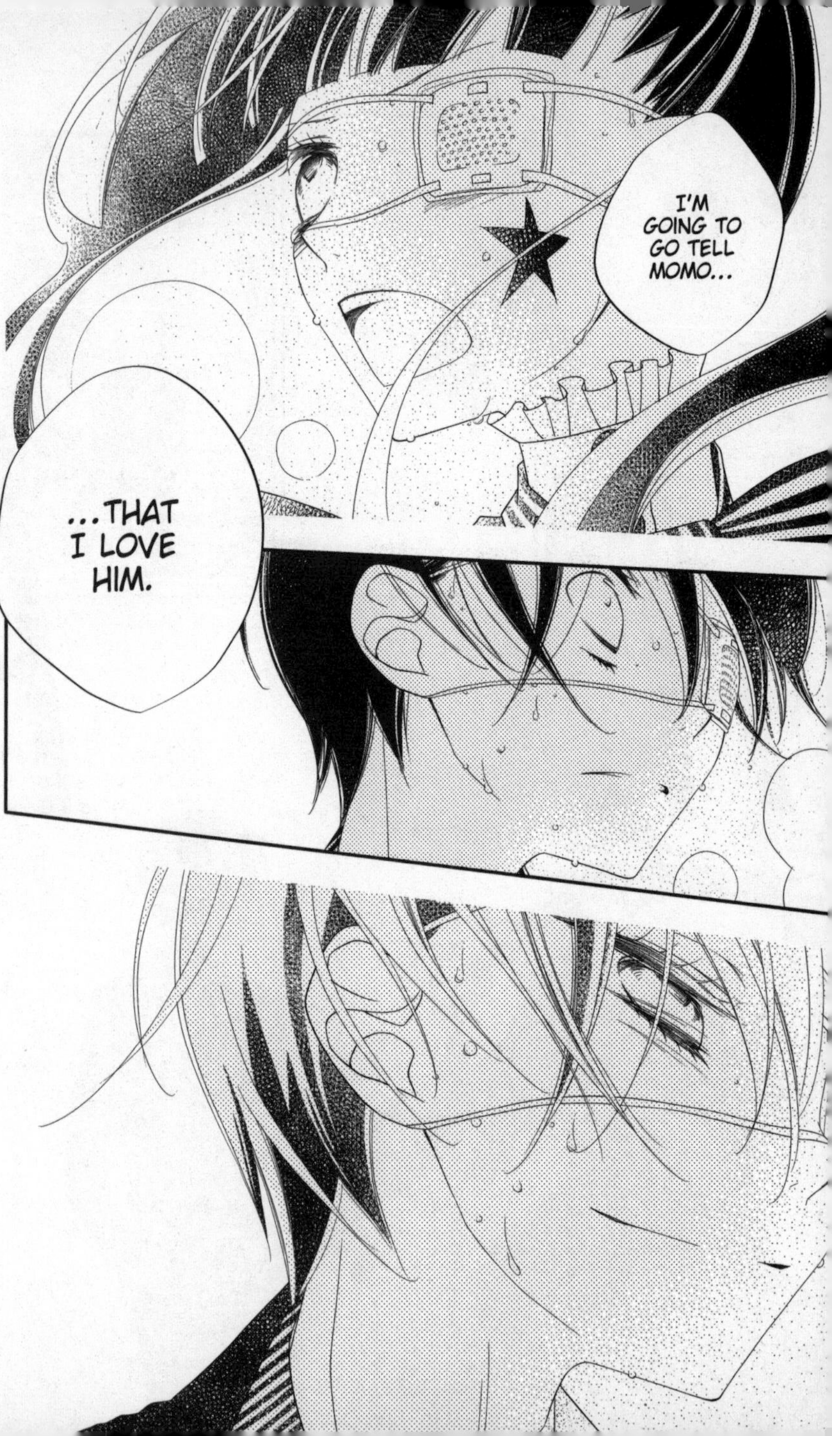
I'M GOING TO GO TELL MOMO...
...THAT I LOVE HIM.

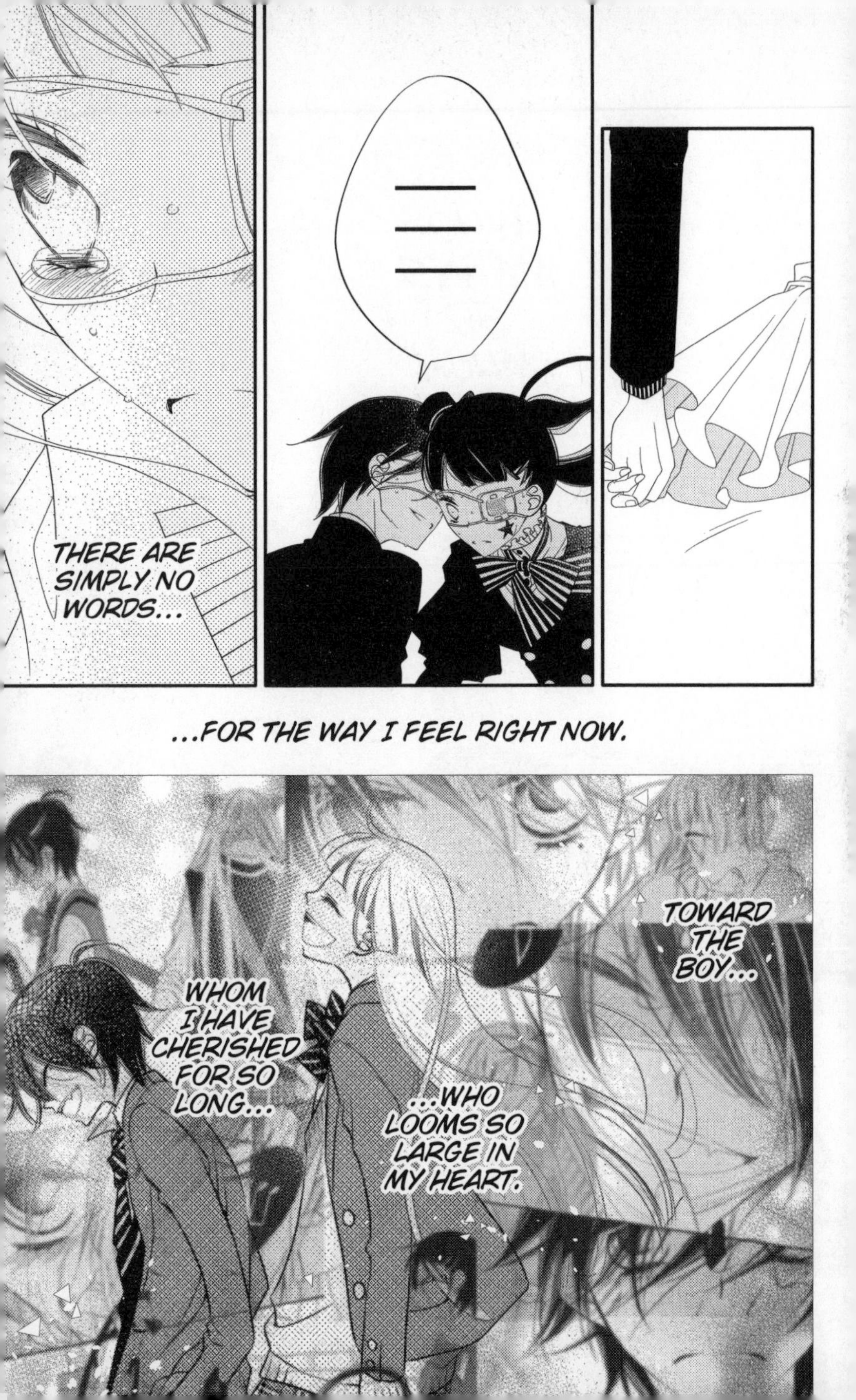
THERE ARE SIMPLY NO WORDS...
...FOR THE WAY I FEEL RIGHT NOW.
TOWARD THE BOY...
WHOM I HAVE CHERISHED FOR SO LONG...
...WHO LOOMS SO LARGE IN MY HEART.

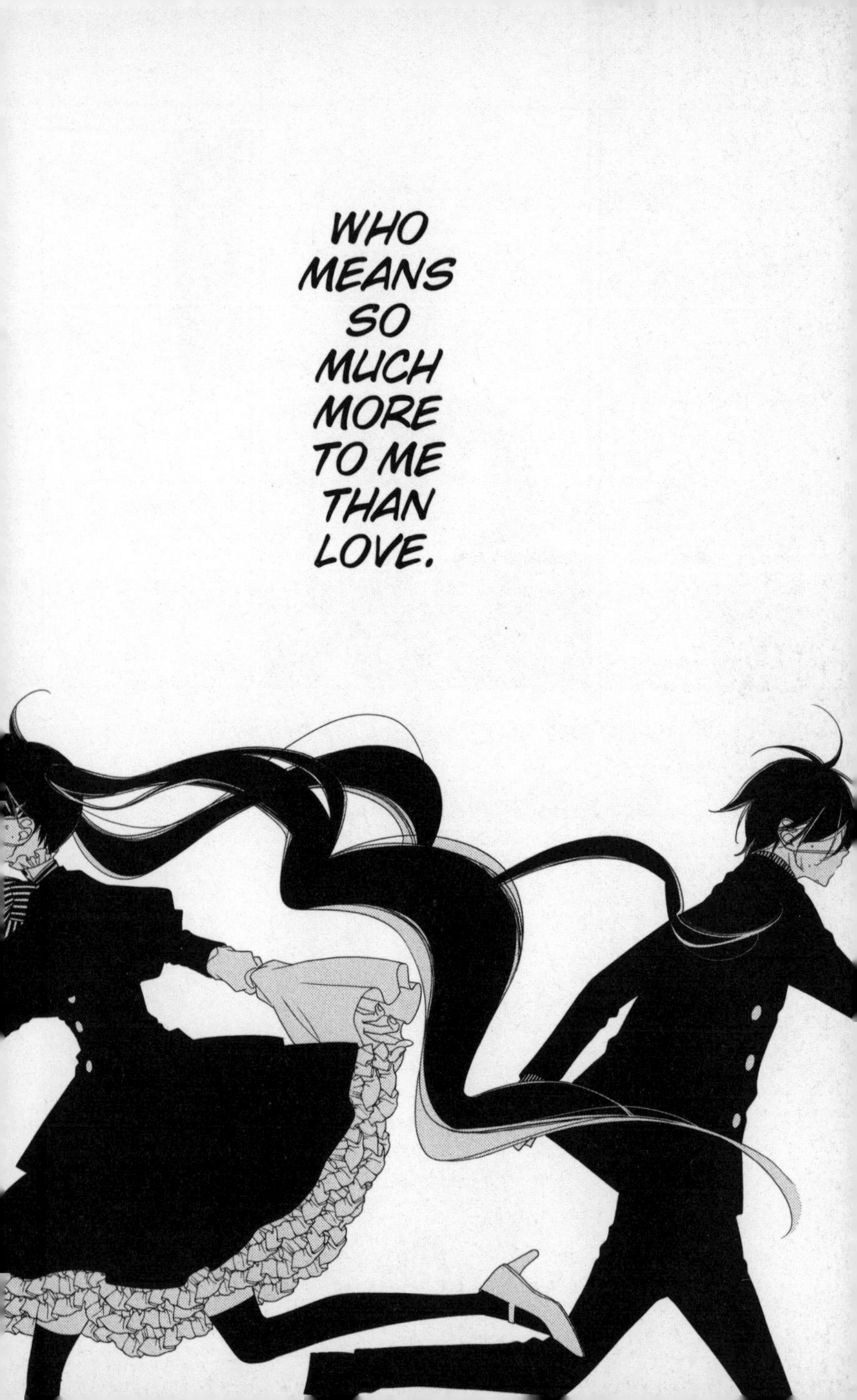
WHO MEANS SO MUCH MORE TO ME THAN LOVE.

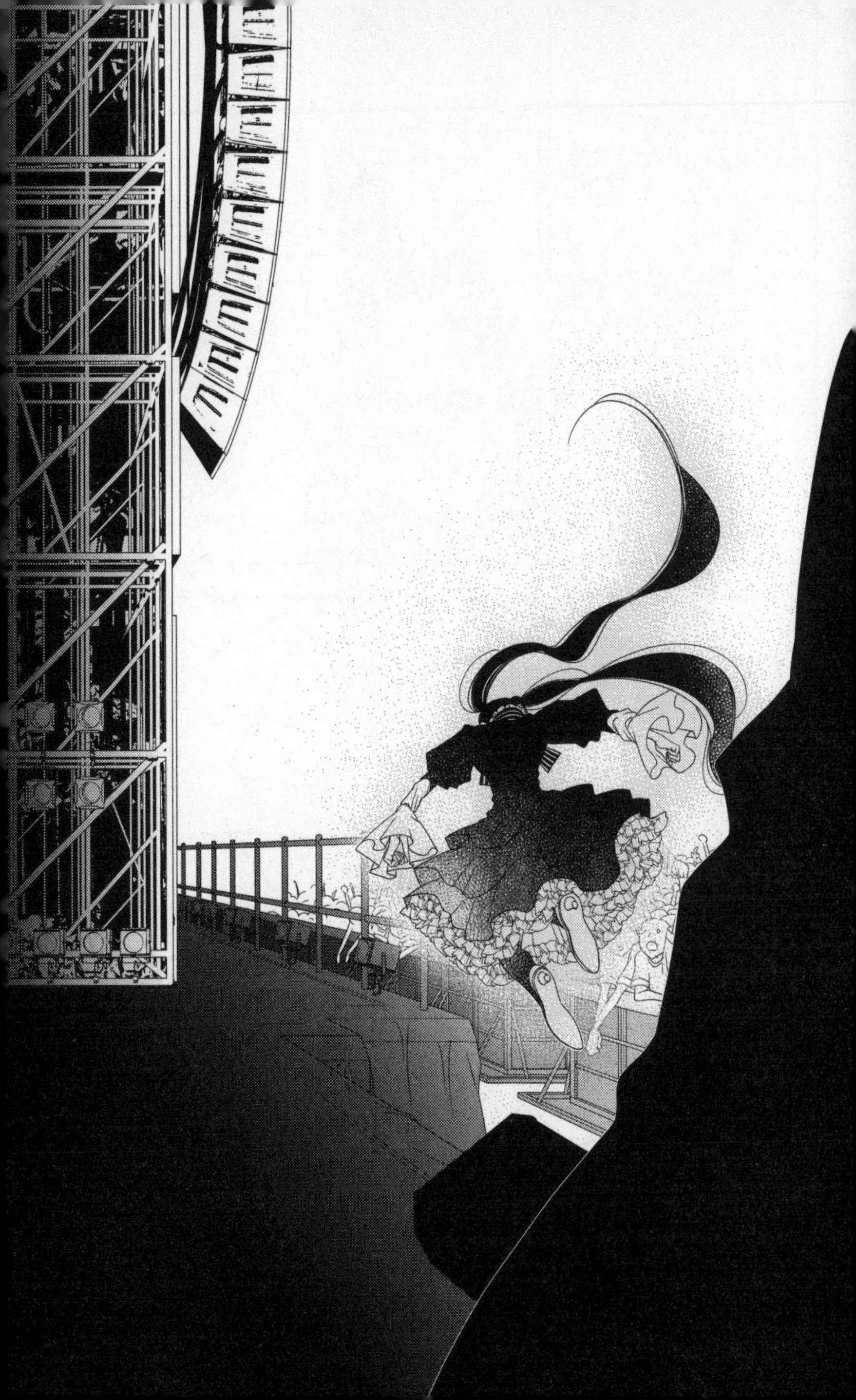

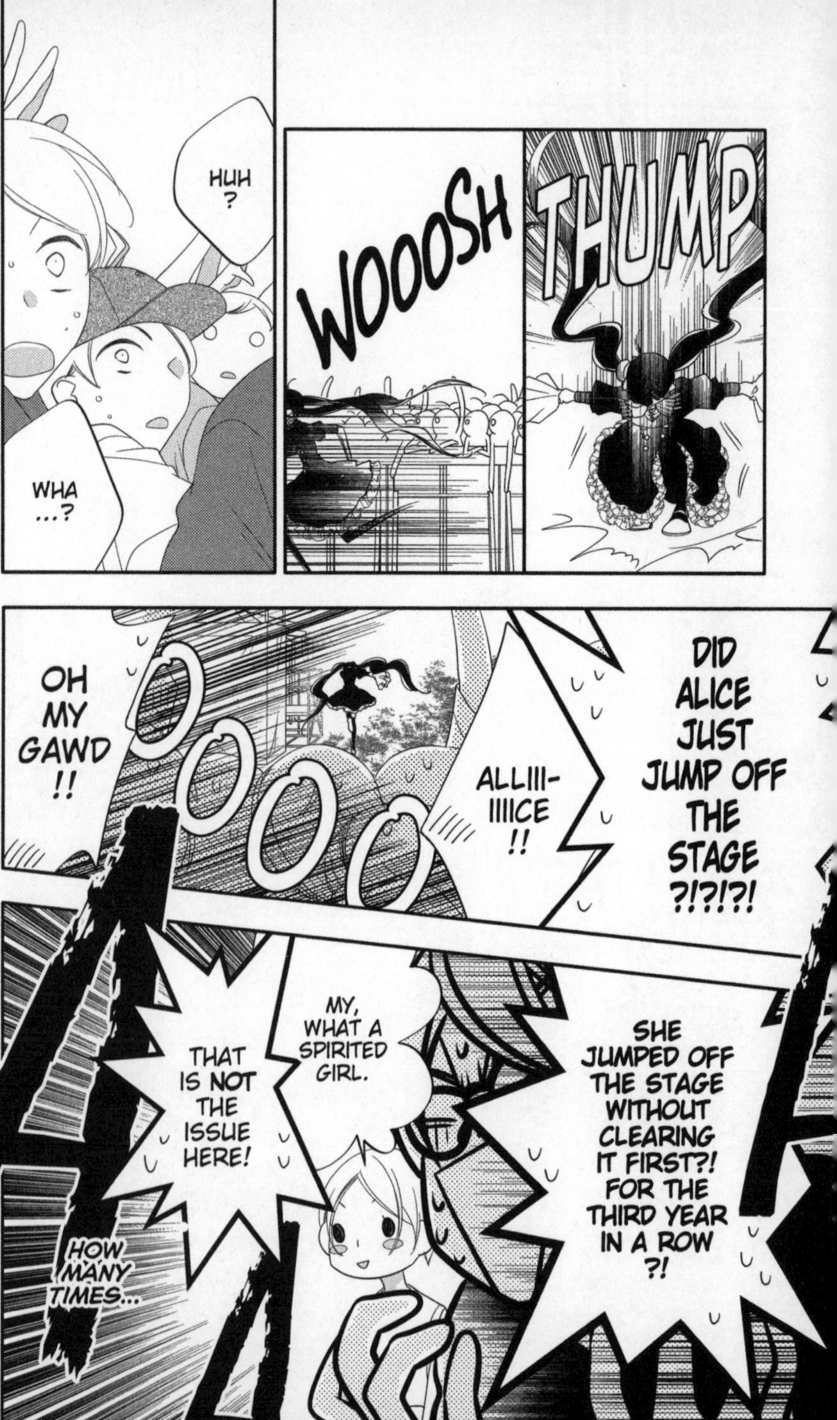
THUMP
WOOOSH
HUH?
WHA...?
DID ALICE JUST JUMP OFF THE STAGE?!?!?!
ALLIIII-IIIICE!!
OOOOO
OH MY GAWD!!
SHE JUMPED OFF THE STAGE WITHOUT CLEARING IT FIRST?! FOR THE THIRD YEAR IN A ROW?!
MY, WHAT A SPIRITED GIRL.
THAT IS NOT THE ISSUE HERE!
HOW MANY TIMES...

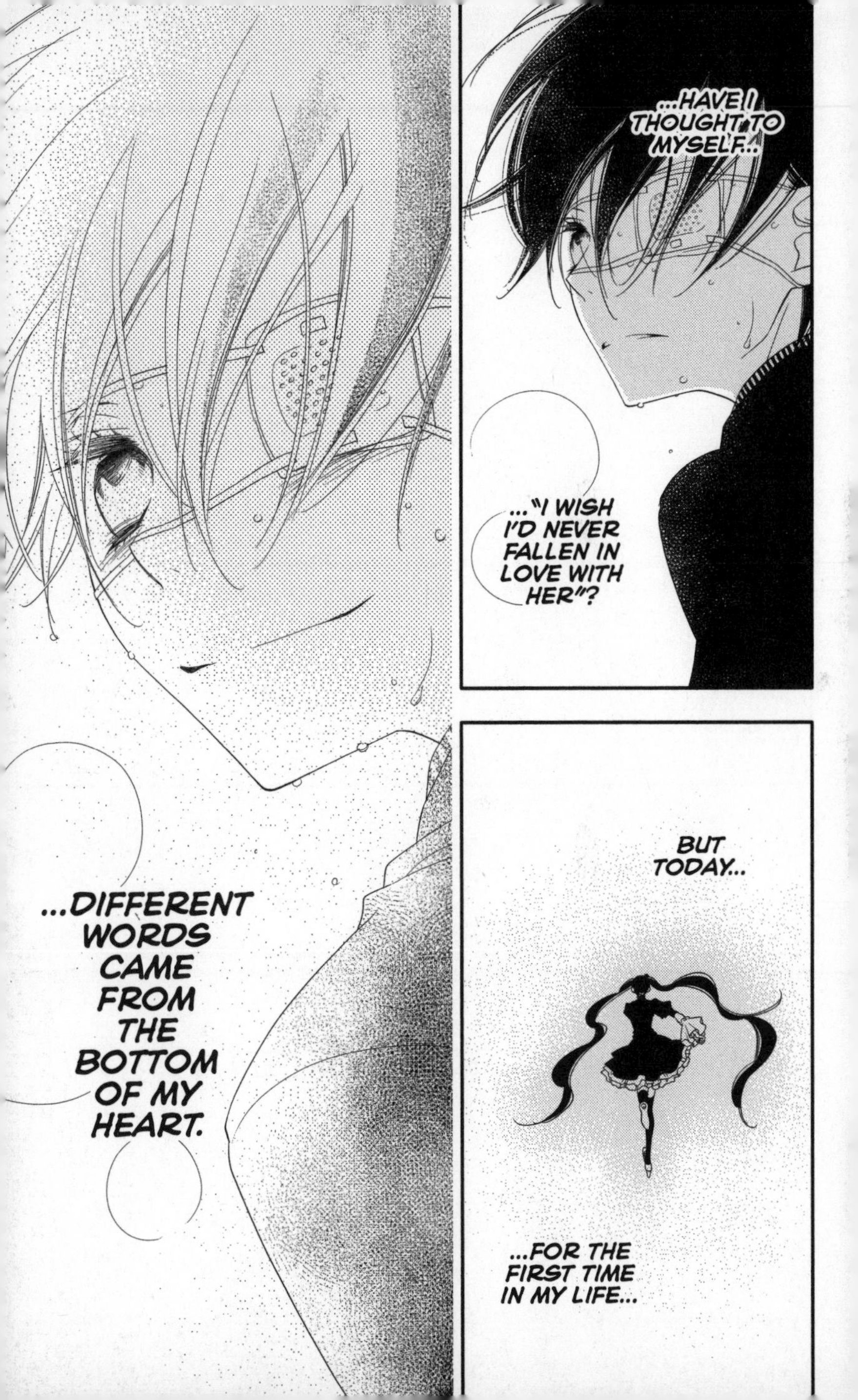
...HAVE I THOUGHT TO MYSELF...
..."I WISH I'D NEVER FALLEN IN LOVE WITH HER"?
BUT TODAY...
...FOR THE FIRST TIME IN MY LIFE...
...DIFFERENT WORDS CAME FROM THE BOTTOM OF MY HEART.

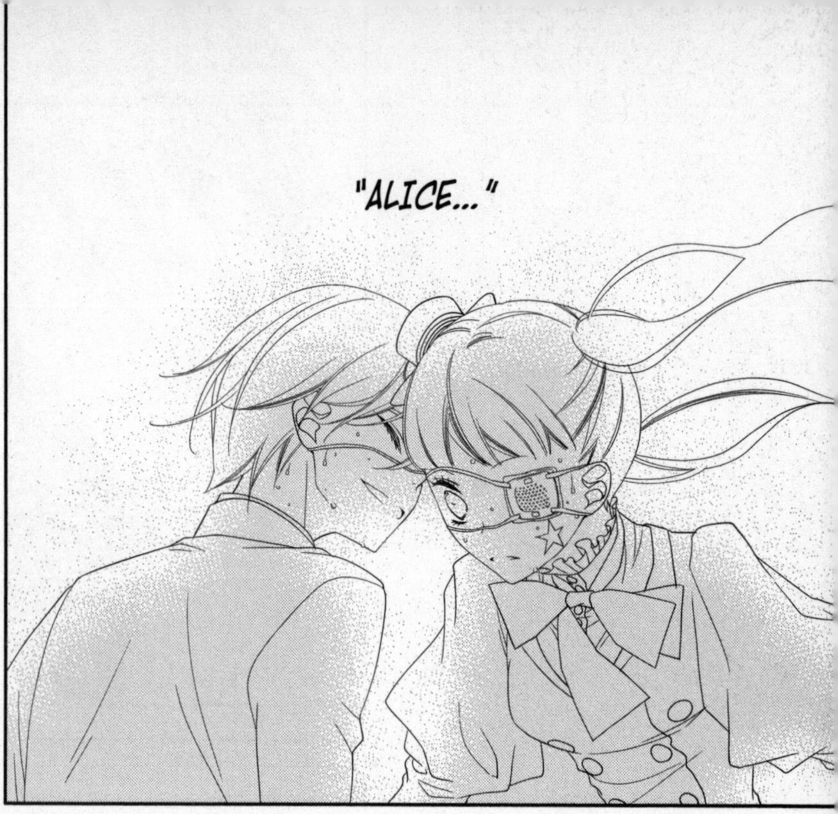
"ALICE..."

"I'M GLAD I FELL IN LOVE WITH YOU."

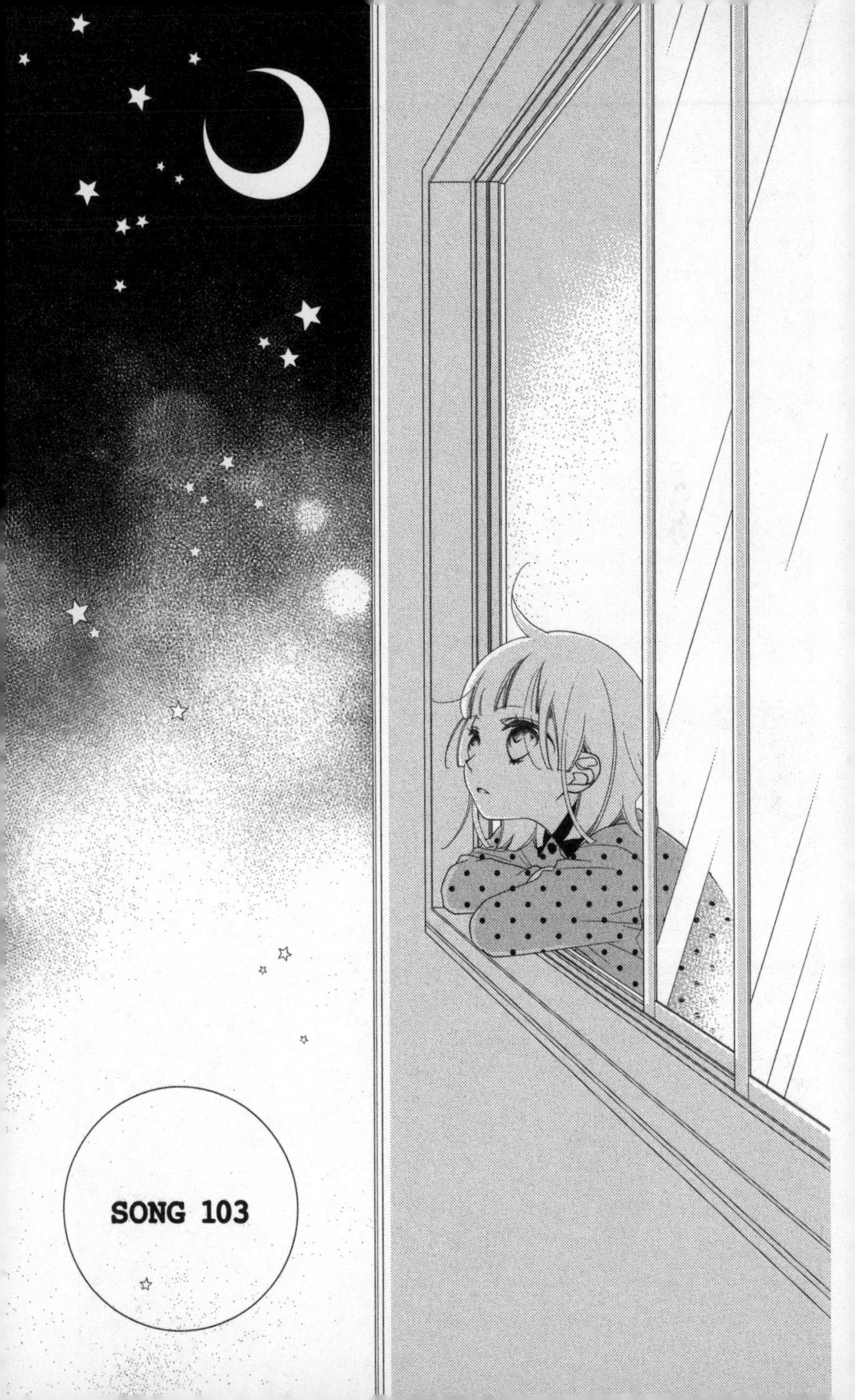
SONG 103

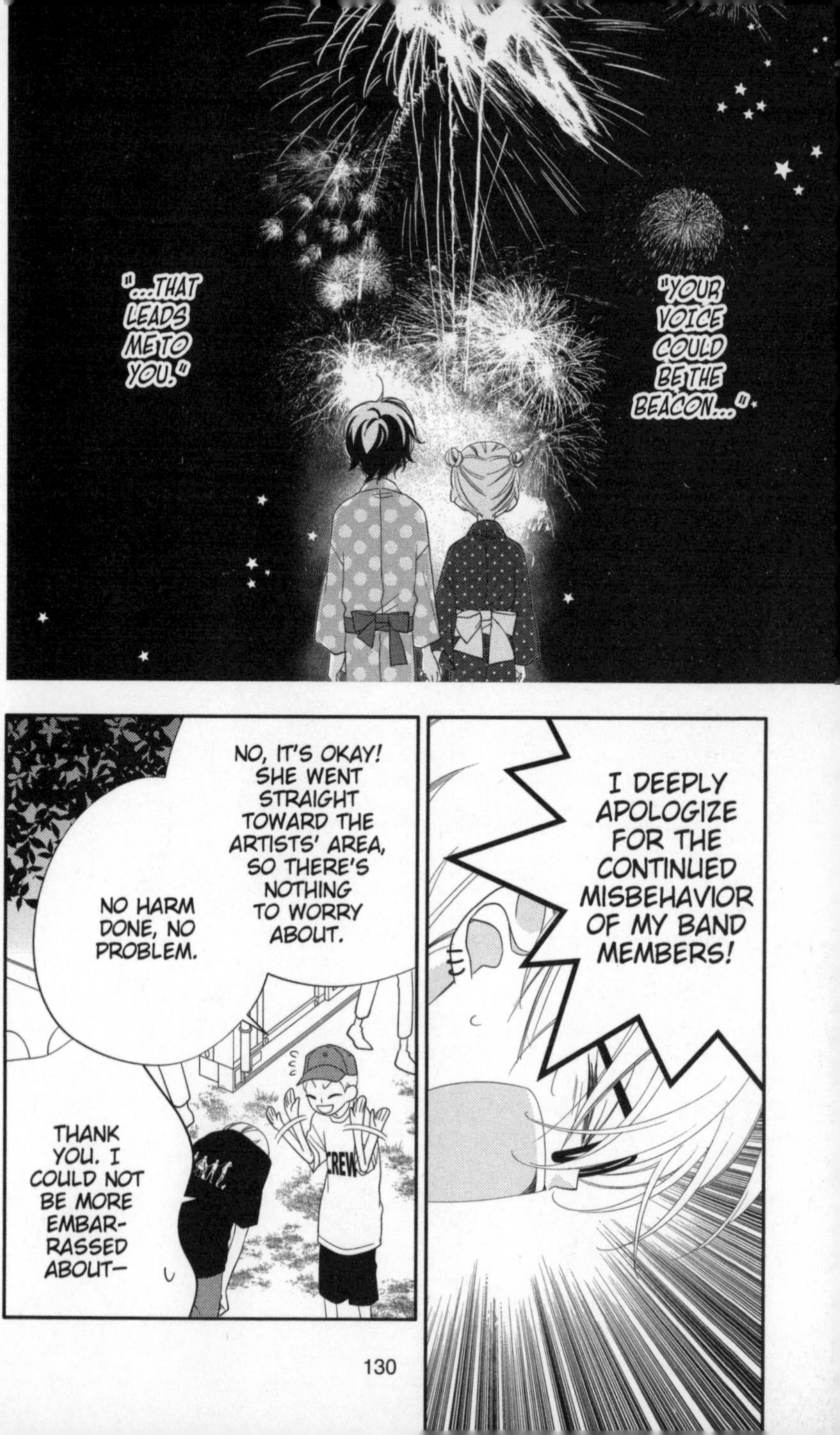
"YOUR VOICE COULD BE THE BEACON..."
"...THAT LEADS ME TO YOU."
I DEEPLY APOLOGIZE FOR THE CONTINUED MISBEHAVIOR OF MY BAND MEMBERS!
NO, IT'S OKAY! SHE WENT STRAIGHT TOWARD THE ARTISTS' AREA, SO THERE'S NOTHING TO WORRY ABOUT.
NO HARM DONE, NO PROBLEM.
THANK YOU. I COULD NOT BE MORE EMBARRASSED ABOUT—
CREW

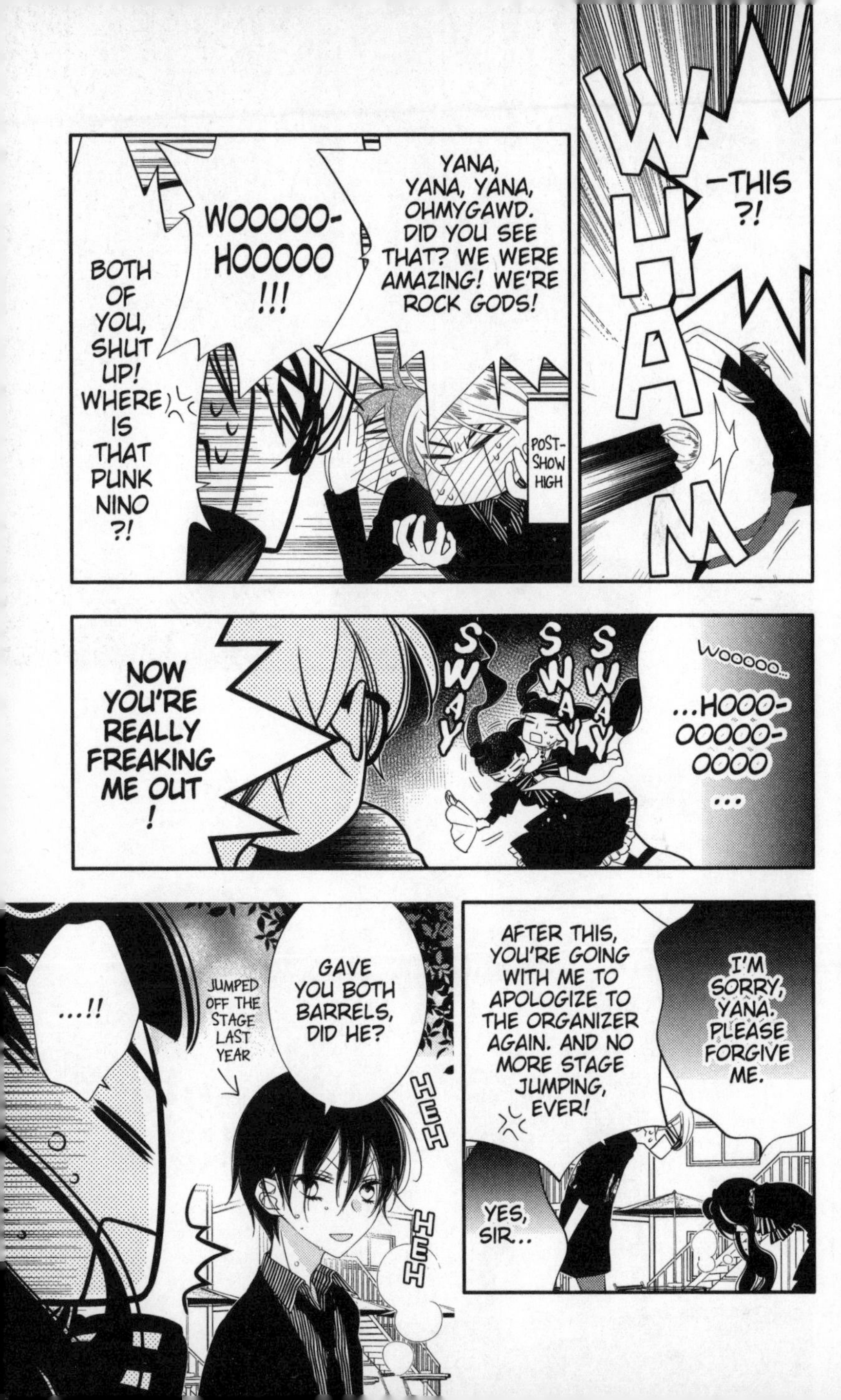
WHAM
-THIS ?!
YANA, YANA, YANA, OHMYGAWD. DID YOU SEE THAT? WE WERE AMAZING! WE'RE ROCK GODS!
WOOOOO-HOOOOO !!!
BOTH OF YOU, SHUT UP! WHERE IS THAT PUNK NINO ?!
POST-SHOW HIGH
WOOOOO...
...HOOO-OOOOO-OOOO ...
SWAY SWAY SWAY
NOW YOU'RE REALLY FREAKING ME OUT !
I'M SORRY, YANA. PLEASE FORGIVE ME.
AFTER THIS, YOU'RE GOING WITH ME TO APOLOGIZE TO THE ORGANIZER AGAIN. AND NO MORE STAGE JUMPING, EVER!
YES, SIR...
GAVE YOU BOTH BARRELS, DID HE?
JUMPED OFF THE STAGE LAST YEAR
HEH HEH
...!!

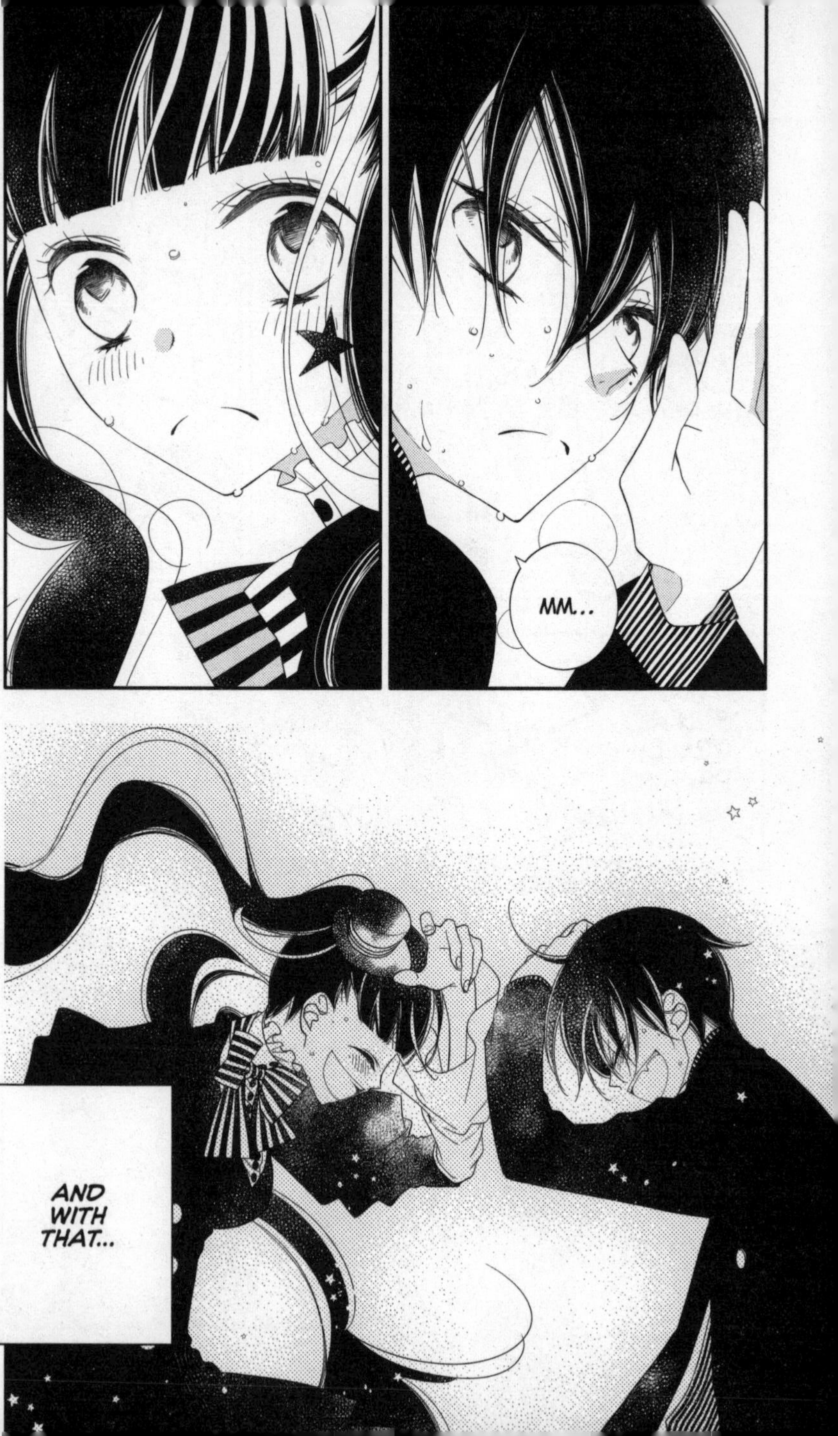
MM...
AND WITH THAT...

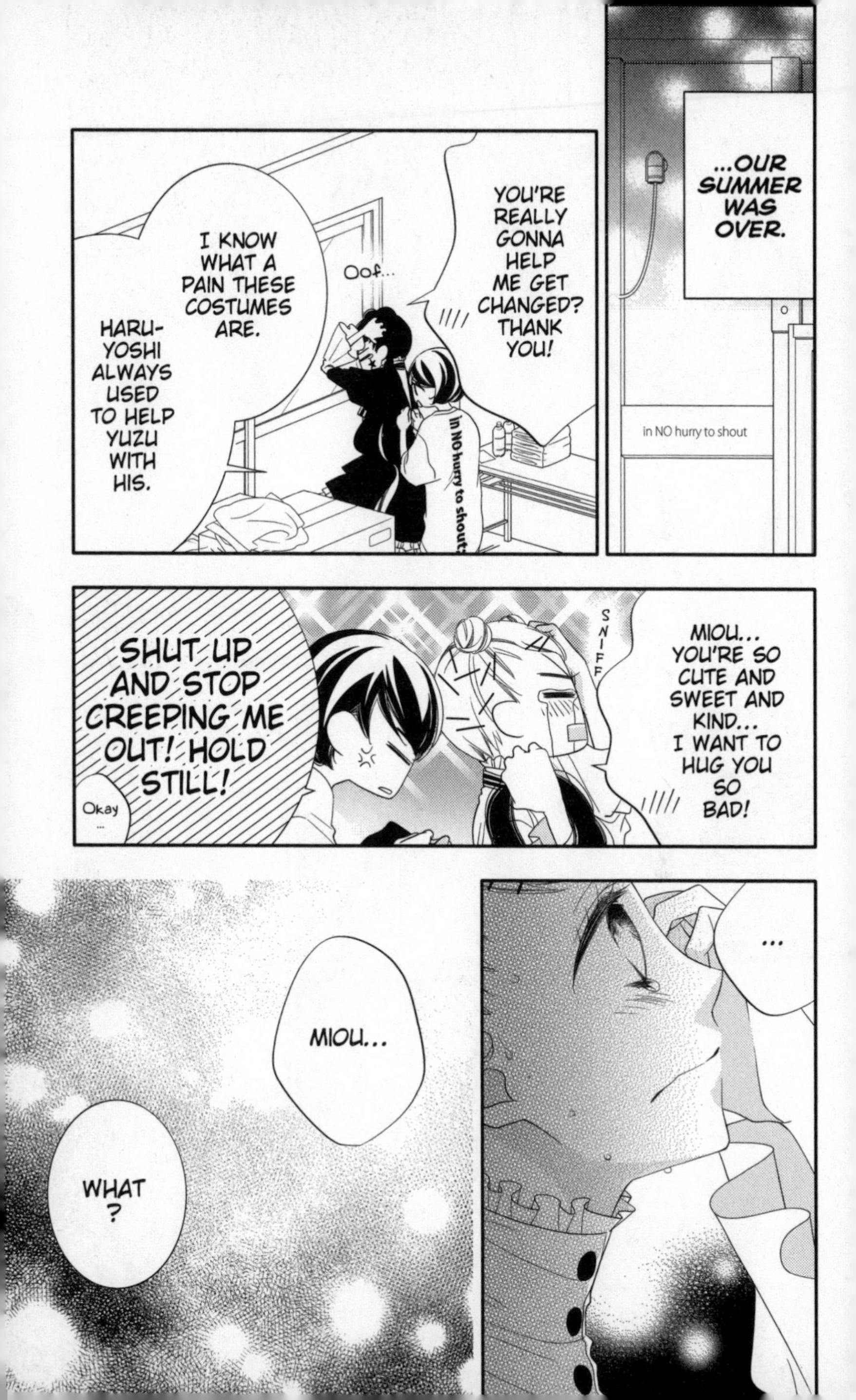
...OUR SUMMER WAS OVER.
in NO hurry to shout
YOU'RE REALLY GONNA HELP ME GET CHANGED? THANK YOU!
Oof...
I KNOW WHAT A PAIN THESE COSTUMES ARE.
HARU-YOSHI ALWAYS USED TO HELP YUZU WITH HIS.
in NO hurry to shout
MIOU... YOU'RE SO CUTE AND SWEET AND KIND... I WANT TO HUG YOU SO BAD!
SNIFF
SHUT UP AND STOP CREEPING ME OUT! HOLD STILL!
Okay ...
...
MIOU...
WHAT?

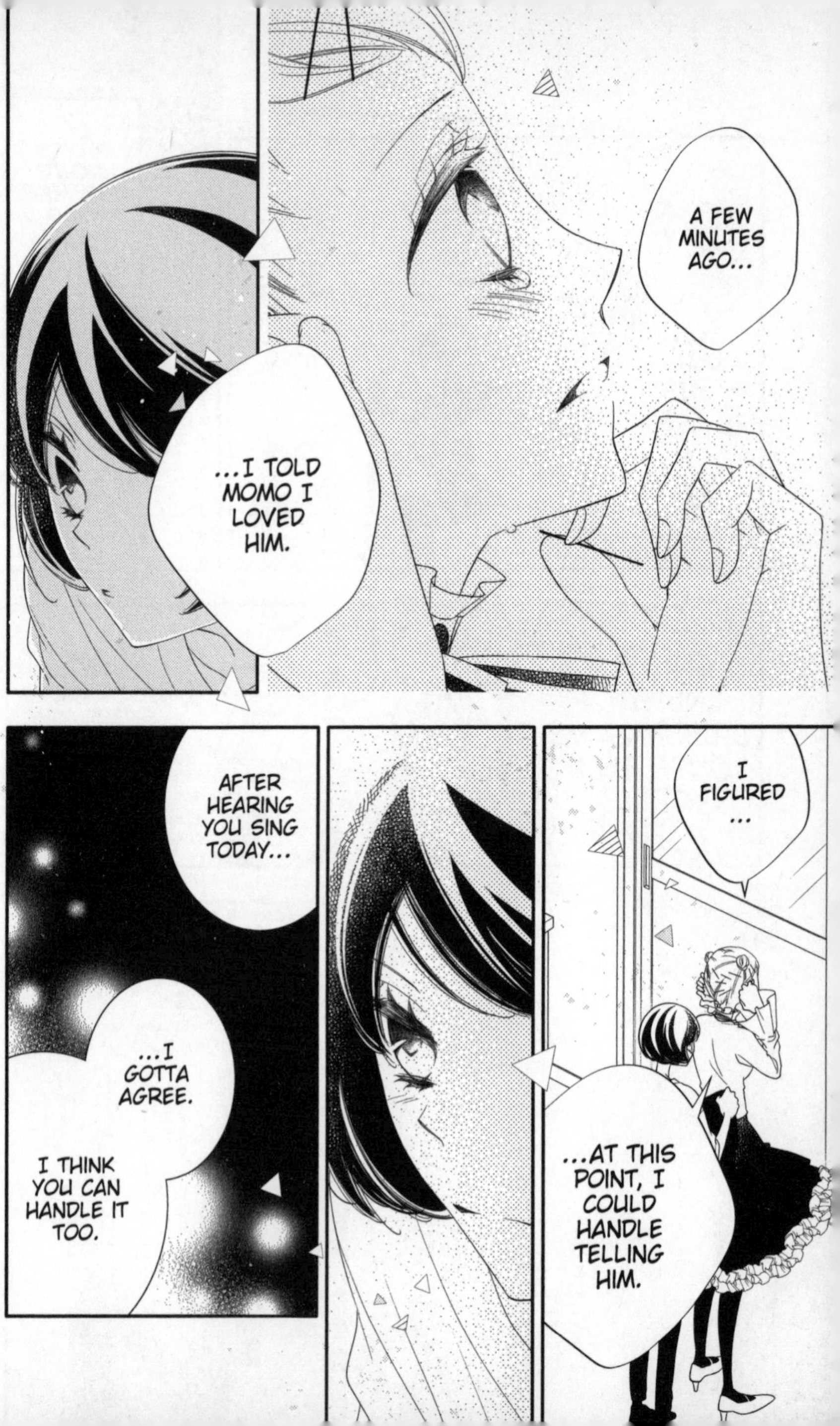
A FEW MINUTES AGO...
...I TOLD MOMO I LOVED HIM.
I FIGURED...
...AT THIS POINT, I COULD HANDLE TELLING HIM.
AFTER HEARING YOU SING TODAY...
...I GOTTA AGREE.
I THINK YOU CAN HANDLE IT TOO.

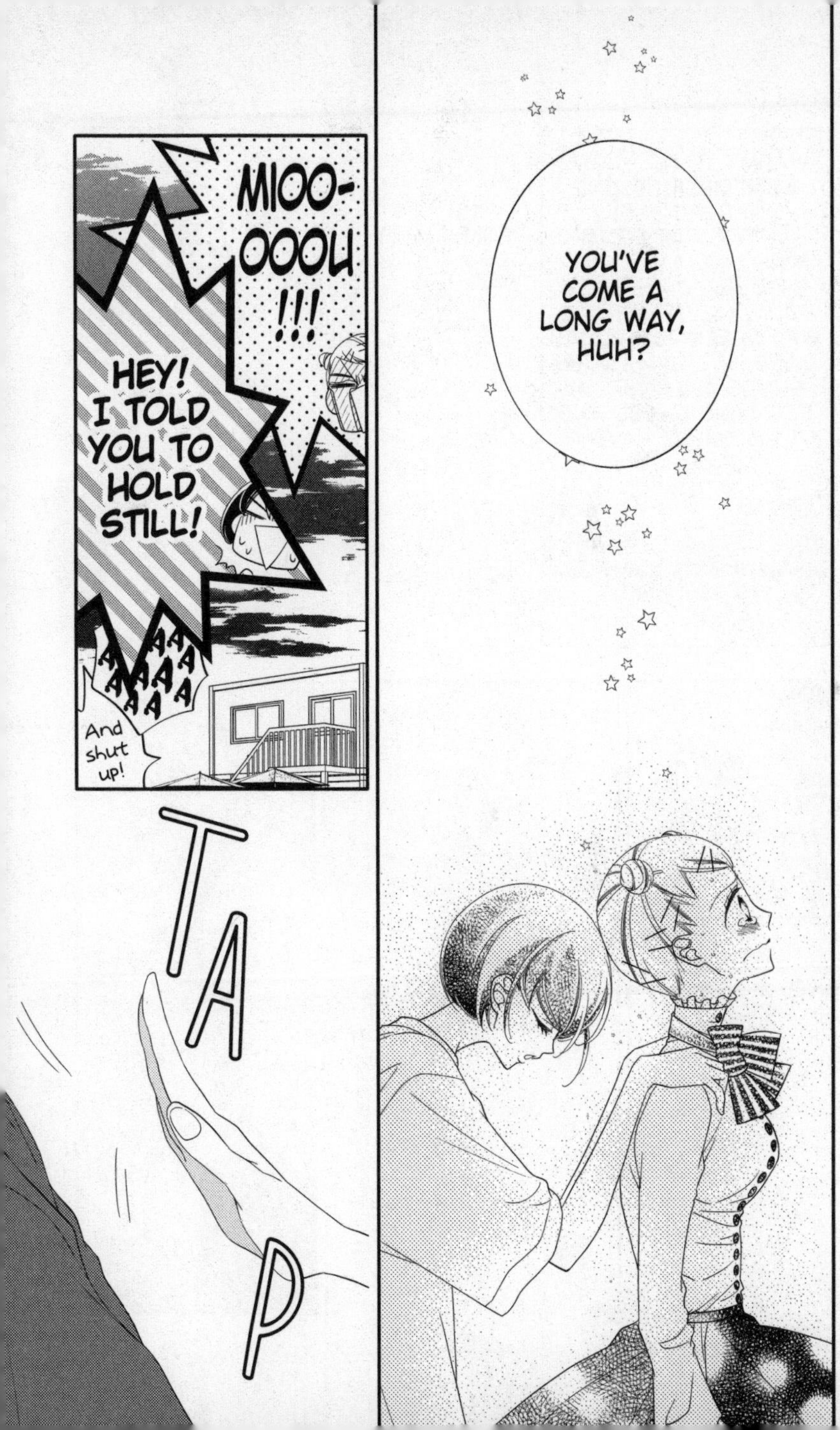
YOU'VE COME A LONG WAY, HUH?
MIOO-OOOU!!!
HEY! I TOLD YOU TO HOLD STILL!
AAAAAAAAAAAAA
And shut up!
TAP

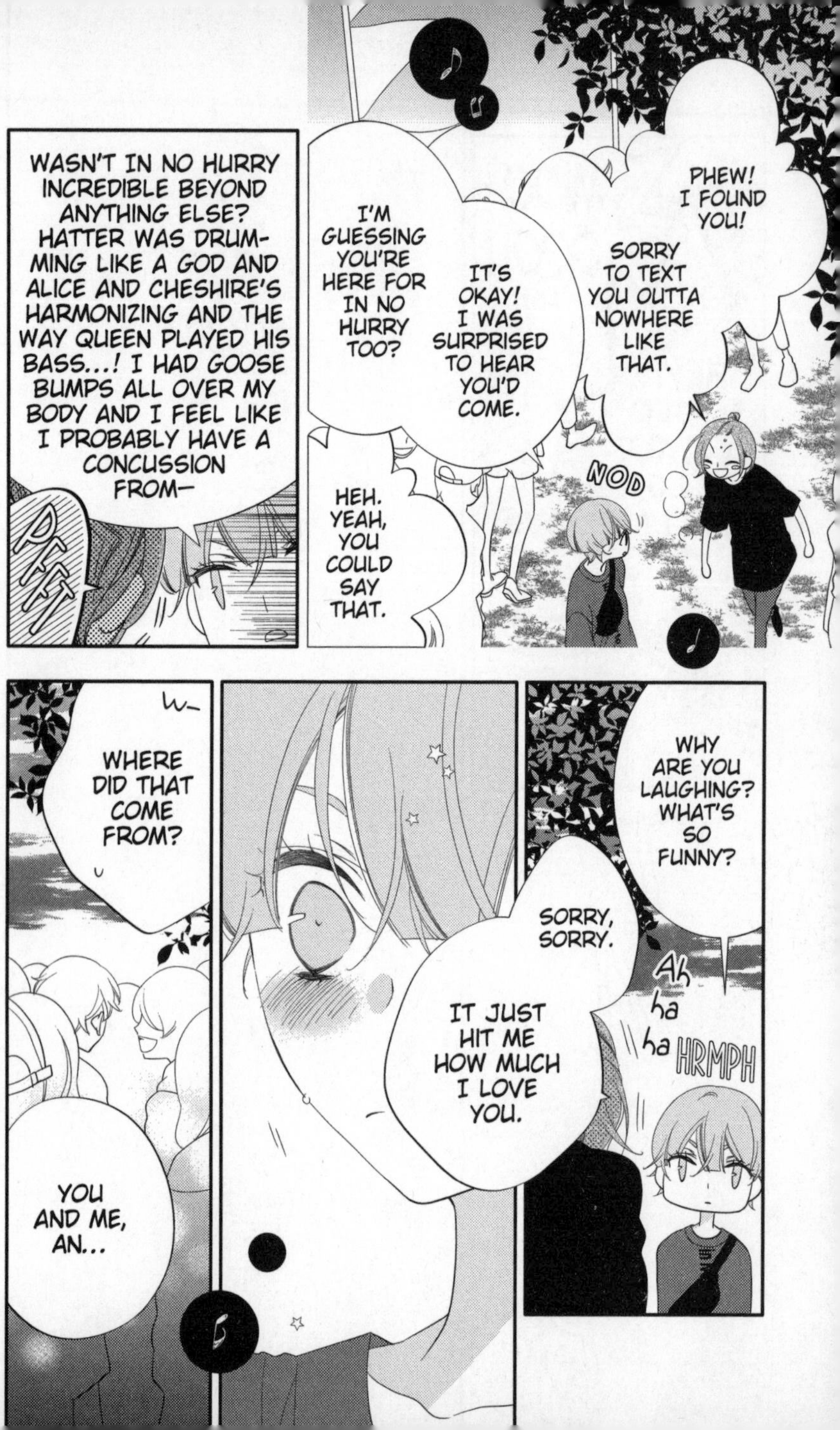
PHEW! I FOUND YOU!
SORRY TO TEXT YOU OUTTA NOWHERE LIKE THAT.
NOD
IT'S OKAY! I WAS SURPRISED TO HEAR YOU'D COME.
I'M GUESSING YOU'RE HERE FOR IN NO HURRY TOO?
HEH. YEAH, YOU COULD SAY THAT.
WASN'T IN NO HURRY INCREDIBLE BEYOND ANYTHING ELSE? HATTER WAS DRUMMING LIKE A GOD AND ALICE AND CHESHIRE'S HARMONIZING AND THE WAY QUEEN PLAYED HIS BASS...! I HAD GOOSE BUMPS ALL OVER MY BODY AND I FEEL LIKE I PROBABLY HAVE A CONCUSSION FROM—
PFFT
WHY ARE YOU LAUGHING? WHAT'S SO FUNNY?
Ah ha ha
HRMPH
SORRY, SORRY.
IT JUST HIT ME HOW MUCH I LOVE YOU.
W—
WHERE DID THAT COME FROM?
YOU AND ME, AN...

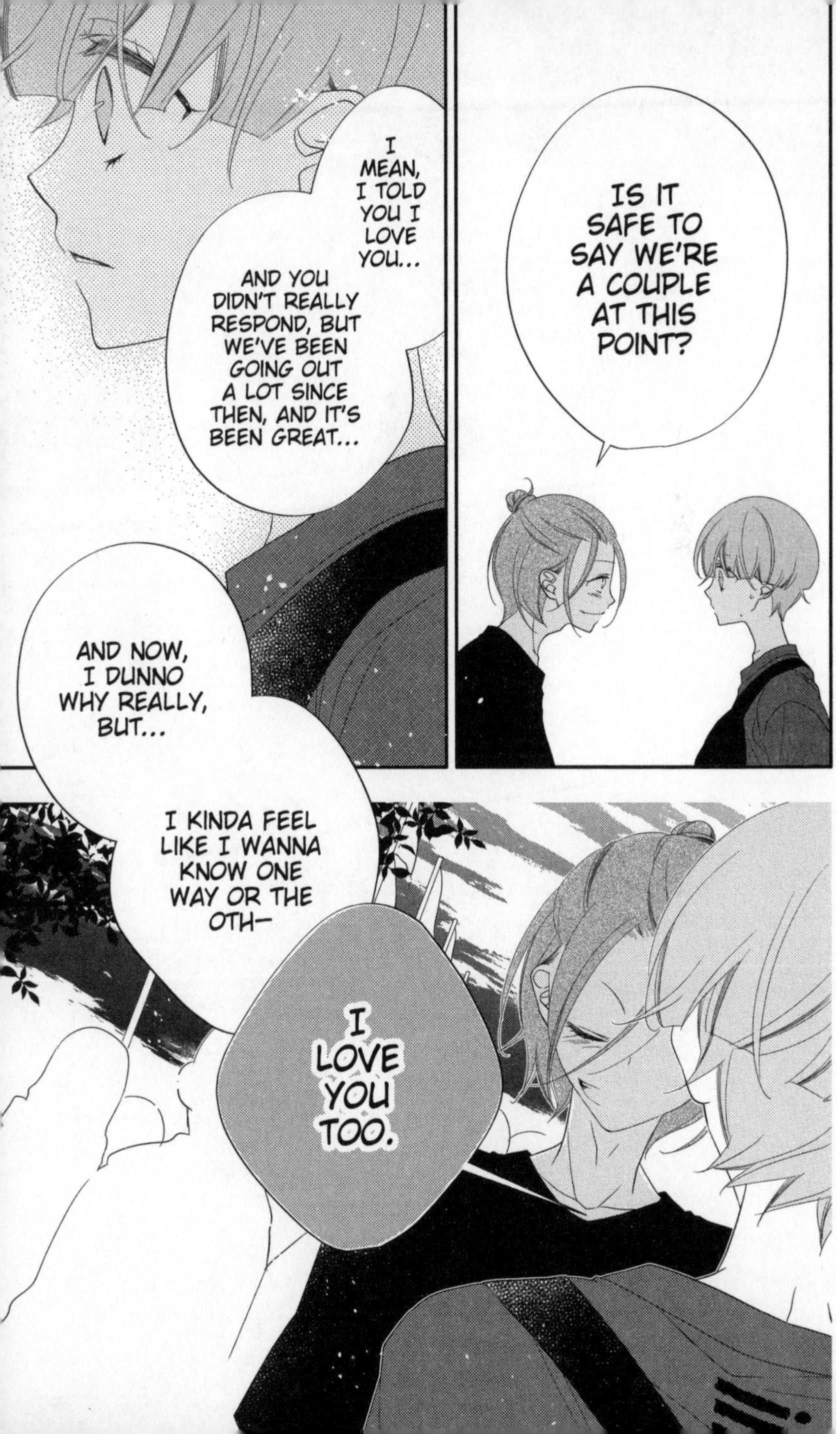
IS IT SAFE TO SAY WE'RE A COUPLE AT THIS POINT?
I MEAN, I TOLD YOU I LOVE YOU...
AND YOU DIDN'T REALLY RESPOND, BUT WE'VE BEEN GOING OUT A LOT SINCE THEN, AND IT'S BEEN GREAT...
AND NOW, I DUNNO WHY REALLY, BUT...
I KINDA FEEL LIKE I WANNA KNOW ONE WAY OR THE OTH—
I LOVE YOU TOO.

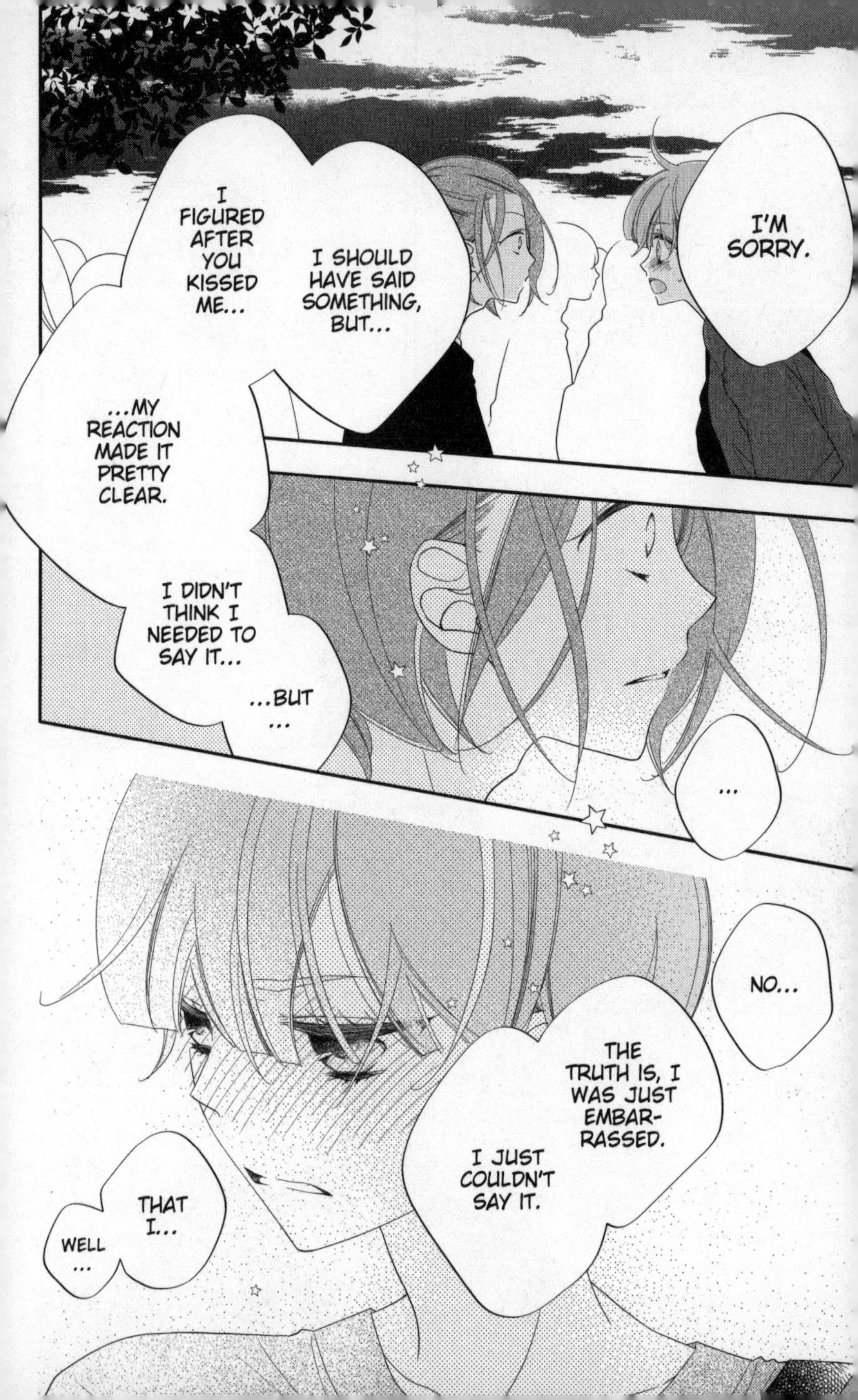
I'M SORRY.
I SHOULD HAVE SAID SOMETHING, BUT...
I FIGURED AFTER YOU KISSED ME...
...MY REACTION MADE IT PRETTY CLEAR.
I DIDN'T THINK I NEEDED TO SAY IT...
...BUT ...
...
NO...
THE TRUTH IS, I WAS JUST EMBARRASSED.
I JUST COULDN'T SAY IT.
THAT I...
WELL ...

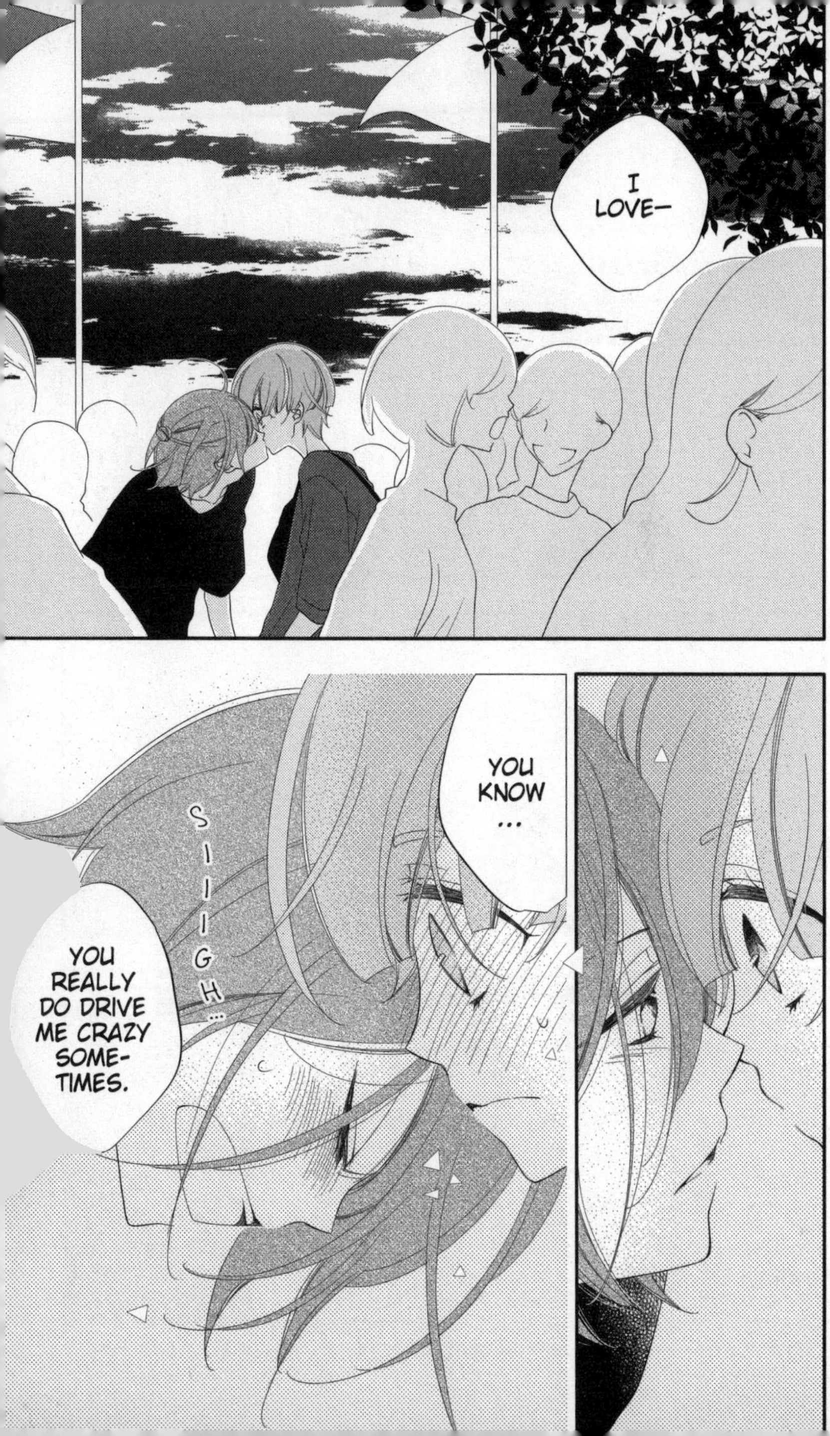
I LOVE—
YOU KNOW...
SIIIGH...
YOU REALLY DO DRIVE ME CRAZY SOME-TIMES.

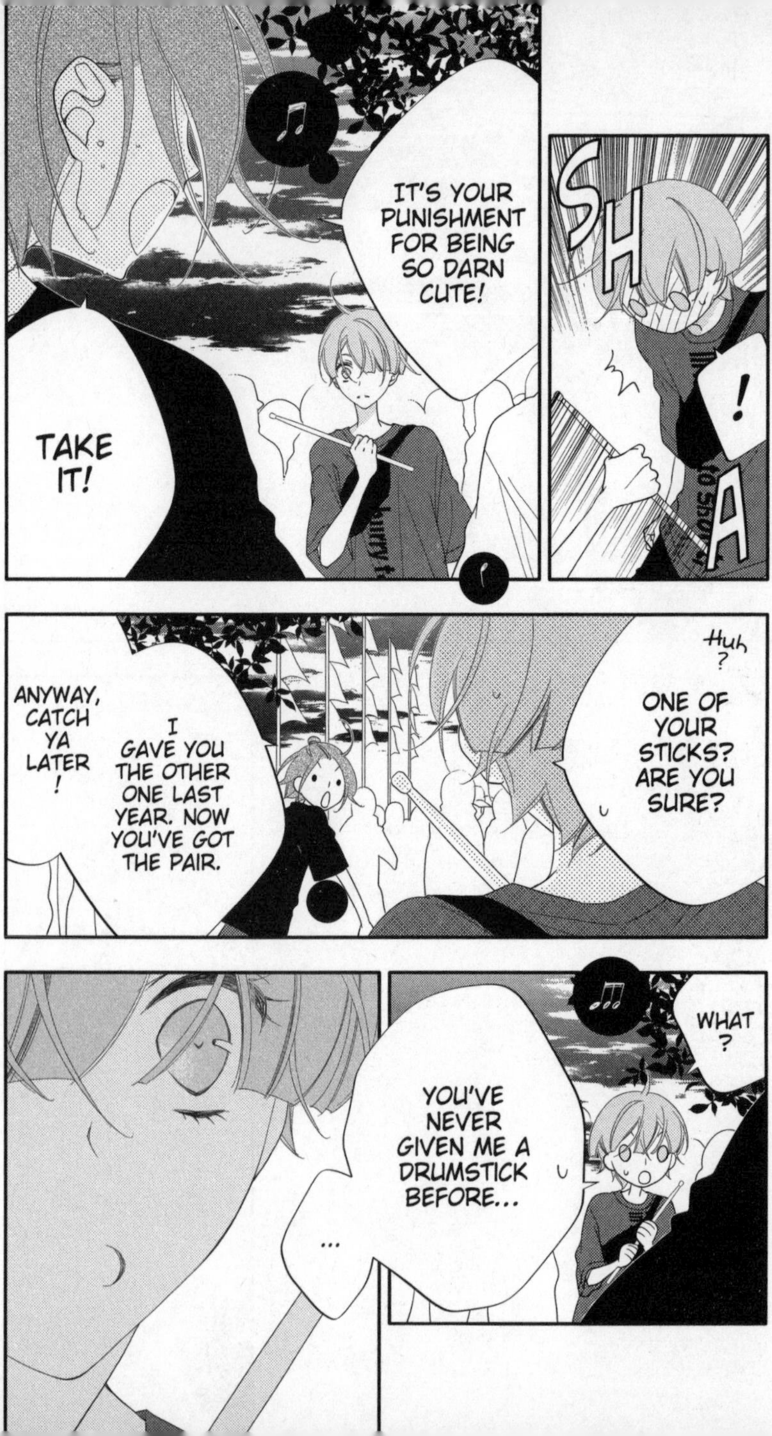
SHA
!
IT'S YOUR PUNISHMENT FOR BEING SO DARN CUTE!
TAKE IT!
Huh?
ONE OF YOUR STICKS? ARE YOU SURE?
I GAVE YOU THE OTHER ONE LAST YEAR. NOW YOU'VE GOT THE PAIR.
ANYWAY, CATCH YA LATER!
WHAT?
YOU'VE NEVER GIVEN ME A DRUMSTICK BEFORE...
...

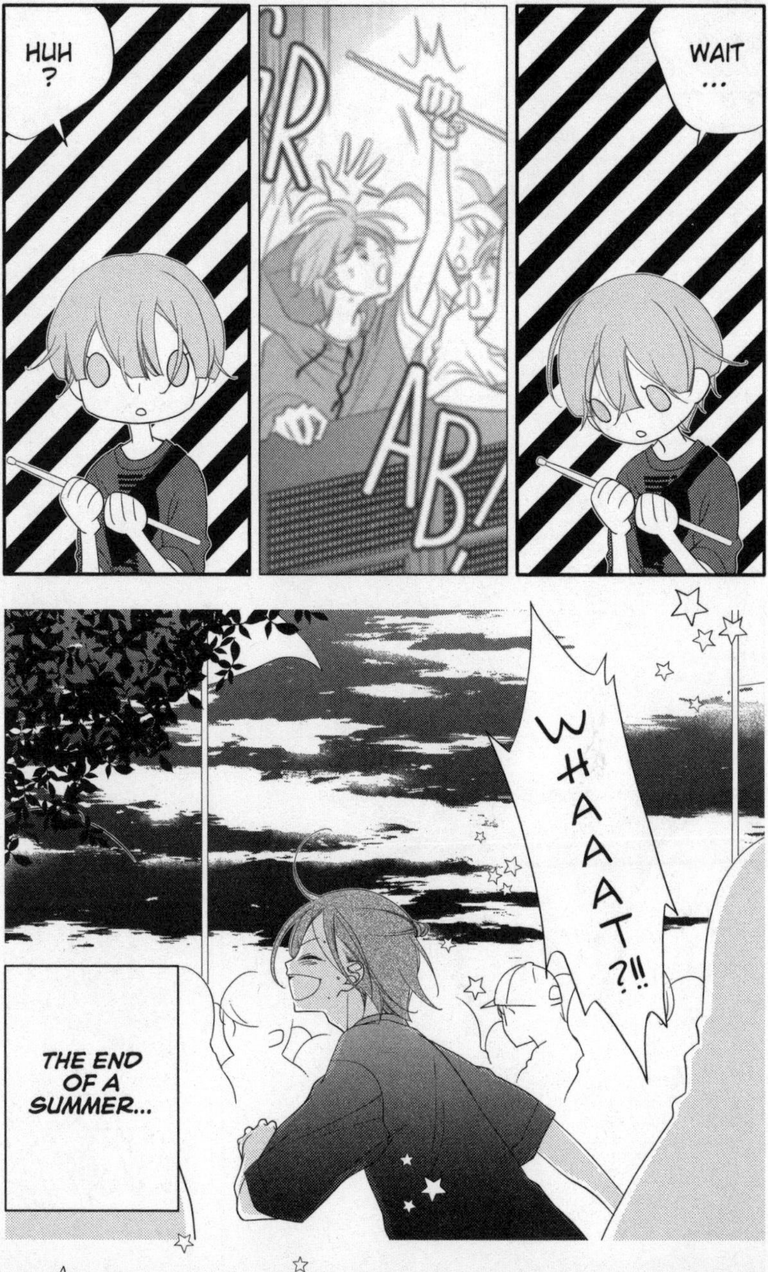
WAIT ...
HUH ?
WHAAAT?!!
THE END OF A SUMMER...

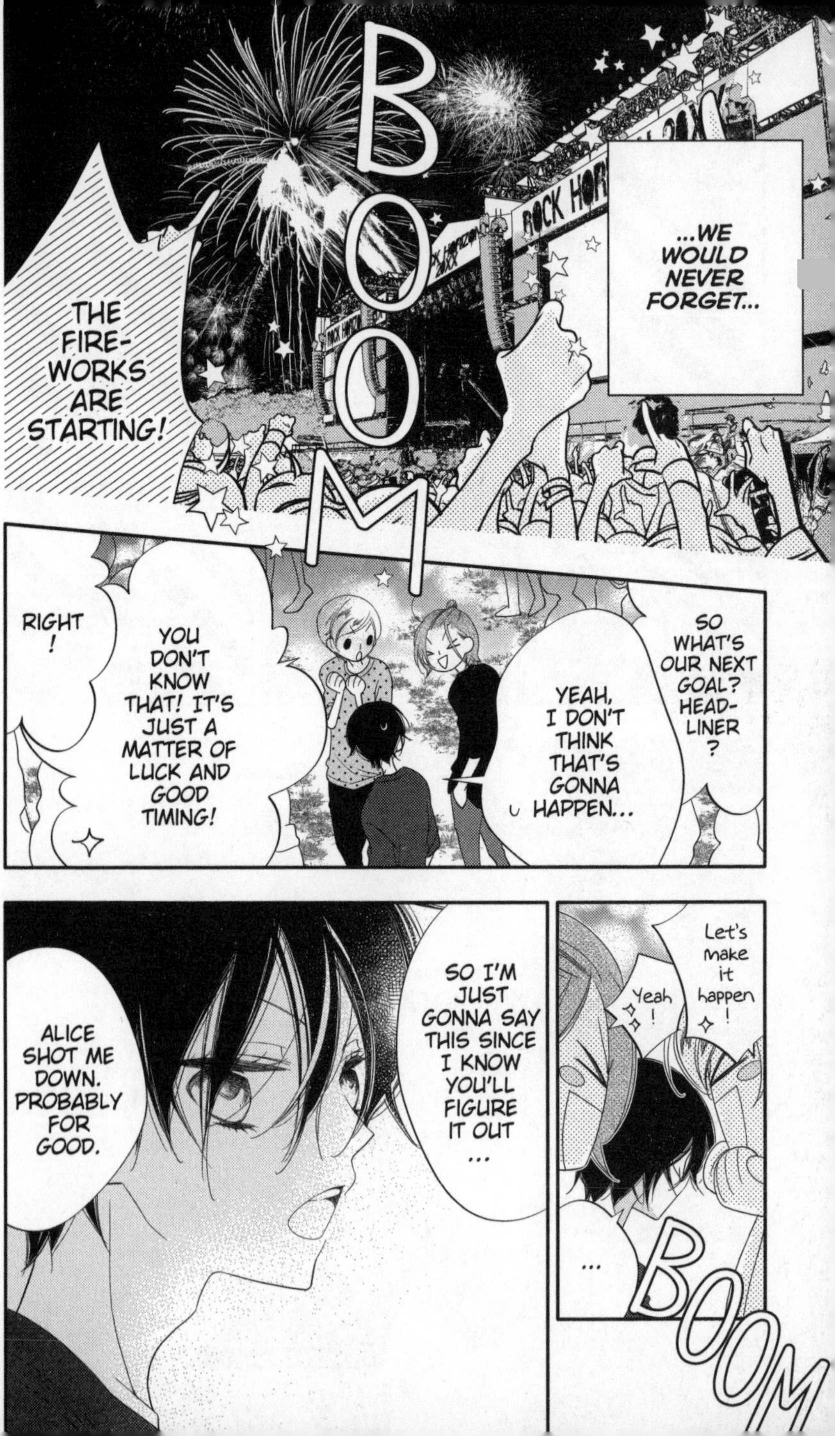
...WE WOULD NEVER FORGET...
BOOM
THE FIRE-WORKS ARE STARTING!
SO WHAT'S OUR NEXT GOAL? HEAD-LINER?
YEAH, I DON'T THINK THAT'S GONNA HAPPEN...
YOU DON'T KNOW THAT! IT'S JUST A MATTER OF LUCK AND GOOD TIMING!
RIGHT!
Let's make it happen!
Yeah!
...
BOOM
SO I'M JUST GONNA SAY THIS SINCE I KNOW YOU'LL FIGURE IT OUT...
ALICE SHOT ME DOWN. PROBABLY FOR GOOD.

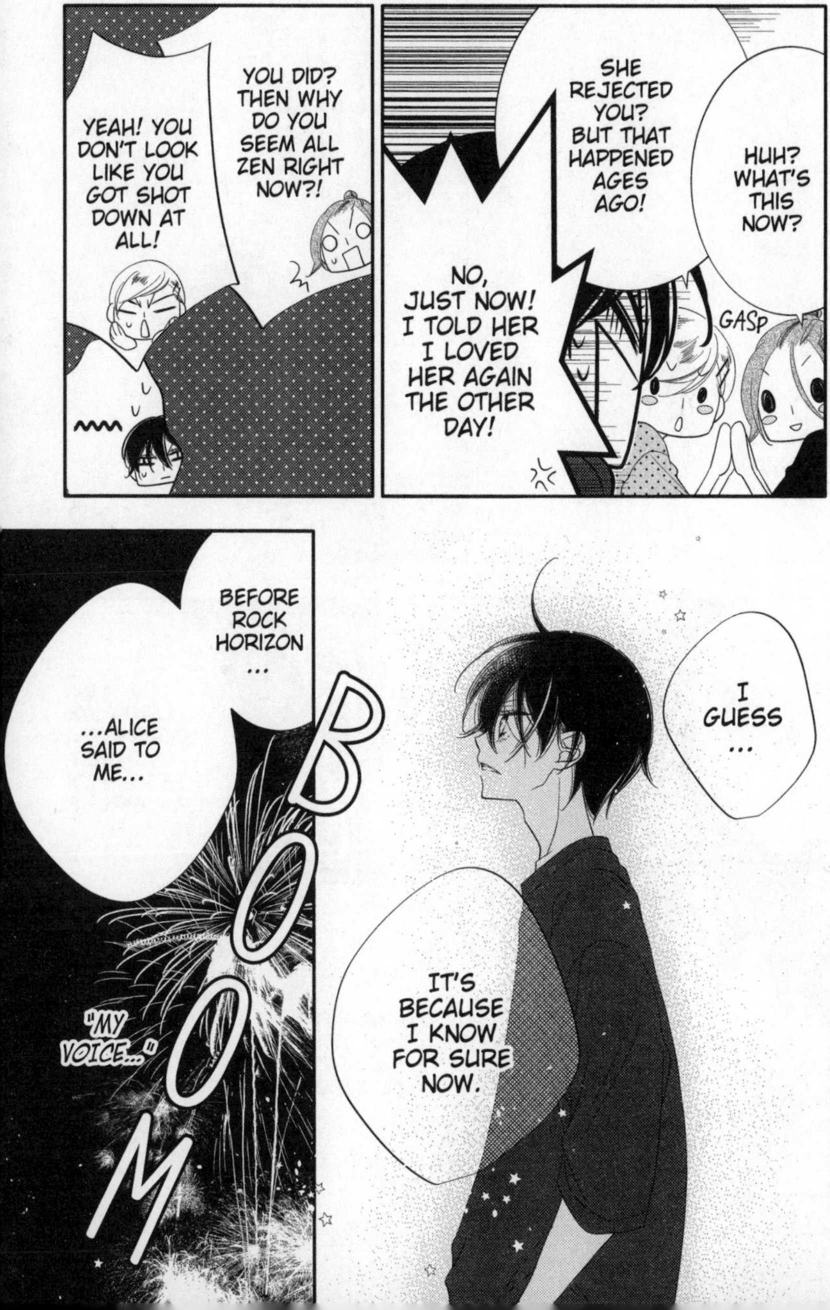
HUH? WHAT'S THIS NOW?
SHE REJECTED YOU? BUT THAT HAPPENED AGES AGO!
GASp
NO, JUST NOW! I TOLD HER I LOVED HER AGAIN THE OTHER DAY!
YOU DID? THEN WHY DO YOU SEEM ALL ZEN RIGHT NOW?!
YEAH! YOU DON'T LOOK LIKE YOU GOT SHOT DOWN AT ALL!
I GUESS...
IT'S BECAUSE I KNOW FOR SURE NOW.
BEFORE ROCK HORIZON...
...ALICE SAID TO ME...
"MY VOICE..."
BOOOM

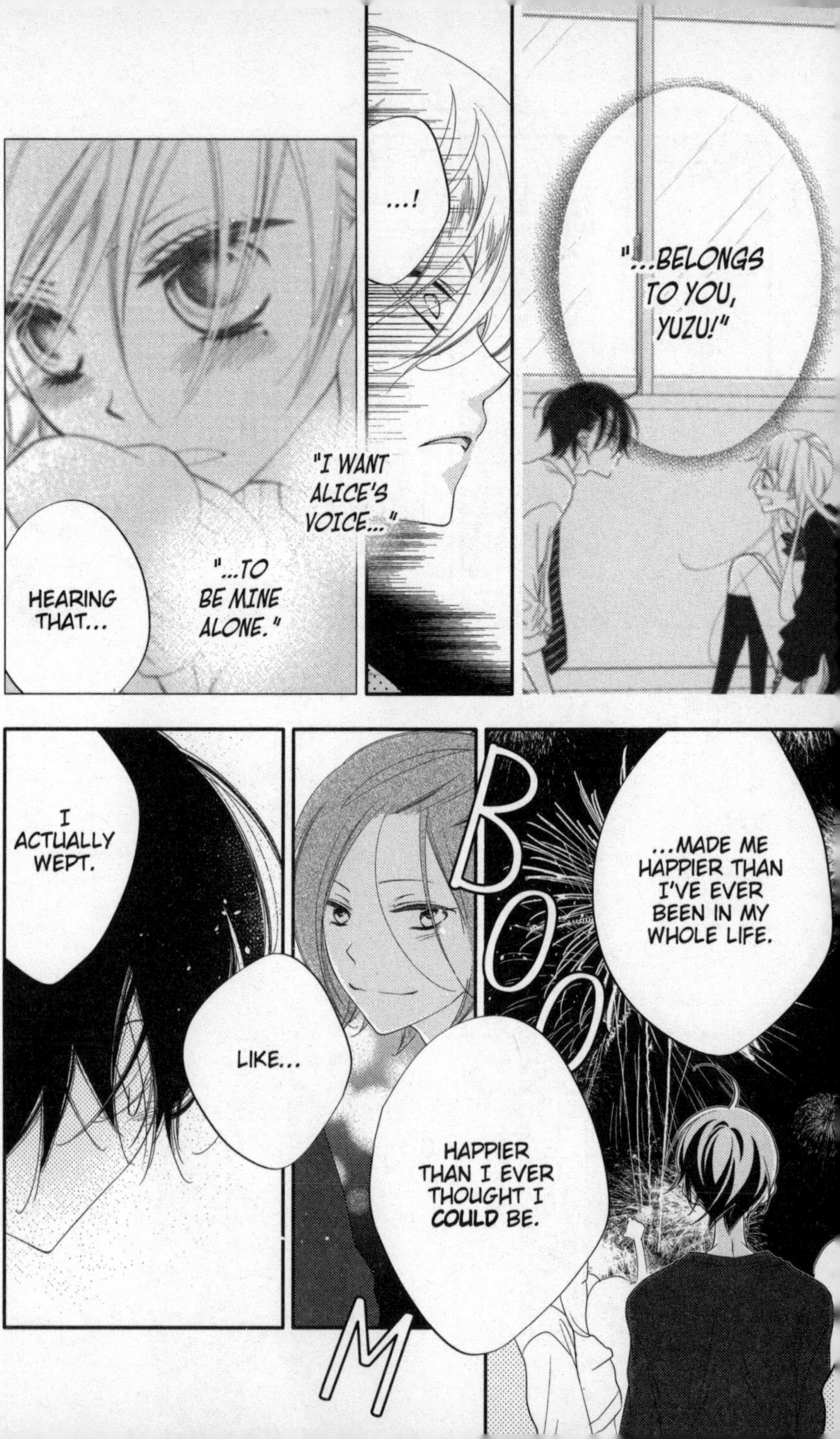
"...BELONGS TO YOU, YUZU!"
...!
"I WANT ALICE'S VOICE..."
"...TO BE MINE ALONE."
HEARING THAT...
...MADE ME HAPPIER THAN I'VE EVER BEEN IN MY WHOLE LIFE.
BOOM
HAPPIER THAN I EVER THOUGHT I COULD BE.
LIKE...
I ACTUALLY WEPT.

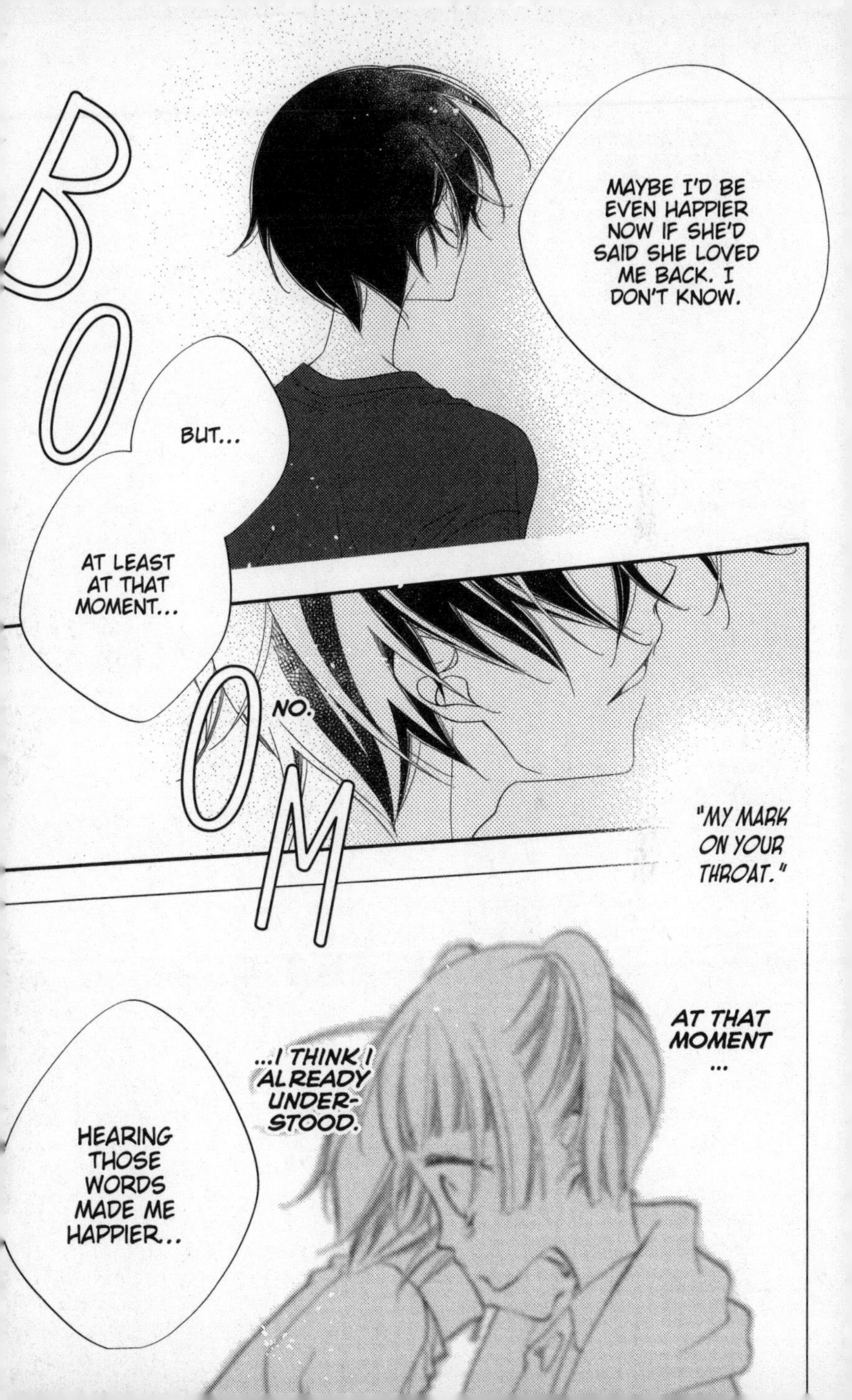
MAYBE I'D BE EVEN HAPPIER NOW IF SHE'D SAID SHE LOVED ME BACK. I DON'T KNOW.
BOOM
BUT...
AT LEAST AT THAT MOMENT...
NO.
"MY MARK ON YOUR THROAT."
AT THAT MOMENT ...
HEARING THOSE WORDS MADE ME HAPPIER...
...I THINK I ALREADY UNDER-STOOD.

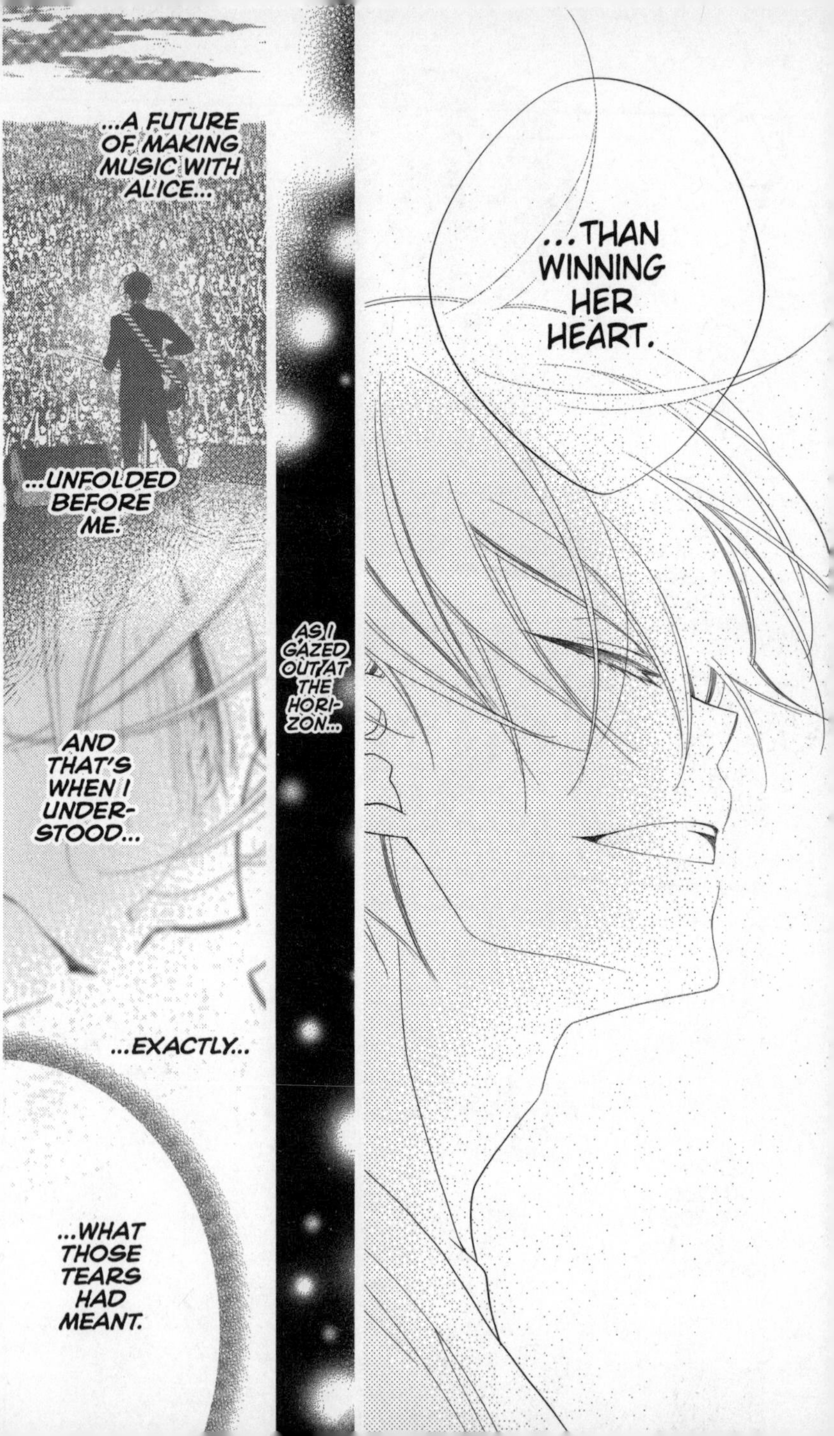
...THAN WINNING HER HEART.
AS I GAZED OUT AT THE HORIZON...
...A FUTURE OF MAKING MUSIC WITH ALICE...
...UNFOLDED BEFORE ME.
AND THAT'S WHEN I UNDERSTOOD...
...EXACTLY...
...WHAT THOSE TEARS HAD MEANT.

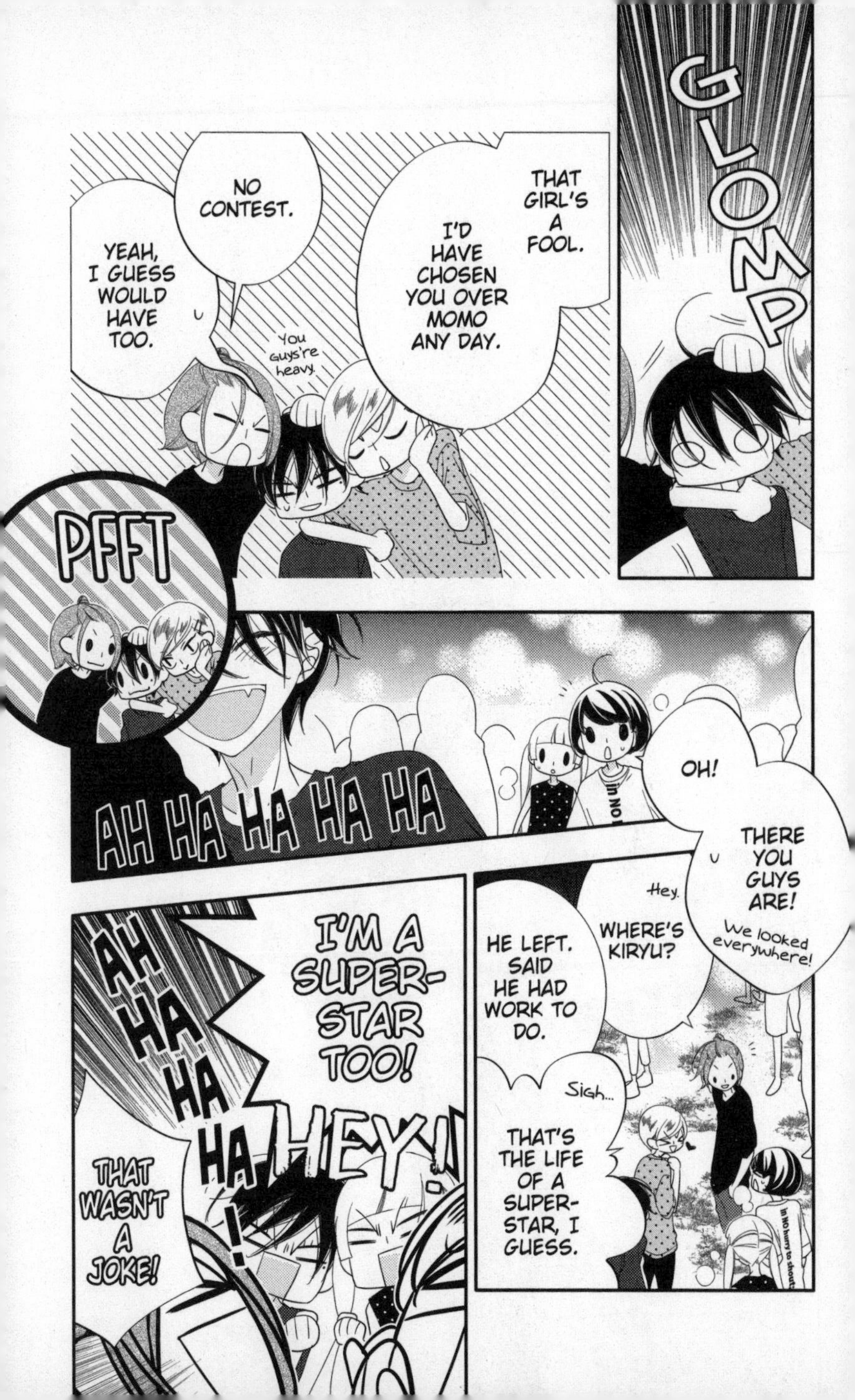
GLOMP
THAT GIRL'S A FOOL.
I'D HAVE CHOSEN YOU OVER MOMO ANY DAY.
You guys're heavy.
NO CONTEST.
YEAH, I GUESS WOULD HAVE TOO.
PFFT
AH HA HA HA HA
OH!
THERE YOU GUYS ARE!
We looked everywhere!
Hey.
WHERE'S KIRYU?
HE LEFT. SAID HE HAD WORK TO DO.
Sigh...
THAT'S THE LIFE OF A SUPER-STAR, I GUESS.
In NO hurry to shout
I'M A SUPER-STAR TOO!
AH HA HA HA HA
HEY!!
THAT WASN'T A JOKE!

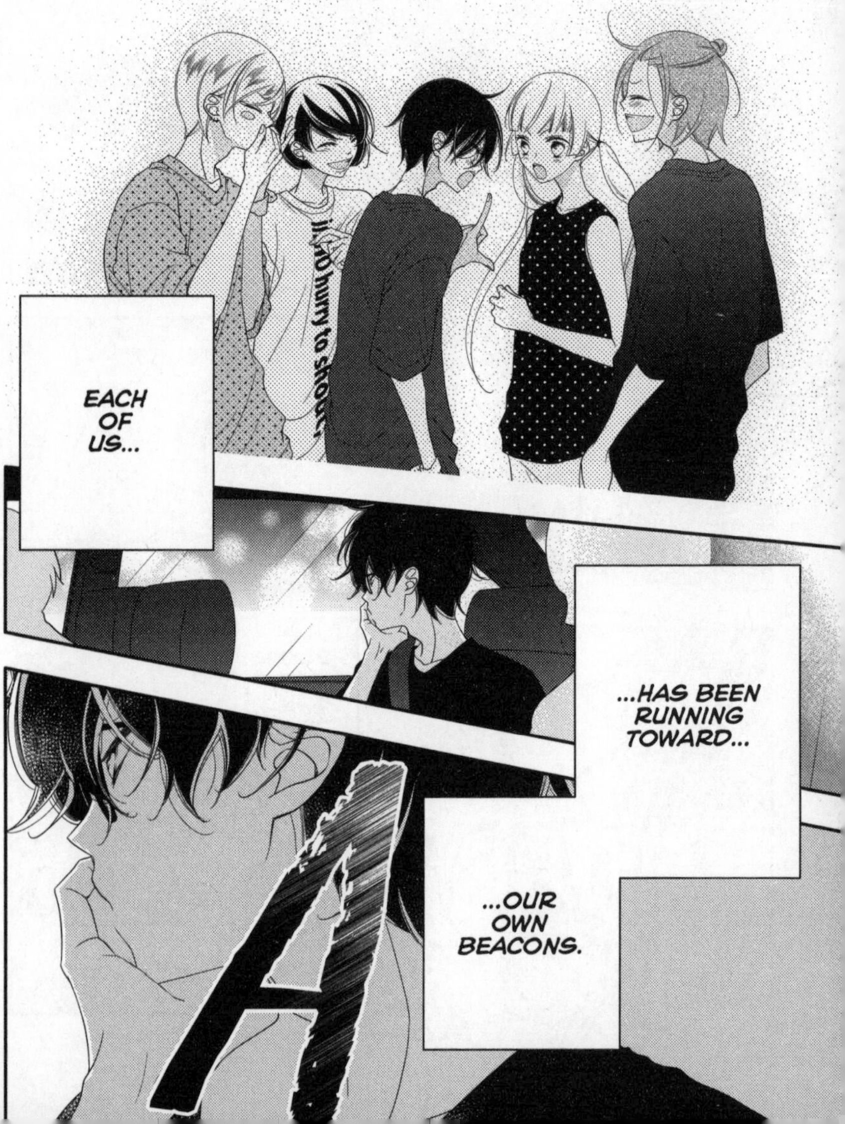
EACH OF US...
...HAS BEEN RUNNING TOWARD...
...OUR OWN BEACONS.

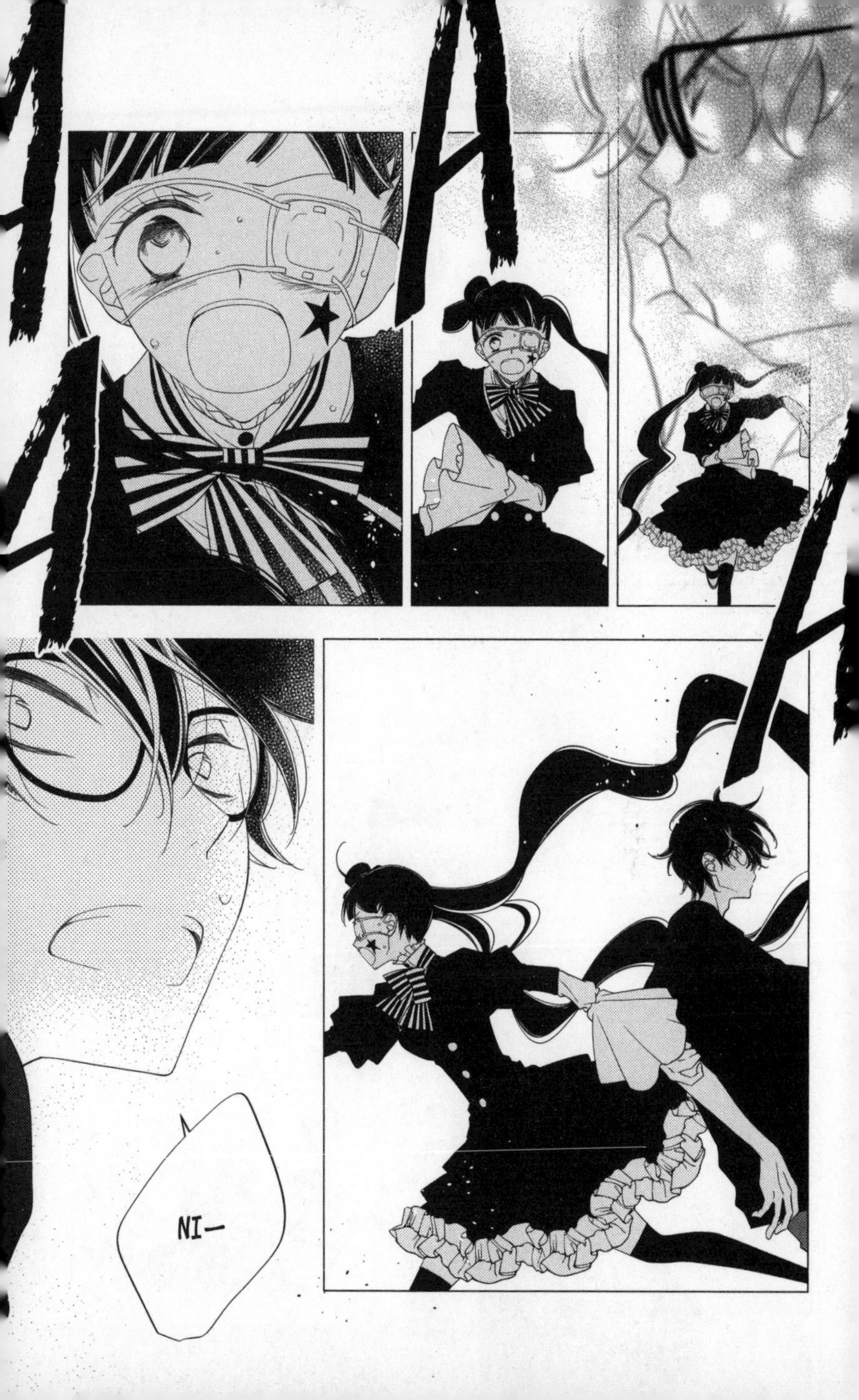
NI—

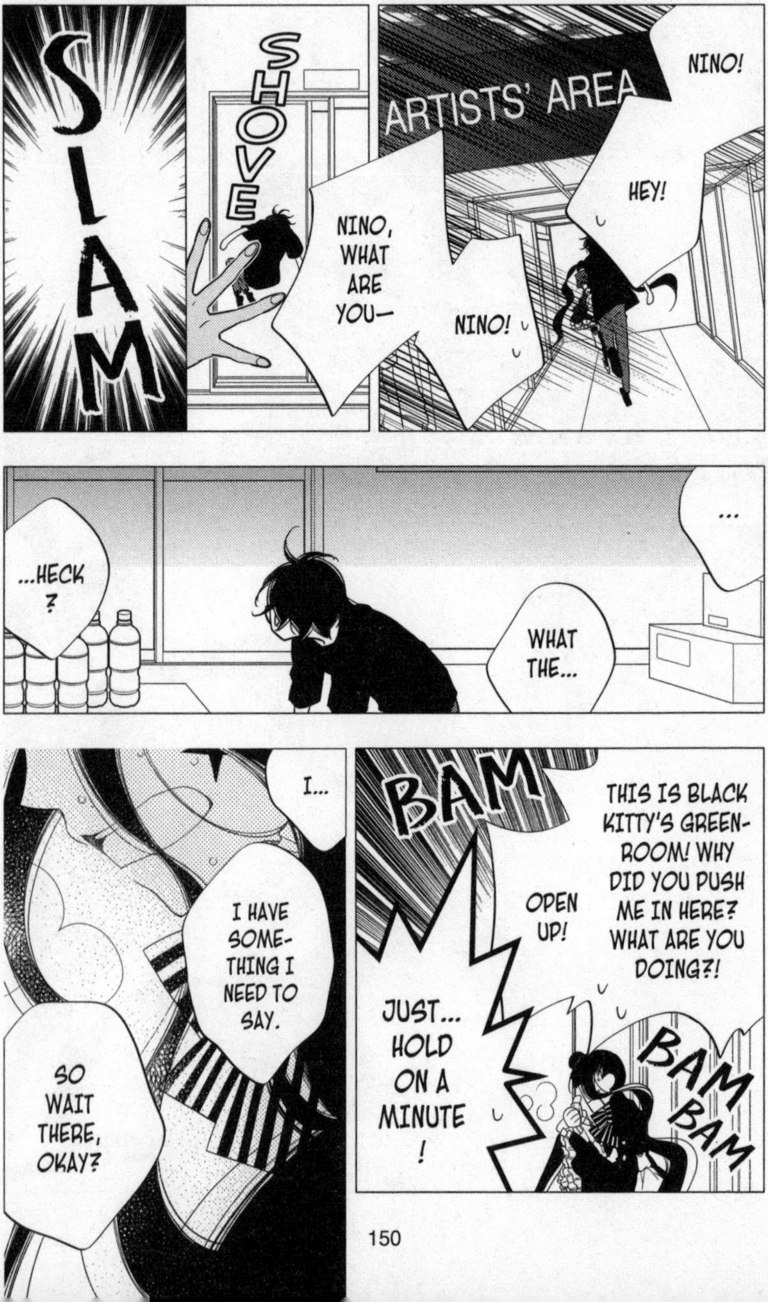
NINO!
ARTISTS' AREA
HEY!
NINO, WHAT ARE YOU—
NINO!
SHOVE
SLAM
...
WHAT THE...
...HECK?
THIS IS BLACK KITTY'S GREEN-ROOM! WHY DID YOU PUSH ME IN HERE? WHAT ARE YOU DOING?!
BAM
OPEN UP!
BAM BAM
JUST... HOLD ON A MINUTE!
I...
I HAVE SOME-THING I NEED TO SAY.
SO WAIT THERE, OKAY?

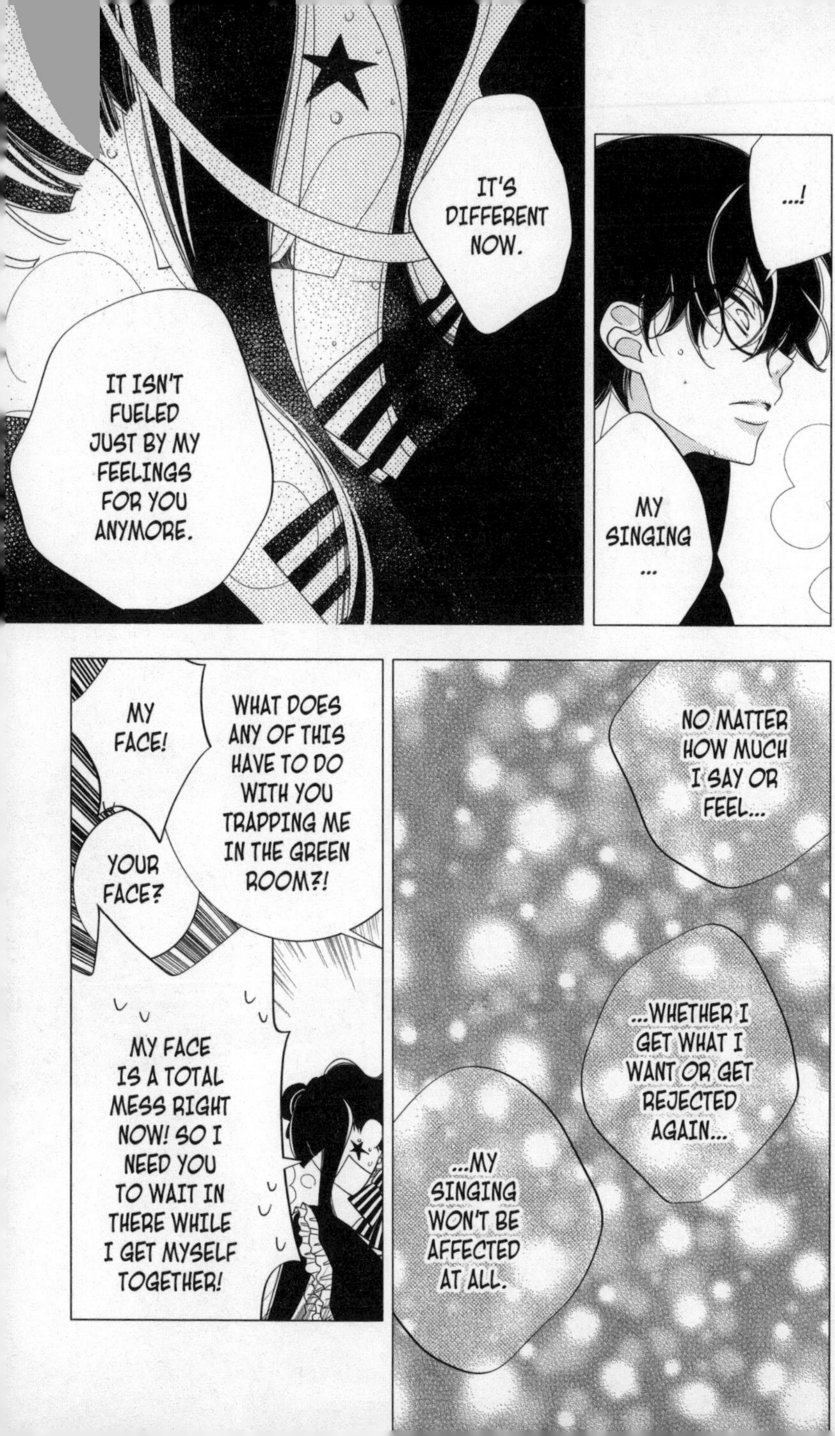
...!
MY SINGING ...
IT'S DIFFERENT NOW.
IT ISN'T FUELED JUST BY MY FEELINGS FOR YOU ANYMORE.
NO MATTER HOW MUCH I SAY OR FEEL...
...WHETHER I GET WHAT I WANT OR GET REJECTED AGAIN...
...MY SINGING WON'T BE AFFECTED AT ALL.
WHAT DOES ANY OF THIS HAVE TO DO WITH YOU TRAPPING ME IN THE GREEN ROOM?!
MY FACE!
YOUR FACE?
MY FACE IS A TOTAL MESS RIGHT NOW! SO I NEED YOU TO WAIT IN THERE WHILE I GET MYSELF TOGETHER!

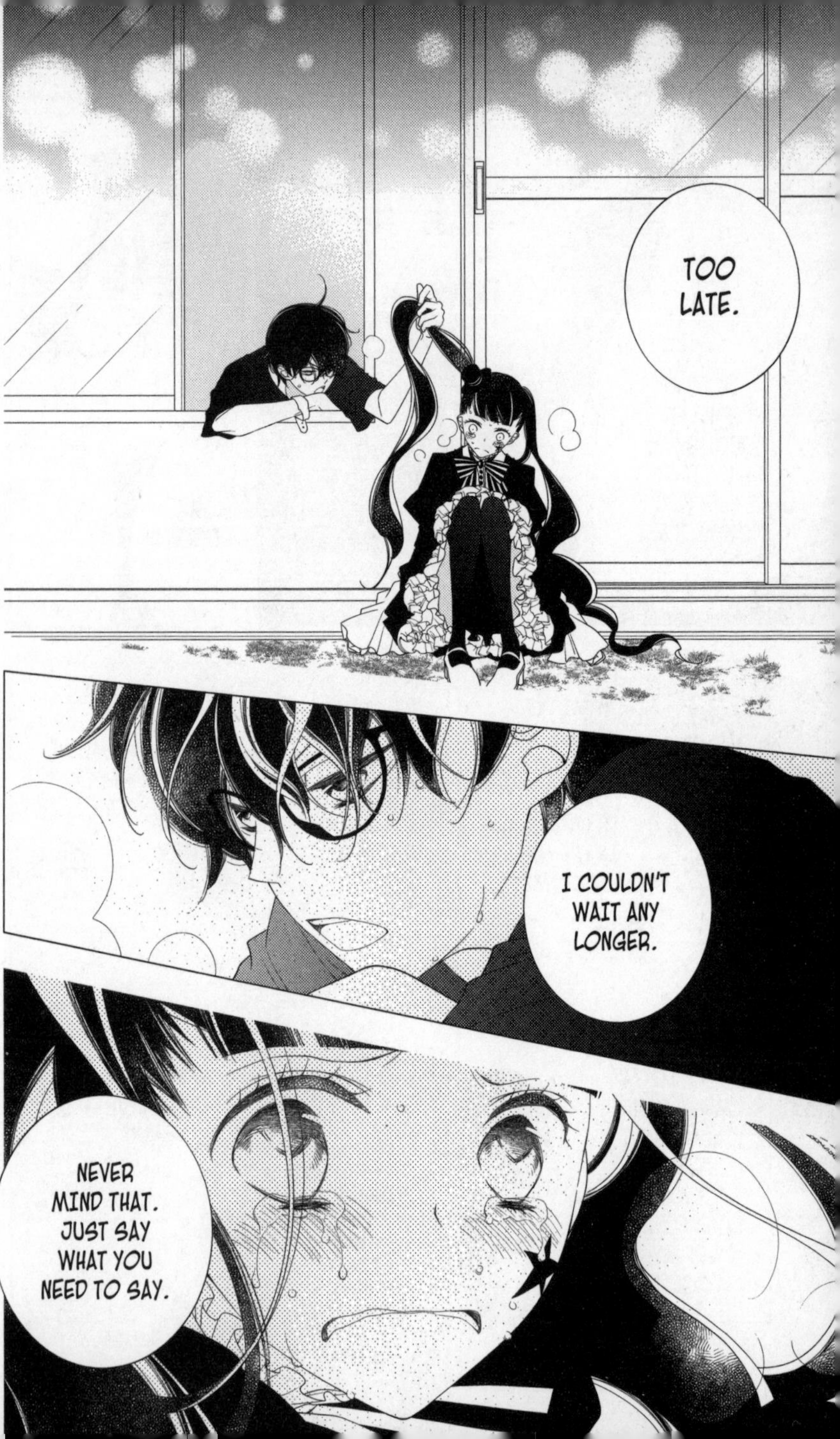
TOO LATE.
I COULDN'T WAIT ANY LONGER.
NEVER MIND THAT. JUST SAY WHAT YOU NEED TO SAY.

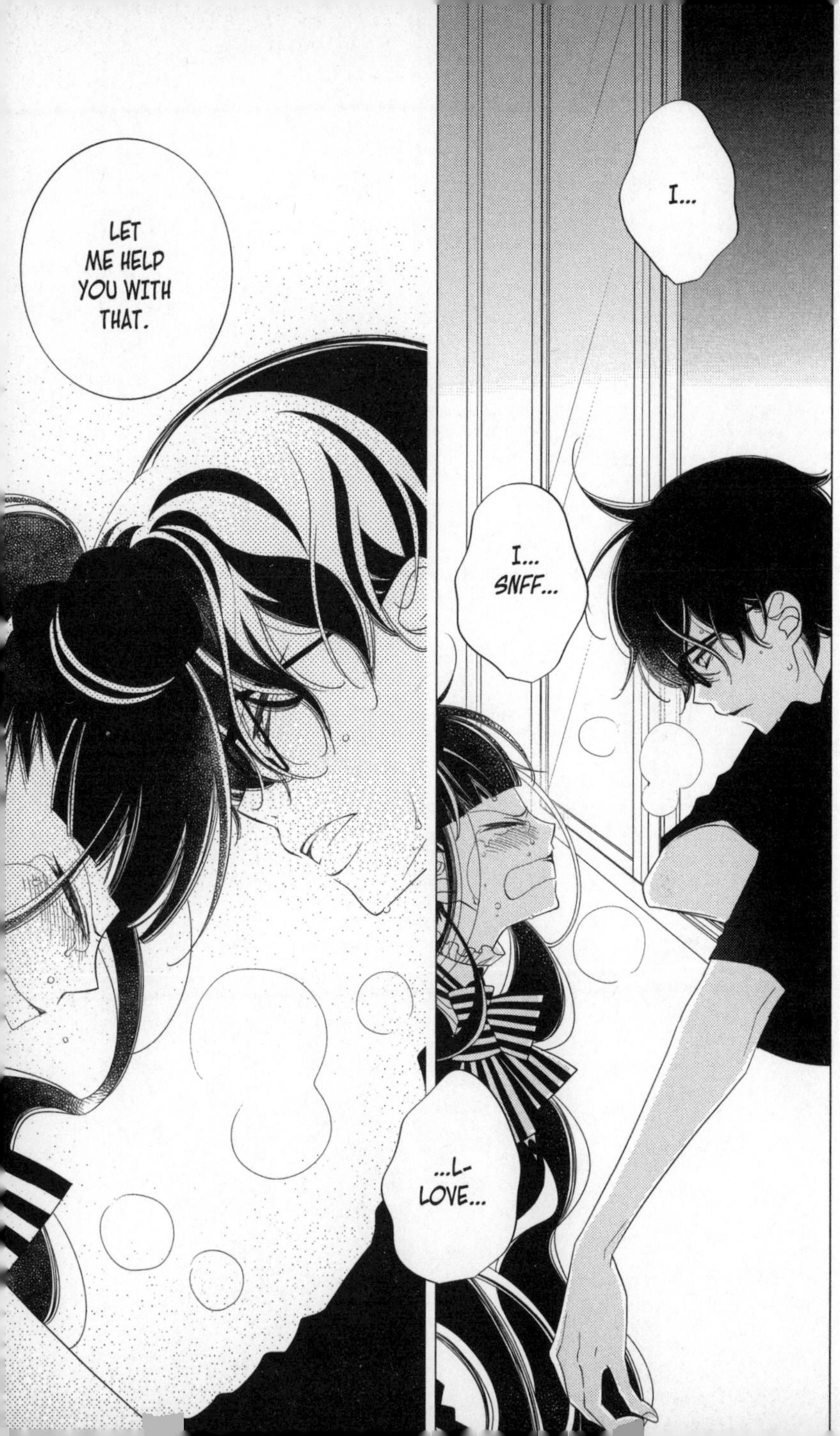
I...
I... SNFF...
...L-LOVE...
LET ME HELP YOU WITH THAT.

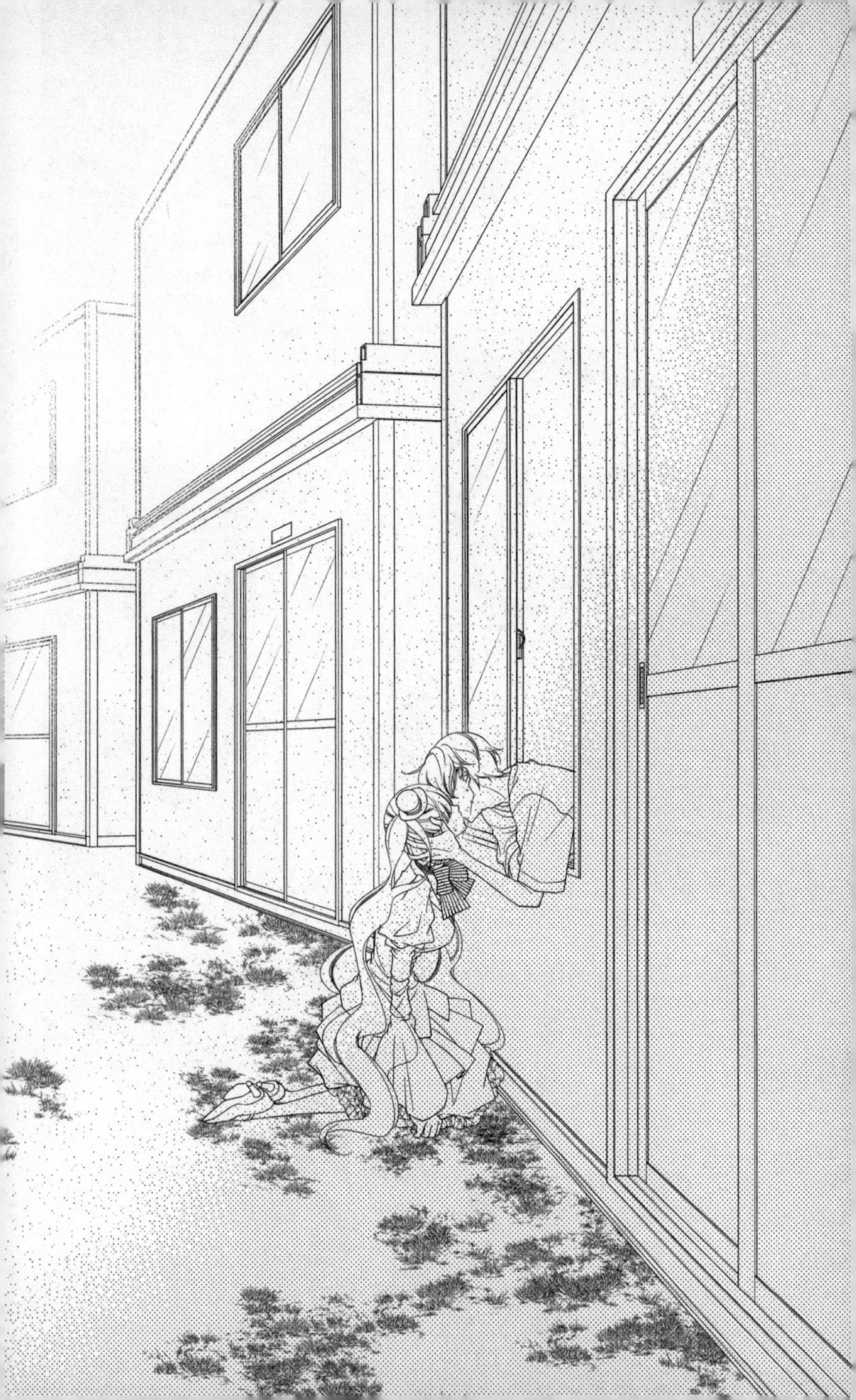

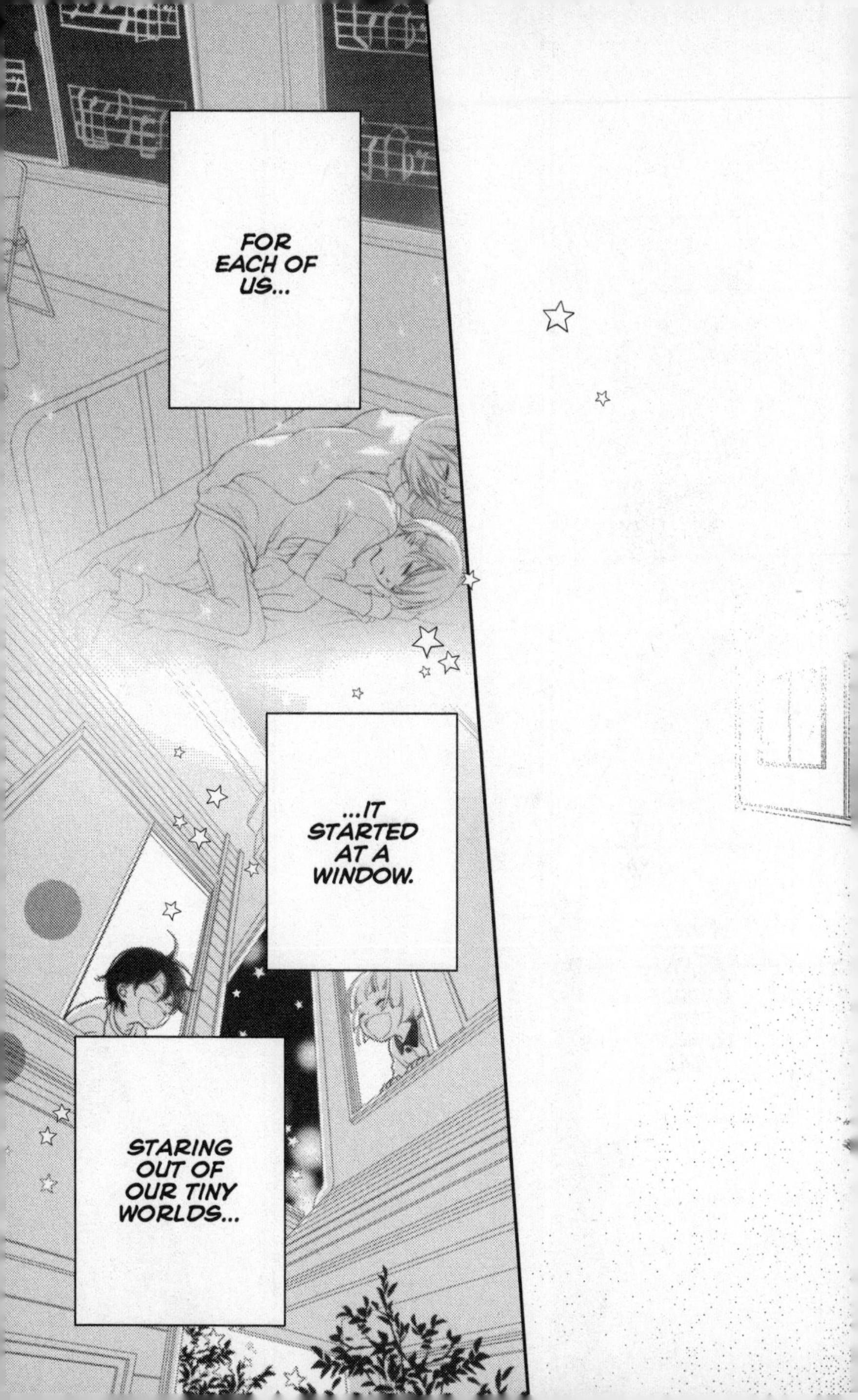
FOR EACH OF US...
...IT STARTED AT A WINDOW.
STARING OUT OF OUR TINY WORLDS...

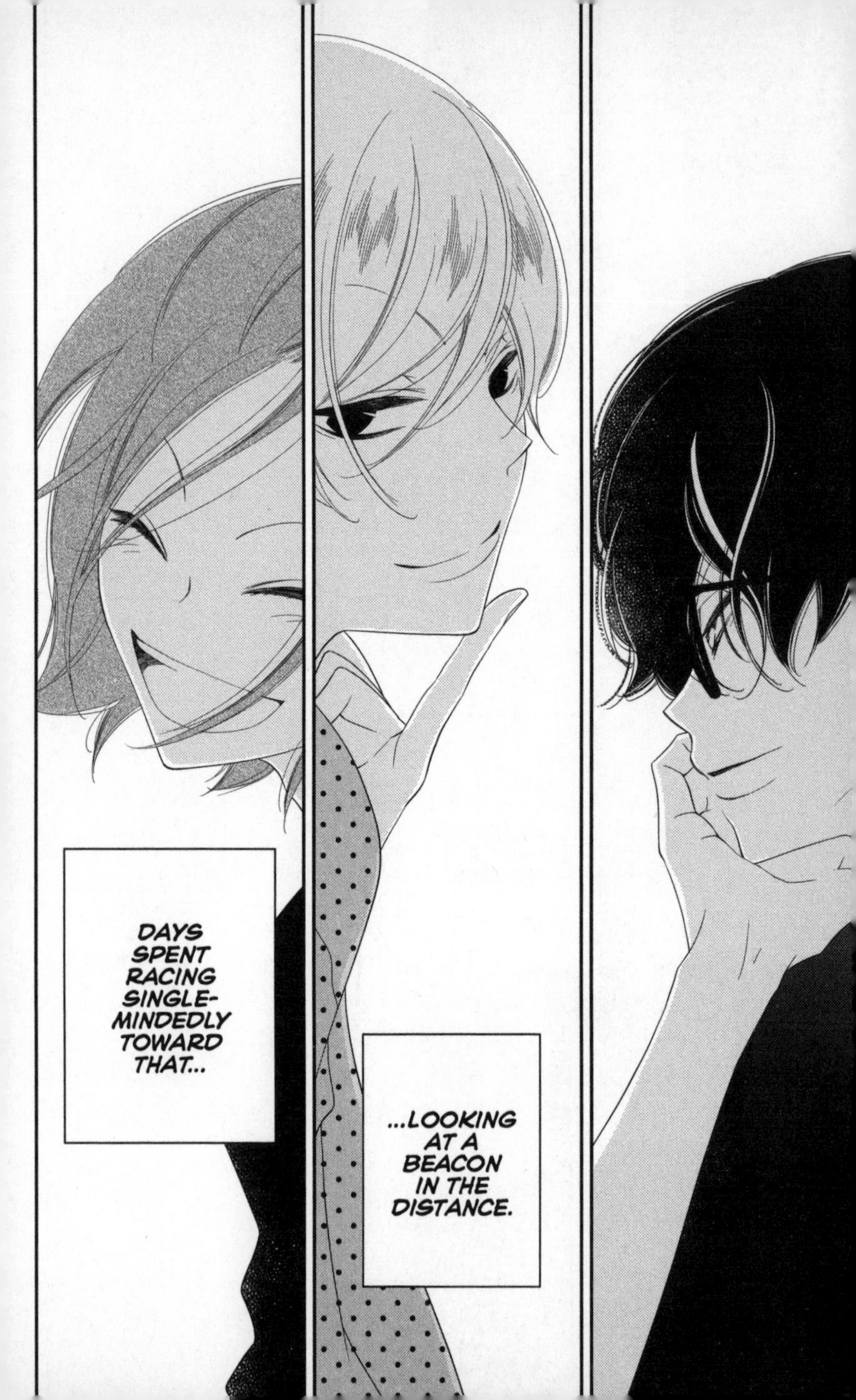
DAYS SPENT RACING SINGLE-MINDEDLY TOWARD THAT...
...LOOKING AT A BEACON IN THE DISTANCE.

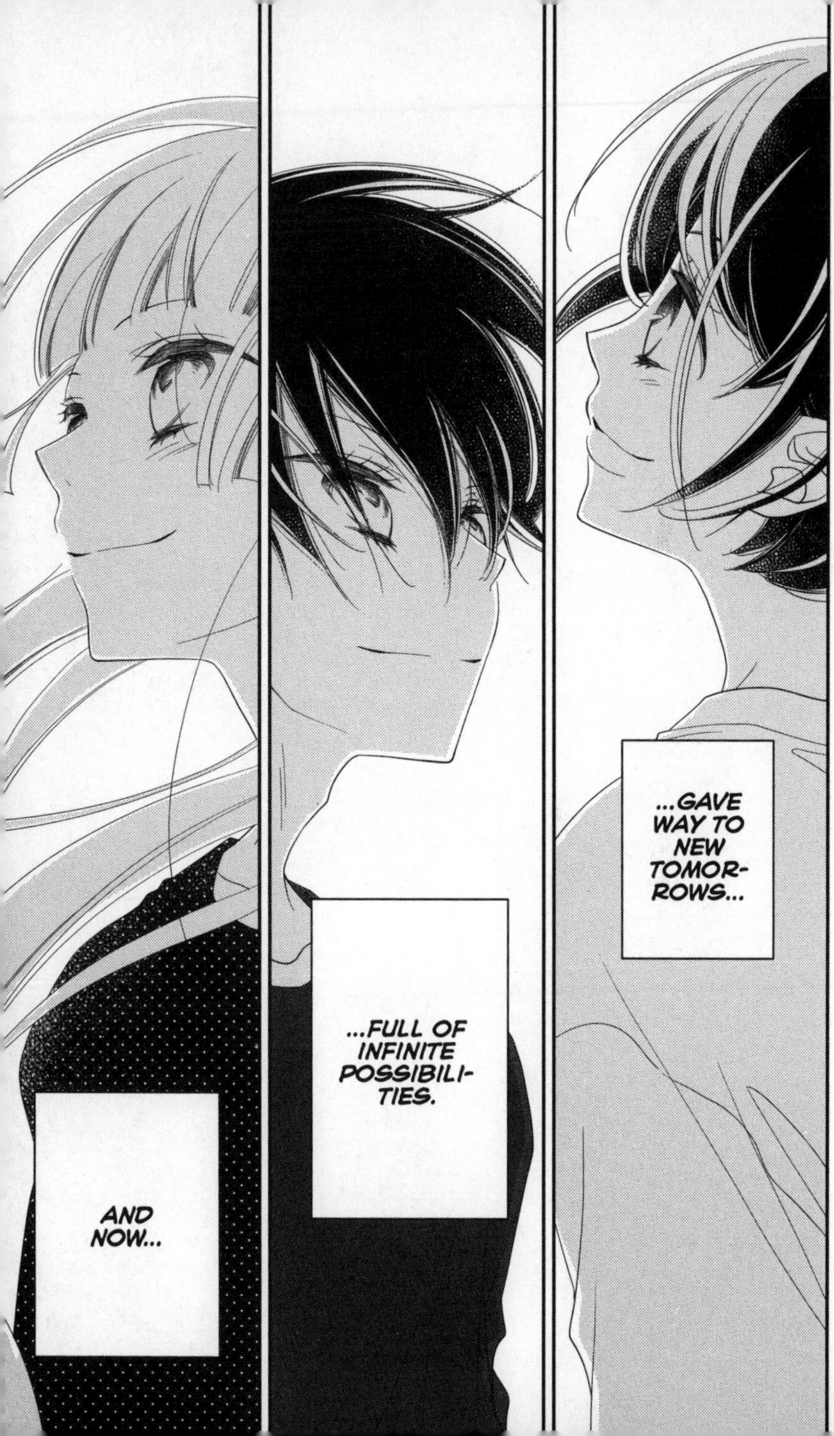
...GAVE WAY TO NEW TOMOR-ROWS...
...FULL OF INFINITE POSSIBILI-TIES.
AND NOW...

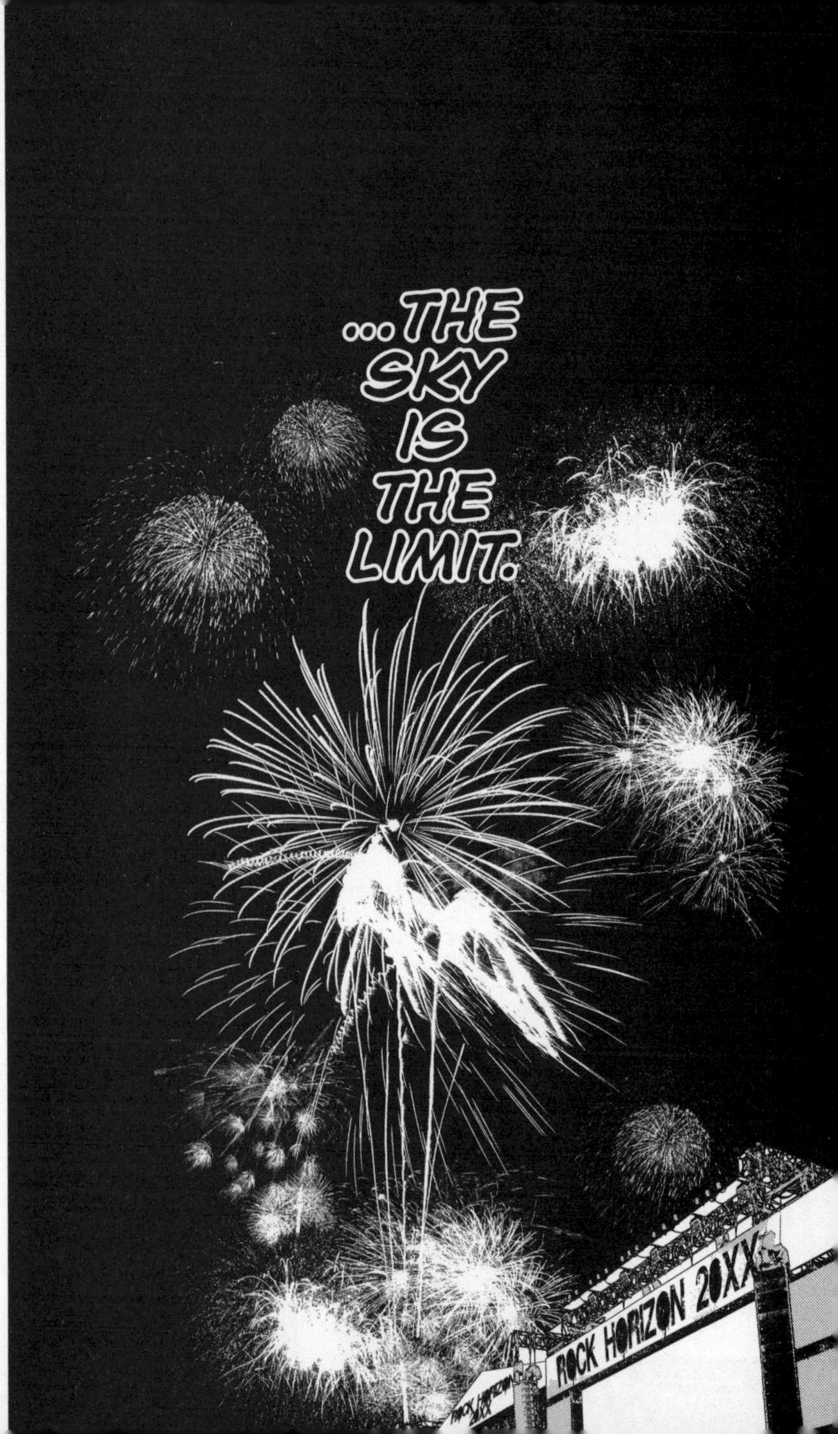
...THE SKY IS THE LIMIT.
ROCK HORIZON 20XX

WE'D
BEEN
HIDING
OUR
TRUE
FEELINGS.

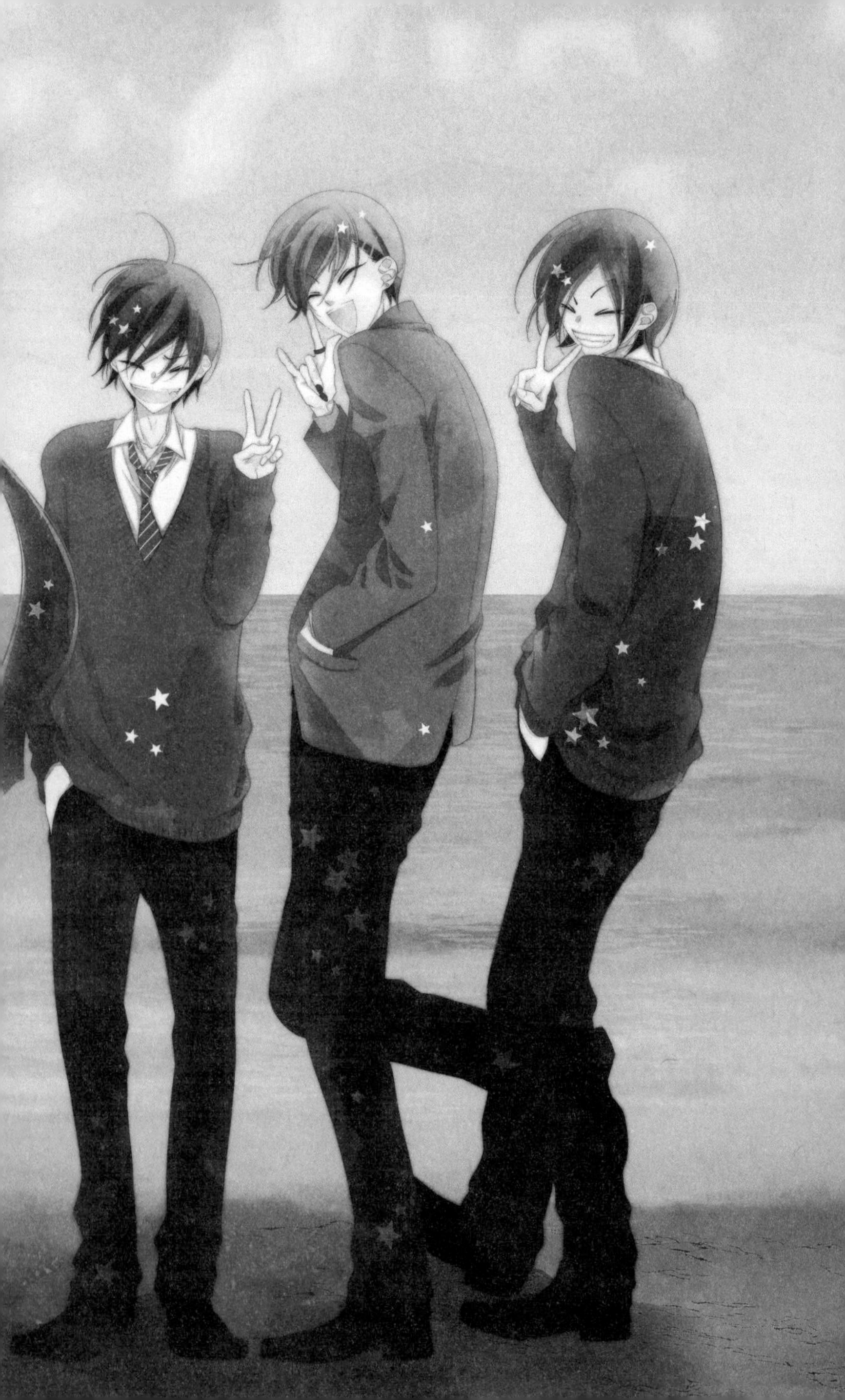

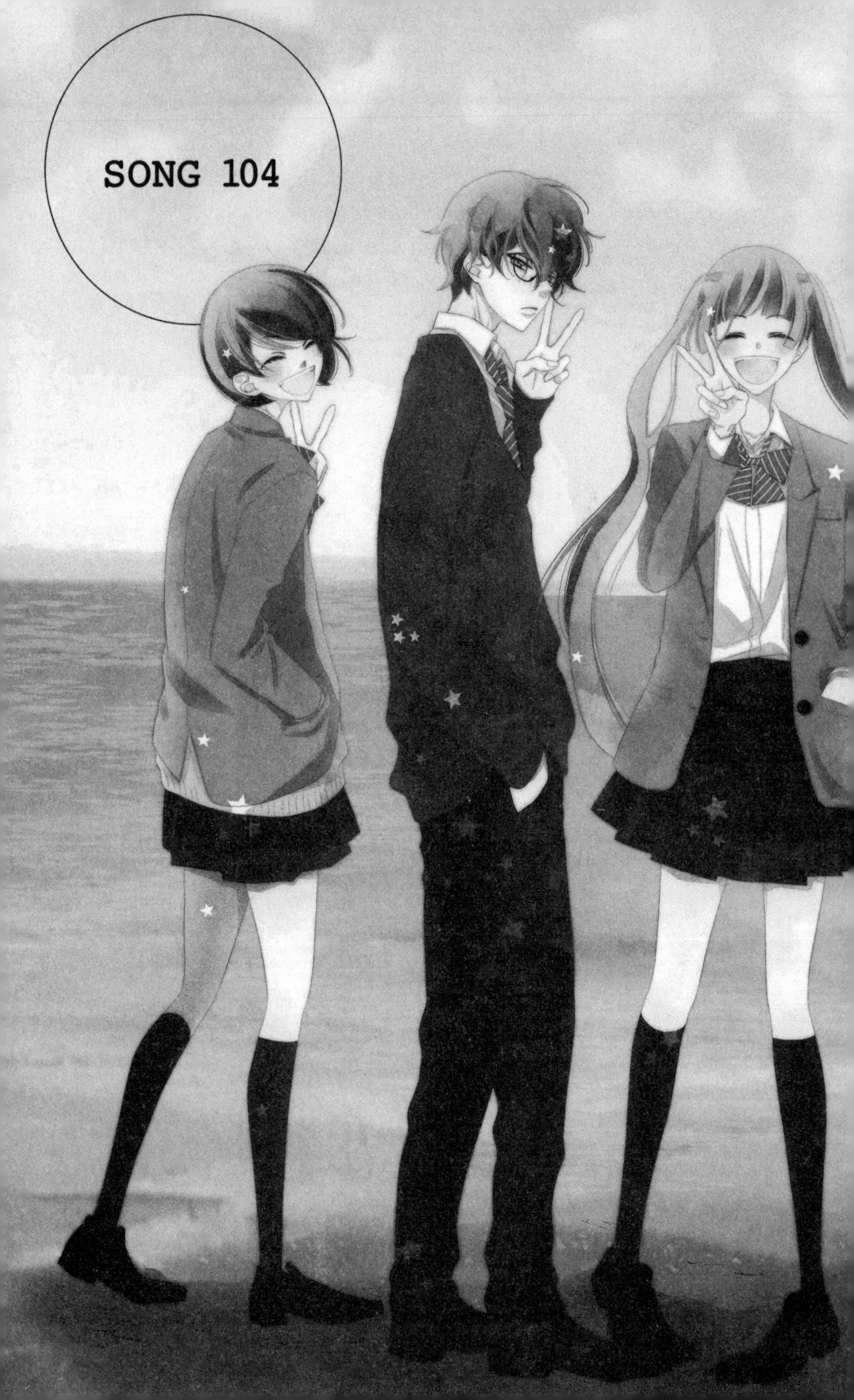
SONG 104

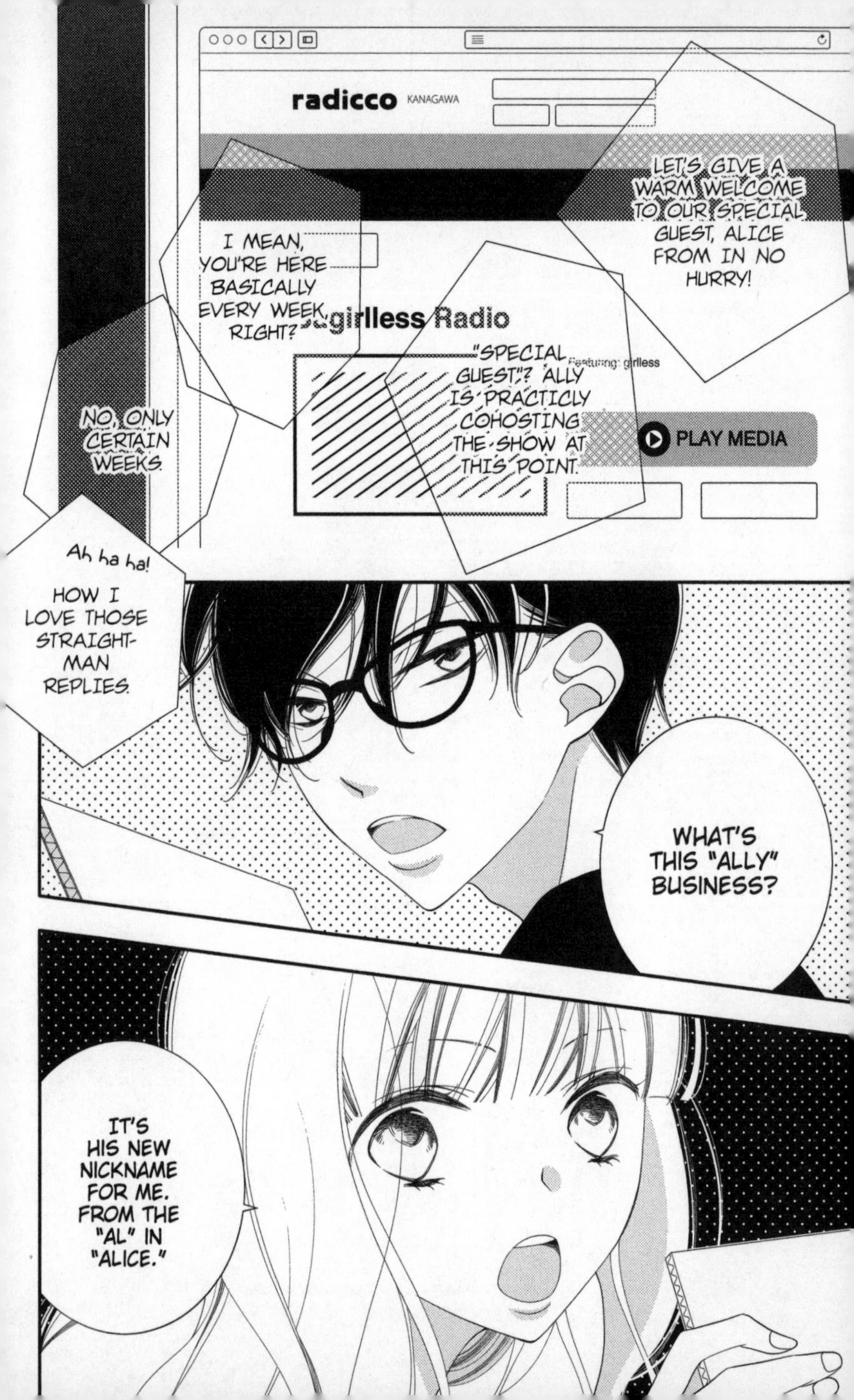
radicco KANAGAWA
girlless Radio
Featuring: girlless
PLAY MEDIA
LET'S GIVE A WARM WELCOME TO OUR SPECIAL GUEST, ALICE FROM IN NO HURRY!
"SPECIAL GUEST"? ALLY IS PRACTICLY COHOSTING THE SHOW AT THIS POINT.
I MEAN, YOU'RE HERE BASICALLY EVERY WEEK, RIGHT?
NO, ONLY CERTAIN WEEKS.
Ah ha ha!
HOW I LOVE THOSE STRAIGHT-MAN REPLIES.
WHAT'S THIS "ALLY" BUSINESS?
IT'S HIS NEW NICKNAME FOR ME. FROM THE "AL" IN "ALICE."

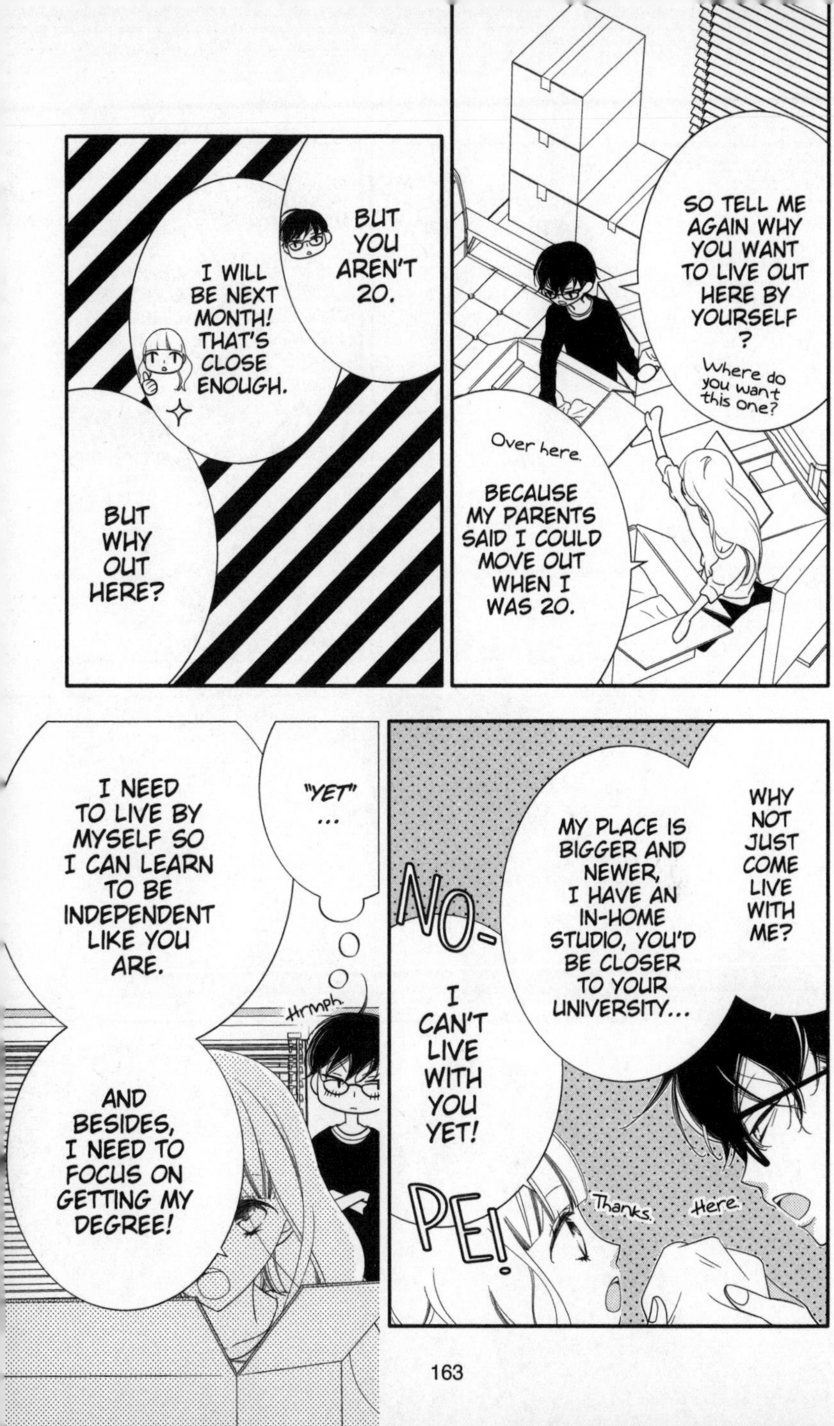
SO TELL ME AGAIN WHY YOU WANT TO LIVE OUT HERE BY YOURSELF?
Where do you want this one?
Over here.
BECAUSE MY PARENTS SAID I COULD MOVE OUT WHEN I WAS 20.
BUT YOU AREN'T 20.
I WILL BE NEXT MONTH! THAT'S CLOSE ENOUGH.
BUT WHY OUT HERE?
WHY NOT JUST COME LIVE WITH ME?
MY PLACE IS BIGGER AND NEWER, I HAVE AN IN-HOME STUDIO, YOU'D BE CLOSER TO YOUR UNIVERSITY...
NO-PE!
I CAN'T LIVE WITH YOU YET!
Here.
Thanks.
"YET"...
I NEED TO LIVE BY MYSELF SO I CAN LEARN TO BE INDEPENDENT LIKE YOU ARE.
Hrmph.
AND BESIDES, I NEED TO FOCUS ON GETTING MY DEGREE!

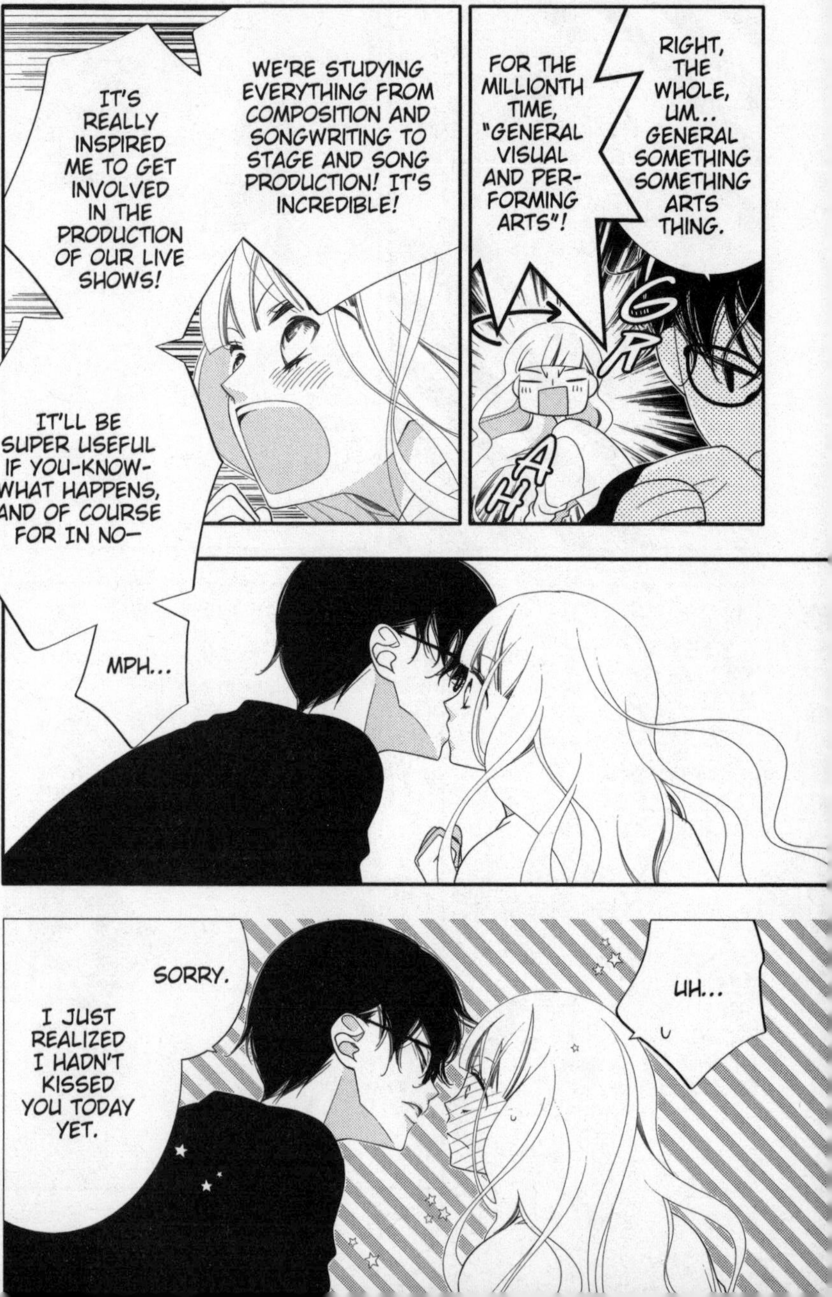
RIGHT, THE WHOLE, UM... GENERAL SOMETHING SOMETHING ARTS THING.
FOR THE MILLIONTH TIME, "GENERAL VISUAL AND PER-FORMING ARTS"!
GR
HA
WE'RE STUDYING EVERYTHING FROM COMPOSITION AND SONGWRITING TO STAGE AND SONG PRODUCTION! IT'S INCREDIBLE!
IT'S REALLY INSPIRED ME TO GET INVOLVED IN THE PRODUCTION OF OUR LIVE SHOWS!
IT'LL BE SUPER USEFUL IF YOU-KNOW-WHAT HAPPENS, AND OF COURSE FOR IN NO—
MPH...
UH...
SORRY.
I JUST REALIZED I HADN'T KISSED YOU TODAY YET.

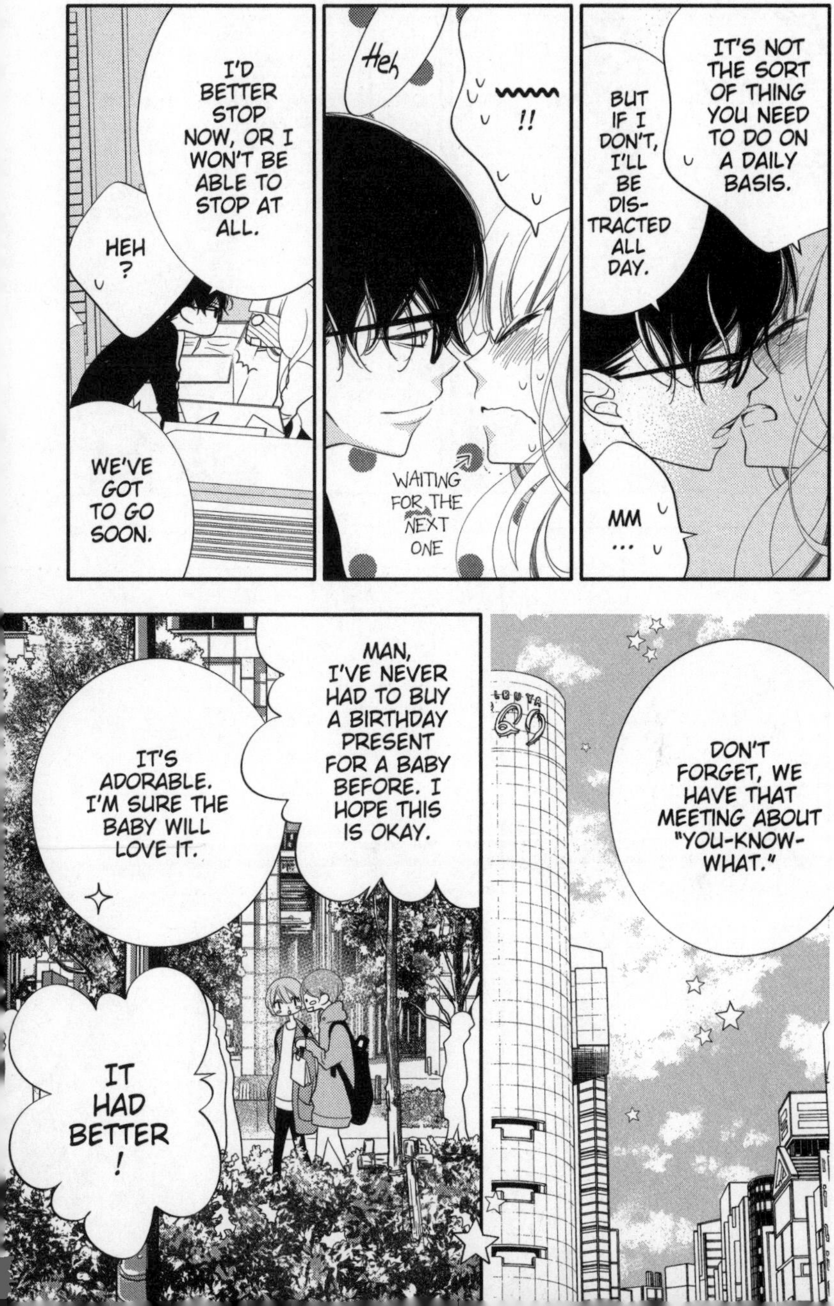
IT'S NOT THE SORT OF THING YOU NEED TO DO ON A DAILY BASIS.
BUT IF I DON'T, I'LL BE DIS-TRACTED ALL DAY.
MM...
Heh
!!
WAITING FOR THE NEXT ONE
I'D BETTER STOP NOW, OR I WON'T BE ABLE TO STOP AT ALL.
HEH?
WE'VE GOT TO GO SOON.
DON'T FORGET, WE HAVE THAT MEETING ABOUT "YOU-KNOW-WHAT."
MAN, I'VE NEVER HAD TO BUY A BIRTHDAY PRESENT FOR A BABY BEFORE. I HOPE THIS IS OKAY.
IT'S ADORABLE. I'M SURE THE BABY WILL LOVE IT.
IT HAD BETTER!

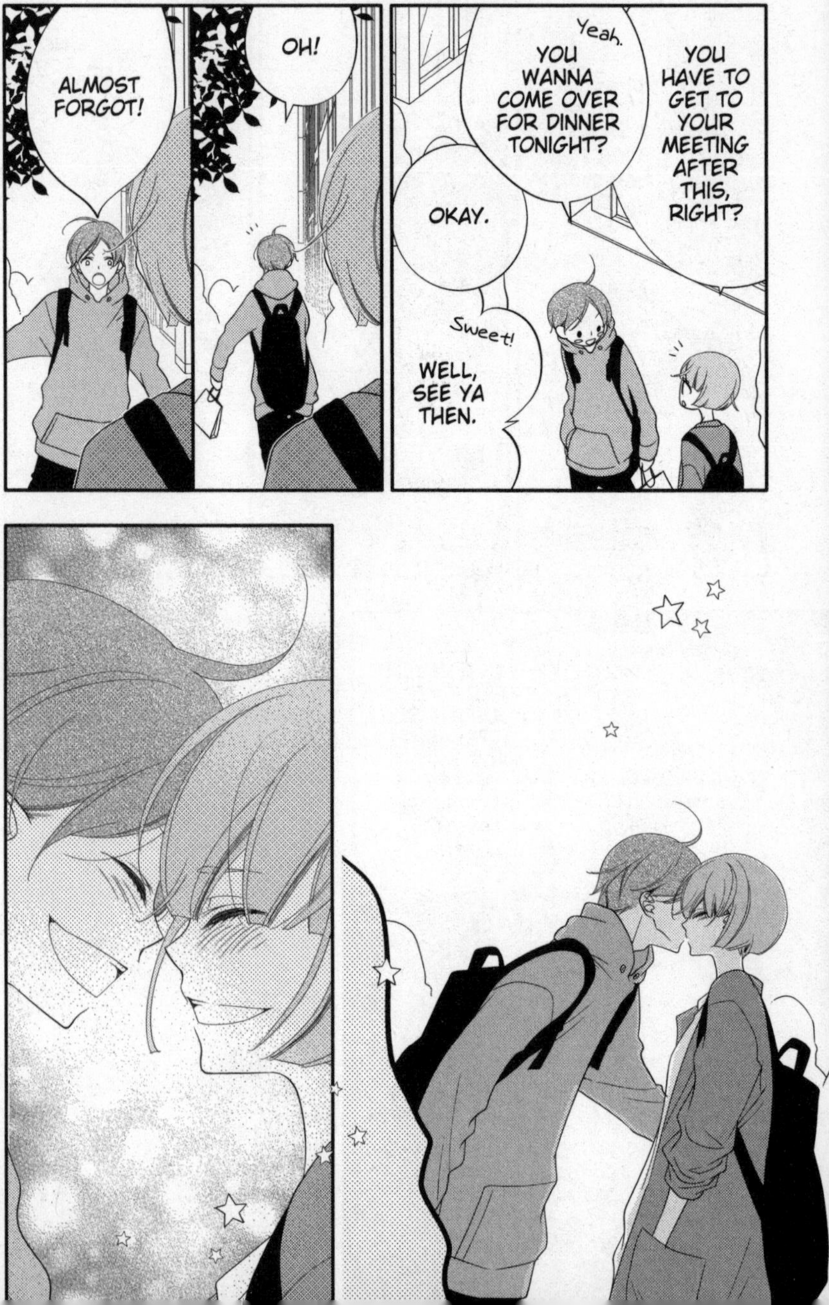
YOU HAVE TO GET TO YOUR MEETING AFTER THIS, RIGHT?
Yeah.
YOU WANNA COME OVER FOR DINNER TONIGHT?
OKAY.
Sweet!
WELL, SEE YA THEN.
OH!
ALMOST FORGOT!

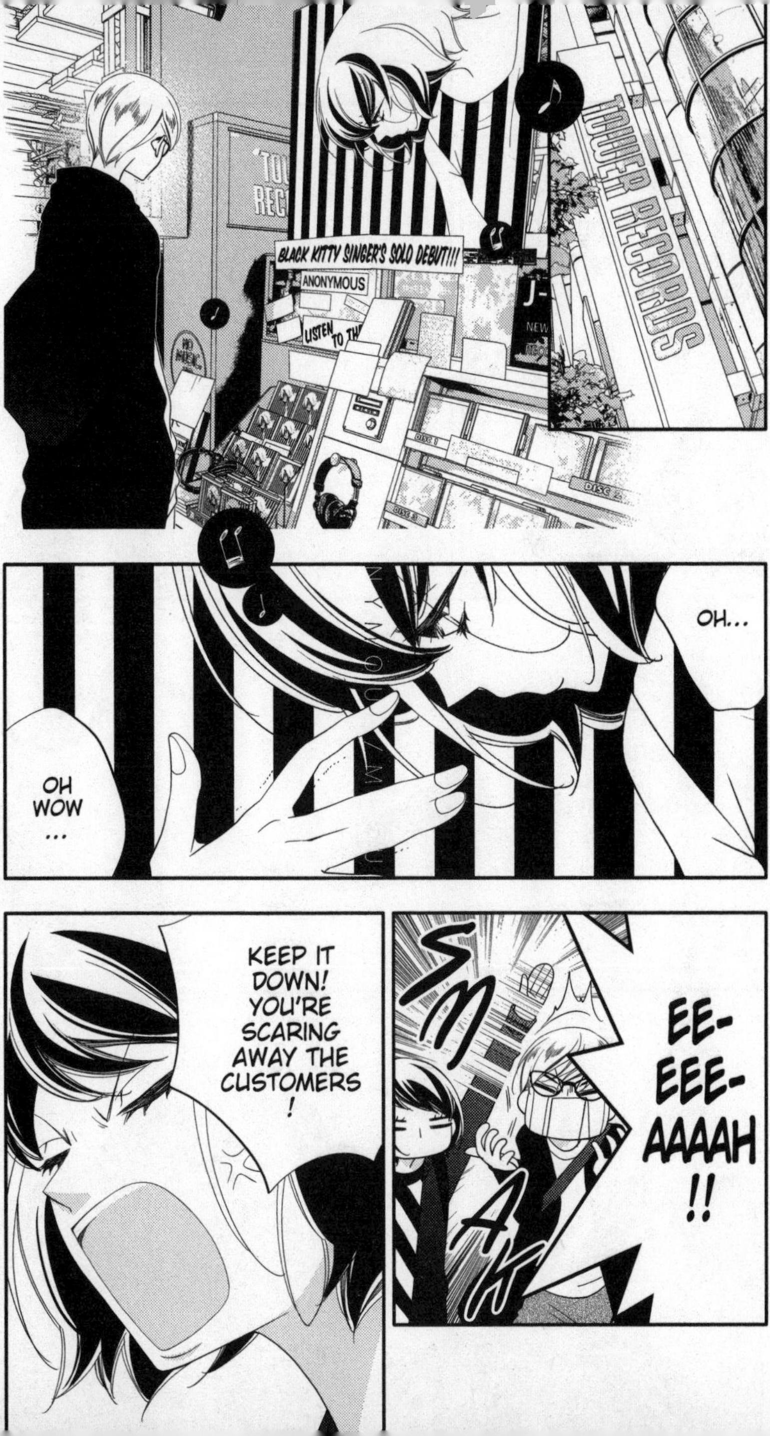
TOWER RECORDS
BLACK KITTY SINGER'S SOLO DEBUT!!!
ANONYMOUS
LISTEN TO TH
OH...
OH WOW ...
EE-EEE-AAAAH !!
SMAK
KEEP IT DOWN! YOU'RE SCARING AWAY THE CUSTOMERS !

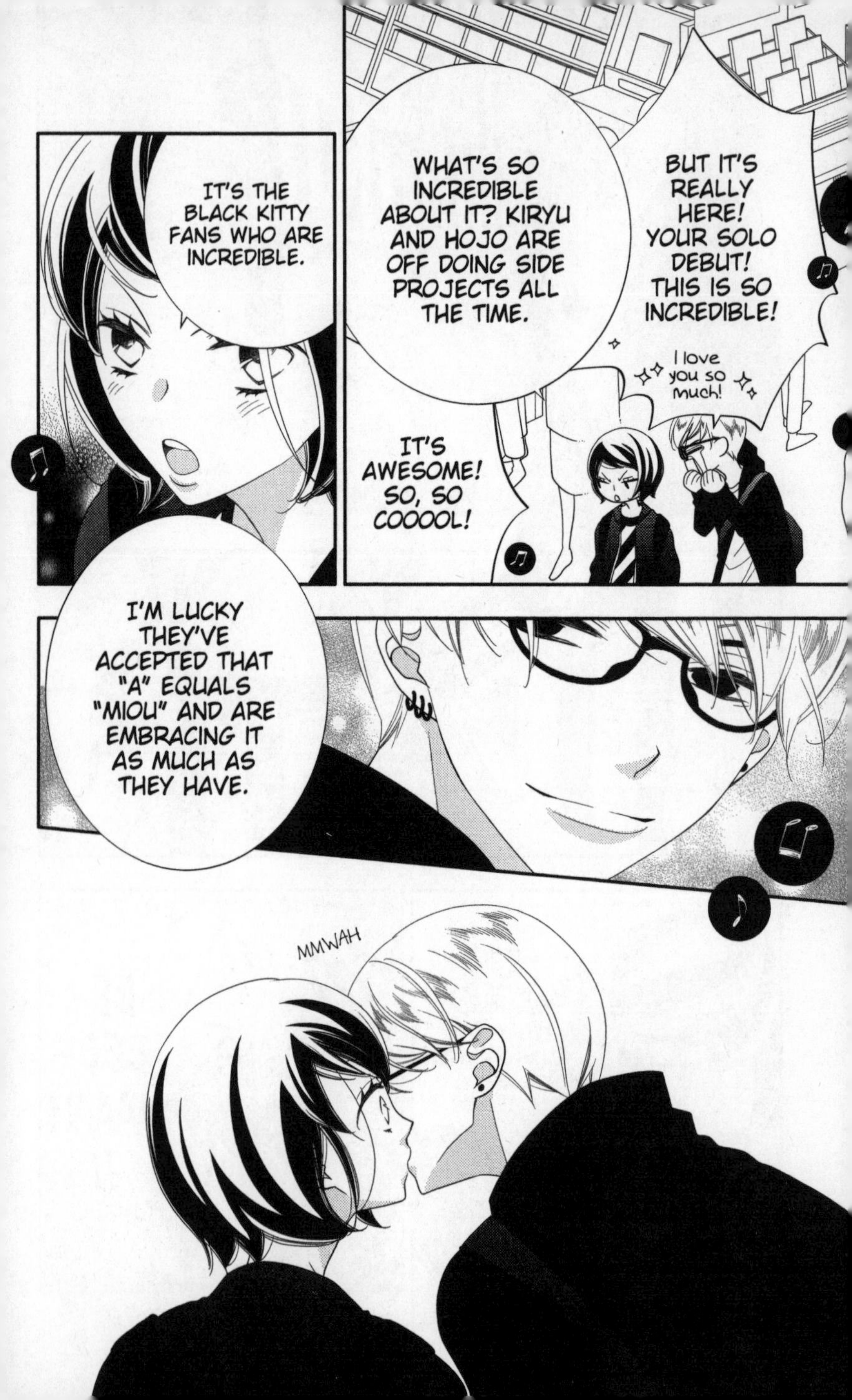
BUT IT'S REALLY HERE! YOUR SOLO DEBUT! THIS IS SO INCREDIBLE!
I love you so much!
WHAT'S SO INCREDIBLE ABOUT IT? KIRYU AND HOJO ARE OFF DOING SIDE PROJECTS ALL THE TIME.
IT'S AWESOME! SO, SO COOOOL!
IT'S THE BLACK KITTY FANS WHO ARE INCREDIBLE.
I'M LUCKY THEY'VE ACCEPTED THAT "A" EQUALS "MIOU" AND ARE EMBRACING IT AS MUCH AS THEY HAVE.
MMWAH

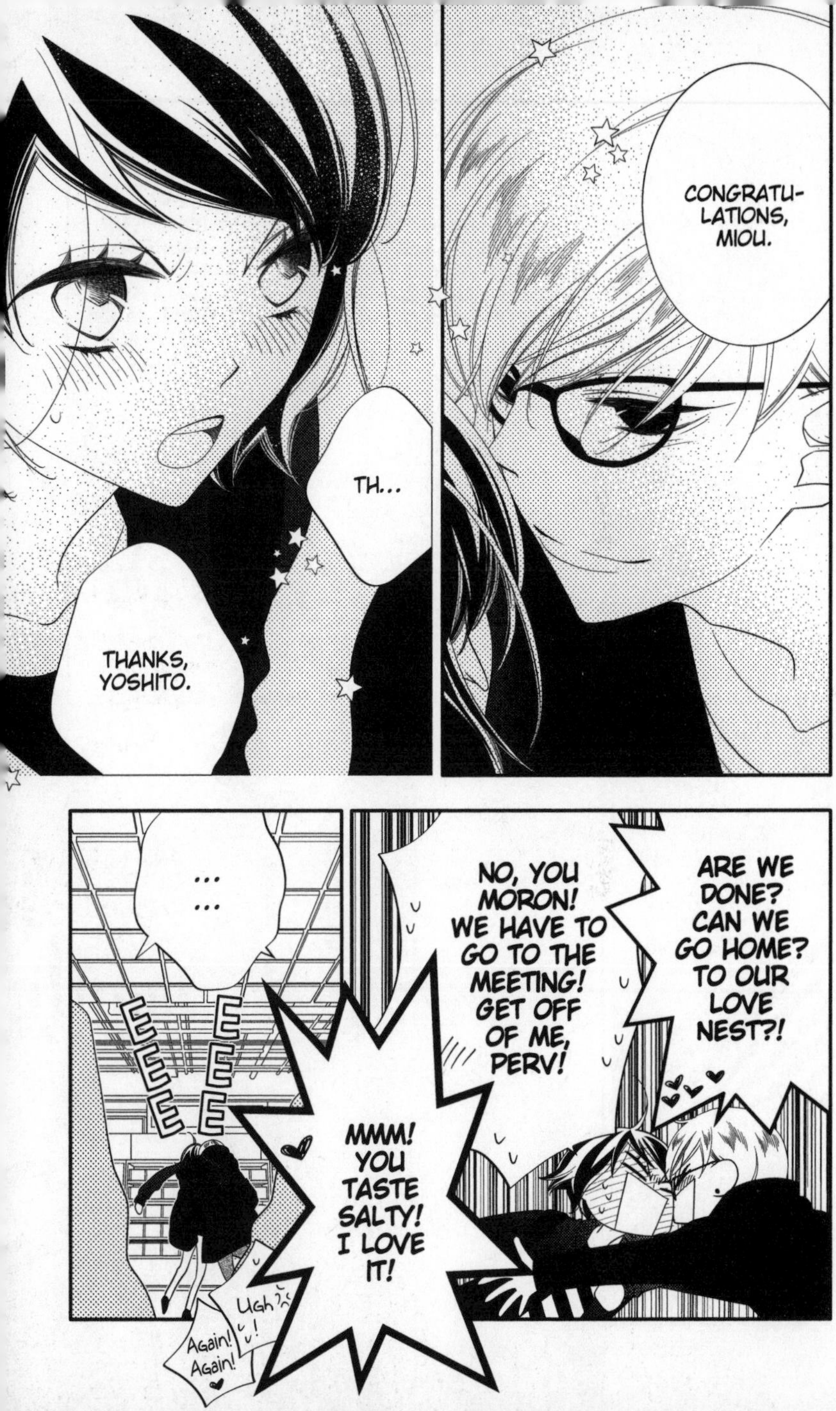
CONGRATULATIONS, MIOU.
TH...
THANKS, YOSHITO.
ARE WE DONE? CAN WE GO HOME? TO OUR LOVE NEST?!
NO, YOU MORON! WE HAVE TO GO TO THE MEETING! GET OFF OF ME, PERV!
MMM! YOU TASTE SALTY! I LOVE IT!
...
...
EEEE
EEEE
Ugh
Again! Again!

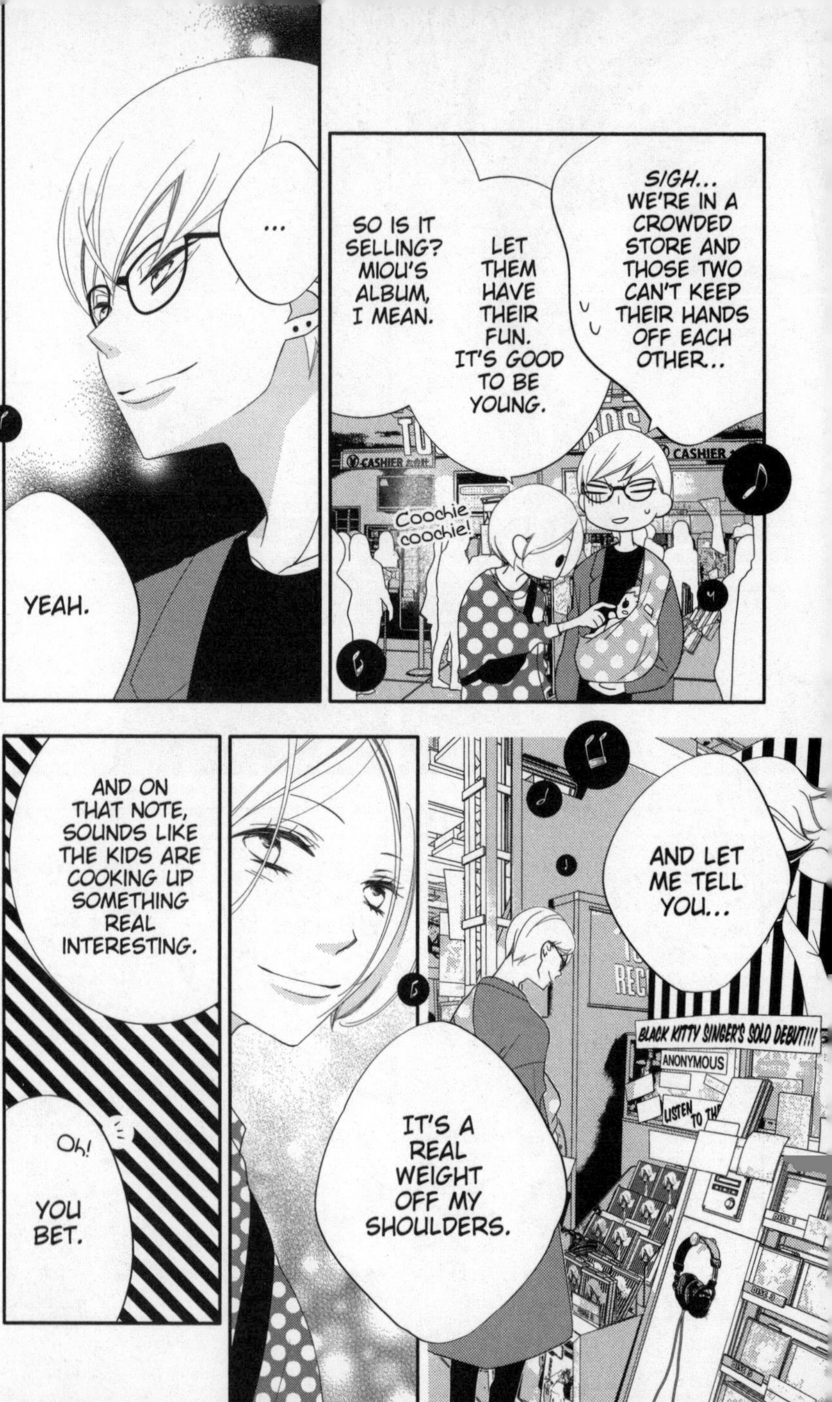
SIGH... WE'RE IN A CROWDED STORE AND THOSE TWO CAN'T KEEP THEIR HANDS OFF EACH OTHER...
LET THEM HAVE THEIR FUN. IT'S GOOD TO BE YOUNG.
SO IS IT SELLING? MIOU'S ALBUM, I MEAN.
CASHIER
CASHIER
Coochie coochie!
...
YEAH.
AND LET ME TELL YOU...
IT'S A REAL WEIGHT OFF MY SHOULDERS.
BLACK KITTY SINGER'S SOLO DEBUT!!!
ANONYMOUS
AND ON THAT NOTE, SOUNDS LIKE THE KIDS ARE COOKING UP SOMETHING REAL INTERESTING.
Oh!
YOU BET.

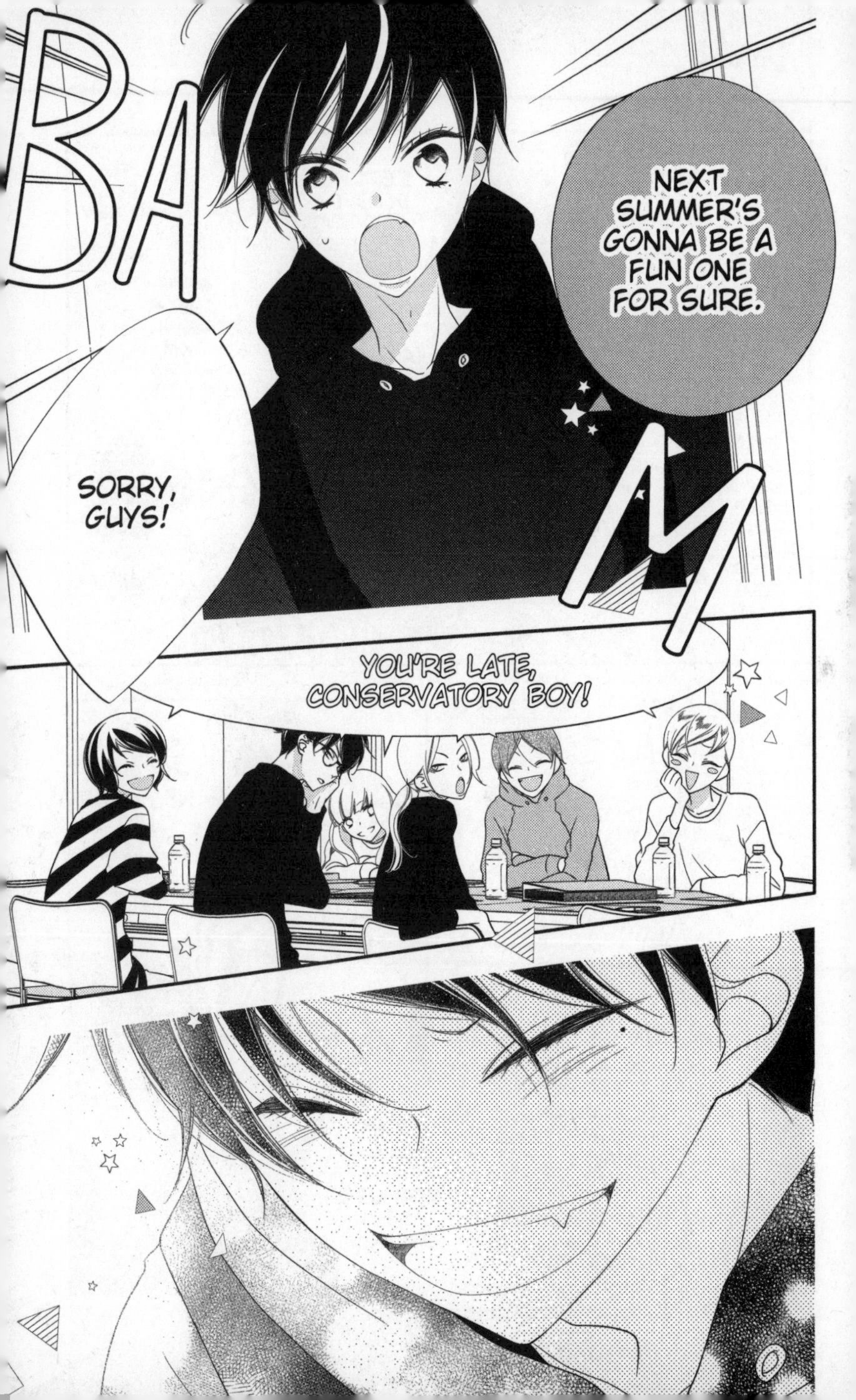
NEXT SUMMER'S GONNA BE A FUN ONE FOR SURE.
BAM
SORRY, GUYS!
YOU'RE LATE, CONSERVATORY BOY!

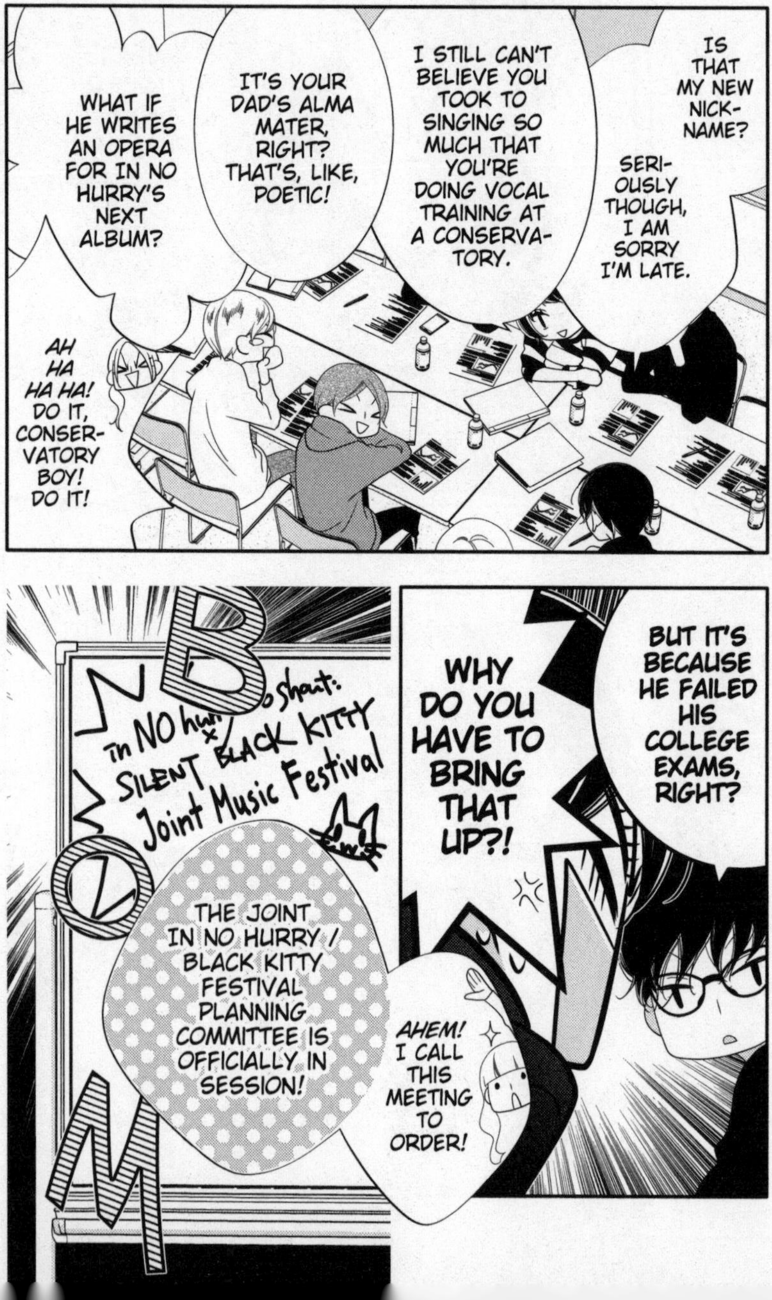
IS THAT MY NEW NICK-NAME?
SERI-OUSLY THOUGH, I AM SORRY I'M LATE.
I STILL CAN'T BELIEVE YOU TOOK TO SINGING SO MUCH THAT YOU'RE DOING VOCAL TRAINING AT A CONSERVA-TORY.
IT'S YOUR DAD'S ALMA MATER, RIGHT? THAT'S, LIKE, POETIC!
WHAT IF HE WRITES AN OPERA FOR IN NO HURRY'S NEXT ALBUM?
AH HA HA HA! DO IT, CONSER-VATORY BOY! DO IT!
BUT IT'S BECAUSE HE FAILED HIS COLLEGE EXAMS, RIGHT?
WHY DO YOU HAVE TO BRING THAT UP?!
in NO
Shout:
× SILENT BLACK KITTY
Joint Music Festival
BOOM
AHEM! I CALL THIS MEETING TO ORDER!
THE JOINT IN NO HURRY / BLACK KITTY FESTIVAL PLANNING COMMITTEE IS OFFICIALLY IN SESSION!

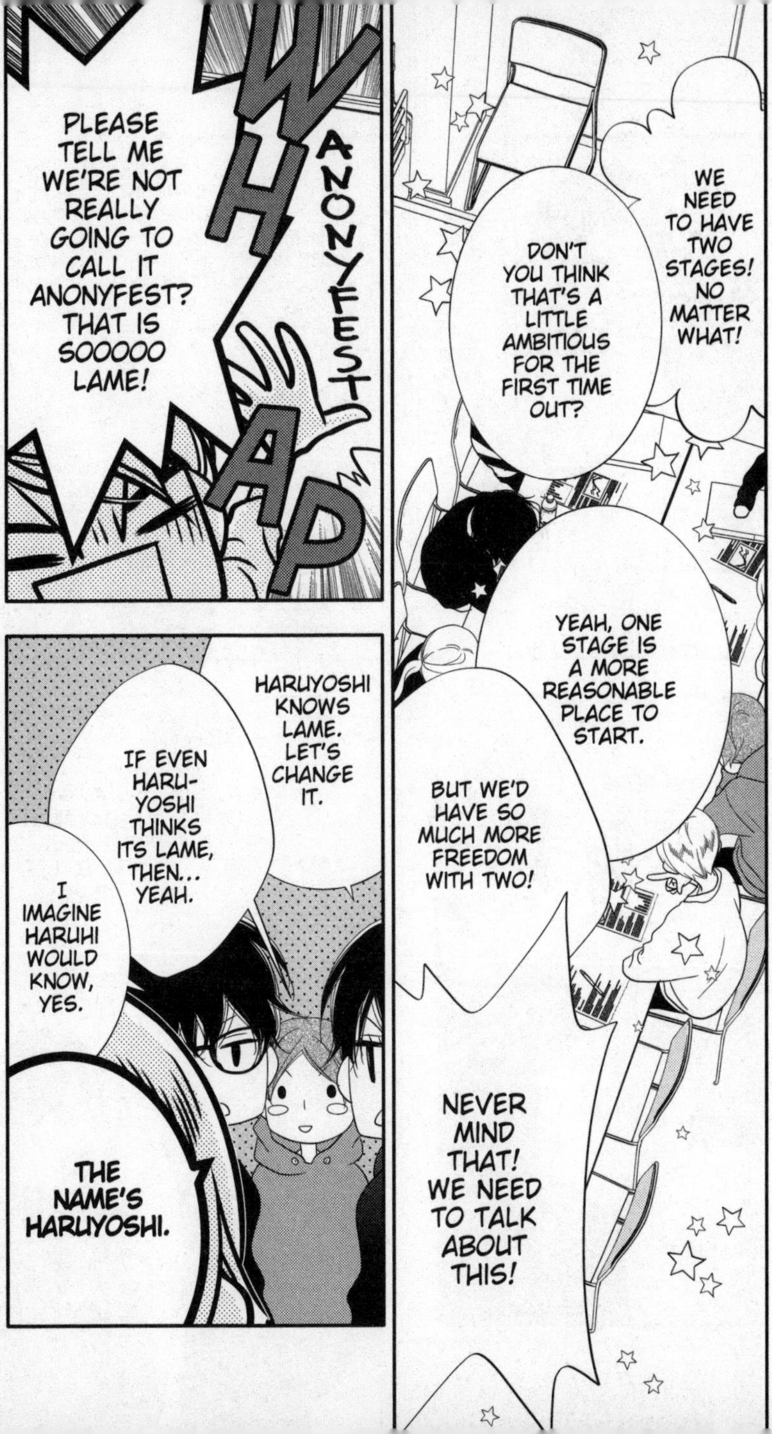
WE NEED TO HAVE TWO STAGES! NO MATTER WHAT!
DON'T YOU THINK THAT'S A LITTLE AMBITIOUS FOR THE FIRST TIME OUT?
YEAH, ONE STAGE IS A MORE REASONABLE PLACE TO START.
BUT WE'D HAVE SO MUCH MORE FREEDOM WITH TWO!
NEVER MIND THAT! WE NEED TO TALK ABOUT THIS!
WHAP
ANONYFEST
PLEASE TELL ME WE'RE NOT REALLY GOING TO CALL IT ANONYFEST? THAT IS SOOOOO LAME!
HARUYOSHI KNOWS LAME. LET'S CHANGE IT.
IF EVEN HARUYOSHI THINKS ITS LAME, THEN... YEAH.
I IMAGINE HARUHI WOULD KNOW, YES.
THE NAME'S HARUYOSHI.

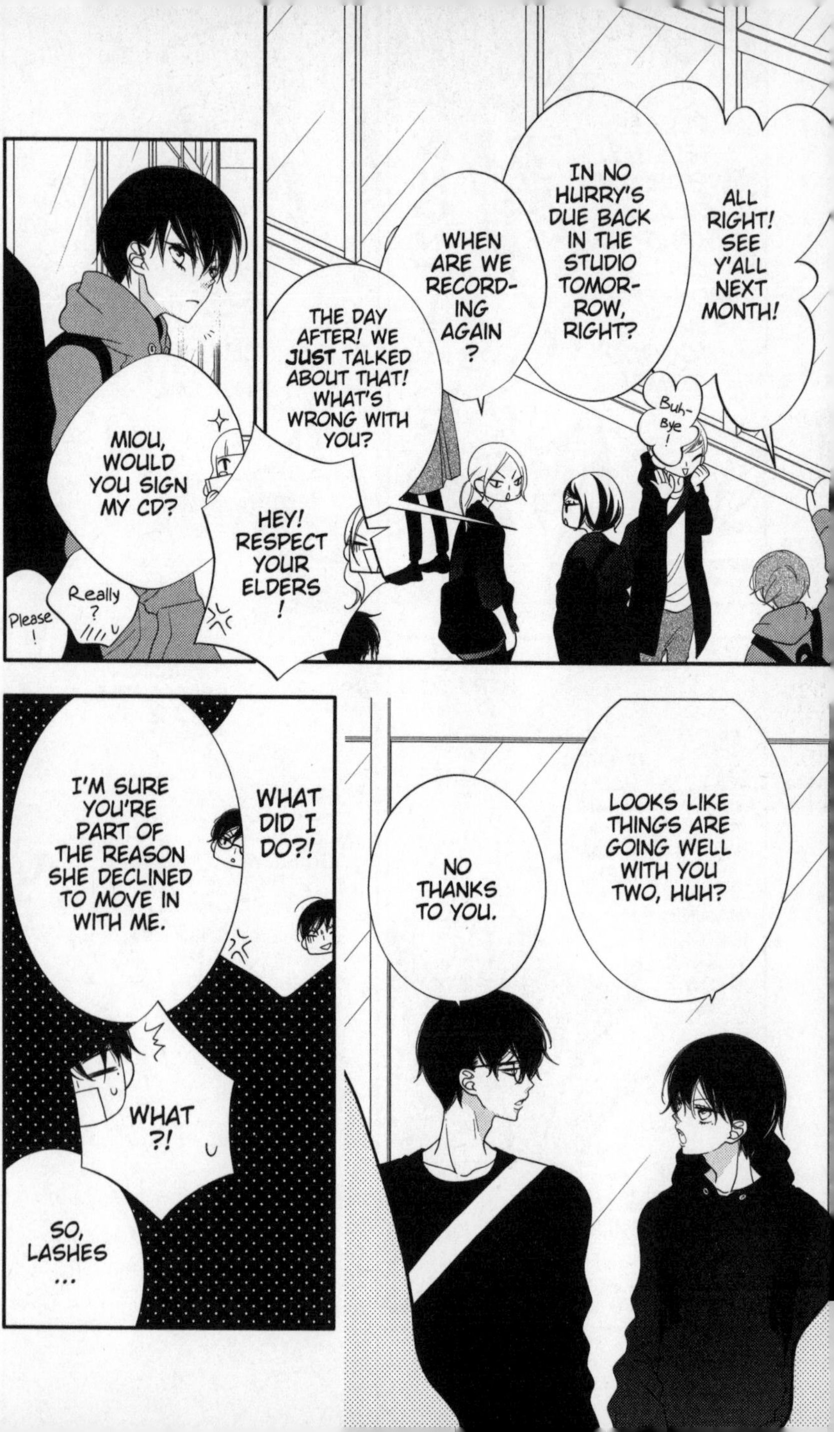
ALL RIGHT! SEE Y'ALL NEXT MONTH!
Buh-Bye!
IN NO HURRY'S DUE BACK IN THE STUDIO TOMORROW, RIGHT?
WHEN ARE WE RECORDING AGAIN?
THE DAY AFTER! WE JUST TALKED ABOUT THAT! WHAT'S WRONG WITH YOU?
HEY! RESPECT YOUR ELDERS!
MIOU, WOULD YOU SIGN MY CD?
Really?
Please!
LOOKS LIKE THINGS ARE GOING WELL WITH YOU TWO, HUH?
NO THANKS TO YOU.
I'M SURE YOU'RE PART OF THE REASON SHE DECLINED TO MOVE IN WITH ME.
WHAT DID I DO?!
WHAT?!
SO, LASHES...

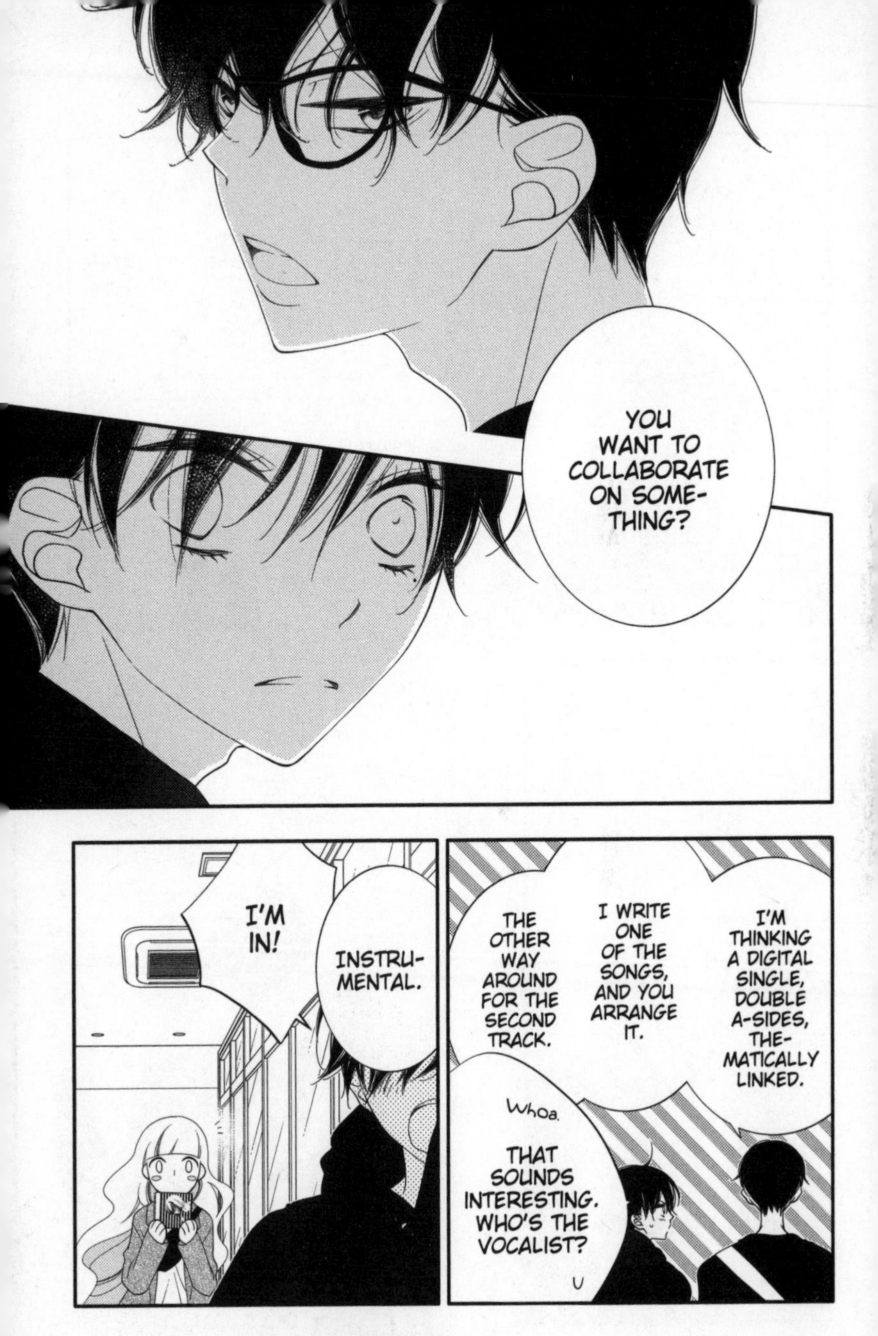
YOU WANT TO COLLABORATE ON SOME-THING?
I'M THINKING A DIGITAL SINGLE, DOUBLE A-SIDES, THE-MATICALLY LINKED.
I WRITE ONE OF THE SONGS, AND YOU ARRANGE IT.
THE OTHER WAY AROUND FOR THE SECOND TRACK.
Whoa.
THAT SOUNDS INTERESTING. WHO'S THE VOCALIST?
INSTRU-MENTAL.
I'M IN!

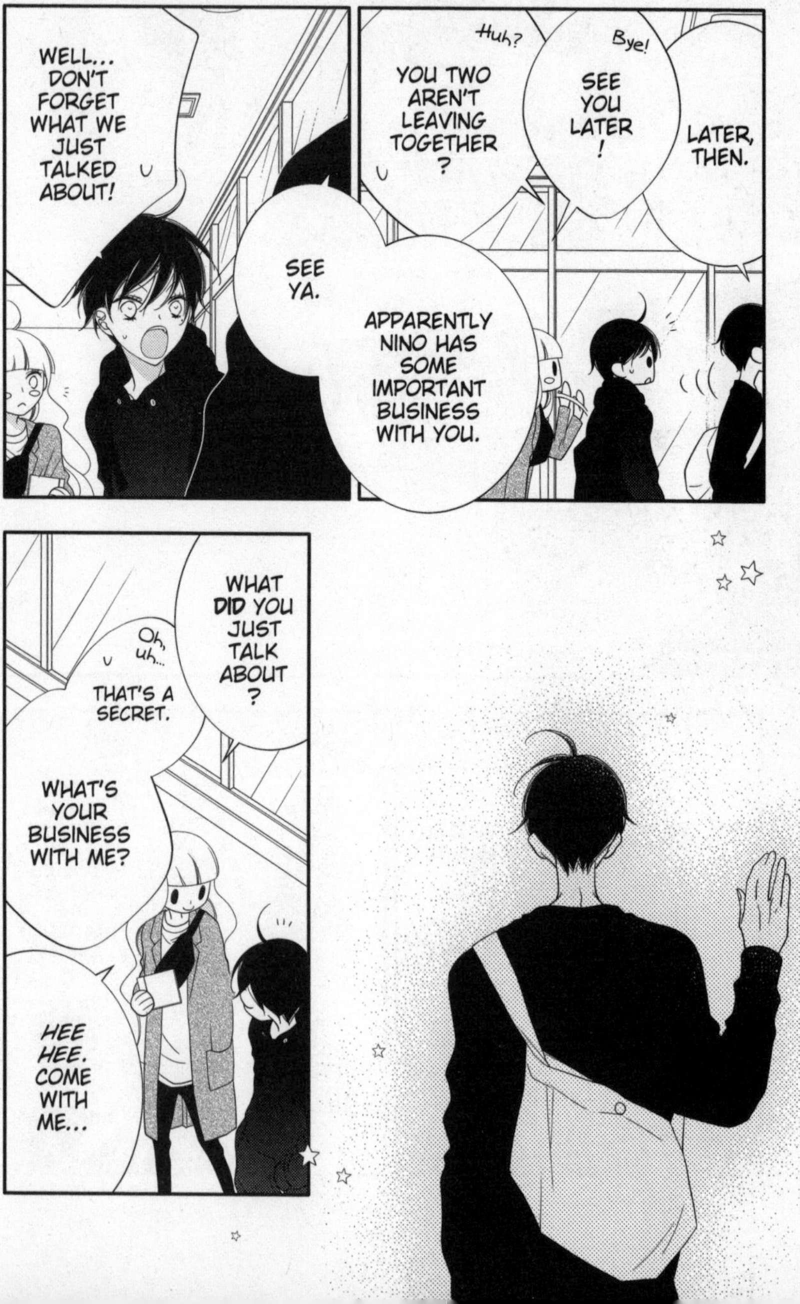
LATER, THEN.
Bye!
SEE YOU LATER!
Huh?
YOU TWO AREN'T LEAVING TOGETHER?
SEE YA.
APPARENTLY NINO HAS SOME IMPORTANT BUSINESS WITH YOU.
WELL... DON'T FORGET WHAT WE JUST TALKED ABOUT!
WHAT DID YOU JUST TALK ABOUT?
Oh, uh...
THAT'S A SECRET.
WHAT'S YOUR BUSINESS WITH ME?
HEE HEE. COME WITH ME...

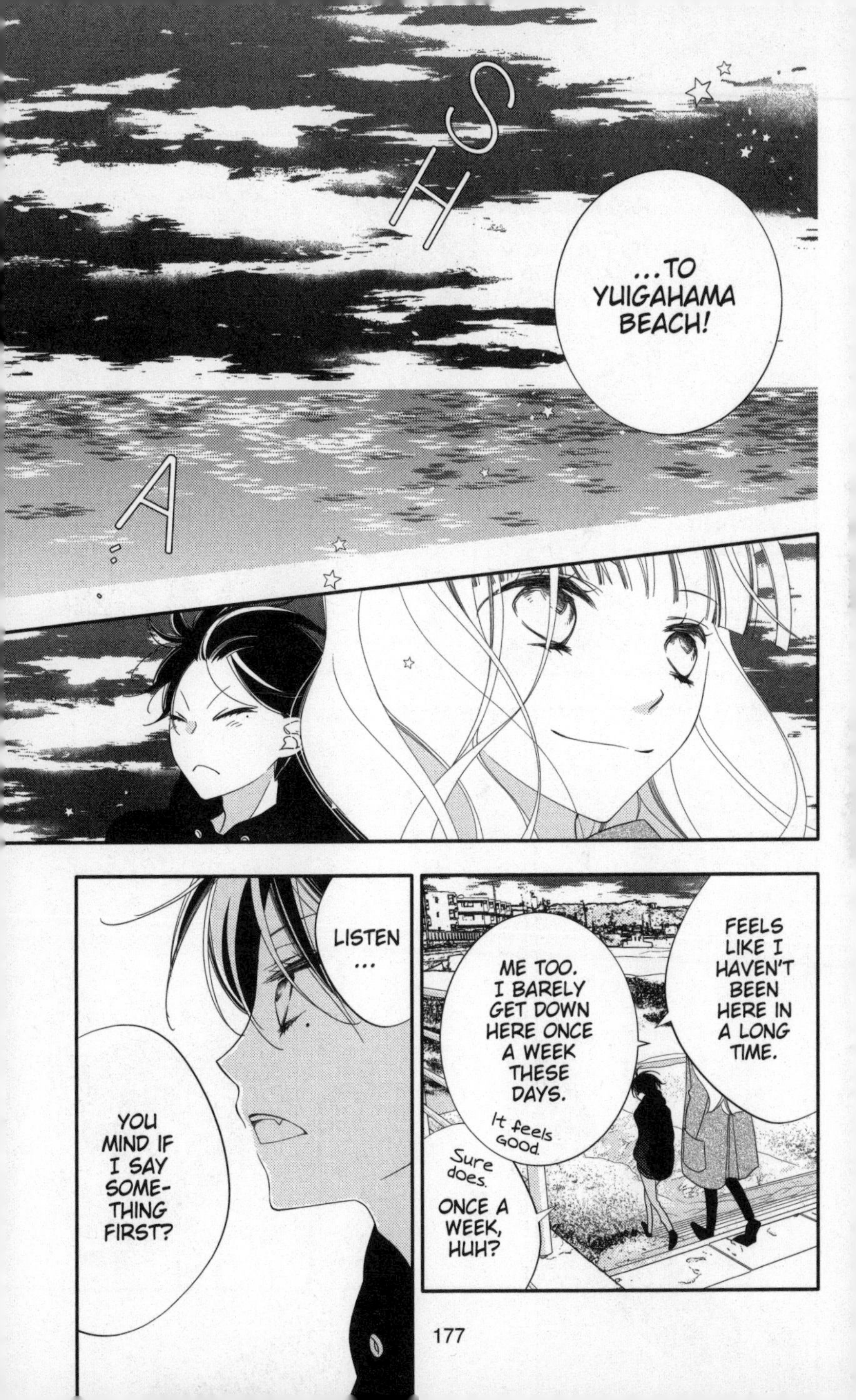
...TO YUIGAHAMA BEACH!
SHA
FEELS LIKE I HAVEN'T BEEN HERE IN A LONG TIME.
ME TOO. I BARELY GET DOWN HERE ONCE A WEEK THESE DAYS.
It feels good.
Sure does.
ONCE A WEEK, HUH?
LISTEN ...
YOU MIND IF I SAY SOME-THING FIRST?

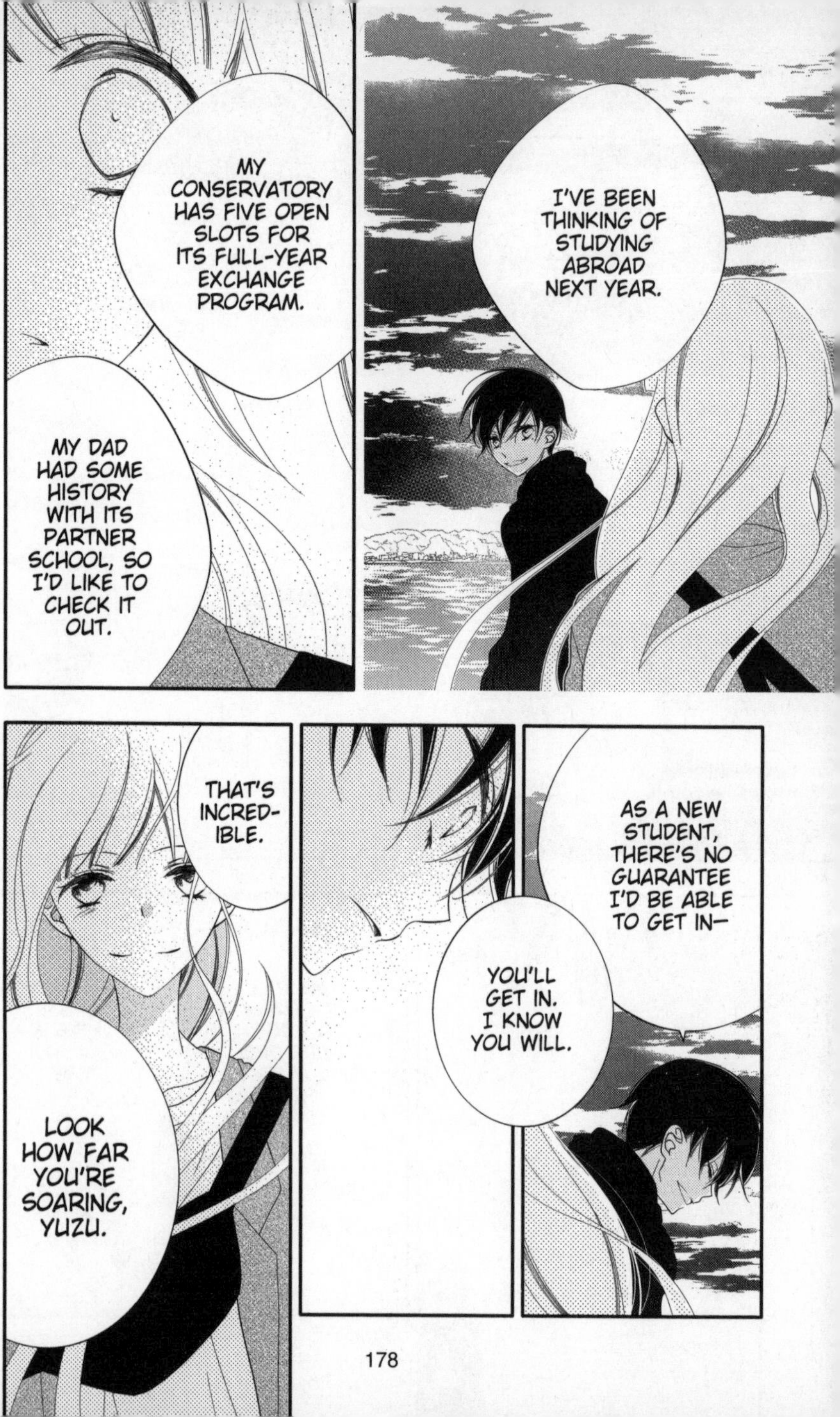
I'VE BEEN THINKING OF STUDYING ABROAD NEXT YEAR.
MY CONSERVATORY HAS FIVE OPEN SLOTS FOR ITS FULL-YEAR EXCHANGE PROGRAM.
MY DAD HAD SOME HISTORY WITH ITS PARTNER SCHOOL, SO I'D LIKE TO CHECK IT OUT.
AS A NEW STUDENT, THERE'S NO GUARANTEE I'D BE ABLE TO GET IN—
YOU'LL GET IN. I KNOW YOU WILL.
THAT'S INCRED-IBLE.
LOOK HOW FAR YOU'RE SOARING, YUZU.

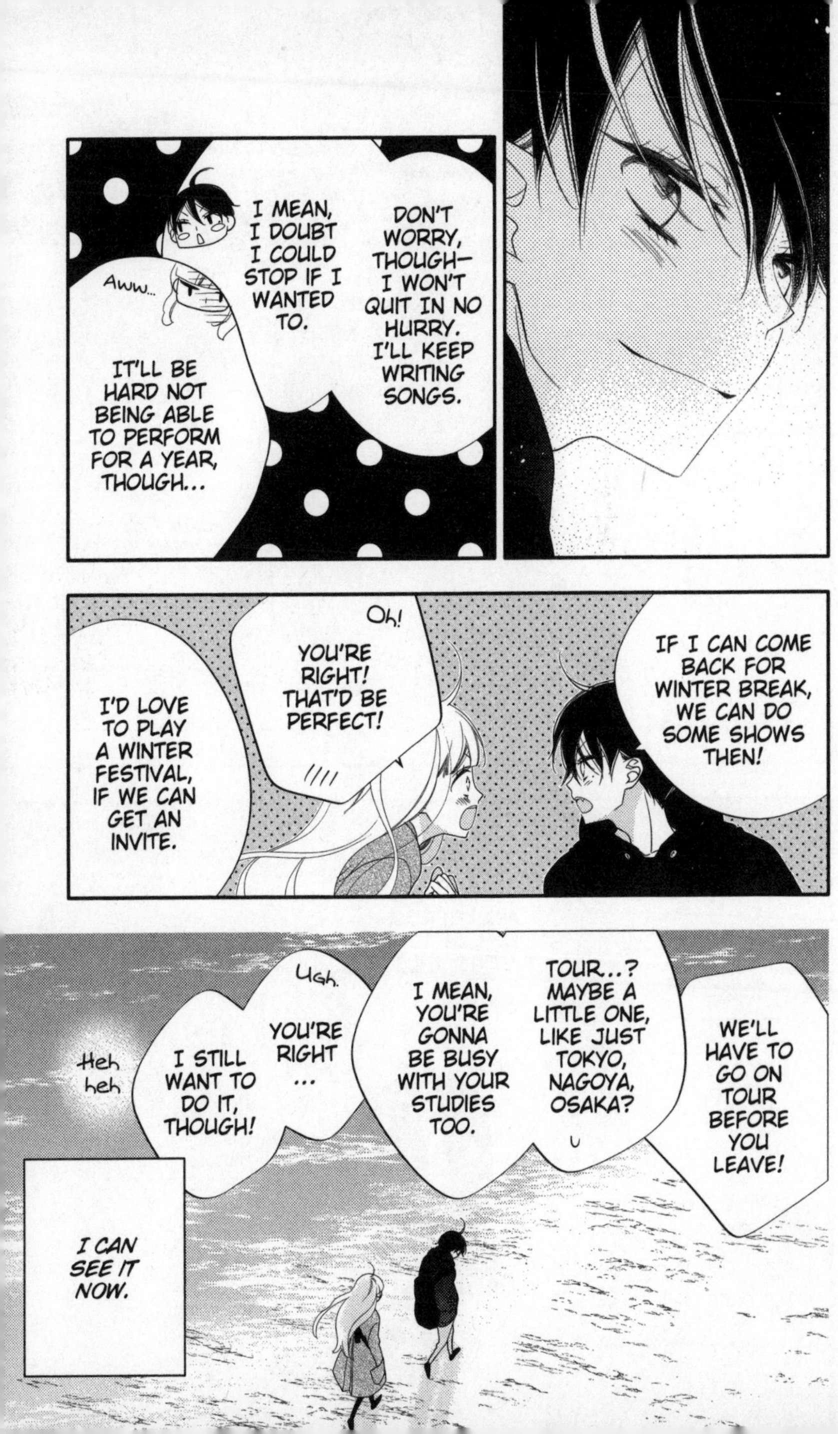
DON'T WORRY, THOUGH— I WON'T QUIT IN NO HURRY. I'LL KEEP WRITING SONGS.
I MEAN, I DOUBT I COULD STOP IF I WANTED TO.
Aww...
IT'LL BE HARD NOT BEING ABLE TO PERFORM FOR A YEAR, THOUGH...
IF I CAN COME BACK FOR WINTER BREAK, WE CAN DO SOME SHOWS THEN!
Oh!
YOU'RE RIGHT! THAT'D BE PERFECT!
I'D LOVE TO PLAY A WINTER FESTIVAL, IF WE CAN GET AN INVITE.
WE'LL HAVE TO GO ON TOUR BEFORE YOU LEAVE!
TOUR...? MAYBE A LITTLE ONE, LIKE JUST TOKYO, NAGOYA, OSAKA?
I MEAN, YOU'RE GONNA BE BUSY WITH YOUR STUDIES TOO.
Ugh.
YOU'RE RIGHT...
I STILL WANT TO DO IT, THOUGH!
Heh heh
I CAN SEE IT NOW.

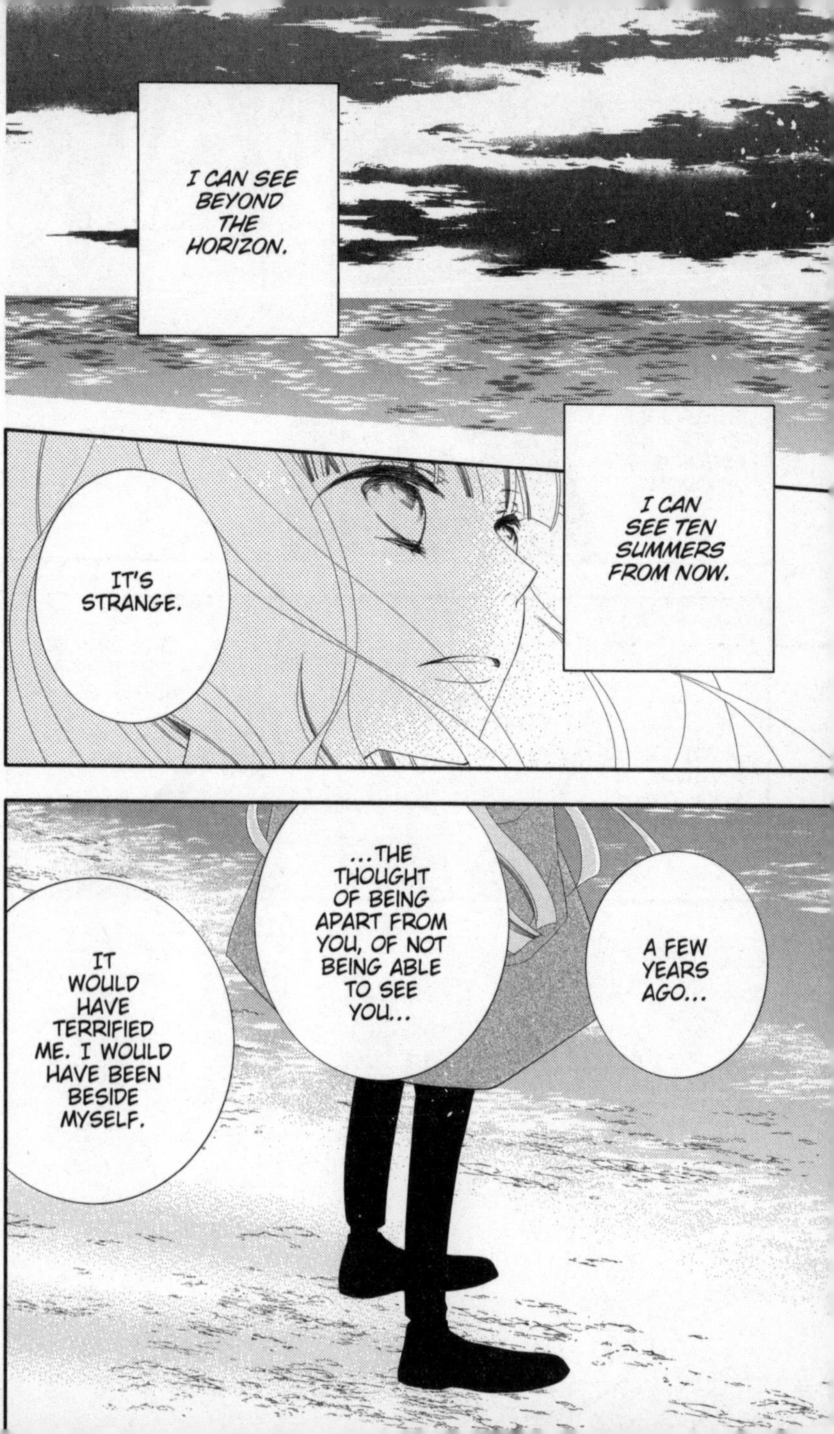
I CAN SEE BEYOND THE HORIZON.
I CAN SEE TEN SUMMERS FROM NOW.
IT'S STRANGE.
A FEW YEARS AGO...
...THE THOUGHT OF BEING APART FROM YOU, OF NOT BEING ABLE TO SEE YOU...
IT WOULD HAVE TERRIFIED ME. I WOULD HAVE BEEN BESIDE MYSELF.

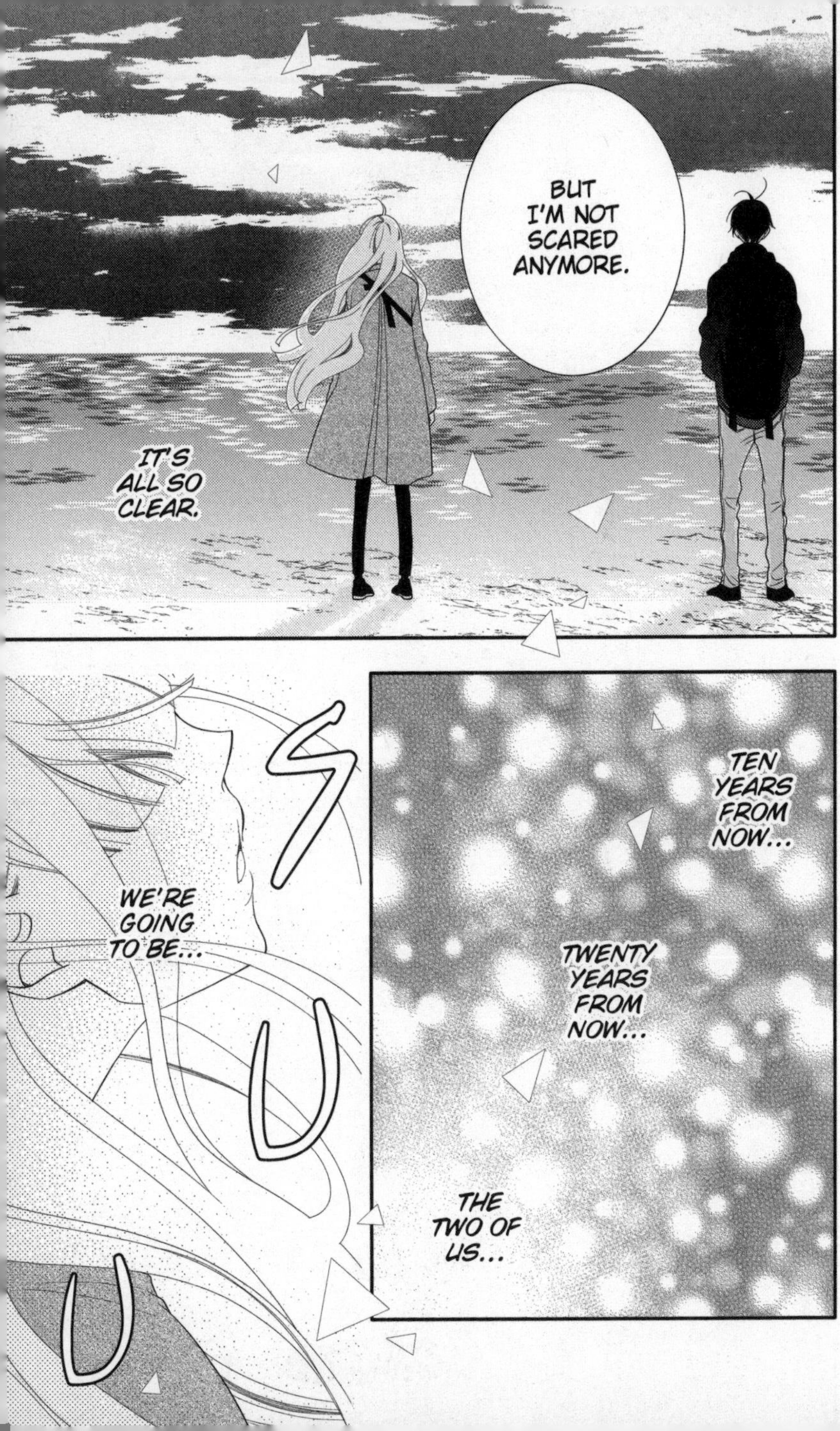
BUT I'M NOT SCARED ANYMORE.
IT'S ALL SO CLEAR.
TEN YEARS FROM NOW...
TWENTY YEARS FROM NOW...
THE TWO OF US...
WE'RE GOING TO BE...
SUU

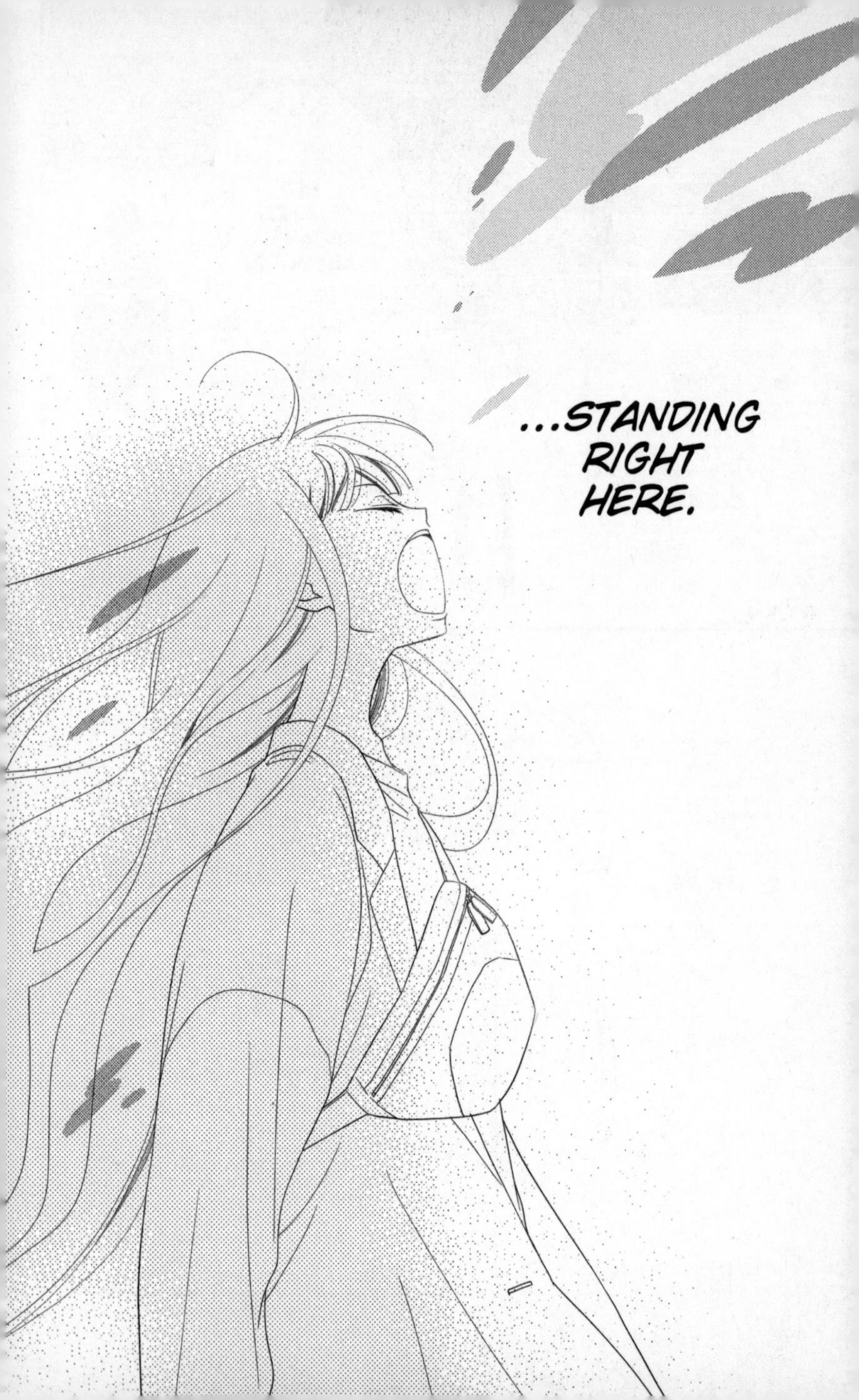
...STANDING RIGHT HERE.

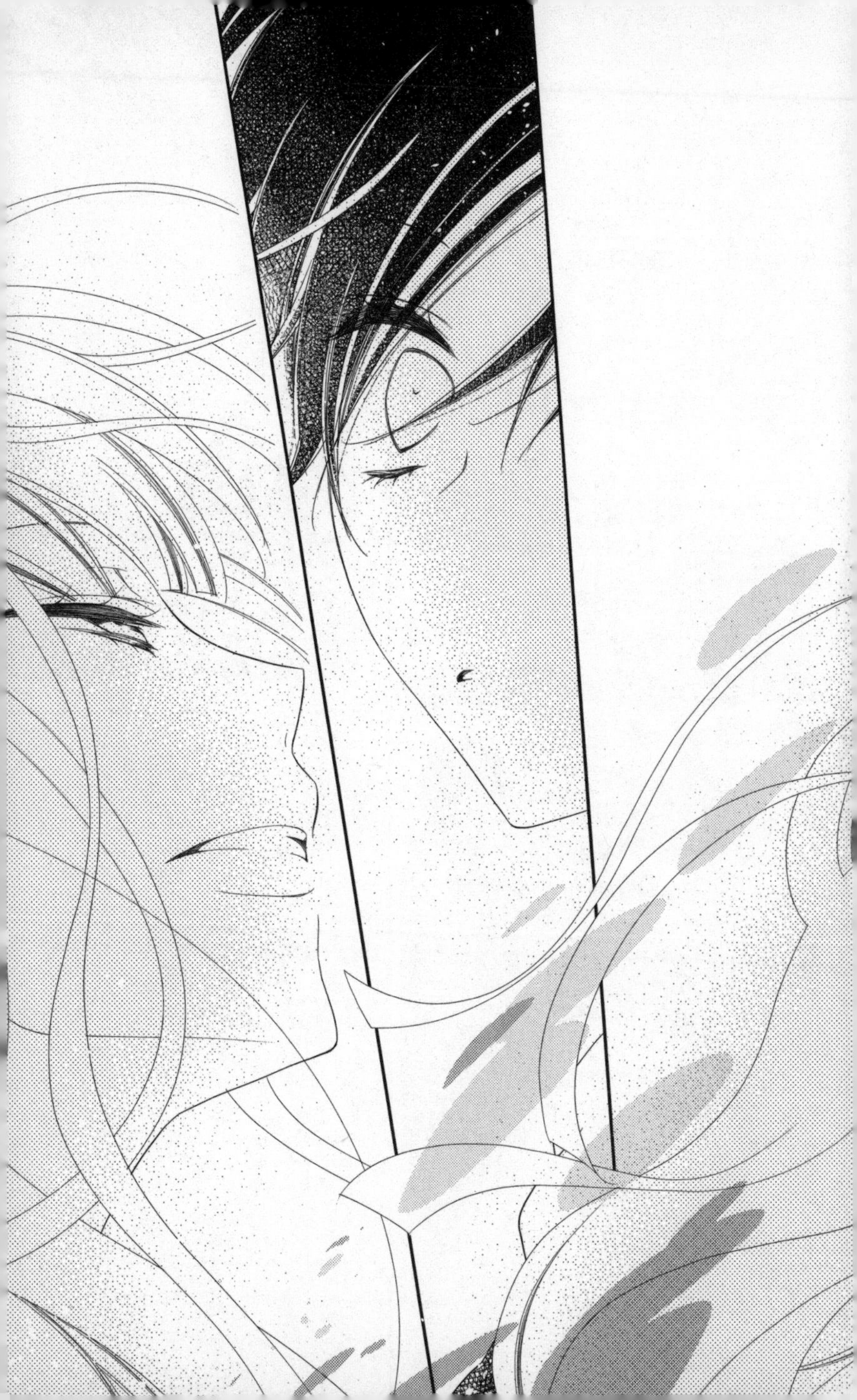

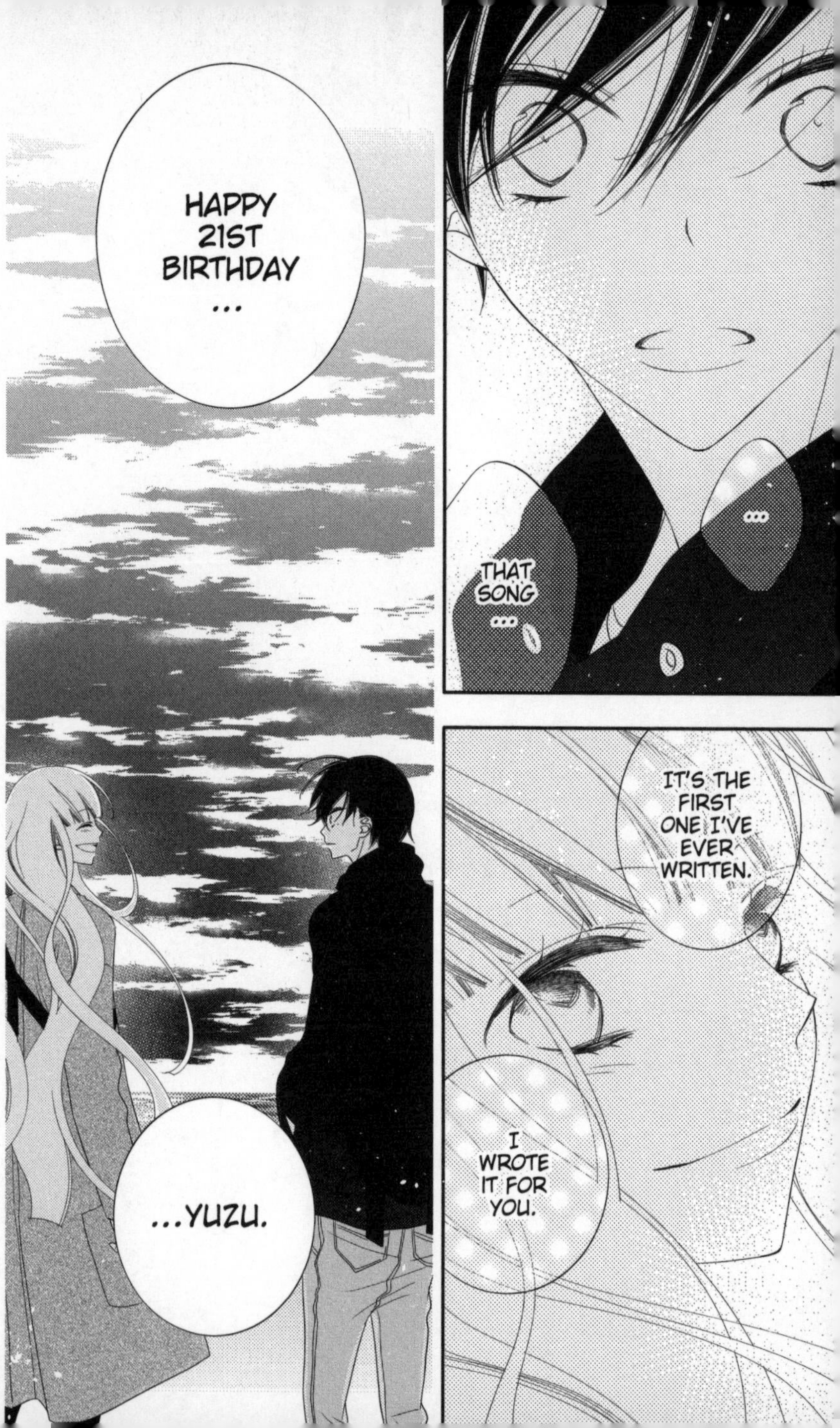
...
THAT SONG ...
IT'S THE FIRST ONE I'VE EVER WRITTEN.
I WROTE IT FOR YOU.
HAPPY 21ST BIRTHDAY ...
...YUZU.

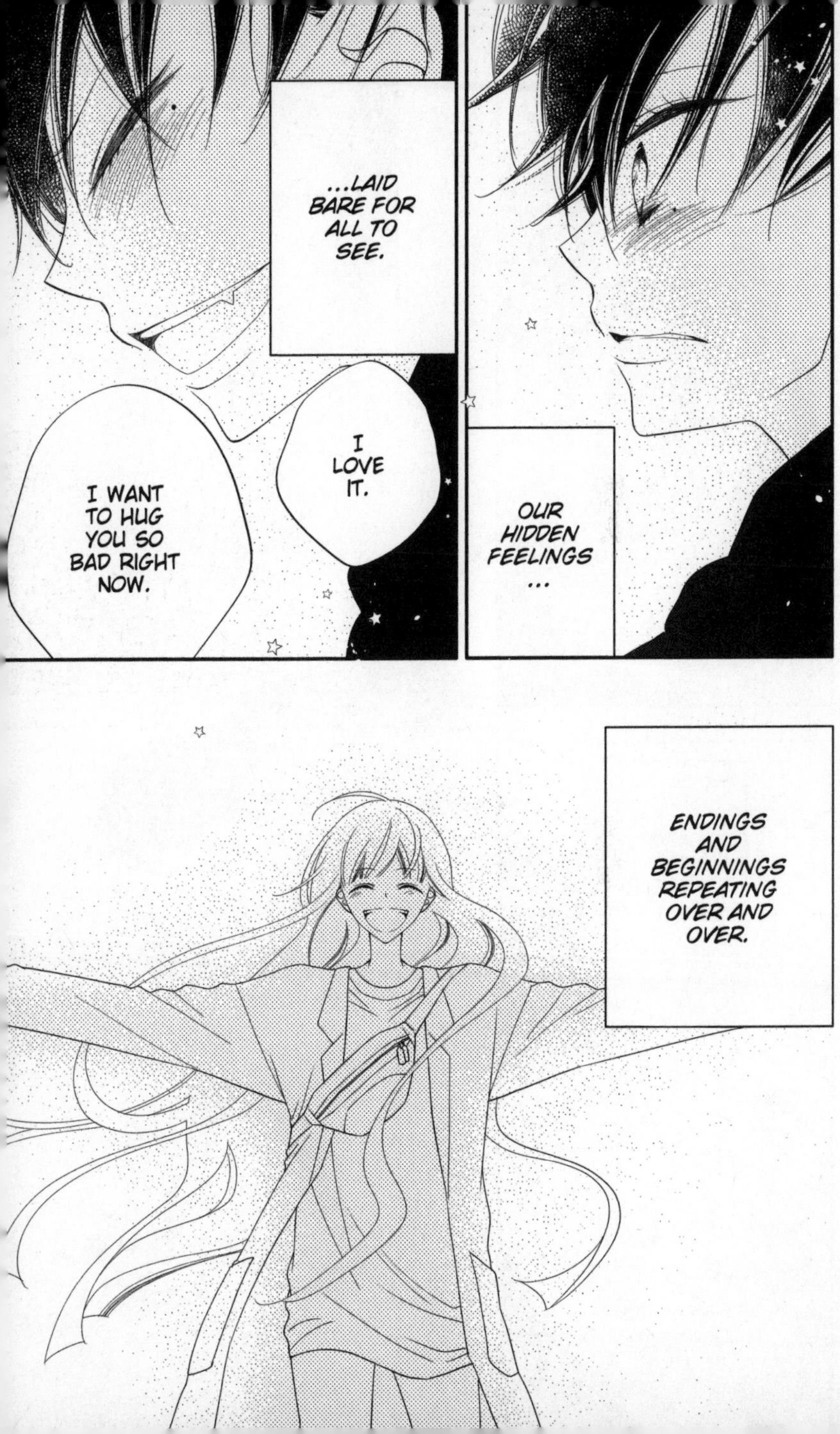
OUR HIDDEN FEELINGS...
...LAID BARE FOR ALL TO SEE.
I LOVE IT.
I WANT TO HUG YOU SO BAD RIGHT NOW.
ENDINGS AND BEGINNINGS REPEATING OVER AND OVER.

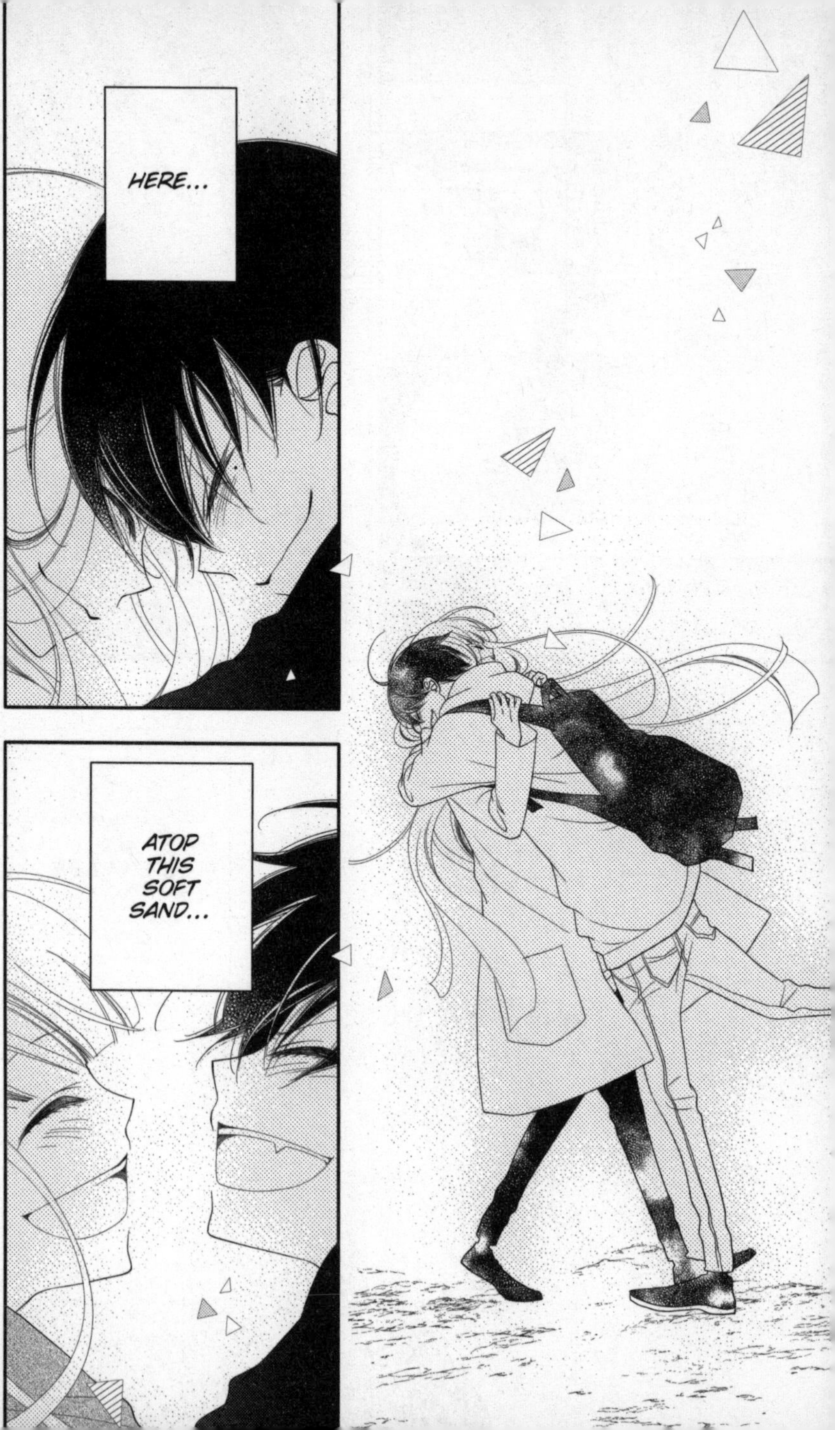
HERE...
ATOP THIS SOFT SAND...

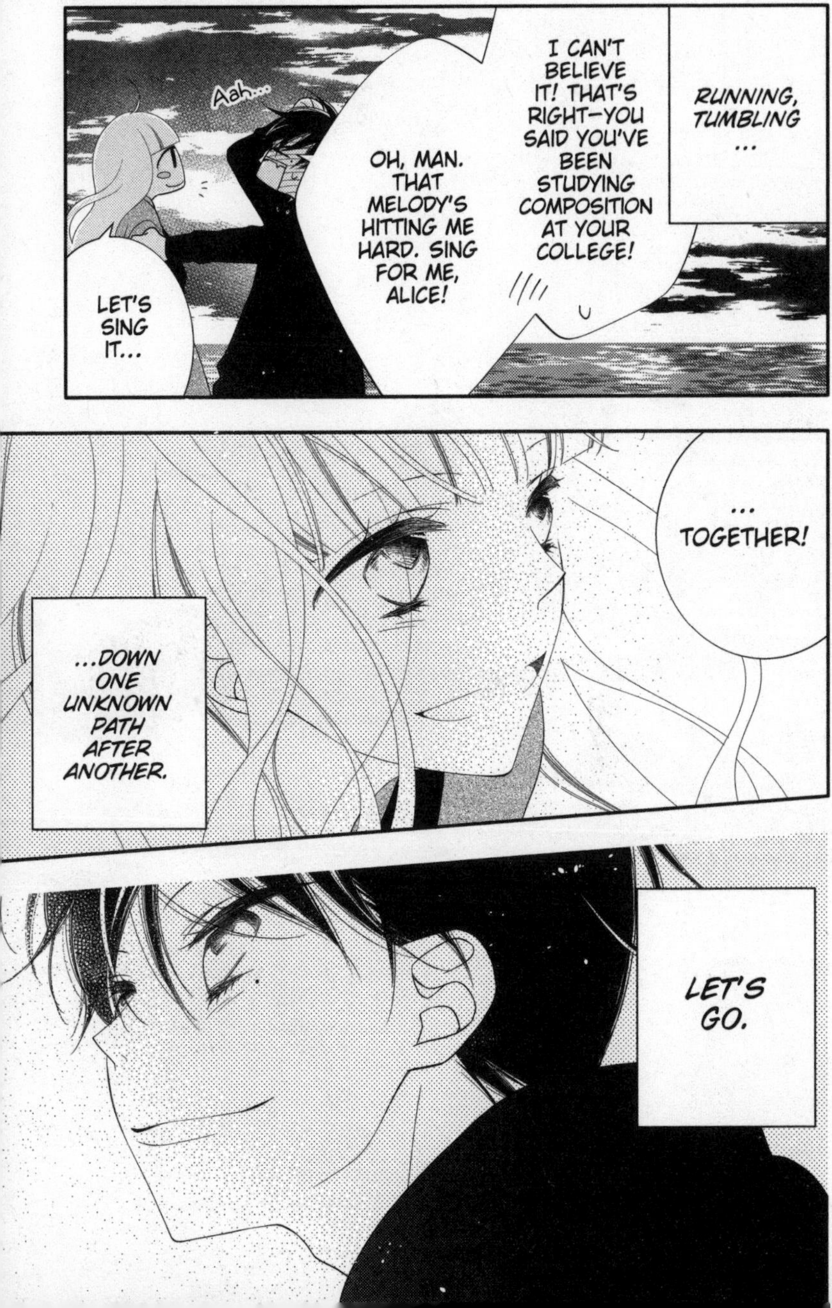
RUNNING, TUMBLING ...
I CAN'T BELIEVE IT! THAT'S RIGHT—YOU SAID YOU'VE BEEN STUDYING COMPOSITION AT YOUR COLLEGE!
OH, MAN. THAT MELODY'S HITTING ME HARD. SING FOR ME, ALICE!
Aah...
LET'S SING IT...
... TOGETHER!
...DOWN ONE UNKNOWN PATH AFTER ANOTHER.
LET'S GO.

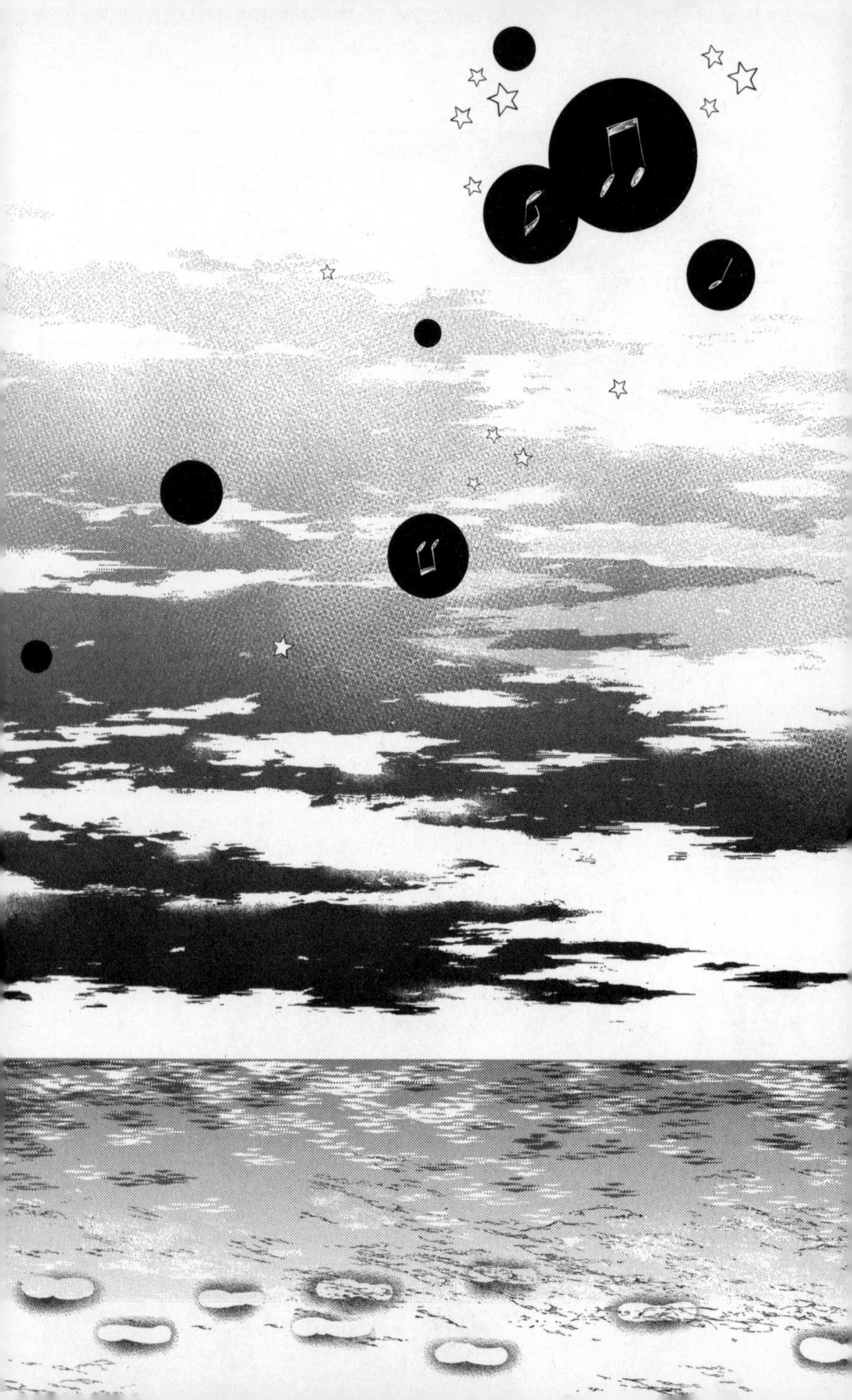

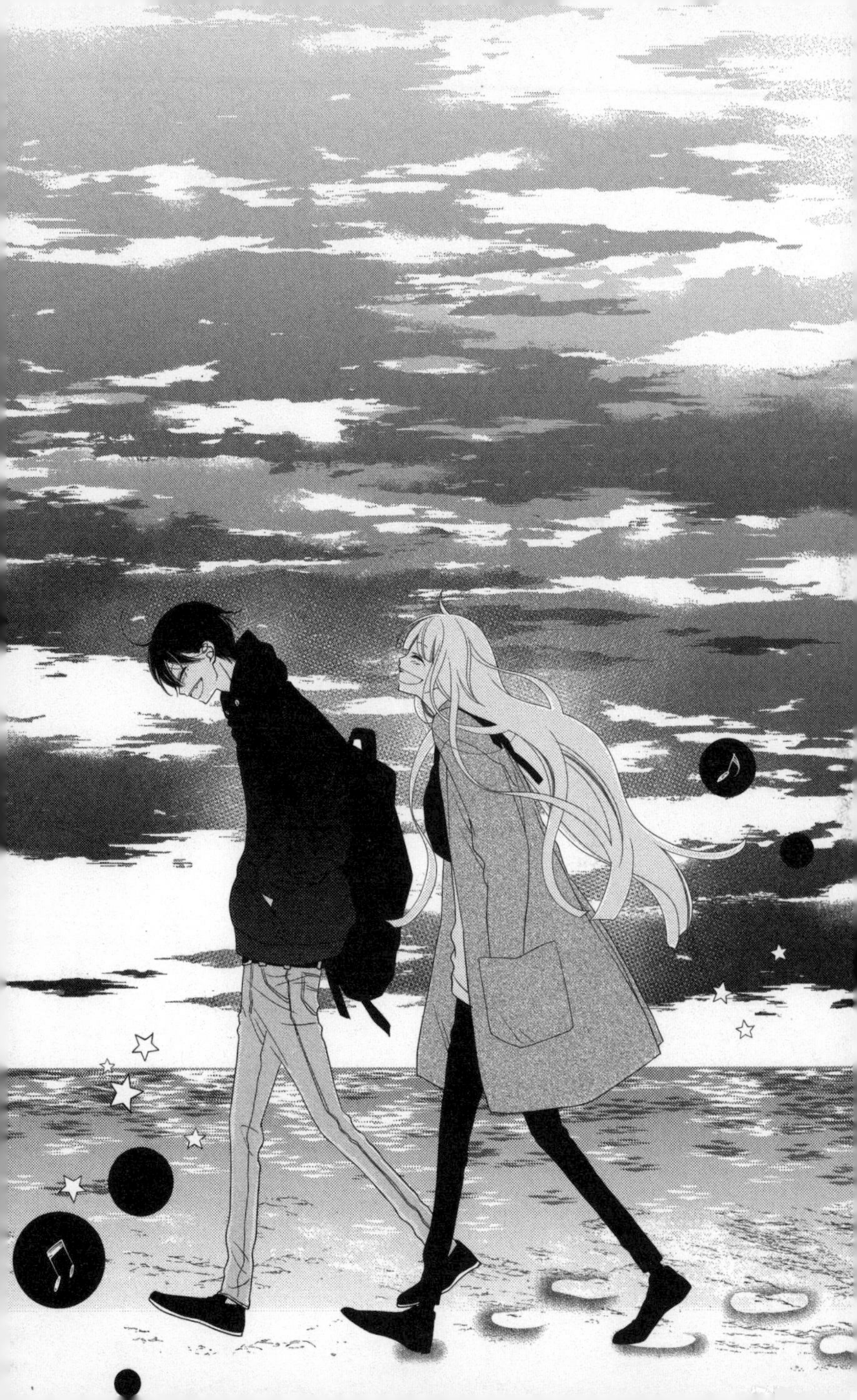

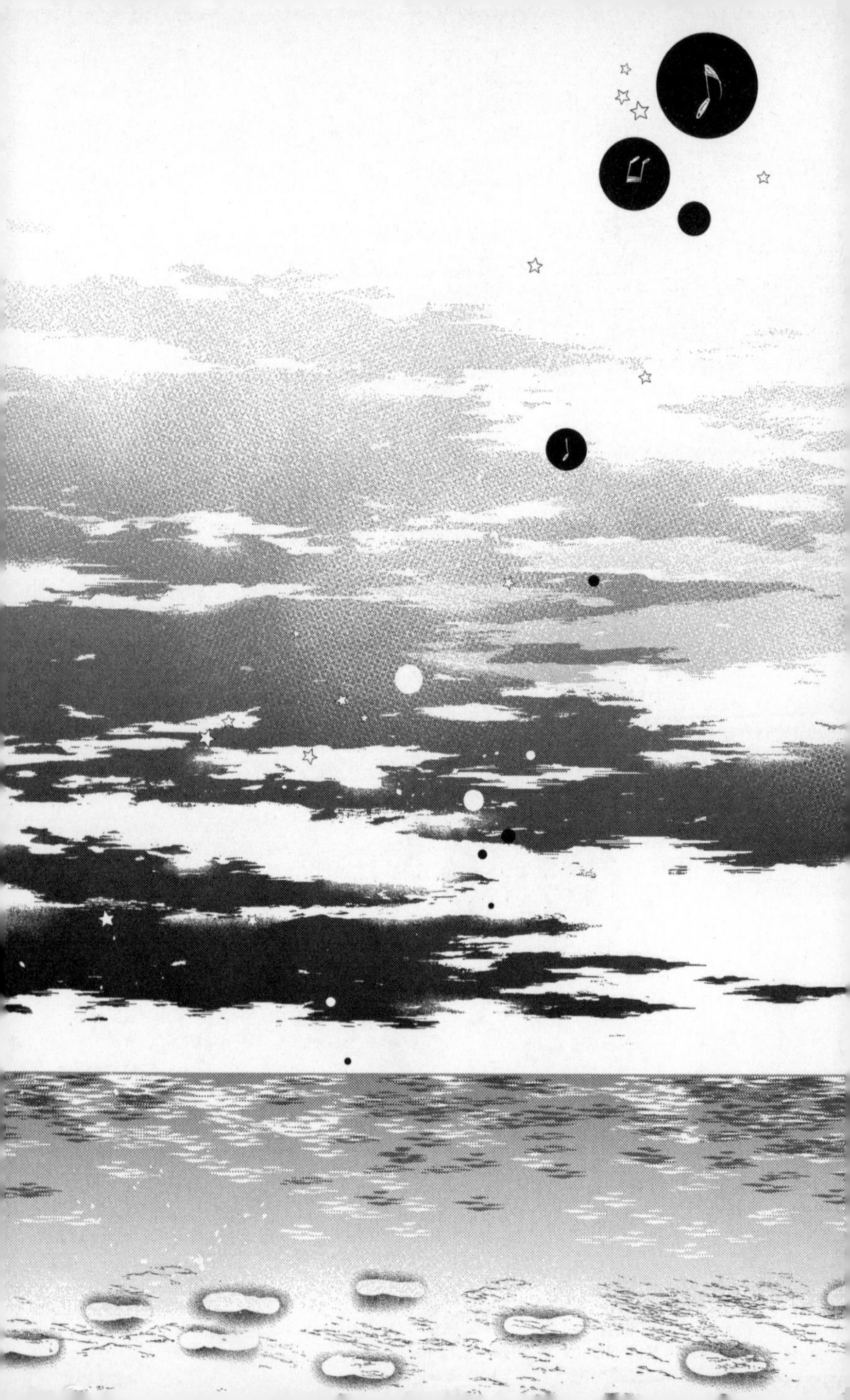

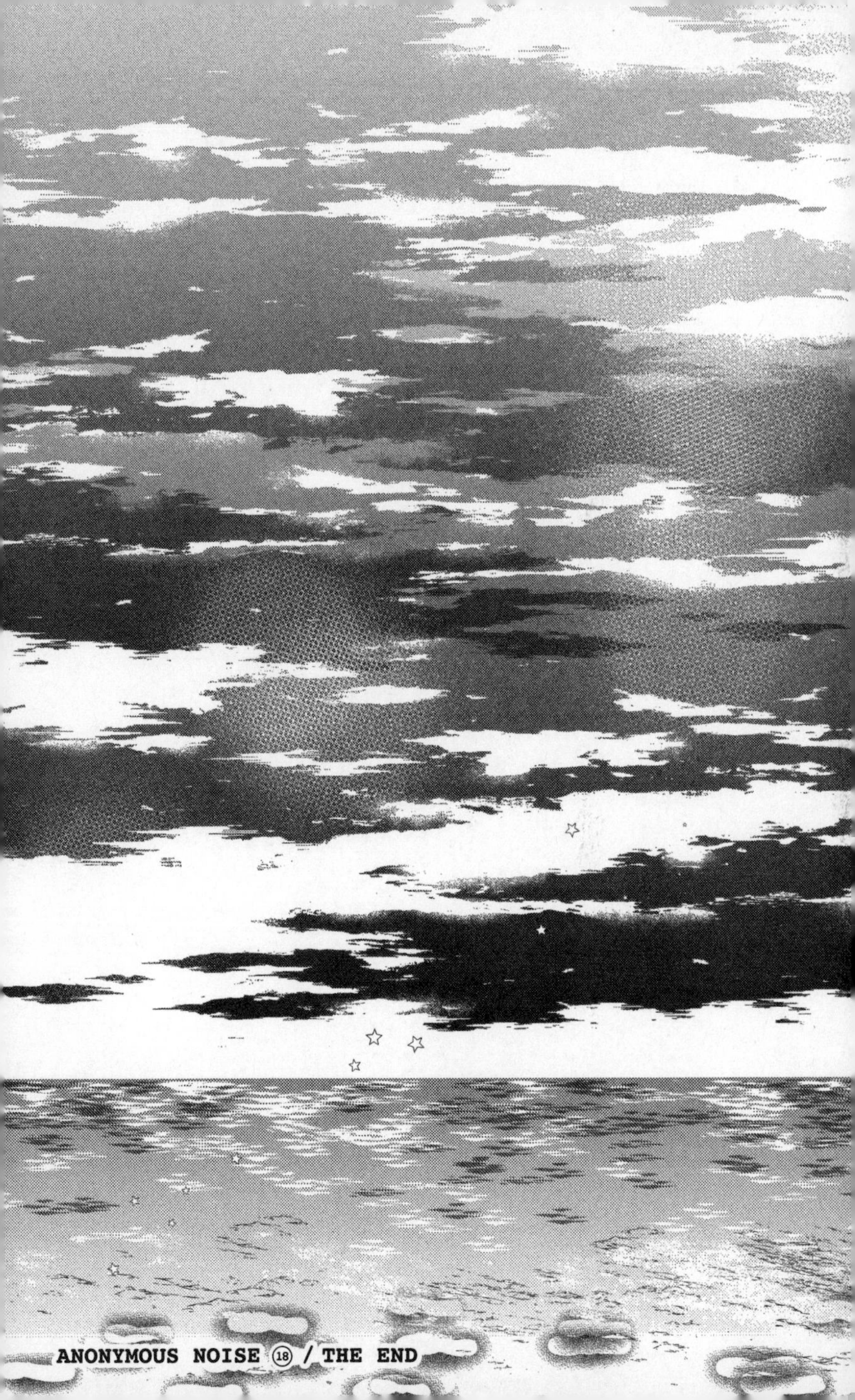
ANONYMOUS NOISE ⑱ / THE END

I have so many powerful emotions about this volume that I haven't even started to process them all yet. But one feeling rings out loud and clear—deep gratitude for the readers who have supported me on this journey. It's only thanks to you that I've made it here at all. From the bottom of my heart, thank you.

- Ryoko Fukuyama

Born on January 5 in Wakayama Prefecture in Japan, Ryoko Fukuyama debuted as a manga artist after winning the Hakusensha Athena Shinjin Taisho Prize from Hakusensha's *Hana to Yume* magazine. She is also the author of *Nosatsu Junkie*. *Anonymous Noise* was adapted into an anime in 2017.

ANONYMOUS NOISE
Vol. 18
Shojo Beat Edition

STORY AND ART BY
RYOKO FUKUYAMA

English Translation & Adaptation/Casey Loe
Touch-Up Art & Lettering/Joanna Estep
Design/Yukiko Whitley
Editor/Amy Yu

Fukumenkei Noise by Ryoko Fukuyama
© Ryoko Fukuyama 2019
All rights reserved.
First published in Japan in 2019 by HAKUSENSHA, Inc., Tokyo.
English language translation rights arranged with HAKUSENSHA, Inc., Tokyo.

The stories, characters and incidents mentioned in this
publication are entirely fictional.

Printed in the U.S.A.

Published by VIZ Media, LLC
P.O. Box 77010
San Francisco, CA 94107

10 9 8 7 6 5 4 3 2 1
First printing, January 2020

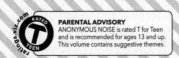

viz.com   shojobeat.com

IDOL dreams

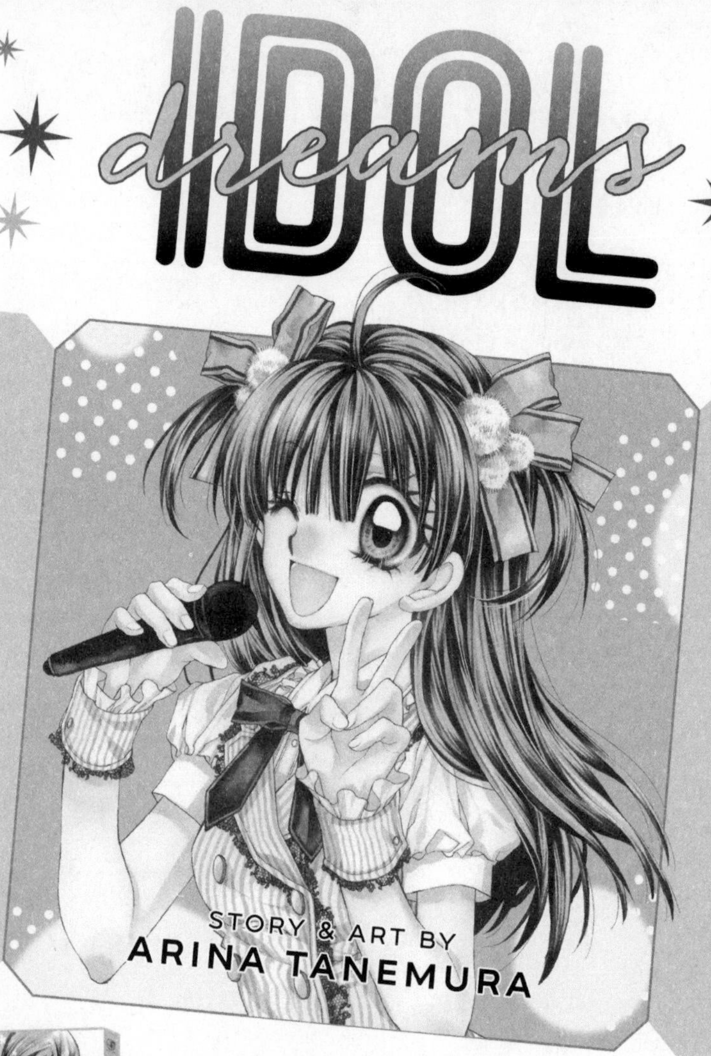

STORY & ART BY
ARINA TANEMURA

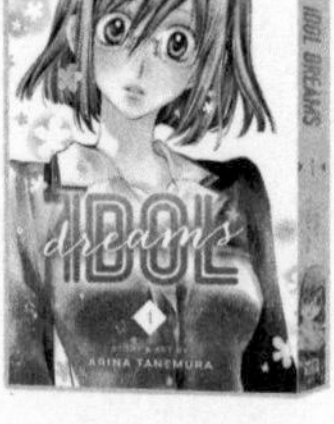
IDOL DREAMS
IDOL
dreams
1
ARINA TANEMURA

At age 31, office worker Chikage Deguchi feels she missed her chances at love and success. When word gets out that she's a virgin, Chikage is humiliated and wishes she could turn back time to when she was still young and popular. She takes an experimental drug that changes her appearance back to when she was 15. Now Chikage is determined to pursue everything she missed out on all those years ago—including becoming a star!

Shojo Beat VIZ RATED T TEEN

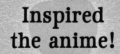

Behind the Scenes!!

STORY AND ART BY **BISCO HATORI**

From the creator of Ouran High School Host Club

Ranmaru Kurisu comes from a family of hardy, rough-and-tumble fisherfolk and he sticks out at home like a delicate, artistic sore thumb. It's given him a raging inferiority complex and a permanently pessimistic outlook. Now that he's in college, he's hoping to find a sense of belonging. But after a whole life of being left out, does he even know how to fit in?!

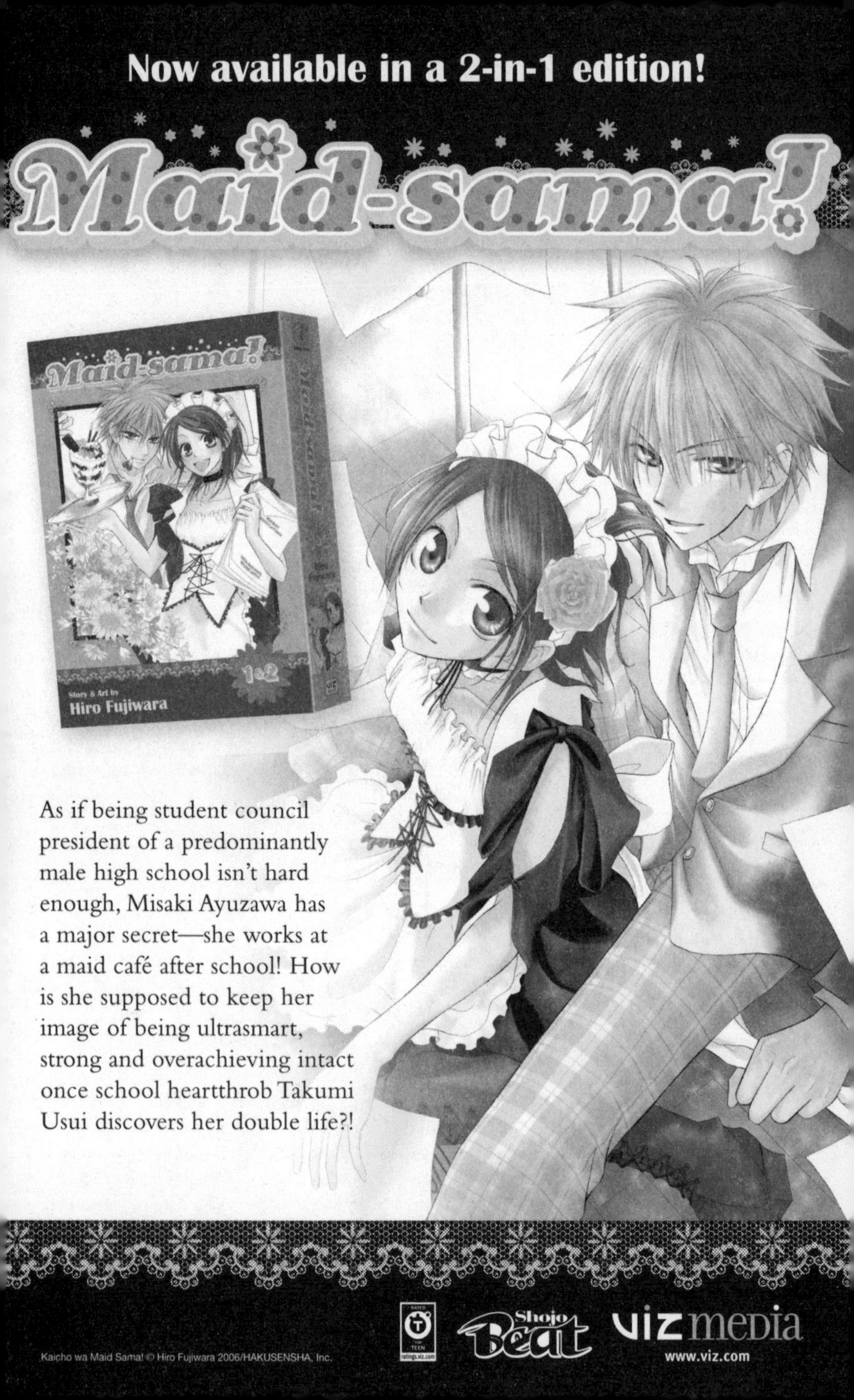
Now available in a 2-in-1 edition!
Maid-sama!
Maid-sama!
1&2
Story & Art by
Hiro Fujiwara
As if being student council president of a predominantly male high school isn't hard enough, Misaki Ayuzawa has a major secret—she works at a maid café after school! How is she supposed to keep her image of being ultrasmart, strong and overachieving intact once school heartthrob Takumi Usui discovers her double life?!
RATED T TEEN
ratings.viz.com
Shojo Beat
VIZ media
www.viz.com
Kaicho wa Maid Sama! © Hiro Fujiwara 2006/HAKUSENSHA, Inc.

FROM THE CREATOR OF VAMPIRE KNIGHT

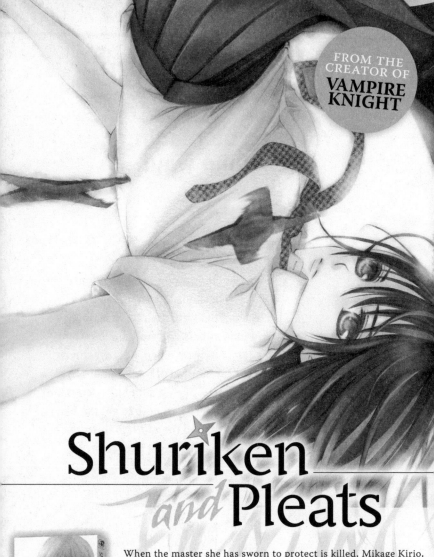

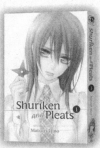

Surprise!

You may be reading the wrong way!

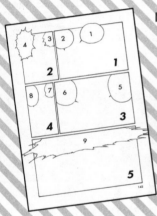

It's true: In keeping with the original Japanese comic format, this book reads from right to left—so action, sound effects and word balloons are completely reversed. This preserves the orientation of the original artwork—plus, it's fun! Check out the diagram shown here to get the hang of things, and then turn to the other side of the book to get started!

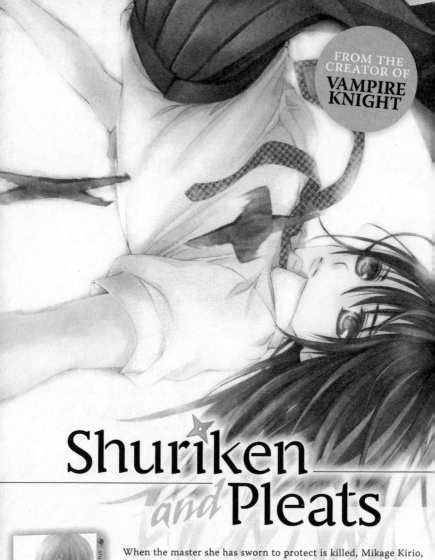

Surprise!

You may be reading the wrong way!

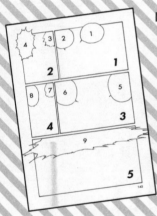

It's true: In keeping with the original Japanese comic format, this book reads from right to left—so action, sound effects and word balloons are completely reversed. This preserves the orientation of the original artwork—plus, it's fun! Check out the diagram shown here to get the hang of things, and then turn to the other side of the book to get started!